HISTORY
OF ORAL HISTORY

HISTORY OF ORAL HISTORY

Foundations and Methodology

Edited by
Thomas L. Charlton, Lois E. Myers,
and Rebecca Sharpless

With the assistance of
Leslie Roy Ballard

ALTAMIRA
PRESS

A Division of Rowman & Littlefield Publishers, Inc.
Lanham • New York • Toronto • Plymouth, UK

ALTAMIRA PRESS
A division of Rowman & Littlefield Publishers, Inc.
A wholly owned subsidiary of
The Rowman & Littlefield Publishing Group, Inc.
4501 Forbes Boulevard, Suite 200
Lanham, MD 20706
www.altamirapress.com

Estover Road, Plymouth PL6 7PY, United Kingdom

British Library Cataloguing in Publication Information Available

Library of Congress Cataloging-in-Publication Data

History of oral history : foundations and methodology / edited by Thomas
L. Charlton, Lois E. Myers, and Rebecca Sharpless, with the assistance of
Leslie Roy Ballard.
    p. cm.
Includes bibliographical references and index.
ISBN-13: 978-0-7591-1085-4 (cloth : alk. paper)
ISBN-10: 0-7591-1085-9 (cloth : alk. paper)
ISBN-13: 978-0-7591-0230-9 (pbk. : alk. paper)
ISBN-10: 0-7591-0230-9 (pbk. : alk. paper)
  1. Oral history—Handbooks, manuals, etc. 2. History—Methodology—
Handbooks, manuals, etc. I. Charlton, Thomas L. (Thomas Lee) II. Myers,
Lois E., 1946– III. Sharpless, Rebecca.

  D16.14.H63 2007
  900—dc22

                                                        2007009711

Printed in the United States of America

∞™ The paper used in this publication meets the minimum requirements of
American National Standard for Information Sciences—Permanence of Paper
for Printed Library Materials, ANSI/NISO Z39.48-1992.

Contents

Acknowledgments

These essays first appeared in 2006 in the reference volume *Handbook of Oral History*. In that publication we acknowledged the contributions of several individuals who deserve equal credit in this derivative textbook.

The advisors and friends who formed our editorial board suggested topics and authors. Contributing their expertise to the planning stages were Albert S. Broussard, Texas A&M University; James E. Fogerty, Minnesota Historical Society; Ronald J. Grele, Columbia University; Robert Perks, British Library; Linda Shopes, Pennsylvania Historical and Museum Commission; Richard Cándida Smith, University of California at Berkeley; and Valerie Raleigh Yow, Chapel Hill, North Carolina.

Baylor University has continued to provide generous and consistent support for the Institute for Oral History, whose faculty and staff assisted the editors in creating both the *Handbook of Oral History* and the current text. We pay special tribute to institute editor Leslie Roy Ballard for his careful proofreading and reference checking and administrative associate Becky Shulda for her kind assistance in correspondence with our authors.

We are grateful for the cooperative spirit of our publisher, AltaMira Press, and we look forward to working with them to produce a companion textbook from the remaining articles in the *Handbook of Oral History*.

Far from being the last word on oral history, these essays are a part of the solid foundation upon which twenty-first-century students will construct an oral history methodology for their own time. We are grateful for the opportunity to instruct future oral historians in the core values of a humanitarian discipline that harnesses technological innovation to preserve and proclaim the historical significance of personal and collective experience.

Introduction

Thomas L. Charlton, Lois E. Myers, and
Rebecca Sharpless

The editors of this volume are pleased to present a collection of
state-of-the-art essays about oral history for both course adop-
tions and advanced practitioners. For many years, there has
been a need for stimulating essays about the essentials of oral
history that could form the basis of interdisciplinary college-
level courses that view oral history as one of the most important
research methodologies available to both academic and public
historians. Also, participants in short courses and workshops
sometimes wonder what sources are available to help them use
oral history concepts at a "higher level"—conceptualized with
theory, informed by historiography, stimulated by new field
methods. It is this need that the editors seek to meet even as they
provide refreshing new ideas for experienced oral historians.

Encouraged by the reception given to the *Handbook of Oral
History* (AltaMira Press, 2006), a comprehensive reference work,
the editors now provide a focused selection from that volume,
by seven of the top scholars in the field of oral history, organized
around the foundations and methodological structures of oral
history studies.

This book joins a host of other appropriate teaching materials available to enrich the pedagogy of a graduate seminar
leader or the curious independent scholar: works on memory
and history, documentary films featuring oral history, scholarly

journal articles, manuals on interviewing and the technical processing of oral history, and interdisciplinary books that remind readers of the strong affinity between social history and oral history. The essays in this collection might well form the core of a lecture series or seminar, especially if supplemented with materials in various media that are already available.

Foundations

In every academic setting, the teacher or discussion leader says something like, "Where to begin is always the question, and in this course we will begin by considering the words of others." The opening section of this book is called "Foundations" for a good reason: Its contents are intended to lay the groundwork for the readings in the second section of the book, called "Methodology."

It is easy to imagine a class of intermediate-to-advanced-level students spending one or two weeks at the beginning of a semester considering, digesting, and thoroughly discussing this book's opening essay, "The History of Oral History" by Rebecca Sharpless, who has much experience as a field interviewer, research administrator, and social historian. Her essay sets the background and tone for the entire book. One way to use this essay in the classroom would be to ask students to give examples of how oral history spread as a movement during the latter half of the twentieth century. Almost every historiographical essay is an unfinished work, but this one goes a long distance in tracing the development of oral history, especially in North America.

Several pleasant surprises await the reader of "Oral History as Evidence" by the cultural historian Ronald J. Grele, one of the movement's leading critics. Enriched by experience in both philanthropic institutions and higher education, Grele is never intellectually better than when he is deep in thought about the evidentiary value of oral history. Those who journey with him in thinking about oral history soon find themselves taking paths that open many new ideas about how oral history has altered the way we think about the discipline of history. Far from an inquiry about evidence as it might be approached in the field of law, Grele probes and explores the interplay between history and memory and the ways in which oral history has enlarged that discussion. Students reading Grele should be ready to ask themselves, "What kinds of examples of the relationships between history and memory are presented by Grele, and how do they seem to fit our new understanding of oral history?" Taken together, the essays by Sharpless and Grele lay the foundation for what is constructed in the following chapters.

Methodology

In the book's second section, "Methodology," readers are guided through the paramount steps of conceptualization, field interviewing, transcription (never an easy task), and archiving. The authors of these essays are (1) a cultural anthropologist (Mary A. Larson) who is also a veteran oral history program administrator in the Southwest; (2) a public historian (Linda Shopes) in the Middle Atlantic region who excels in critical thinking about topics as diverse as community history and academic oral historians' jousts with institutional review boards that must approve human subject research; (3) a New England–bred oral historian (Charles T. Morrissey) whose acclaimed research projects on U.S. presidential, congressional, philanthropic, and medical histories are without peers; (4) a preeminent archivist (James E. Fogerty) who is also highly respected for his administrative career in a major state historical society in the Great Lakes region; and (5) a senior editor at a university-based institute in Texas (Elinor A. Mazé), who, as a regular monitor of traffic on H-Oralhist, keeps her finger on the pulse of oral history practitioners.

Mary Larson's "Research Design and Strategies" contains a finely reasoned lesson that begins with oral historians' approaches to their research subjects. Far from prescriptive, this essay lays out the various ways to conceptualize either an individual interview or a series of interviews. Larson keeps an eye on the needs of individuals and organizations as she presents a strong case that theoretical considerations must be dealt with before an oral history research project can move through other essential steps and phases of development. It is important to emphasize that while this essay is written by a university-based oral historian, its genius lies in its thoughtful, clear, and practical presentation. It is easy to imagine a professor assigning this essay to students, asking, "According to the Larson essay, what are the keys to well-designed oral history?" Why not take the time to design oral history research carefully and well?

One of the oral history profession's premier theoreticians, Linda Shopes, is the author of "Legal and Ethical Issues in Oral History"—a subject essential for thoughtful oral historians. Shopes's approach in this highly important essay starts with an assumption that much oral history has an archival purpose and destination. But Shopes strives for much broader coverage of her subject, providing readers with some of the best available discussion of federal issues in oral history practice, along with the ins and outs of copyright, signed agreements, and the concept of informed consent. Shopes leads her readers through a fascinating consideration of how legal and ethical issues are integrally connected. Shopes's experience and expertise in dealing with the U.S. federal government over the ongoing issue of whether institutional review boards should have oversight over academic oral history interviewing projects, as they do over other interviews of human subjects, adds greatly to her authority and credibility. Among the many questions that oral history students might ponder is this one: "In the absence of case law, why is so much attention paid to the legal side of oral history?"

The essay "Oral History Interviews: From Inception to Closure" by Charles T. Morrissey is almost certain to be a favorite for students and other readers. Beginning with his first experiences in oral history at the Harry S. Truman Presidential Library, Morrissey shares secrets he has accumulated during his lengthy and distinguished career. This chapter reads like the account of a highly experienced oral historian interviewing himself critically. Morrissey walks the reader through a set of detailed, comprehensive steps leading from the first thoughts about conducting an oral history interview to the final considerations. In this way, a relatively inexperienced oral historian can vicariously accompany Morrissey on his research rounds. Morrissey—whose well-documented and highly varied career as a contract oral historian has taken him into the boardrooms of corporate giants, the offices and homes of former congressmen, the vacation resorts of confidantes of U.S. presidents, the secluded get-aways of philanthropists, and the laboratories and offices of medical geniuses—has the experience and characteristics of the quintessential American oral historian: affable, gentle but focused, full of good humor, and determined to succeed on every interview occasion. Students might imagine themselves alongside Morrissey as he conducts an interview and ask themselves, "What are Morrissey's very best practices and moves as he glides through an interview?" There are many; students can learn much from him.

James E. Fogerty's "Oral History and Archives: Documenting Context" is far more than a recipe for storing and preserving oral history recordings and transcripts. He has taken this opportunity to expand the view of the reader and the teacher into a vista beautifully landscaped with many aspects of what he calls "context," which is essentially the general purpose and setting of an interview. Fogerty also spills much ink considering the basic question of the final product(s) of an oral history and what might need to be archived and preserved. We are grateful for his insight into many of the archive-related issues, and students might be wise to pursue the following questions as they read his essay: "What are the most basic issues related to preserving oral history records and transcripts for future research?" And, "Why should *all* oral history products be considered historical documents?"

Elinor A. Mazé, a wordsmith and editor par excellence, gives us a most helpful contribution in "The Uneasy Page: Transcribing and Editing Oral History," the essay that closes this text. She offers astute observations about the nature of oral history in all its forms, examples of how to handle difficult transcribing hurdles, and sophisticated definitions of professional editorial steps. Mazé is perhaps at her best in looking at what the future may bring to oral history projects. While few college and university faculty members teaching oral history courses may be aware of all the latest ideas regarding editorial work in the oral history office, they can appreciate the trend toward digitization that Mazé knows so well and urge their students and others to move into the digital age. Like other authors in this volume, Mazé refers readers to the Oral History Association's *Oral History Evaluation Guidelines*, whose standards and principles have greatly helped thousands of oral history practitioners at every level. An appropriate question to guide readers might be, "According to Elinor Mazé, what is the future of electronic media insofar as oral history is concerned?" To that question might be added a second: "What should rising oral historians know about the World Wide Web and its potential for increasing access to oral history?" Rapid change is in order for oral history, but the essence of the interview as historical evidence is safe and will remain at the core of all studies about oral history.

The editors are proud to be associated with this publication and the stellar cast of authors who have stretched our minds with intellectually stimulating essays about key elements of the oral history profession. Our sincere hope is that the lessons provided by these leaders in the field of oral history will take their places in the lengthy but growing historiographical record that the most serious oral history researchers will be citing and discussing well into the future.

Many thanks to all who have labored to make this work possible. Special thanks to colleague and friend Lois Myers of the Institute for Oral History at Baylor University, whose intimate, steadfast commitment to this project kept it alive during many months of delays; truth be told, she is the editor-in-chief of the entire project.

I

FOUNDATIONS

1

The History of Oral History

Rebecca Sharpless

Oral history has its own history and as a modern movement has its roots in many locations, over many centuries. In the twentieth century, the methodology rose from several directions. Since the 1940s, however, the practice of oral history has been relatively unified in the Western academic world, with a high level of agreement on basic matters. This essay traces the historiography of oral history.

Practitioners of the modern oral history movement enjoy contemplating its ancient origins, sometimes pointing out with glee that all history was oral before the advent of writing. From the Greek side come the historians Herodotus, who employed first-person interviews in gathering information for his account of the Persian Wars in the fifth century BCE, as well as Thucydides, who interrogated his witnesses to the Peloponnesian War "by the most severe and detailed tests possible." In the Zhou dynasty of China (1122–256 BCE), the emperor appointed scribes to record the sayings of the people for the benefit of court historians. Africanists point to the *griot* tradition in recording history, in which oral traditions have been handed down from generation to generation. Historian and anthropologist Jan Vansina highlighted the Akan (Ghanaian) proverb *Tete ke asom ene Kakyere*: "Ancient things remain in the ear." In the Western hemisphere, observers point to Bernardino de Sahagùn, a sixteenth-century

Franciscan missionary to New Spain who brought together about "a dozen old Indians reputed to be especially well informed on Aztec lore so that he and his research assistants might interrogate them." Sahagùn and his colleagues produced a text and 1,850 illustrations.[1]

Despite the traditional prevalence of orally transmitted historical sources, such traditions fell into disfavor in the scientific movement of the late nineteenth century, and there arose a prejudice against oral history that remained strong for more than fifty years. Nineteenth-century German historian Leopold von Ranke, protesting moralization in history, said that the task of the historian was "simply to show how it really was (*wie es eigentlich gewesen*)," and other historians enthusiastically took up his cause.[2] Some historians, however, were never won over by the scientific approach. Californian Hubert Howe Bancroft, for example, recognized that missing from his vast collection of books, journals, maps, and manuscripts on western North America were the living memories of many of the participants in the development of California and the West. Beginning in the 1860s, Bancroft hired assistants to interview and create autobiographies of a diverse group of people living in the western part of the U.S. The resulting volumes of "Dictations" ranged from a few pages to a full five-volume memoir. Bancroft eventually entrusted his collection to the University of California at Berkeley, and it became the core of the library that bears his name.[3]

During the first third of the twentieth century, other historians began to see oral history accounts as valid. The Federal Writers' Project, part of the Works Progress Administration during the New Deal, emerged from the project administrators' democratic impulses to portray America in its cultural diversity.[4] W. T. Couch of the University of North Carolina Press decided to expand the Federal Writers' Project to collect life stories. Taking notes, the writers collected from ordinary Americans more than ten thousand first-person narratives, most of which were deposited in the Library of Congress. From this body of interviews, Couch published in 1939 a selection of interviews with ordinary Southerners as *These Are Our Lives*. Explaining his purpose, Couch wrote, "The idea is to get life histories which are readable and faithful representations of living persons, and which, taken together, will give a fair picture of the structure and working of society. So far as I know, this method of portraying the quality of life of a people, of revealing the real workings of institutions, customs, habits, has never before been used for the people of any region or country. . . . With all our talk about democracy it seems not inappropriate to let the people speak for themselves."[5] Folklorist B. A. Botkin focused on the Former Slave Narratives portion of the project in his 1945 work, *Lay My Burden Down: A Folk History of Slavery*. In his introduction, Botkin wrote: "From the memories and the lips of former slaves have come the answers which only they can give to questions which Americans still ask: What does it mean to be a slave? What does it mean to be free? And, even more, how does it *feel*?" The first-person narratives in the Federal Writers' Project answered at least in part such intimate questions.[6]

At the same time, but from a completely different vantage point, Columbia University historian Allan Nevins, formerly a "newspaperman," in 1938 decried a historical field that lacked life and energy. In his influential work *The Gateway to History*, Nevins called for a popularization of history and the creation of an organization that would make "a systematic attempt to obtain, from the lips and papers of living Americans who have led significant lives, a fuller record of their participation in the political, economic and cultural life of the last sixty years." Nevins cherished the idea of "the immense mass of information about the more recent American past . . . which might come fresh and direct from men once prominent in politics, in business, in the professions, and in other fields; information that every obituary column shows to be perishing."[7] He kept his idea and his dream alive for more than a decade during the difficult years of World War II.

American military historians used oral history extensively to gain contemporary accounts of World War II. The U.S. Army brought professionally trained historians into each theater to collect sources and write studies. A historian assigned to cover the Pacific theater, Lieutenant Colonel (later Brigadier General) S. L. A. Marshall, pioneered the army's oral history effort as he brought together participants shortly after the fighting (often within a few hours) and conducted group interviews. After the Allied invasion of Normandy in June 1944, Marshall traveled to

France to interview combatants from the 82nd and 101st Airborne Divisions. He then traveled throughout Europe collecting firsthand accounts of recent battlefield experiences. Hundreds of historians conducted similar interviews, the majority of which took place a week to ten days after the action or sometimes even later. The best-known field historian, Forrest C. Pogue, spent D-Day aboard a landing ship interviewing wounded soldiers who had participated in the assault. Historians assigned to the European theater alone collected more than two thousand interviews by the end of the war. The notes and transcripts from these endeavors eventually came to the National Archives.[8]

After World War II, Allan Nevins continued to pursue his interest in oral history research. He persuaded his friend Frederic Bancroft, a librarian with a family fortune, to leave Columbia University $1.5 million for the "advancement of historical studies." With a portion of the Bancroft funds, Nevins launched "the oral history project" at Columbia in 1948.[9]

A graduate student took notes in longhand for the first interviews, conducted by Nevins. The Columbia colleagues soon learned of a recent invention, the wire recorder, and lost no time in acquiring one. The process then moved much faster, and they began transcribing the interviews as a convenience to researchers. The first American-made tape recorders (as opposed to wire), modeled on a captured German Magnetophon, were launched in 1948, but tape recorders did not become widely available until several years later.[10]

Nevins selected the first oral history projects at Columbia because of their potential for external funding. The earliest projects included oil wildcatting, the Book-of-the-Month Club, the Ford Motor Company, and the timber industry, all chosen because of their potential to bring in payment from the corporations or individuals interviewed for the small department. The project focused on elite subjects, resulting in a group of biographies of powerful white males.[11]

As the Columbia project picked up speed, others in the United States began to employ the new recording equipment. At the University of Texas in 1952, archivist Winnie Allen organized and supervised a project to record stories of pioneers of the oil industry. Noted folklorists William Owens and Mody Boatright served as interviewers and project directors.[12] In the 1940s, the Forest History Society began taking notes on the reminiscences of veterans of the forest products industry. The society started tape recording in the early 1950s and gradually expanded its interviewee pool to include forestry educators, government employees, and conservationists.[13]

The University of California at Berkeley created its Regional Oral History Office in 1954. In the mid-1940s, George Stewart at Berkeley conceived the idea of continuing Hubert Howe Bancroft's interviews. In 1952, James D. Hart, director of the Bancroft Library, decided to interview author Alice B. Toklas, then living in Paris. After the next interviews, with the founder of the bohemian community of Carmel, California, the Berkeley program formally received funding in 1954. Willa Baum became its head in 1958 and remained so until 2000.[14] In 1959, the regents of the University of California at Los Angeles (UCLA) established the UCLA Oral History Program, upon the urging of historians, librarians, and other members of the UCLA community. Appropriately for its southern California location, the project focused strongly on the arts.[15] The first university-based oral history programs in the United States were well under way by 1960.

The National Archives of the United States began formal oral history work through the presidential libraries, starting in 1961 with the Harry S. Truman Library, in Independence, Missouri, and expanding rapidly with the John F. Kennedy Library in 1964, the Herbert Hoover Oral History Program in 1965, and the Lyndon B. Johnson and Dwight D. Eisenhower projects beginning in 1967. The presidential projects were monumental in scope and size. By 1969, the year after Lyndon Johnson left office, his oral history project already had 275 tapes.[16] The presidential projects played a crucial role in once again bringing the federal government into the oral history movement, and they also broadened the definition of political history, featuring interviews with ordinary people as well as the movers and shakers from the various White House administrations.

Throughout the 1960s, oral history research expanded dramatically. Part of this expansion was due to the availability of portable cassette recorders, first invented by the Philips Company in 1963. The philosophical underpinnings of the oral history

movement, however, lay with the democratic impulses of the social history movement. The civil rights movement, protests
against the Vietnam War, and the feminist movement all raised
questions about American history based on the deeds of elite
white men. Contesting the status quo, social historians began to
explore the interests of a multiracial, multiethnic population with
an emphasis on class relationships. As they sought to understand
the experiences of ordinary people, historians turned to new ways
of discovering the pluralistic "mind of the nation," in the words
of historian Alice Kessler-Harris. Oral history, easily accessible
and useful for talking with almost any type of person, became a
primary tool for documenting the lives of ordinary people.[17] As
Ronald Grele notes elsewhere in this volume, historians in England led the way in documenting lives of ordinary people, as
Americans tended to focus their interviews on elites, but clearly a
sea change was under way. Historians of the left hoped that, by
giving voice to the voiceless, they could foster social change.

By 1965, the oral history movement had reached a critical
mass. *Oral History in the United States*, a report published in that
year by the Columbia University Oral History Research Office,
identified eighty-nine oral history projects nationwide. Practitioners realized a need for standardization of practices and procedures, which Gould Colman, an archivist and oral historian
at Cornell University, articulated in an article in the *American
Archivist*.[18] The time seemed appropriate to call a gathering of
people calling themselves "oral historians."

With the urging of Allan Nevins, James V. Mink, university
archivist and director of oral history at UCLA, convened a nationwide meeting at Lake Arrowhead, California, in September
1966. Seventy-seven people came for the three-day "National
Colloquium on Oral History," a lively gathering of archivists, librarians, historians, members of the medical profession, and
psychiatrists from across the United States and including international participants from Lebanon. The colloquium consisted of
panel discussions aimed at gaining consensus on definitions of
oral history, the uses of oral history, directions for future work,
techniques for interviewing, and professional objectives and
standards.[19] The debates were prescient, highlighting some of
the issues that would remain under discussion in oral history

circles almost forty years later. In other areas, the attendees at Lake Arrowhead were able to reach consensus quickly.

The first area of consensus was on keeping the cumbersome term *oral history*. Louis Starr, the director of the Columbia oral history program, observed the phrase had "gone generic. The *New York Times* and even the *New York Daily News*, that ultimate authority, use it in lower case now."[20]

The discussions at the first meeting were lively and wide ranging. The opening discussions centered on exactly what constituted oral history—was it the tape? The transcription? Did it have to be recorded? Philip Brooks of the Truman Library argued that it did: "Now I think that a tape recorder is important enough to oral history to constitute almost a part of the definition. . . . I think I can take pretty good notes, and I could recreate pretty well what they said, but my notes do not constitute actually what they said, a record of their oral statements."[21] Brooks and like-minded colleagues carried the argument, and recording became a standard part of the definition of oral history in the U.S.

Some early programs, notably the Truman Library and Columbia University, recorded their interviews but did not believe in saving the tapes, making transcription crucial.[22] There was great worry about how to represent the memoirist in the final product: Should ungrammatical utterings be edited? What about material that the interviewee deleted from the transcript? Elizabeth Dixon of UCLA argued for destroying the tapes: "One thing is economy. You keep buying tape, and we're back to the budget again! We can't afford it. Another thing, as Dr. Brooks has said, is that many people would not give you such candid tapes, if they thought you were going to keep them forever because they may not like the way they sound on tape."[23] Louis Shores, dean of the library school at Florida State University, countered by pleading for "more serious consideration of the tape itself as a primary source. Strongly I urge that all of us who are developing oral history collections protect the master of the original tape for replaying by later researchers, and for the possibility that some new truth may be discovered from the oral original not revealed by the typescript."[24] Most programs assumed early on the right of the interviewee to close their memoirs, putting a time seal on interview materials to be made public at some future date. Some returned transcripts to the interviewees for their editing, while others wanted to let the first transcription stand in its original form. Still others destroyed their first drafts.[25] Programs varied on methods of dissemination. While some kept their transcripts as tightly controlled, rare items, the University of California at Berkeley distributed its completed transcripts to a number of selected depositories.

Underlying the arguments about the conduct of oral history programs was a deep concern with the ethics of oral history interviewing. To that end, attendees at the first oral history colloquium in 1966 vigorously debated a list of possible objectives and standards. The standards included issues over recording fidelity, verbatim transcriptions, the right of interviewees to review and change their transcripts, appropriate training of interviewers, and related materials to accompany the transcript.

The discussion of the need for a code of ethics began as early as 1967, stirred in part by William Manchester's controversial use of intimate interviews with the Kennedy family in his book *The Death of a President*. At its third meeting, in 1968, the Oral History Association adopted its first set of standards, labeled "Goals and Guidelines." The final document included three guidelines each for the interviewee and interviewer and one for sponsoring institutions. The first clearly stated the right of the interviewee: "His wishes must govern the conduct of the interview." Others stressed the mutual understanding between interviewer and interviewee regarding the conduct and outcome of the interviewing process. The "Goals and Guidelines" indicated a spirit of compromise regarding arguments about the retention of tape recordings and the need for transcription.[26] These guidelines stood unchanged for more than a decade.

As oral historians crystallized a common set of goals and standards, they worked to disseminate scholarship on oral history. The new Oral History Association, chartered in 1967, published the proceedings of its first meetings, then broadened the publication to an annual journal, titled the *Oral History Review*, in 1973.[27] Practitioners also realized the importance of spreading the gospel of high-quality oral history, and they began actively teaching others how to conduct projects according to the new standards. With funding from the Higher Education Act, for example, UCLA offered an eleven-day oral history institute in July 1968.[28] Beginning in 1970, the Oral History Association Colloquium (as the annual meetings were first called) also featured a workshop component.[29] Willa Baum, director of the Regional Oral History Office at the University of California at Berkeley, published *Oral History for the Local Historical Society*, the first how-to manual on oral history, in 1969. Numerous others soon followed.[30]

During the late 1960s and 1970s, oral history projects rode the crest of increasing grant funding for such work and fed directly into the social history movement in the United States. The National Endowment for the Humanities (NEH) and state humanities councils, founded at almost the same time as the Oral History Association (OHA), generously funded oral history projects through the early 1980s. A 1981 issue of the *Oral History Association Newsletter* listed thirty-two NEH grant awards, ranging from $400,000 to a local historical society in Nebraska to $2,500 to a youth center in Rochester, New York.[31] Funding from humanities organizations on both the national and state levels enabled academics and local communities alike to engage in oral history activities.

Oral history research reflected the social changes of the 1960s and 1970s. The growing acknowledgment of the importance of various ethnic groups in American society fueled an interest in their histories. One of the earliest such oral history endeavors was the Doris Duke project on Native American history. Between 1966 and 1972, tobacco heiress Duke gave a total of $5 million to the universities of Arizona, Florida, Illinois, South Dakota, New Mexico, Utah, and Oklahoma. The funding established multiple oral history centers to document the diversity among Native Americans, making possible interviews, for example, with members of every Native American tribe in Oklahoma. Portions of the South Dakota interviews were published in 1971 in a volume titled *To Be an Indian*.[32]

The civil rights movement gave impetus to numerous oral history projects on African American history. Noted author Alex Haley conducted numerous interviews with Malcolm X for his *Autobiography of Malcolm X*, published shortly after Malcolm X's assassination.[33] Between 1967 and 1973, Howard University gathered more than seven hundred interviews as part of its Civil Rights Documentation Project.[34] With funding from the Rockefeller Foundation, Duke University historians William Chafe and Lawrence Goodwyn between 1972 and 1982 specifically trained doctoral students as oral historians. Their interviews then created source material with which to rewrite the history of the U.S. in its multiracial complexity.[35]

Two of the most celebrated uses of oral history in African American history gained national recognition in the mid-1970s. Historian Theodore Rosengarten, conducting field research on the Alabama Sharecroppers Union, found in Ned Cobb an ideal interviewee. He conducted 120 hours of interviews with Cobb, which he published, to great critical acclaim, as *All God's Dangers: The Life of Nate Shaw*.[36] And Alex Haley traced his family's stories back to Gambia, publishing the results of his quest as *Roots: The Saga of an American Family*, which won the Pulitzer Prize. The ensuing television miniseries based on Haley's book set industry records for numbers of viewers when it aired in January 1977.

The women's movement also found oral history to be congenial to its aims. Some of the earliest work in that movement concentrated on women who had been active in the woman suffrage movement. The University of California at Berkeley interviewed leaders such as Alice Paul, while the Feminist Oral History Project, led by Sherna Gluck, focused on rank-and-file suffragists.[37] Radcliffe College launched its Black Women Oral History Project in 1976, interviewing seventy-two women of remarkable achievement.[38] Oral history proved to be a tool uniquely suited for uncovering women's daily experiences. In 1977, Gluck wrote, "Refusing to be rendered historically voiceless any longer, women are creating a new history—using our own voices and experiences. We are challenging the traditional concepts of history, of what is 'historically important,' and we are affirming that our everyday lives *are* history."[39]

Historians of labor and working-class people also realized early the potential for oral history. Between 1959 and 1963, Jack W. Skeels of the University of Michigan and the Wayne State University Institute of Labor and Industrial Relations interviewed fifty-four people to document the creation of the United

Auto Workers.[40] Labor activists Alice Lynd and Staughton Lynd interviewed rank-and-file workers about their experiences in the labor actions of the 1930s and 1940s, demonstrating that workers organized themselves rather than waiting for union officials to act.[41] Peter Friedlander relied on the memories of Edmund Kord, president of Local 229 of the United Automobile Workers in Detroit to produce an in-depth study of the founding and emergence of one union local.[42] Tamara Hareven employed numerous oral history interviews to portray life in a New Hampshire mill village in *Amoskeag: Life and Work in an American Factory-City*.[43] Across the U.S., significant archives arose containing oral histories of labor activists.

Community historians also soon realized the value of interviewing in documenting local history. With community history came attempts to "give back" history to the people. The idea also flourished that helping people record their local history would give those people efficacy in their lives, or empower them. In many locations in the United States, oral historians interviewed community members and created public programming from the interviews. Books, pamphlets, slide-tape shows, and readers theaters abounded. A typical project described in the *Oral History Association Newsletter* in 1981 was the Neighborhood Oral History Project in Lincoln, Nebraska. The project employed student interns to record the histories of Lincoln neighborhoods. Each neighborhood had a history committee that created a slide–tape presentation, and an oral historian–storyteller created stories to present to children. Director Barbara Hager expressed her hope that "through sharing cultural heritages while working on the project, participants will transfer their energies to revitalization and preservation of their neighborhoods."[44] One particularly creative, sophisticated application of oral history to community history was Project Jukebox, initiated in 1988 by the University of Alaska Fairbanks (UAF). UAF staff members conducted oral history interviews and loaded the transcripts, along with other materials, onto interactive "jukebox" players accessible to interviewees.[45]

Oral historians and folklorists also made common cause, discussing oral tradition as historical evidence. Folklorist Lynwood Montell used oral history to study a former community of mixed-blood people settling amid the white farmers in the Cumberland hills of southern Kentucky after the Civil War. In his introduction to *The Saga of Coe Ridge*, Montell makes a passionate argument for the use of oral tradition, where no written documentation exists, to produce "folk history."[46]

Such broad applications of interviewing methods unnerved traditional historians, many of whom were already uncomfortable with social history. As researchers began taking to oral history interviewing with great enthusiasm, traditionalist historians leveled criticisms at the methodology. Most notable was renowned historian Barbara Tuchman, who feared the type of history that oral sources buttressed. She compared the tape recorder to "a monster with the appetite of a tapeworm," and argued that it facilitated "an artificial survival of trivia of appalling proportions." "We are drowning ourselves in unneeded information," Tuchman said.[47]

Yet criticism of oral history also came from those who wished for more radical uses of interviewing. Historian Nathan Reingold critiqued established programs in his talk at the Oral History Association colloquium in 1969: "It would be very useful if people got away from these great men and deliberately looked for people, trends, and events that *are* largely bereft of conventional documentation." Reingold was responding to the uses of oral history in the biographies primarily of powerful white males, such as Forrest Pogue's four-volume work on General George Marshall and T. Harry Williams's study of Huey Long, which won both the Pulitzer Prize and the National Book Award.[48]

Reingold also raised the issue of validity, a concept that has continued to concern oral historians for many years: "I think you all know that if there is a contemporary letter saying one thing and an oral history saying the opposite and there are no other evidences whatsoever on this point, nine out of ten historians will take the contemporary letter."[49] Critiques such as Reingold's set up a continual challenge for oral historians: defending the reliability (the consistency with which an individual will tell the same story repeatedly) and validity (the agreement between the interview and other types of historical sources) of interviews.[50]

The expense of oral history worried some early critics. In 1967, Philip A. Crowl defended the expense of the John Foster

Dulles Oral History Project. He observed that 280 interviews, conducted over a period of three years at an expense of almost $67,000, were well worth the cost: "Oral history . . . is not meant to serve as a substitute for the documentary record. It does in fact supplement the record by producing some information not hitherto documented. But more important, it can provide guidelines to assist the historian through the jungle of data that confronts him."[51]

By the late 1960s, oral history was gaining popularity with the general public and academics alike. Chicago radio talk-show host Studs Terkel first used taped interviews in book form in *Division Street: America*, a study of seventy ordinary people in Chicago. He followed this with *Hard Times: An Oral History of the Great Depression* and *Working: People Talk about What They Do All Day and How They Feel about What They Do*. Terkel's work garnered widespread acclaim in the popular press. Terkel's methods remained in tension with the "Goals and Guidelines" of the Oral History Association, for he edited heavily and rearranged his interviews and made no provisions for archiving them.[52] Terkel nonetheless epitomized oral history for many Americans.

Another variety of oral history began when a desperate young school teacher enlisted students in his English class to gather the folklore around their home in Appalachian Georgia. The students and teacher, Eliot Wigginton, created a magazine known as *Foxfire*, which became wildly popular upon its initial publication in 1966. Doubleday published the first compilation in 1972, and it was followed by ten subsequent editions.[53] Foxfire created an intersection between oral history and pedagogy, as Wigginton used the project to teach numerous language-arts topics. The success of Foxfire gave rise to numerous other similar projects, several of which persisted into the twenty-first century.[54] It also created an industry of its own, including a 1982 Broadway play for which Jessica Tandy won a Tony Award for her portrayal of Aunt Arie Carpenter.

In 1975, the Oral History Association published a revised *Bibliography on Oral History*, enumerating ongoing work in the United States. The compiler, Manfred Waserman, observed that in 1965 there were 89 reported projects. By 1975, the number had risen to 230, with an additional 93 planned. Waserman commented, "In

1972 it was estimated that there were some 700 oral history centers in 47 states and several foreign countries. The literature on oral history, consisting of about 80 articles in 1967, more than doubled by 1971, and increased to around 300 through 1974. Publications incorporating oral history material have multiplied to the point where the presence of 'oral history' in a title is no longer uncommon." Waserman observed that the items in the bibliography were "products of oral history broadly defined and were produced by a wide spectrum of oral history practitioners extending, in the particular instance of academe, from scholars to high school students." The material varied greatly in quality and included "social, political, and cultural subject matter" as well as folklore and oral tradition. Waserman concluded, "While the merit of these works must be judged on an individual basis, this extension of the oral history phenomenon, with its publications, programs, and related literature has, nevertheless, blurred rather than defined and delineated the origins and scope of the subject."[55] As an acknowledgment of the growing appeal of the practice, the *Journal of Library History*, beginning in 1967, and *History News* (published by the American Association for State and Local History), beginning in 1973, featured regular articles on oral history.[56]

As a field of critical inquiry, oral history began to mature in the 1970s, influenced by cultural studies scholars such as Clifford Geertz. Postmodernism and oral history were well suited for one another, as oral texts easily moved away from positivism.[57] One of the first thoughtful responses to the interviewing phenomenon was "Oral History and *Hard Times*: A Review Essay," in which Michael Frisch used Studs Terkel's work to examine the nature of memory and the significance of recollecting an earlier time amid the turmoil of the 1970s. Frisch observed, "To the extent that *Hard Times* is any example, the interviews are nearly unanimous in showing the selective, synthetic, and generalizing nature of historical memory itself. . . . These capacities are shown to be not only present, but central in the way we all order our experience and understand the meaning of our lives."[58]

Ronald J. Grele edited *Envelopes of Sound: The Art of Oral History*, published in 1975. The outcome of a session at the 1973 Organization of American Historians meeting, *Envelopes of Sound* featured two major papers. One, by Grele himself, examined an interview through linguistic analysis, studied the interaction between the interview participants, and considered the cultural "problematic" brought into the interview by the subject. The second, by Dennis Tedlock, explored rendering narrative as poetry. An interview with Studs Terkel and dialogue between him and the OAH panelists, including chair Alice Kessler-Harris and commentators Jan Vansina and Saul Benison, further broadened the discussion.[59] Conversations about oral history began to move away from the literal process and the content to the theory behind the interview.

Intellectual cross-fertilization with trends in Europe, particularly England, increased in the 1970s as well. In his studies of East Anglia, George Ewart Evans argued for the relevance of oral tradition in supplementing written records.[60] Paul Thompson, oral historian at the University of Essex, published *The Voice of the Past: Oral History* in 1978, demonstrating how oral evidence can change the standard historical narrative. The development of the Oral History Society in England, which published its first journal in 1971, paralleled that of the Oral History Association in the U.S.

Even as it took on international dimensions, oral history became increasingly accessible to local and family historians. Many projects, often limited in scope, flourished in local historical societies, voluntary associations, and so on. Such projects often escaped the attention of academic historians but held deep significance for their communities of origin. As the number of practitioners grew at the grassroots level, regional and state-level oral history groups sprang up across the United States. The first, the New England Association for Oral History, began in 1974, while Oral History in the Middle Atlantic Region formed in 1976. The Michigan Oral History Council was founded in 1979. The Southwest Oral History Association was created in 1981, the Texas Oral History Association in 1982, the Northwest Oral History Association in 1983, and the Oral History Association of Minnesota in 1985. Each of these organizations fostered local history research while promulgating the highest standards of oral history practice, offering workshops, and giving awards for exemplary research.

Discussions over the nature and practice of oral history continued apace. While some issues easily coalesced into agreement, others remained contentious. In 1979, a selected group of Oral History Association members came together at the Wingspread Conference Center in Wisconsin to build upon the original "Goals and Guidelines" and to formulate a set of guidelines to "impart standards to oral history projects that were just beginning and to provide critical appraisal to established projects that wished review and advice from professional peers."[61] The resulting *Evaluation Guidelines*, an official publication of the Oral History Association, promulgated basic criteria for programs and projects. The guidelines included analyses of purposes and objectives; selections of interviewers and interviewees; availability of materials; finding aids; management, qualifications, and training; ethical and legal guidelines; tape and transcript processing guidelines; interview content guidelines; and interview conduct guidelines. The guidelines proved an invaluable touchstone for practitioners seeking to conduct interviews of the highest quality and provided a common ground for discussion.

Recording technology expanded beyond audio equipment with the appearance and spread of video recording, which appeared in professional discussions as early as 1970. Once again, oral historians debated over the nature of the product and how it changed when visual images were added to the verbal record.[62] The debate over videotaping continued into the 1980s, when the Alfred P. Sloan Foundation awarded the Smithsonian Institution funds to examine videohistory's effectiveness. By 1991, Smithsonian historians had completed more than 250 hours of tape in several different projects. Evaluator Stanley Goldberg expressed reservations about the increased administrative costs and the expense of high-quality recording, while Carlene Stephens commented on video's usefulness for documenting material objects and processes. Producer Brien Williams declared that preliminary audio interviews were critical to success. Their conclusions seemed to point to a limited but valuable role for video in oral history interviewing.[63]

Scholarship in oral history continued to mature. In 1984, Willa Baum and David Dunaway compiled and edited *Oral History:*

An Interdisciplinary Anthology. The reader brought together thirty-four germinal articles in the field, beginning with early writings by Allan Nevins and Louis Starr, and continuing with articles on interpreting and designing projects, applied oral history, the relationships with other disciplines, education, and libraries.[64] Writings on oral history became increasingly sophisticated. In 1986, Linda Shopes analyzed book reviews on oral history and concluded that a sustained critical voice was emerging.[65] Bibliographer David Henige's *Oral Historiography* (1982) investigated how oral historians shape "the past they reconstruct," looking at the role of the historian in selecting, recording, and interpreting sources.[66] In the field of communication studies, Eva McMahan and her colleagues pioneered studies in oral history as a rhetorical device, examining the interview as a communicative event and speech act.[67] Michael Frisch in 1990 published his collected essays in a volume evocatively titled *A Shared Authority: Essays on the Craft and Meaning of Oral and Public History.* Frisch's essays included thoughtful discussion of the collaboration between interviewee and interviewer.[68] In 1987, the *Journal of American History*, the quarterly publication of the Organization of American Historians, began an annual section on oral history, which was edited by Linda Shopes and Michael Frisch for ten years and then by Michael Gordon and Lu Ann Jones. The oral history section served as part of the journal's examination of resources available to historians. Over the next sixteen years, oral historians provided a mixture of topical and reflective essays designed not to be theoretical or methodological, but to "foster a more thoughtful evaluation of oral history source materials and a more self-conscious historical practice."[69]

Increasingly, American oral historians came to be influenced by scholars outside the U.S. The *International Journal of Oral History*, edited by American Ronald J. Grele, began publication in 1980, focusing on comparative approaches, cross-disciplinary or interdisciplinary approaches, and theoretical and methodological discussions, all within an international context. In 1992, the journal merged with *Life Stories* from the British Oral History Society to become the *International Yearbook of Oral History and Life Stories*, which published several thematic issues of mostly European and American scholarship in the mid-1990s.[70] The work of scholars such as Elena Poniatowska and Luisa Passerini began influencing American readers with their nuanced readings of oral interview data.[71] A group of oral historians from around the world met in Essex, England, in 1979, sharing their common interests. The group organized formally at its 1996 meeting in Göteborg, Sweden, as the International Oral History Association, held biennial meetings, and published a bilingual journal titled *Words and Silences/Palabras y Silencios*.

Historian Alessandro Portelli, whose research included Americans in Appalachia as well as his fellow Italians, published his important work *The Death of Luigi Trastulli and Other Stories* in 1991. Portelli's study of the versions of the death of steelworker Luigi Trastulli brought new questions to bear on the issues of validity and reliability in oral history. Portelli posited that the way that people remember is as important as what they remember: "Oral history has made us uncomfortably aware of the elusive quality of historical truth itself."[72] Trained in the field of literary studies, Portelli was keenly attuned to analysis of texts, and he significantly influenced the ways in which historians interpreted their sources. In the same year, Sherna Gluck and Daphne Patai edited *Women's Words: The Feminist Practice of Oral History*, a collection of thirteen essays by women in several academic disciplines. The authors reflect on personal politics, power dynamics, and race and ethnicity as well as gender. Elizabeth Tonkin's *Narrating Our Pasts: The Social Construction of Oral History* (1992) investigated the question of oral history and narrative, as Tonkin argued that narratives are both social constructions and individual performances.[73]

The breadth of oral history research continued to be one of its prime strengths. In 1988, Twayne Publishers, acknowledging the wide appeal of oral history, started its Oral History Series, edited by Donald A. Ritchie. Twenty-six books, on an expansive array of topics, appeared between 1990 and 1998, testimony to the span of the usefulness and applicability of oral history. The Twayne volumes centered around interview transcripts, carefully contextualized.[74] As gay and lesbian studies emerged in the U.S. academy, oral history again became a prime tool for documenting people and movements. Among the earliest titles in the field were Allan Berube's work on World War II soldiers, Lillian Faderman's general study of lesbians, and Elizabeth Kennedy and Madeline Davis's research on working-class lesbians.[75]

Two major manuals for oral history research appeared in the mid-1990s: *Doing Oral History*, by Donald Ritchie, and *Recording Oral History*, by Valerie Yow. Both books, each excellent in its own way, demonstrate the consensus that oral historians shared regarding standards and methods, the differences in approaches, and the vast possibilities for applications.[76] In 1998, British historians Robert Perks and Alistair Thomson pulled together much of the best scholarship of the late twentieth century into *The Oral History Reader*, considering critical developments, interviewing, advocacy and empowerment, interpretation, and "making histories."[77]

In the mid-1990s, technological issues took center stage as digital recording raised anew issues of representation of the interviewee's voice.[78] The issue of accessibility, widely discussed since the late 1960s, became even more pressing as the World Wide Web made possible unlimited distribution of oral history transcripts and sound files.[79] The Internet and e-mail also made possible digital exchanges between oral historians. Terry Birdwhistell of the University of Kentucky launched an Internet discussion list, OHA-L in 1993. It became affiliated with the rapidly growing organization known as H-Net in 1997 under the name H-Oralhist. Almost two thousand subscribers worldwide can communicate electronically about issues of mutual interest. The Internet has also facilitated a massive oral history initiative by the Library of Congress: the Veterans History Project. Spurred by the loss of World War II veterans, the project enlists volunteers nationwide to conduct interviews and deposit them in the Library of Congress. By May 2003, more than seven thousand interviews had been submitted to the project.[80]

Oral historians have long been concerned with issues of memory, particularly how people remember and what shapes their memories. Early works by Michael Kammen and John Bodnar raised the questions of public participation in the formulation of historical memory, opening the floodgate of later scholarship.[81] By the turn of the twenty-first century, discussions of memory pertained to the physical process not of a given individual but rather of society at large—what a society remembers and what that means.

Writing using oral history has continued to grow in sophistication. The Palgrave Studies in Oral History published its first volume in 2003. Edited by Linda Shopes and Bruce Stave, the Palgrave books are designed to look at oral history interviews in depth, to place them "in broad historical context and engage issues of historical memory and narrative construction."[82]

In 2005, oral history methodology continues to flourish. Both the Oral History Association and the International Oral History Association are thriving, and their publications continue to increase in quality. The methodology continues to prove itself useful in a broad array of topics, and applications continue to become more creative. As the World Wide Web grows in scope and influence, it undoubtedly will have an impact on the dissemination of oral history. But the basic dynamic, two people sitting and talking about the past, has remained largely unchanged. Despite the sophistication of analysis and interpretation, a middle-school student can still do a legitimate oral history interview. Where individuals communicate, oral history will continue to be useful.

Notes

I thank Bruce Stave and Thomas Charlton for their careful reading of and suggestions for this chapter.

1. Starr, "Oral History," 4; Moss, "What Is It," 5; Strassler, *Landmark Thucydides*, 15; Vansina, *Oral Tradition*, xi (originally published as *Oral Tradition: A Study in Historical Methodology*); Haley, "Black History," 12, 14–17; Hanke, "American Historians," 6–7. For an overview of historiography in Europe and Africa, see Henige, *Oral Historiography*, 7–22.

2. Carr, *What Is History?* 3.

3. Hart, *Catalogue*, vii–viii.

4. Hirsch, *Portrait of America*, 6. Hirsch provides an elegant discussion of the intellectual impulses behind the Federal Writers' Project.

5. Couch, preface to *These Are Our Lives*, ix, x–xi.

6. Botkin, *Lay My Burden Down*, ix. Ann Banks discusses the history of WPA project anthologies in her 1980 collection of eighty previously unpublished

interviews in *First Person America*, xi, xiii, xv. Later, in 1993, Theda Perdue published *Nations Remembered*, a selection of WPA interviews with Native Americans. An extended debate over the veracity of the slave narratives took place in the *Oral History Review*. See Soapes, "Federal Writers' Project"; Rapport, "Life Stories"; and Terrill and Hirsch, "Replies."

7. Nevins, *Gateway to History*, iv. See Hirsch, *Portrait of America*, 141–47, for a contrast between the Federal Writers' Project and Nevins's approach to collecting personal narratives.

8. Everett, *Oral History Techniques*, 4–7; Pogue, *Pogue's War*, 99.

9. Nevins, "How and Why," 31–32.

10. Starr, "Oral History," 8–9, 22.

11. Nevins, "How and Why," 32; Starr, "Oral History," 10–11.

12. Boatright and Owens, *Derrick Floor*, ix–x.

13. Annotations of the Forest History Society interview collection first appeared in Holman, *Oral History Collection*, and are now available online at Forest History Society Oral History Program, Understanding the Past for Its Impact on the Future, http://www.lib.duke.edu/forest/Research/ohiguide.html (accessed January 31, 2005).

14. Hart, *Catalogue*, vii–viii.

15. Grele, introduction to *UCLA Oral History Program*, 1. See also UCLA Oral History Program, History and Description, University of California at Los Angeles, http://www.library.ucla.edu/libraries/special/ohp/ohphist.htm (accessed January 31, 2005).

16. Starr, "Oral History," 12; Herbert Hoover Presidential Library and Museum, Research Collections: Historical Materials, Oral History Transcripts, http://www.ecommcode2.com/hoover/research/historicalmaterials/oral.htm l (accessed January 26, 2005); Truman Presidential Museum and Library, Oral History Interviews, http://www.trumanlibrary.org/oralhist/oral_his.htm (accessed January 26, 2005); Eisenhower Presidential Library Information Archives, Eisenhower Library Information Resources: Oral Histories, http://www.ibiblio .org/lia/president/EisenhowerLibrary/oral_histories/Oral.html (accessed January 26, 2005); John F. Kennedy Library and Museum, Historical Materials in the John F. Kennedy Library: Oral History Interviews, http://www.cs.umb.edu/ ~serl/jfk/oralhist.htm (accessed January 31, 2005); Lyndon Baines Johnson Library and Museum, Oral History Collection, http://www.lbjlib.utexas.edu/ johnson/archives.hom/biopage.asp (accessed January 26, 2005).

17. Kessler-Harris, "Social History," 233–34, 237.

18. Colman, "Oral History," 79–83.

19. Dixon and Mink, *Oral History at Arrowhead*.

20. Dixon, "Definitions," 14.

21. Ibid., 6.

22. Ibid., 5. By the mid-1970s, 70 percent of U.S. programs were transcribing their interviews, opposed to British and Canadian programs, which left theirs in recorded form only. Louis Starr concluded, "This is not so much because those who favor the transcript have the better of the argument on theoretical grounds as because of practical convenience." Starr, "Oral History," 7.

23. Dixon, "Definitions," 22.

24. Nevins, "Uses," 40.

25. Dixon, "Definitions," 19; Dixon and Colman, "Objectives and Standards," 78, 80.

26. "Oral History Association Adopts Statement about Goals and Guidelines during Nebraska Colloquium," *Oral History Association Newsletter* 3, no. 1 (January 1969), 4. The "Goals and Guidelines" were subsequently revised in 1975.

27. Editors to date are Samuel Hand, 1973–1978; Richard Sweterlitsch, 1978–1980; Arthur A. Hansen, 1981–1987; Michael Frisch, 1987–1996; Bruce M. Stave, 1996–1999; and Andrew J. Dunar, 2000–2005. *Oral History Review* began publishing twice yearly with volume 15 in 1987.

28. *Oral History Association Newsletter* 2, no. 2 (April 1968): 1.

29. *Oral History Association Newsletter* 4, no. 3 (July 1970): 6.

30. Other significant manuals prior to the 1990s included Moss, *Program Manual*; Davis, Back, and MacLean, *Tape to Type*; Ives, *Tape-Recorded Interview* (1980); Charlton, *Oral History for Texans* (1981); and Sitton, Mehaffy, and Davis, *Guide for Teachers*.

31. *Oral History Association Newsletter* 15, no. 1 (1981): 6–7.

32. Cash and Hoover, *To Be an Indian*.

33. Haley, "Black History," 7–8; X, *Autobiography*.

34. Browne, "Civil Rights," 90–95.

35. Jefferson, "Echoes from the South," 43–62.

36. Rosengarten, *All God's Dangers*, xiii–xxv.

37. Bancroft Library Regional Oral History Office, Oral History Online: Suffragists Oral History Project, University of California at Berkeley Library, http://bancroft.berkeley.edu/ROHO/projects/suffragist/ (accessed January 31, 2005); Gluck, *Parlor to Prison*.

38. Hill, *Women of Courage*, 3–4.

39. Gluck, "What's So Special" (1984), 222.

40. Starr, "Oral History," 12; Walter P. Reuther Library, Oral History Collections: UAW Oral Histories, Wayne State University College of Urban Labor and Metropolitan Affairs, http://www.reuther.wayne.edu/use/ohistory.html#uaw (accessed January 26, 2005).

41. Lynd and Lynd, *Rank and File*, 3.

42. Friedlander, *UAW Local*.

43. Hareven and Langenbach, *Amoskeag*.

44. "Neighborhood OH Changes Lives," *Oral History Association Newsletter* 15, no. 2 (1981): 6.

45. University of Alaska Fairbanks Oral History Program, Project Jukebox, Elmer E. Rasmuson Library, University of Alaska Fairbanks, http://uaf-db.uaf.edu/Jukebox/PJWeb/pjhome.htm (accessed January 26, 2005). Following Baum's early community history guide, *Oral History for the Local Historical Society*, the Oral History Association produced its own guide by Mercier and Buckendorf, *Using Oral History in Community History Projects*. For a particularly good example of a community history, see Fee, Shopes, and Zeidman, *Baltimore Book*.

46. Montell, *Coe Ridge*, ix–xxvii.

47. Tuchman, "Distinguishing the Significant" (1984), 76.

48. Reingold, "Critic Looks at Oral History," 219. Pogue, *George C. Marshall*; Williams, *Huey Long*.

49. Reingold, "Critic Looks at Oral History," 217.

50. Hoffman, "Reliability and Validity." Hoffman has continued her work for several decades, particularly with her husband Howard Hoffman's memories of his service during World War II. See Hoffman and Hoffman, *Archives of Memory*.

51. Philip A. Crowl, "The Dulles Oral History Project: Mission Accomplished," *American Historical Association Newsletter*, February 1967.

52. For Terkel's discussion of his editing, see Grele, "Riffs and Improvisations," 31–39.

53. Wigginton, *Foxfire Book*. For a description of how the Foxfire movement began, see Wigginton, *Shining Moment*.

54. Two of the most successful projects include Loblolly, Gary, Texas, and The Long, Long Ago Oral History Project, Suva Intermediate School, Bell Gardens, California. See Sitton, *Loblolly Book*, and Brooks, "Long, Long Ago." High school students in Lebanon, Missouri, published *Bittersweet: The Ozark Quarterly* from 1973 to 1983. See Massey, *Bittersweet Country*.

55. Waserman, *Bibliography*, rev. ed., iii–iv.

56. The *Journal of Library History* articles ran twice yearly from 1967 (Volume 2) to 1973 (Volume 8) and were often descriptions of oral history projects and activities. *History News* articles appeared occasionally through 1976.

57. Bonnell and Hunt, introduction to *Beyond the Cultural Turn*, 2–3, 4.

58. Frisch, "Oral History and *Hard Times*" (1990), 13.

59. Grele, *Envelopes of Sound* (1975).

60. Evans, *Where Beards Wag All*.

61. Oral History Association, *Evaluation Guidelines*, 1. The guidelines were updated in 1989 and again in 2000.

62. Frantz, "Video-Taping"; Colman, "Where to Now?" 2; Charlton, "Videotaped Oral Histories."

63. Goldberg, "Manhattan Project Series," 98; Stephens, "Videohistory," 107; Williams, "Recording Videohistory," 143–44.

64. Dunaway and Baum, *Oral History* (1984).

65. Shopes, "Critical Dialogue."

66. Henige, *Oral Historiography*, 128.

67. McMahan, *Elite Oral History Discourse*.

68. *Oral History Review* 30, no. 1 (Winter/Spring 2003) featured essays by seven authors commenting on the collaborative process.

69. Frisch and Shopes, "Introduction," 593. The annual oral history sections of the *Journal of American History* began in 1987 (Volume 74) and continued through 2002 (Volume 89). The editors were Michael Frisch and Linda Shopes (1986–1996) and Lu Ann Jones and Michael Gordon (1997–2002).

70. Grele, "Editorial," 2. The first *International Yearbook* was Passerini, *Memory and Totalitarianism*.

71. Poniatowska, *Nothing, Nobody*; Passerini, *Fascism in Popular Memory*.

72. Portelli, *Death of Luigi Trastulli*, viii–ix. Portelli followed with the equally engaging *Battle of Valle Giulia* and *Order Has Been Carried Out*.

73. Tonkin, *Narrating Our Pasts*.

74. Donald A. Ritchie, e-mail message to author, January 26, 2004. The first Twayne volume was Lewin, *Witnesses to the Holocaust*.

75. Berube, *Coming Out*; Faderman, *Odd Girls*; Kennedy and Davis, *Boots of Leather*.

76. Ritchie, *Doing Oral History* (1995); Yow, *Recording Oral History* (1994). The 2003 revised edition of Ritchie, *Doing Oral History*, contains a significant bibliography. The second edition of Yow's manual, updated and enlarged, appeared in 2005.

77. Perks and Thomson, *Oral History Reader*.

78. Gluck, Ritchie, and Eynon, "New Millennium."

79. Large oral history programs produced printed guides to their collections. In the mid-1980s, the Southwestern Oral History Association produced a unified database of interviews in the region. See Gallacher and Treleven, "Online Database." The importance of this issue is demonstrated by the heated arguments in late 2003 on H-Oralhist, the Internet discussion list, regarding plans for a database by the Alexander Street Press.

80. Veterans History Project News and Events, Veterans' Stories Online for Memorial Day, Library of Congress American Folklife Center Veterans History Project, http://www.loc.gov/folklife/vets//news-courage.html (accessed January 26, 2005).

81. Kammen, *Mystic Chords of Memory*; Bodnar, *Remaking America*.

82. The first volume is Polishuk, *Sticking to the Union*. The call for manuscripts is located online at Palgrave Global Publishing at St. Martin's Press, Palgrave Studies in Oral History, University of Connecticut Center for Oral History, http://www.oralhistory.uconn.edu/palgrave.html (accessed January 31, 2005).

2

Oral History as Evidence

Ronald J. Grele

The question of evidence is as good a one as any, and probably better than most, around which to organize a few thoughts about oral history. What follows is a series of short discussions about the history and some of the unique characteristics of oral history, organized to highlight some interesting ways to discuss the context of the evidence produced by the oral history interview.

When asked to give a brief definition of evidence, a cynical lawyer friend claimed it was whatever the judge allowed. Now, the issue is much more complex, but it is useful to be reminded that a good deal of what is admissible (accepted) depends upon the gatekeepers, those who sanction the evidentiary value of whatever statements of fact or interpretation are offered in support of an argument or proposition. But those gatekeepers; their values, attitudes, and power; and the institutions they inhabit and structure change over time. Thus what historians consider evidence changes as well. To understand the ways in which oral history has been used as evidence it is necessary to sketch the larger and more complicated milieu of its history, a history now recognized as both international and interdisciplinary.

There are two themes to that history: the transformation of oral history from a source of information (data) to the production and interpretation of texts, and the alteration of the view of the oral historian/interviewer from objective and contemplative observer to active participant in the process. These two changes, which took place within a set of attitudes and traditions that structured the work of historians in general, and oral historians in particular, define our project. As the practice emerged after World War II, the attitudes and traditions within which it did so reflected the tension between those who saw oral history as archival practice and those who envisioned oral history as the handmaiden of social history.

From early reports and brief descriptions of oral history at particular institutions and in various parts of the world, the tension between archival projects and efforts in social history emerges clearly.[1] While there are distinctions to be made, complications to be noted, and silences to be explored, the general consensus is that the origin of oral history in the United States lay in archival practice, while in Europe the origin was the work of social historians. Therefore, those who followed the North American model established archival projects, and those following the European model accented the importance of social history.[2] Even a cursory examination indicates, however, that in the U.S. there was a good deal of oral history interviewing as part of the thrust of the new social history and that in most European countries many oral history projects did, indeed, spring from archival concerns. Although oral history efforts in various parts of the world responded to unique local traditions and particularistic pressures,[3] the archives–social history distinction seems to have been the general case, and it is still a useful way to categorize oral history in order to understand the evolution of its uses as evidence.

Oral History as Archival Practice

In the U.S. and those areas of the world affected by trends or institutions in the U.S., those who articulated, or tried to articulate, a definition of oral history linked that definition to archival practice. Worried that in the age of the telephone and an era when men of affairs no longer kept diaries or wrote memoirs, the founders of oral history in the U.S., those who gathered in California in 1967 to found the Oral History Association, argued that personal interviews, properly researched and processed, on file in manuscript collections and archives, would provide the basis for historical research and for the publications of historians and others in the future. The goal of this effort was to complement the existing written record with information gleaned from interviews and fill in the gaps in that record in the same manner that letters, journals, and diaries had done since the dawn of widespread literacy. According to Allan Nevins, the founder of the Columbia University Oral History Research Office, this effort sought to "hold in view the publishable book."[4] The implication was twofold: oral history interviews were to be collected to become the basis of the publication of more history books by people other than the people who gathered the interviews, and the individual oral history itself was to be treated as a book.[5] The oral history was to be transcribed, indexed, and edited as if it were a publication. In some cases this transcript was called a memoir, and it was often edited just as a publishable manuscript would be edited. For example, in the project Nevins led at Columbia University, where editing by project staff was minimal, the date of submission (completion of the process), not the date of the conduct of the interview, was the officially cataloged date of the interview, mimicking the world of publishing.[6] In all of this it was clear that the final product was to be offered to the historical profession as a document upon which, when complemented with written materials, books could be based. In line with this modest goal, Arthur M. Schlesinger Jr. spoke for many of his colleagues in seeing the value of oral history as "essentially supplementary evidence. What it is good at is to give a sense of the relations among people—who worked with whom, who liked whom, who influenced whom. . . . The recollected material cannot pretend to the exactitude of, say, the White House tapes of the Nixon years."[7] Many other members of the profession, however, thought the end result was minimally useful, providing only color or anecdote.[8]

Thus it was not extraordinary that most of the earliest American oral history projects were situated in archives, libraries, or manuscript collections, either academic or governmental, rather than within history departments at major universities, and that a great deal of attention was spent on questions of access, copyright, processing, and cataloging. Obviously, one of the major reasons for such a concern was to make the information contained in the interviews easily available. Scholars would not have to spend hours in a laborious effort to listen to the original tapes, and since tapes were not to be listened to, in some cases they were destroyed. Transcripts could much more easily be indexed, and in addition, transcribing imposed a standard for citation and quotation. It was also a way to enable archivists to apply all of the traditional standards that had been applied to written sources to these new sound recordings.[9] A secondary concern, but an important one, was to protect the interviewee from any embarrassments that the spontaneous interviewing technique might engender. Thus the transcripts were returned to the interviewees for their correction. While a case could be made that this produced a much more reliable document and therefore more reliable evidence because it included a second, more measured consideration on the part of the person interviewed, the major consideration seems to have been the feelings of unease on the part of archivists about the collection of potentially embarrassing, if not slanderous, material. Oral history evidence, since it was to be publicly available through the auspices of an institution, was to be evidence that would pass muster in line with the canons of the respectable publishing world. In addition, the concern with the rights of authors, in this case those interviewed, meant that the evidence produced by oral histories was to be subject to the ethics and legalities of the traditions of Anglo-American publishing.[10] The positive side of this practice was the fact that the document was to be made widely available, thus encouraging multiple interpretations and countering any tendency toward source monopoly.

The most striking characteristic of this effort was the concentration upon movers and shakers, those who ordinarily would have amassed a written record of their activities through saving of correspondence or in the minutes of meetings or other documents. This was certainly the case in various governmental projects, such as those at the presidential libraries, but was also true of those at the major universities. Even projects in labor history were more than likely to center their activities on union leaders rather than rank-and-file members of those same unions. In terms of who was to be interviewed, most projects were elitist to the core.

The experience and prestige of American oral history institutions, especially those connected to the federal government or located at major universities, such as Columbia, the University of California at Berkeley, and the University of California at Los Angeles, acted as a spur to oral history efforts in other nations. In some cases, such as Israel, the connection was direct. Elsewhere, such as in Malaysia, the connection was a U.S.-trained archivist who established the first organized government project. In other countries, such as Brazil and Indonesia, early efforts were funded by American foundations and purposely modeled on American practice.[11] In Mexico, France, and Canada, all areas with deep traditions of social history, many early projects were nonetheless located in archives, and archival concerns were an important part of the debates over the usefulness of oral history. In Singapore, David Lance, one of the few in the British oral history movement at the time concerned with archives and a recent arrival in the republic, was instrumental in assisting in establishing the first governmental archival projects. In other nations, such as Spain, Germany, the Philippines, and New Zealand, contacts between scholars using oral history and American archival projects were much more informal, but instrumental.[12] All of this activity meant that by the mid-1970s there was a flourishing of the collection of oral history recordings to be placed in archives or other depositories.

Oral History and Social History

If in the U.S. the original impetus for the development of the field was a concern for creating documents to fill a perceived vacuum in the existing record, elsewhere oral history emerged from the traditional practices of historians who had long used interviews as part of their effort to research the past. While the actual practice was nothing new, the name was, as was the mission, which as formulated for the most part by New Left historians was double edged: to create a history of the everyday lives of those who had heretofore been ignored by historians and thereby produce a "better" history, and to radicalize the practice of history by contesting a "hegemonic" view of agency and power.

The most thoroughly articulated description of the conjoined evolution of oral history and the "new" social history is *The Voice of the Past* by Paul Thompson.[13] In Thompson's view, oral history was the latest stage of a long tradition in the use of "oral evidence" to uncover the history of everyday life, in the fullest sense of "everyday," from the minutest aspects of the interior world of the family to the largest propositions of oppositional culture. Starting with Herodotus, including Jules Michelet's study of the French Revolution, and moving through folklore studies, the traditions of social reportage, such as Henry Mayhew and Beatrice and Sidney Webb, the work of the Chicago school of sociology, and the Works Progress Administration's American slave narratives, Thompson traced a long lineage for oral history.[14] If archival oral history came into its own as something new with the invention of the tape recorder, oral history in social history had always been a part of historical studies. Its patrimony was social history with a small *s*. No longer the story of Lady Millicent and Lord Gotrocks and their comings and goings on their estates or in their town houses, this was the history of the ordinary and everyday life of the working class and its constituent components, such as women, children, and racial and ethnic minorities, those whose stories had been ignored in the traditional tale of political and economic power. Oral history was, thus, to play a vital role in the culturalist formations of social history being articulated by British and American social historians, most notably E. P. Thompson, Eric Hobsbawm, Herbert Gutman, and Eugene Genovese.[15] It was to be a part of the struggle to produce a history from below.[16]

Practitioners believed that not only would this use of oral history produce a better history, one more attuned to the real tensions of the social order, but it would also provide the base for a reorientation of the discipline of history. At a minimum, oral history would aid in the transformation of history from a discipline to an activity.[17] At its most ambitious, the claim was that the study of history would become a tool for the reconstruction of the social order, a method of consciousness raising, and that the oral history interview would be both another moment in that consciousness raising and the basis for the articulation of a radical vision among activists.[18] Those studied would be radicalized by the process of recalling their pasts and its oppressions, and those studying would become part of the ongoing struggle against oppression. Radical and dissenting traditions would be revived and become a part of current social movements. This double vision was an integral part of the thrust of oral history not only in Great Britain and Scandinavia but also in many parts of the world where historians were attempting to understand the legacy of oppression, such as with fascism and Nazism or Stalinism in continental Europe, apartheid in South Africa, locally repressive regimes such as those then existing in various parts of Latin America, or the lasting effects of a brutal colonialism.[19] Unsurprisingly, the *History Workshop Journal*, one of the loci of oral history in Great Britain, was founded by, and titled itself a journal for, socialist historians.

The differences in the two approaches to the collection of oral history interviews were clear. There seemed to be little consensus on such questions as who was to be interviewed, who was to do the interviewing, and what should be done with the interview. Broadly speaking, in one view, those who left a record as a research base were to be the subjects of an interview while in the other the exact opposite was the goal. Archival projects separated the creation of the interview from the end use, while social historians argued that those who did the interviews should also be responsible for their use and interpretation, thereby introducing one of the most crucial distinctions between oral history and other forms of historical research: the fact that in this case historians themselves were creating the very documents that they were called upon to interpret. Although the claim may bring a smile today, the charge made by Philip C. Brooks of the Truman Library at the founding meeting of the U.S. Oral History Association, that "the person who is collecting a stock of evidence for other researchers to use is almost by definition to be doing a more objective job than the one who is writing his own book, especially the one who has a case to prove," clearly demonstrated that there is a fundamental, unresolved theoretical and methodological issue involved in the practice.[20]

There was also dispute as to the final disposition of the interview. While archivists and manuscript librarians were deeply concerned with the ways in which the interview was to be processed and made available to the public, this was not a major concern for practicing historians. Nor, did it seem, was source monopoly a particular issue.

It might be easy to draw too sharp a geographical line between these two forms of oral history. As noted above, there were any number of archival projects in various European and Latin American nations, Australia, and South Africa and, likewise, many U.S. projects in social history, particularly at the University of North Carolina and Duke University.[21] The arguments, however, could become personal and heated.[22] In time, interest in these distinctions, which once seemed so important, waned. As more researchers working in archives began to make use of their interviews for various purposes, sometimes even publishing monographs using the interviews, as more projects in social history were founded as both archives and publishing ventures, and as more historians sought to locate their interviews in various repositories, the controversy faded.[23] But the division between the two forms of oral history persisted, and rightly so, for they do define real differences in approach, use, and audience.[24] Interviews collected in an archive are used by historians several steps removed from the process of creation, and historians who deposit their interviews find that they are used and interpreted by others in ways sharply at odds with their creation. These differences are important considerations in the resolution of the debates over all aspects of the oral history process. In time, however, even with these concerns in mind, one was able to discern, from a different perspective, ways in which both oral history as archival practice and oral history as social history shared a set of assumptions about historical practice.

A Common World

Looking back at the ways in which the practice of oral history emerged in the 1960s and 1970s, it now seems clear that—whatever the forms—the thought and actual work were based upon a set of common interests and assumptions. Chief among these were a concern with local history, a view of the relation of oral history to the historical profession, and a common set of epistemological assumptions. Each of these commonalities contained its own unique problems and possibilities.

For differing but complementary reasons, both strands of thinking in oral history had a great interest and effect upon efforts at local history. Those who sought to build archives of oral documents often encouraged local libraries, historical societies, or voluntary agencies to initiate projects to collect interviews with local leaders. Building upon long traditions of local history, it was quite natural that oral history would become a part of the surge to know one's local history and to create a documentary basis for that history. So, too, the thrust of social history to move beyond the history of the political center or the capital gave a political urgency to local efforts to document daily life. If, for example, the new agricultural history was to move beyond parliamentary debates or national markets to a study of daily farming practices, it was to the local that one would have to turn for evidence; so, too, with all the other subfields of social history. In the long run, it may be that the greatest glory of oral history was its role in the revivification of local history. But this was also a new local history, one that sought to inculcate pride and identity as well as political agency in the local.[25] In this sense, community historians introduced a new concept of evidence into the discussions of oral history and revealed the tension within social history between some academic professionals and community historians.

A corollary of this interest in local and community history was the use of oral history as a teaching tool on the elementary and high school levels. Especially in the Anglo-Saxon world, teachers received encouragement to send their students into the community to conduct interviews and found welcome within the major national and regional associations, most of which very early established separate education committees to promote such a use for oral history.[26]

Both the new social historians and archivists building collections also shared the assumption that the evidence produced by oral history interviewing was similar to other evidence used by historians and thus could be tested and analyzed in the same manner as historians had done in the past. For many local historians this was also the case. But community historians saw the world somewhat differently, as the term *community* indicates. Community implied that there was some emotional or symbolic (subjective) relationship between people in a local area, and between the historian who was working in that area collecting interviews and the people he or she was interviewing. Oral history evidence was therefore evidence of those connections. Despite the fact that it proved very difficult to come to any general or theoretical understanding of or definition of "community," advocates claimed that oral history was to have uses far beyond the creation of historical texts, and those uses were many and varied, ranging from political mobilization to forms of therapy.[27]

The overlap between social historians and archivists was also, and most importantly for the issues of this essay, apparent in their shared vision of what kind of historical work was to be privileged, what a historical document was, and how it was to be read. While it is important to recognize the differences in attitude between the archival view of oral history and the social history view, ironically enough, spokespeople for both shared a basic assumption that the end result to be privileged, even among some local and community projects, was the published monograph. The leaders in the field recognized the vitality of oral history collection for purposes of museum exhibits, radio programming, or community programs, but when assessing the value and achievements of oral history, it was the listing of monographs published from interviewing that remained the focus. A close look at Thompson's chapter on the achievement of oral history and at the footnotes to that chapter, and an equally close look at the various annual reports written by Louis Starr and published by the Columbia University Oral History Research Office, will immediately reveal the similarity.[28] In both cases, there is a defensive posture that seeks, since oral history was then still seen as a marginal practice, a certain respectability by reference to its usefulness to the profession's traditional heart.

This defensiveness speaks to the marginality of oral history at that time, which in turn helps to explain the traditionalism of the description of what an oral history interview was, how it was created, and how it was to be read.[29] Oral history interviews were seen as documents similar to all other documents, to be treated by the historian in the same manner as he or she would treat any other source. Thus, theorists argued, there was an understandable gap between the historian and the source (the person interviewed). The historian as interviewer and interpreter was a distanced and contemplative observer in the same manner as someone examining a manuscript. The source was what was to be observed. The knowledgeable and "objective" historian was to use the tools of a traditional historiography to discover the "truth" that resided in the sources in the guise of facts that were to be extracted. These facts were transparent in their meaning and could be tested for their accuracy, verifiability, and representativeness by the historian, whose role was unquestioned and whose cultural position in a world of production was invisible. Knowledge lay in the accumulation of the facts, the interconnectedness of which was assumed to be discoverable by the properly trained outside observer, and the problems of those using oral history were the same for those using all sources and were matters of technique. The goal was the production of information, which could be weighed by the traditional methods of historical inquiry for its reliability and verifiability.

It is not unusual that the fullest description of a discourse rests with the critique of that discourse. In this case, the clearest exposition of the view of interviews as data can be found in two critical analyses of *The Voice of the Past*: one by the Birmingham Centre for Contemporary Cultural Studies Popular Memory Group and the other by John Murphy for the Australian journal *Historical Studies*.[30] Both critiques were deeply skeptical of what they saw as the empiricism and positivism of Thompson's view of oral history, especially his emphasis on accuracy and his unwillingness to see the oral history as a cultural artifact. It must be noted, however, that Thompson was hardly alone in this view. Therefore, it is somewhat unfair to single him out for criticism. Brooks, as noted earlier, articulated the same vision in the U.S. in the early deliberations of the Oral History Association, as did Nevins, who went even further than Thompson in claiming that interviewers must settle for no "evasions," and that it was their "duty" to get "clear and veracious answers" through a "rigid" and "severe" "cross-examination."[31] Essays by Alice Hoffman, William Cutler, and William Moss made the same points, although a bit more subtly. The same assumptions could be found in most reports from the field in any number of national publications.[32] They informed most of the handbooks and primers published during these years, either explicitly with reference to works in the social sciences or implicitly, as if such a view was to be beyond question.[33]

The general lack of theoretical introspection about such issues resulted in endless discussion of the techniques of interviewing. There was, to be sure, a naïve realization that the oral history interview was somehow different because it exhibited certain unique characteristics in its reliance upon memory and the social relations of the interview, which involved the historian directly in the face-to-face creation of the documents that he or she would later use or that would be used by others at some later date. But the discourse focused on how the interview situation could be manipulated to overcome this relationship or how it could be used to obtain the most valid document. The problems presented by the interview were solvable within the traditions of common sense that historians applied to all sources. Such an articulation of the task was the common discourse among oral historians.

Despite these theoretical limitations and despite the seeming cogency of the criticism that the narrow view of the practice resulted in the failure by those who collected and used oral history interviews to realize the full potential of oral history to challenge the traditional strictures of the historical profession or to realize its radical promise, it was clear by the early 1970s that both oral history approaches—archival and social history—had attained a popularity and respectability beyond question. Even looking with a skeptical eye over the various bibliographies touting the practice, it was a remarkable product. More and more historians, especially former 1960s activists who had entered the academy and were creating the subfields of working-class, women's, African American, and ethnic history were using oral history collections or conducting interviews for their monographs. Oral history had, indeed, creatively expanded the horizons of the new social history by producing new evidence or new ways to read old evidence. Colleges and universities in large numbers were offering courses in the technique, and increasing numbers of foundations were willing to fund work in oral history. It took no one by surprise when the Oral History Association in the U.S. titled its 1974 annual meeting "Oral History Comes of Age." It was simply one echo of the self-congratulatory tone that was creeping into discussions among oral historians.

Academics and Activists

The hesitancy to join in this chorus of praise for the academic uses of oral history came, for the most part, not from traditional historians, although there were some holdouts to this euphoria, but from community historians and especially those with a New Left political agenda, who argued that the increasing use of oral history for academic purposes had put the practice out of reach for ordinary people. In addition, the increasingly abstract nature of the language used and the high prices of academic publications posed a barrier to effective politics. Such charges reflected the tensions between academic and activist historians.[34]

As noted above, community historians and political activists had long recognized that the intimate relationship engendered in the interview situation was as important as the reading of the texts it produced, and many had come to argue that that relationship now made it possible to gather history "pure." If the academy had failed to produce a history of the heretofore excluded, one reason was that academicians had not been willing to listen to them. Now it was possible to get a history from, as some said, "the horse's mouth," directly from the people without the intervening ideology of the professional caste of historians and sociologists. The radicalism of oral history lay in the fact that it gave a voice to the people themselves. This became a very potent argument in the world of oral history.[35]

Because there was, with few exceptions, no deeper dialogue, the discussion of the interview relation devolved into the debate over, on the one hand, the practice of "professional" historians and archivists seeking to produce works that neutralized the relationship between the parties to an interview while retaining the right of interpretation for the historian versus, on the other, the reification of the experience in the name of consciousness raising. The contrast between these two attitudes was brilliantly dissected by Michael Frisch. Reviewing Studs Terkel's *Hard Times*, Frisch raised fundamental questions about the nature of oral history as it had emerged from the 1960s as a source for information and insight to be used in traditional ways and as a way of bypassing historical interpretation. Frisch found in the enthusiasm surrounding oral history a contradictory set of attitudes toward history, neither of them very historical and both deeply conservative in their implications. The first was the view that oral history was more history, simply piling on more and more data. The second was the populist drive to escape history embedded in the articulated mission to somehow go beyond professional historians and get a purer history from the voices of the folk. Neither posture, he argued, spoke to the potentials of oral history or to the issues of the ways in which memory and historical construction guided the ways in which people made their histories and lived their lives in history. The real issue for Frisch was how readers are "to understand the variable weave of pure recall and reflective synthesis—historical statements as well as historical information—that characterize almost all of the interviews" in Terkel's work.[36] Neither more history nor no history speaks to the larger issues of the understanding of consciousness. Instead, Frisch saw a much more complex task for oral history:

> By studying how experience, memory, and history become combined in and digested by people who are the bearers of their own history and that of their culture, oral history opens up a powerful perspective; it encourages us to stand somewhat aside of cultural forms in order to observe their workings. Thus it permits us to track the elusive beasts of consciousness and culture in a way impossible to do from within. . . . Although it is so tempting to take historical testimony to be history itself . . . the very documents of oral history really suggest a different lesson.[37]

It was clear that oral historians were being called upon to rethink the practice in ways that would move the theory of evidence beyond the search for data about events and force a consideration of the dynamic and dialectic relationship of interviewer and interviewee in the creation of what could only be called a text.

The Transformation

The approach that Frisch took toward reading an oral history interview was one of a number of new ways of understanding and speculating upon the practice that emerged in the mid- to late 1970s that would transform the field: the transformation, already noted, from the search for information to a search for a method of reading the text as more than simply a document. This in turn was a part of a much wider and deeper shift in historical studies from social history to cultural studies.[38]

From the earliest days, there had always been voices urging a more complex reading of oral histories. In England, Elizabeth Tonkin in her concern with "oracy" sought to combine social anthropology, ethnomethodology, and literary analysis to understand the sense of history underlying oral testimony, while in the U.S., Corinne Gilb urged archivists collecting oral history interviews to use those interviews for insights into cultural construction. In another example, Saul Benison talked about the interview as a first interpretation and noted that the mutual creation of the interview is both the strength and the weakness of the document.[39]

One of the most interesting early examples of the changing nature of the discourse about oral history is the work of Martin Duberman in *Black Mountain*, a study of an experimental college in North Carolina that flourished in the 1930s and 1940s. Elsewhere, I have gone into some detail about *Black Mountain*.[40] My reading of the book is that Duberman found himself caught between the traditional expectations of the historical profession as to how evidence should be mobilized and the creative possibilities of oral history fieldwork, a tension so severe that he himself admits he had to put the work aside for a number of years because he had to break through the boundaries of the discipline. His problem was how he could explore and represent the reactions of those he interviewed to their own historical experiences and his own at the same time. The following excerpt catches his dilemma:

> My journal, Monday, August 3, 1970: The data is taking over again. Or rather, my compulsiveness about being totally accurate and inclusive. I start letting myself go . . . [but] get deflected into incorporating . . . material into earlier sections; mostly additional citations to footnotes rather than changing interpretations—just the kind of silly "iceberg" scholarship . . . that I rhetorically scorn. By the time I come back to the question that had started to excite me, I am leaden with repetitive information to other people's reactions to other issues. How can I explore theirs and mine simultaneously? I don't want to evade and distort their views, but I don't want fidelity to theirs to take over, to obliterate mine. . . . It's an example of how destructive so-called "professional training" can be: it initiates you into and confirms the rightness of techniques previously used by others. Yet . . . there aren't any techniques, only personalities.[41]

Today this tension is termed the quest to understand intersubjectivity. That Duberman could not fully resolve the contradictions is not surprising, but the effort is a wonderful example of a moment in the history of oral history. Harshly criticized when first published,[42] the book has become one of the classic texts in oral history.

By the mid- to late 1970s, the questions that captured Duberman's attention were being asked by more and more historians using oral history or doing oral history interviews. If oral history interviews were evidence of the ways in which one understood the past, they were unique documents. The intervention of the historian in the very document he or she was called upon to interpret was something new. In addition, it was clear that oral histories were documents of the here and now about the then and there, fusing past and present in a complex web of interpretation. Also, with the fascination with "reconstituting the small details of everyday life" and "the shift from 'places to faces,' from topographical peculiarities to the quality of life,"[43] in the words of Raphael Samuel, oral history ran into all of the problems of the individualizing tendencies of biography. The oral history interview also brought subjectivity, the subject's view of himself or herself as a cultural actor, to the fore. In their dialogical creation, layers of interpretation, and varied uses, oral history interviews raised fundamental historiographical questions.[44]

It was clear that the interview did uncover what happened in the past and that oral history did expand the realm of what was studied, but it was also clear that the interview was evidence of the ways in which history lived on in the present and the ways in which the present informed a view of the past. In the words of Alessandro Portelli, "The unique and precious element which oral sources force upon the historian and which no other sources possess in equal measure (unless it be literary ones) is the speaker's subjectivity; and therefore if the research is broad and articulated enough, a cross-section of the subjectivity of a social group or class. They tell us not what people did, but what they wanted to do, what they believed they were doing, what they now think they did. . . . Subjectivity is as much the business of history as the more visible facts."[45] In accepting this view, however, it was necessary to accept the view that those interviewed were more than just repositories of facts to be gathered by the historians. It was necessary to see interviewees, if not as direct voices from the past, as in some manner their own historians, capable of elaborate and sometimes confusing methods of constructing and narrating their own histories.

What then was the nature of the relationship between the past as expressed in the interview and the present in which the interview was being conducted, and in what ways did the interaction of the interviewer and interviewee influence or determine these relationships? Also, how is the interviewer to understand the testimony given when it was clearly more than a simple recitation of what happened in the past, but also articulated complicated mental reconstructions? While the arguments over these questions have a very convoluted and complex history, in brief, these issues merged with a New Left concern with questions of subjectivity—not only the subjective areas of mental life, such as ideology, memory, consciousness, and myth expressed by both interviewer and interviewee in the interview, but also the question of how the subject is formed in history, the structured and structuring of consciousness. In Italy, Luisa Passerini merged the fieldwork she undertook interviewing working-class Italians in Turin with the questions of subjectivity as asked by George Lukács and Antonio Gramsci in order to understand the complicated interweaving of the work ethic and silences about the fascist period in Italy. This allowed her to talk about those silences as a deep wound in worker consciousness of their acceptance of fascism and, in the process, raise fundamental questions about the ability of the traditional categories of social history to deal with such subjectivity. In those same years, Portelli began to apply the concerns of narrative theory to the oral history interview in order to see the telling of a story as a cultural practice with consequences for an understanding of consciousness.[46]

In England, the Birmingham Popular Memory Group in its critique of Thompson called for a new and more radical way of thinking about oral history in order to understand the struggles over popular memory. The manifesto of that group was the most explicit in denying the epistemological basis of both the traditional methods of the profession and the new social history, in particular.[47] In *Envelopes of Sound*, I tried to merge a concern with the structure of the interview and the work of Louis Althusser to understand the social, linguistic, and ideological structure of the historical text, which I termed a conversational narrative. The goal was to capture the two dimensions of our interest: the nature of the story and its creation through the interaction of the two parties to the interview.[48] Work with a similar concern with text, work that significantly enlarged the boundaries of the discussion about oral history, was done by Tonkin in Great Britain, Lutz Neithammer in Germany, and Phillipe Joutard in France.[49] By 1979, the *History Workshop Journal* could editorialize: "Recent developments in the methodology [of oral history] suggest that the potential exists for a more speculative and analytic approach to the evidence. For Marxists [the particular audience for the *Journal*], conversely, they show that theoretical categories and questions can be transformed in light of a critical interpretation of the evidence."[50]

All of this produced a very lively and complicated mix. Recognizing the potential of oral history to radically alter the ways in which history was understood led some scholars to ask new questions about memory and consciousness, while others began to think of new ways to teach history and new ways to mobilize sound and the new media in that teaching. Others saw in oral history the potential for historical drama or therapy. The inherent interdisciplinarity of the practice was evident.[51]

While it would take the rest of this volume to list the various sources of this new view of the possibilities of oral history, a few publications should be noted. The work of Passerini and Portelli, already mentioned, is crucial for an understanding of the explorations of subjectivity as well as the relationship between interviewer and interviewee. Portelli's chapter in *The Death of Luigi Trastulli*, on oral history as an experiment in equality, Michael Frisch's *A Shared Authority*, and the various essays in *Interactive Oral History Interviewing*, edited by Eva McMahan and Kim Lacy Rogers, explore in different ways the problems of the fieldwork relationship that so vexed Duberman.[52] Again, Portelli's various volumes have been instrumental in developing our thinking on the role of narrative in oral history, collective and individual memory, and the politics of history. Peter Friedlander, Virginia Yans-McLaughlin, and Samuel, concentrating on the relationship between individual biography and collective consciousness as expressed in the interview, contributed to a much more complex understanding of the nature of autobiography and political militancy. *Amoskeag*, by Tamara Hareven, explored the interstices of industrial and labor history. The essays compiled by Sherna Gluck and Daphne Patai in *Women's Words*, as well as the essays by Sally Alexander, Anna Davin, and other feminists writing in *History Workshop* and other journals, explored the crucial and variegated relations between feminist theory, subjectivity, narrativity, and oral history. All of this work has been predicated upon the proposition that oral history, while it does tell us about how people lived in the past, also, and maybe more importantly, tells us how that past lives on into and informs the present.[53]

One area in which oral historians were confronted with questions about the ways in which this tension between past and present expresses itself is trauma studies, a genre in itself. Centered at first among those who were interviewing Holocaust survivors, the concerns with issues of trauma were quite naturally extended to interviews with survivors of political torture, experiences such as rape, or other horrendous events. On such projects it was clear that the historian could not remain a contemplative presence, that the interview process itself as an experience became a moment in the resolution of the conflicts over the past, or a moment in the revivification of the original emotions of powerlessness and victimization and all the attendant consequences of that re-emergence. While these issues cannot be explored here in any great detail, it is important to keep them in mind in any discussion of what kinds of evidentiary uses of oral history are possible, any discussion of subjectivity in the interview, and our later discussion of memory. As stated by Jay Winter and Emmanuel Sivan, "Under specific conditions and occasionally long after the initial set of 'traumatic events,' . . . extrinsic contexts can produce overwhelming recall. At this point memory crowds out everything else; it is potentially paralytic."[54] Dominick LaCapra has been particularly insightful about the consequences for the oral historian (and, by implication, the challenges for historical reconstruction and dialogic exchange) of the ways that the past is reworked in Holocaust testimonies.[55] Many of these issues will be noted again in the discussion of the uses of oral history in the post–Cold War era.

The collective effect of work in oral history in the 1970s and 1980s that sought to move from issues in social history to cultural studies, as previously noted, was summed up in 1990 by Samuel and Thompson in their introduction to *The Myths We Live By*, a compilation of papers delivered at the Sixth International Oral History Conference held at Oxford, England, in 1987. "This volume," the authors argued,

> suggests how far the concerns of oral historians have shifted over the last decade. When we listen now to a life story, the manner of its telling seems to us as important as what is told. We find ourselves exploring interdisciplinary territory alongside others for whom the nature of narrative is a primary issue: among the anthropologists, psychoanalysts, historians . . . who recognize history itself as a narrative construction, literary critics who read metaphors as clues to social consciousness. This new sensitivity can strengthen some of the earlier purposes of oral historians. . . . As soon as we recognize the value of the subjective in individual testimonies, we challenge the accepted categories of history.[56]

When one examines the content of that volume, there is no disputing the claims of the editors. For anyone interested in the ways in which oral history interviewing, when creatively conceived and used, can open new avenues of thought about historical processes, many of the essays in the volume provide the starting point. The essays excite the reader with how myth, memory, narrative, and history are interwoven with an insight into how biography and testimony, in both manner and mode, can penetrate into the ways in which language becomes history. Certainly, there are questions to be asked about some of the points raised by the particular uses of myth in these essays, but gone are the tentativeness and apologetics that governed much of the early work with oral history interviews. Present is a comfort with subjective evidence and the ways in which it can be conceived theoretically.[57]

This transformation of oral history was, of course, part of a much larger transformation, one that has come to be called the "linguistic turn," "the historical turn," or the turn to cultural studies.[58] To detail these changes in any depth is beyond the charge of this essay. Essentially what was involved was the acceptance of a set of assumptions about the study of history, many of which had a period of long gestation. Grounding all else was the concept that history (knowledge about the past) was not something to be discovered in the facts or in the events of the past. It was, rather, a historically and culturally specific construction, and the ways in which it was constructed had to be comprehended for it to be understood and analyzed. Foremost, history, as all knowledge, was constructed through the agency of language and discourse. Historical narratives were not evinced in the ways in which events related to one another in a system of causality, but in the ways the imagination of the historian used words to create a symbolic world. It was through language that one discerned what Clifford Geertz called the "ensemble of texts" that composed a culture.[59] Language was structured and structuring. Thus, social history, with its accent upon what was now seen to be a narrow, class-based sociology, was to be invigorated with a new cultural vision. In part, this was a reaction to the trends of the 1960s arguing that historical studies must make way for issues of race, gender, and sexuality, which could not be explained within the traditional categories of social history.

In this view it was not the facts of experience but the "experience of experience" that was of interest. There was no master narrative but only stories and ambiguities. In a world where the personal was the political, one was concerned with the interrogation of such categories as nation, race, and gender to capture how understanding was revealed in practice. Thus data was interpretation. Gone was the objective observer, and politics was to be understood as the process by which plays of power and knowledge constitute identity and experience.

Oral historians, increasingly concerned with issues of narrative and subjectivity, found a comfortable milieu in cultural studies and a new sense of security about what it is they were studying and how they wished to study it: thus the optimism of the *History Workshop Journal* 1990 introduction. This optimism was confirmed by the privileged place given oral history in a special 1989 edition of the *Journal of American History* devoted to the analysis of memory. In that issue, David Thelen, the journal's editor, stressed the importance of oral history in studying memory and encouraged the profession to examine the rich literature then emerging.[60] To a large degree it was obvious that if the historical profession had gatekeepers who determined what was and what was not evidence, oral history had been admitted to the bar.

Thus, in the mid-1980s, three new critiques of the practice of oral history went almost totally ignored, despite the fact that they were offered by three major figures in the profession who under ordinary circumstances would have been considered gatekeepers. In the first case, Dominique Aron-Schnapper, in her comments at the Fourth International Conference on Oral History in Aix-en-Provence, France, argued that oral historians should not concern themselves with elaborate constructions to understand subjectivity but should return to and concentrate upon the archival task of filling in the gaps in the written record. In the second case, Louise Tilly, then president of the Social Science History Association in the U.S., speaking from the perspective of quantification and social history, criticized both oral history and people's history. And Patrick O'Farrell, in Australia, argued that the whole mission, either of social history or community history, was a waste of the historian's time for little gain:

a feckless effort to fill the pages of history with the history of "ordinary" people, whose history, basically, is uninteresting.[61]

The most cogent of these critiques was that of Tilly because it stated the case so clearly. The task of social science history, she argued, is "research that attempts generalizations of some breadth verified by . . . quantitative analysis when appropriate."[62] The concern with subjectivity and the claims made by oral historians and people's historians rested upon a "radical passivity" mixed with a concept of "subjectivity" and would never produce a valid historiography. In particular, she argued, the emphasis upon the individual testimony as an insight into collective representations and cultural identities is "ahistorical and unsystematic."[63] The responses from a number of oral historians, and then Tilly's response to those comments, all of which were published in the *International Journal of Oral History*, offer a wonderful insight into the then current debates over the nature of the evidence produced by oral historians and its uses.[64]

While these critiques are now of some historical interest, they did little to alter the direction of oral history. That direction was clear: oral history was becoming increasingly interdisciplinary, increasingly international, increasingly focused upon issues of subjectivity, and increasingly interested in how to use the potential of the interview and the language of the interview to understand that subjectivity, whether it was memory, ideology, myth, consciousness, identity, desire, or any other such attributes. One caution from that time, however, must be noted and is addressed below. In his review of the English version of Passerini's *Fascism in Popular Memory*, Richard Cándida Smith warned that in viewing the oral history interview as a cultural form that merges subjectivity and the narrative mode, "further thought needs to be given to how oral history can be read for evidence of the interaction of culture and political action."[65]

Narrative

Because it has always been first and foremost a fieldwork practice, oral history had always looked to other disciplines for guidance, if not standards. Its early practitioners were particularly interested in similar work in sociology, behavioral psychology, law, applied anthropology, or journalism.[66] This was a natural crossover for those concerned with gathering and using evidence that for the most part was to be transposed into written form or into measurable or statistical relationships and therefore could meet the judgment of verifiability, reliability, validity, and representation as defined by the dominant intellectual strictures of the time. Even when one recognized the natural affinity for biographical and autobiographical studies, as Nevins obviously did, the basic approach mirrored the empiricism of these disciplines. A clear example of this connection is Thompson's first major work, *The Edwardians*, in which he tried to meld his oral history interviewing with a selection of interviewees based upon a properly drawn sample derived from early twentieth-century censuses.[67] By the mid-1980s, however, attention was directed toward disciplines such as cultural anthropology, linguistics, literary studies, philosophy, folklore, and cultural studies, which were more likely to attract students of language and culture broadly defined.[68] To be sure, many, if not most, studies using oral history were still concerned with the ways in which individual recitations of experience could be related to collective behavior, but such studies would now also note the importance of language and story in the formation of the connection. This resulted, among other things, in a new fieldwork stance. Whereas in the search for a "scientific" procedure for interviewing the traditional advice was to urge the interviewer into a contemplative and distanced relation with the person interviewed, oral historians now argued for a closer and more interactive response. In the language of the time, the shift was from transactional to intersubjective.[69] In this shift the role of the conception of narrative was fundamental.

When I talked about a conversational narrative in *Envelopes of Sound*, I had in mind a very unsophisticated idea of what was meant by narrative. Essentially, I defined it simply as the telling of a tale of change over time. If any theory was involved, it was quite simple. The story, however conceived, began with a description of a state of stasis, then some disruptive event or experience was introduced to upset that stasis, and finally some resolution that restored stasis was forthcoming. Even a brief examination of the use of narrative by oral historians today, such

as Passerini, Portelli, Daniel James, and especially Tonkin, reveals how naïve that earlier insight was, especially its implication of the unity of action and meaning.[70]

Passerini describes her interviews in various places as oral
narratives, but the actual relationship between those interviews
and narrative theory is embedded in the detailed discussion of
particular interviews and the forms that they take. The interview, she says, is "a semi-structured conversation, which is . . .
more concerned with drawing out forms of cultural identity and
shared traditions than with the factual aspects of social history."[71] The most concise statement of Passerini's idea of a narrative can be found in the Smith review already noted, in which
he pulls together the discussion of narrative inherent in
Passerini's treatment of fascism. In that review, Smith notes how
"the ideas, images and linguistic strategies found in oral narratives constitute what Passerini calls 'the symbolic order of everyday life.'"[72] This view allows Passerini to open her investigation
to the ways in which traditional oral sources provided a repertoire for and merged into the new telling of the story for the historian, the ways in which silences become a part of the narrative,
and the possibilities of understanding collective memory and
thought through the oral narrative.

Portelli is equally concerned with the search for the subjective in oral narratives, but his use of narrative theory is much
more, by his own admission, ad hoc and inductive, seeking to
find in the stories themselves the structures of form. He uses, he
says, "literature, folklore, and linguistics to develop a method
for the study of subjectivity by focusing on the implications of
the verbal strategies used by the narrators. . . . Oral historical
sources are *narrative* sources. Therefore the analysis of oral history materials must avail itself of some of the general categories
developed by narrative theory in literature and folklore. This is
as true of testimony given in free interviews as of the more formally organized materials of folklore."[73] Some of the elements of
narrative Portelli suggests one look for are shifts in velocity, distance, perspective, folk elements, digressions, anecdotes, and
other recurring structures.

Portelli is also intrigued with the dialogic nature of the interview, his own role in the process, and the ways in which nar-

ratives emerge through this dialogue.[74] Because his use of narrative is ad hoc, it appears throughout his by now fairly large corpus, but a casual glance at any number of essays will reveal to the reader the constant and steady negotiations between oral expressions and literary works and traditions, and how those works and traditions help explain and, in turn, are explained by the dialogic nature of the oral history interview.[75]

It should be clear that narrative in an oral history interview does not mean a clearly articulated story that runs in precise chronological pattern. In fact, the request for that kind of narrative might be precisely the wrong kind of question for an interviewer to ask.[76] Rather, the oral historian must follow the patterns set by the people interviewed, which is not that difficult to do since it is the form of every conversation—to follow the gist. The more complex story is usually reconstructed at a later time. In other words, the narrative is constructed syntagmatically.[77]

Drawing upon the oral history work of Passerini and Portelli and the writings on narrative of a wide range of scholars from various disciplines, James succinctly states the case in his life history of an Argentine working-class militant, with reference to David Carr's *Time, Narrative, and History*: "The 'recent blurring of the genres' has induced an increased sensitivity among historians—perhaps most intensively among oral historians—to the importance of narrative as an ordering, sense-making device at both the collective and individual level. As Carr argues, 'At the individual level, people make sense of their lives through stories that are available to them, and they attempt to fit their lives into the available stories. People live by stories.'" James adds, "At a more general level, communities, too, adopt narratives that inculcate and confirm their integrity and coherence over time."[78] In this view, narrative has become the central characteristic and organizing principle for the oral history interview. In essence, the narrative itself becomes a fact of historical interest.

The most complex and nuanced recent treatment of oral history and narrative form is Tonkin's work in *Narrating Our Pasts*, wherein she sets for herself the difficult task of understanding "the mode or genre in which temporal accounts occur in order to grasp the character of the interlocutors' social action and to evaluate the information that the account conveys."[79] Quoting Karin Barber, Tonkin outlines the paradoxical complexity of the task:

"To grasp their historical intent we need to view [representations of pastness] as literature; to grasp their literary mode we need to view them as part of social action; to grasp their role in social action we need to see their historical intent."[80] Assuming that the historian who uses the recollections of others cannot just seek facts, "like currants from a cake," because those facts are embedded in interpretations and therefore can only be understood by understanding the representation, its ordering, its plotting, and its metaphors, Tonkin raises most of the basic issues of narrative analysis of oral accounts—their structuring, the ways in which they relate to social conditions, the performative nature of orality (or oracity, as she calls it), which distinguish oral from literary accounts—and explores questions of memory ("the dialectical interlocking of recall and social nexus") and time.[81] All of this is done within a keen grasp of the interwoven aims and ambitions and social conditions of both parties to the fieldwork experience. *Narrating Our Pasts* must now be the starting point for any discussion of the role of narrative in the understanding of the meaning of the evidence produced in an oral history interview.

In his 1984 critique of Thompson, John Murphy calls for an interpretative reading of oral history texts. In particular, he argues for attention to the problems of the interaction between language and memory and for the centrality of metaphor, since "metaphor is the dominant mode in which oral history functions . . . and a key to a cultural reading on how the past is remembered."[82] Just how far in that direction oral history work has come can be seen in the essays in *Narrative and Genre*, edited by Mary Chamberlain and Paul Thompson, that examine narrative from a variety of perspectives, including literary studies, anthropology, philosophy, folklore, and communications theory, and that, in most cases, begin their analysis with references to Tonkin. The editors' introduction is an excellent posing of the problems and potentials of genre studies of oral autobiography.[83] These and other such studies, almost by necessity, point us to other much more fundamental considerations of narrative, such as those posed by Carr, Jerome Bruner, Donald Spence, and Donald Polkinghorne.[84]

Narrative was a vital part of the so-called cultural turn, and issues raised by narrative, genre, storytelling, and autobiography became an important part of the discourse across disciplinary boundaries.[85] It is far from the task of this essay to parse the subtle similarities and differences between these authors, particularly as to the issue of the discontinuity or continuity between narrative and everyday life, but a few general points should be noted. Narrative means more than simply the mode of the telling of a story that can be studied in a manner abstracted from the life of the person telling the story. Narrative has come to be described as an act of mind, one that, as Carr stated, "arises out of and is prefigured in certain features of life, action, and communication."[86] Karen Halttunen explains, "For Carr, our narratives reflect a fundamental property of human consciousness; they are part of the fabric of human life."[87] In this sense, it is narrative that lends structure to the experience of experience and unites the individual to the collective practically, cognitively, and aesthetically, and therefore encompasses a social relationship and identity. Integral to the construction of memory, narrative is the "organizing principal of human experience," according to Polkinghorne.[88] In the transformation of oral history from a concern with data to a concern with narrative, what one considers evidence also shifted. The question now is, how are metaphor, emplotment, sequence, and all the other attributes of narrative understood as evidence, and of what are they evidence? The issue has moved from historiography to historical cognition. As Bruner says, "Eventually the culturally shaped cognitive and linguistic processes that guide the self telling of life narratives achieve the power to structure perceptual experience, to organize memory, to segment and purpose-build the very 'events' of a life. In the end we *become* the autobiographical narratives by which we 'tell about' our lives."[89]

In *Envelopes of Sound*, I traced out some of the tactical and epistemological consequences of the concern with narrative among oral historians.[90] In brief, I noted that the telling of the story being recorded is not, in most cases, the first time the story was told,[91] that each time it was told it was told within the linguistic, logical, and factual limits of the time of the telling as well as the limits of public and private memory, and thus each time it was told it changed. It is the oral historian's task, through research, to understand the history of these tellings and then to explore the contradictions within the story, contextualize the telling, and thereby help the narrators create the fullest narrative possible at this moment of time. This will allow the researcher to, in the words of Paul Ricoeur, "appropriate the text." "What has to be appropriated," Ricoeur argues, "is the meaning of the text itself, conceived in a dynamic way as the direction of thought opened by the text. In other words, what has to be appropriated is nothing other than the power of disclosing a world that constitutes the reference of the text, . . . the disclosure of a possible way of looking at things, which is the genuine referential power of the text."[92]

In this appropriation one can begin to plumb all the contradictions inherent in ideology, memory, and language. The most obvious explorations of the errors, elisions, and evasions (inaccuracies) that are a part of the different ways of looking at things are the essays that form *The Death of Luigi Trastulli*, by Portelli. The key essay noted in any discussion of the book explores the meaning of the misdating of the death of worker militant Trastulli and why, despite the fact that evidence of the correct date is right at hand, narrators insist Trastulli died on a different date. For Portelli, this insistence becomes a key to understanding the consciousness of his narrators and the ways in which they make sense of their own history.[93]

Of course, common sense tells us, errors, elisions, and evasions can only be understood and be given meaning within some context the reader or listener has constructed. Thus a consciousness of the historicity of the historian as well as the interviewee is vital in making such judgments. Far from being absolved of the sometimes onerous tasks of research and interpretation, oral historians must, in order to realize the potential richness of the oral history document, extend themselves even further into that study.

Documenting International Human Rights

No mention of the growth of oral history in the last decades of the twentieth century can ignore the consequences of the politics of the post–Cold War world and new uses for oral evidence in documenting human rights abuses. Oral historians, especially in

Europe and Latin America, had been, from the start of the practice, interested in documenting political oppression, in particular the history of fascism, Nazism, and colonialism. Oral histories of Holocaust survivors, as already noted, made up a large portion of the organized oral history projects throughout the world long before the recent interest of the Shoah Foundation. The late 1980s and 1990s, however, saw an efflorescence of projects interviewing those whose histories had been stripped from them by repressive regimes. With the collapse of the Communist governments of the Soviet Union and Eastern Europe and other dictatorships, such as those in Latin America, projects were organized almost immediately to rescue the memory of daily life. Sometimes organized with the assistance of Western oral historians, many times rising spontaneously in community groups or university history or sociology departments, there was a rapid expansion of the global reach of oral history. In addition, with the collapse of the apartheid regime in South Africa, oral history came to play a new role as part of the effort to document the history of Africans long denied a history and to assist in efforts at truth and reconciliation. Then, with a new outbreak of general slaughter of populations in areas such as Cambodia and the former Yugoslavia, oral history projects were mounted to document war crimes and other traumatic experiences, such as genocide, torture, and rape, and to provide firsthand testimony of oppression to be offered as evidence at international tribunals or in order to gain reparations.[94]

Many of these projects resonated with issues raised by Holocaust interviews. First and foremost was the necessity and primacy of oral testimonies, given the distorted or nonexistent written record, which if it did exist, by definition lacked any evidence of the extent and detail of the apparatus of oppression and its effects upon ordinary citizens, that is, the subjectivity of oppression. Second, such interviewing narrowed the gap between history and therapy as it documented the trauma of severe dislocations, such as torture or the disappearance of loved ones, and gave a new life to traumatic memories. As noted earlier, such questions were new for oral historians, and the consequences for the definition of the practice remain controversial to this day.

An equally new and sometimes uncomfortable role for oral historians involved questions of human rights and reparations. Long committed to a politics against oppression, their work was now to be used as evidence in trials or tribunals of varying power and potency. Oral history interviews conducted in the 1960s and 1970s on the history of Nazism and fascism were, by and large, conducted at a time long enough removed from the terrors of World War II to provide some space for reflection. In addition, the war crimes tribunals following that war had seemingly settled the case for juridical punishments and, in many cases, reparations. The currency of events at the close of the twentieth century, new calls for reparations, and the revival of old claims such as Native American land rights, however, posed new definitions of oral evidence and therefore new problems for the oral historian.

The growing internationalization of the oral history movement brought to the fore other major theoretical and methodological issues. Was it possible to maintain European and North American notions of narrative and subjectivity, given the development of the field in Latin America, Africa, and Asia, with their own historiographical traditions and modes of oral transmission of the memories of the past? And how were the tools and interpretations developed in the past twenty years to be used in understanding the violence of a new era? In the first case, the debates over the relationship of oral history to the study of oral traditions in Africa indicate how complicated the issues are, and those debates are the debates of Western scholars, for the most part.[95] In the second case, could the telling of one's history aid in the break from a "rigid and limiting constellation of violence"?[96]

Intersubjectivity

In her analysis of the oral history interview as a hermeneutic act, McMahan argues for the centrality of intersubjectivity, which, following Alfred Schutz, she describes as a "precondition for human symbol-using activity." Quoting Schutz, she notes, "The world 'is intersubjective because we live in it as men among other men, bound to them through common influence and work, understanding others and being understood by them.'"[97] The concept, used in this way to describe communication in the oral history interview as a search for understanding, is the logical extension of the concern with issues of subjectivity and narrative, encompassing both. Building upon the work of Hans-Georg Gadamer, McMahan lists three suppositions upon which a "hermeneutic" conversation (Gadamer's term) is based. First, interpretation is "always performed within the universe of linguistic possibilities and . . . these linguistic possibilities as performed mark out the historicality of human experience."[98] Or, in the words of Martin Jay, "Our finitude as human beings is encompassed by the infinity of language."[99] Second, McMahan says, "Interpretation . . . always is guided by the biases that an interpreter has at a specific moment in time." Jay agrees, stating, "It is only through prejudices that our horizons are open to the past."[100] Third, McMahan claims, "'An act of interpretation must always be concerned directly with the historical phenomen[on] itself, e.g., not with an interviewee's intended meaning but what the intended meaning is about.'"[101] At any one moment, intersubjectivity is limited by language, bias, and the nature of the object of investigation. As Jay says, "Understanding is not a reproductive procedure, but rather always a productive one."[102] In this manner the interactive nature of the oral history interview becomes a cooperative effort to interpret the past through the recognition of the role of the historicity of both parties to that interview.

In his usual perceptive manner, Portelli, noting the consequences of this subjectivity, describes the interview situation as "an exchange between *two* subjects; literally a mutual sighting. One party cannot really *see* the other unless the other can see him or her in turn. The two interacting subjects cannot act together unless some mutuality is established. The field researcher, therefore, has an objective stake in equality, as a condition for a less distorted communication and a less biased collection of data."[103] This, he argues, is the basis for the view of oral history as an "experiment in equality," an equality that is based upon the recognition of difference, since equality and sameness are not interchangeable. Thus, intersubjectivity in the interview rests upon two pillars: difference and equality. The various ways oral historians have described and worked with this tension tells us much about how evidence is dialectically and dialogically produced in the interview and for what purposes.

The most popular and easily understood description of this process is Michael Frisch's, given at length and with many wonderful examples in *A Shared Authority*. The idea of shared authority is the means whereby Frisch resolves the tension he earlier describes between more history and the populist attempt to bypass history. Noting the dual meaning of authority encompassing both authorship and power, the idea of shared authority allows Frisch both to note the creative role of the interviewee as well as the interviewer and to make the political point for the necessity of the sharing of interpretative power in the process. Frisch, however, leaves the issue open as to exactly how that sharing will work out in the interview.[104]

The basic assumption of both McMahan and Frisch is that there is a set of differences between interviewees and interviewers that must in some form be negotiated in order for the interview to be conducted and to continue once begun. As Portelli argues, this "joint venture" is an experiment in equality.[105] Far from erasing the gulf between interviewer and interviewee, however, the actual procedure, despite the search for the "reciprocity of perspectives," McMahan explains, is a "tension-laden" one. The interview is therefore a situation of "contrariety."[106]

In this view, because of the wide differences in social power between the parties to the interview, fieldwork equality, as Portelli notes, is difficult to achieve. But these differences are more than simply social power. They include all the cultural assumptions and biases that march in the wake of that power. Thus the historian and the person being interviewed must, on even the most rudimentary level, recognize the rights of the other in the dialogue.[107] At the least, the interviewee must agree that the aims and ambitions of the historian in his or her project are worthy and in some manner even useful to pursue, while the historian must recognize the autonomy of the view of the interviewee. The complexity and the depth of the difficulty of achieving this understanding I have tried to spell out elsewhere by examining the different languages and attitudes that both parties bring to the interview: the historian's professional language of analysis, which in turn reflects his or her professional identity and politics, and the interviewee's historically located language of narrative in which the experience is embedded. Thus the quality of an interview, rather than being the result of the resolution of the basic tension in the process, is determined by the ability or inability of each participant to enter the world of the other.[108]

James, in his life history of Doña María, shows in practice how difficult this is. Other examples of the tension abound. Essays in a recent issue of the *Oral History Review* devoted to the exploration of the idea of shared authority, now defined to encompass much more than simply authorship, reveal the complexities of the relationship in community history projects, ranging from a situation of sympathetic and cooperative political involvement and consensus between historians and members of the community to a situation of near total breakdown of the interview relationship because of the inability to overcome the tension between historian and interviewee.[109] In another study, Glen Adler in his interviews with South African union members under apartheid has documented the enormity of the gulf between even the most well-meaning historian and the interviewees in situations of political repression.[110] A more recent, interesting example of the negotiations between the parties to the interview involved in the search for the winding path of the skein of a life through the various modes of self presentation, evasion, and even lies of a narrator can be found in Sandy Polishuk's introduction to *Sticking to the Union*.[111] If one is to engage in any fieldwork, he or she must agree with Henry Glassie that people, when they tell their stories, do attempt to get the facts of their lives and communities as correct as they can.[112] One must also, however, recognize that the idea of what is accurate and what history should know is not an easily agreed upon conclusion. Very often what is involved is the deep, sharp, and conflicted view of the relationship of self and society on the part of each party to the interview. This is the case, I would argue, even in situations where the relationship comes perilously close to resembling a psychoanalytic session of transference and countertransference.[113]

Enrica Capussotti expresses a more optimistic view of understanding the disruptions of intersubjectivity, based upon the ways in which these contradictions emerge. In summing up her fieldwork experiences interviewing Kosovar Albanians and Kosovar Romany, she states:

> One could say that throughout the 1970s, oral history was written from within a movement which would have liked "to give words" to the subaltern (the working class, for example) and women. In our times, however, oral history is capable of prefiguring the relationships between different subjectivities and cultures and revealing the contradictions between the individual and the community. Oral history can therefore be used to criticize the mechanism of inclusion or exclusion, and the process of identity construction based upon national values. The tensions between the voice of the individual and the dominant discourses of the public sphere, which legitimize the declaration and self position, emerge in every one of the testimonies, and might serve as a powerful "weapon" with which to enter the critical debate on public memory and the political use of the past.[114]

As Passerini notes in her comments on Capussotti's essay, it is optimistic and legitimate "precisely because it presupposes a heterogeneity of subjectivities."[115]

Sound

The direct relationship of interviewer and interviewee is not the only unique trait of the oral history interview. The oral history interview is also unique because it exists as sound. This fact has been noted and commented upon, again, since the early days of oral history. Much of that discussion centered upon four distinct but interrelated problems: modes of presentation, recording practices, preservation, and the distinctions between literacy and orality. In the first case, the question was how to present in an accessible form the essential aural content of the interview. This discussion had two components: the question of transcribing and radio uses of oral history. In the first case, it was obvious, despite the pressures and need for transcription in order to make the interview easily accessible to the widest number of researchers, that the transcript could not catch the fullness of the conversation.[116] It was, recalling Samuel, a mutilation of the word. Transcription leveled the language, put everything in place, could not indicate the tone, volume, range of sound, and rhythms of speech, and as Portelli claimed, denied the orality of oral sources.[117] Arguing for the saving of tapes, Benison noted that "the physical voice helps give a rounded psychological portrait of the man or woman being interviewed and contributes a truth to the oral history account that the typed page can never convey."[118] In addition, the expense of transcription led many to seek new ways of preparing the recordings for listening, such as the TAPE system developed at the Wisconsin Historical Society or, later, various digital indexing systems.[119] These systems for the most part concentrated upon what were seen as traditional users of oral histories, for the most part academic professionals.

Radio was seen as the most compatible medium for the use of oral histories as sound material to reach larger audiences, and many oral historians and projects naturally gravitated to various kinds of radio production, a form of activity that has generated a fairly extensive literature.[120] But it should be noted that even with radio productions, as Peter Read has pointed out, problems of presentation came to the fore. Production for the media meant that silences had to vanish, whole minutes of talk would be transposed, certain speaking styles did not lend themselves to reproduction or interest, and there was no way to convey the intimacy of the interview in a mass medium.[121] Recording practices and preservation are in large part determined by the particular equipment one uses and the particular recording media, factors covered in many manuals and guidebooks.[122]

The topic of orality of oral sources spawned a rich and complex literature on the differences between spoken and written narratives, in particular the work of Walter Ong and Deborah Tannen.[123] Giving primacy to the spoken word, and in some cases to the tape over the transcript, the literature set about to understand the rules of rendition in oral transmission, or the "communicative repertoire." The goal was to understand what was spoken and its performative context and to draw a distinction between spoken and written genres of storytelling.[124] If scholars paid attention to listening, it was to urge historians to pay attention to what was said and how it was said.[125] One of the most interesting comments about the role of sound in the oral history interview was Dennis Tedlock's argument that the dialogue could best be understood as poetry and his experimentation with ways to transcribe an interview in order to catch the cadences and rhythms of a poem.[126] Here again, the goal was to better understand the oral performance.

There is no doubt that some of the most interesting, important, and insightful debates in oral history have addressed themselves to the complicated dialectic between oral and literate cultures, or more centrally to the dialectic between orality and literacy within both literate and oral cultures.[127] But such issues do not exhaust our concern with the phenomenon of sound in the oral history interview, especially in the so-called digital age.[128] To extend these concerns, one must shift attention to sound itself and then speculate on the ways in which the intersubjectivity of the interview is constructed through listening.

What unites the discussion of sound thus far is the focus on speech. It is speech that must be understood, either in spoken or written form; it is speech that must be presented to a larger audience; it is speech that must be recorded properly in order to be understood; and it is spoken genres that define orality. It is the focus on speaking that has led oral historians to be so unconcerned with sound itself.

Listening is to hearing as reading is to sight.[129] Our first object of interest is the sense of sound—hearing. But we have to be clear as to what we are listening. The point that the critics of transcribing seem to be making is that in the concentration upon speech we are missing the full range of voice. It is those aspects of voice that are not speech that we lose in the application of a written orthography. It is also clear, although the point does not seem to have been made, that in the concentration on speech we have ignored the ways in which communication by other aspects of voice is often based upon class, race, and gender differences.[130] Even with the best of intentions in transcribing or in various modes of aural presentation, however, a selection process takes place in which it is somehow determined that certain vocalisms are not to be included in the document and others are. A conversation is full of burps, groans, laughs, sighs, beeps, whistles, and other sounds. Oftentimes in a transcript a laugh or a pause or a sob might be noted (as long as it is not considered embarrassing), while in radio production, in the name of efficiency, only a few of these characteristics are retained. But, it must be noted, each time such editing takes place it is an interpretative act. We must also be aware that the first selection has come in the very act of recording, for the technology itself has selected, out of the total range of sound, both of the voice and the audio world of the voice, only that which can be heard by the microphone. Therefore, even listening to the tapes rather than reading a transcript, although it may get one closer to the phenomenon of the interview, does not replicate the interview fully.[131] In the present age, one must remember, most of what one hears and listens to is media produced and thus edited.

Charles Hardy has been particularly inventive in imagining ways in which oral historians can mobilize the digital media in order to create what he calls "aural art," or sound montages of oral histories, archival recordings, and sound elements, to create a "soundscape." Soundscape here has two dimensions: the recording of the world of sound in which the interview takes place and the presentation of the recorded interview within the context of other sounds from the period under discussion or of the events being discussed. Hardy lists a number of radio presentations that have attempted to merge these two dimensions and points to the possibilities for creative uses of future three-dimensional sound recording. He also notes the limits to such work posed by our print biases, the marginality of radio, and the lack of exposure to high-quality sound recording. There is also a limit in the ways in which we have imagined the world of sound.[132]

Bruce R. Smith, in his study of the acoustical world of early modern England, summarizes recent work on the phenomenology of sound as a sensory experience. He notes four ways to think about sound: as a physical act, as a sensory experience, as an act of communication, and as a political performance.[133] For the most part, oral historians have said little about the first two and focused upon the last two. As a physical act, the sound of a voice arises from within the speaker and surrounds the listener. We have two voices: one we hear and one others hear. We hear ourselves within ourselves and others from without; there is a hereness and thereness. While we cannot go into the kind of detail that Smith recounts, it is important to note three characteristics of an auditory field: surroundability, directionality, and continuity.[134] All of this is posed in direct opposition to sight and reading. Visualized objects stay outside of one. Sound penetrates the body; sound is inescapable. We close our eyes, and we do not see. If we bore of a book, we simply shift focus and look elsewhere. We cannot escape the voice of an interviewee droning on. We may not listen, but we always hear. Sight knowledge is presented to exist quite apart from the body of the knower; in sound one is immersed. Reading is ontological; listening, phenomenological.[135]

Several points follow for the oral historian. As noted, a recording, however faithful, cannot reconstruct the sound world of the interview. It, too, captures only a part of that world. Second, shifting our focus to the ways in which the physical fact of sound becomes a psychological experience reveals an added fullness to the intersubjectivity of the interview, for the aural world is also culturally and historically situated. The project now is to see in which ways we can manipulate new ways of recording in line with new ways of envisioning the world of sound in order to redefine the evidence of the interview. How can we understand evidence derived from a sense other than sight?

Memory, Myth, Ideology, Consciousness

Writing in 1992, James Fentress and Chris Wickham, in one of the few works devoted to memory that directed specific attention to oral history, took oral historians to task for their emphasis upon the analysis of their documents that accented "more or less true statements about the lived past" rather than explaining "how social identities are actually constructed by this or that version of the past" or searching "memories for their social meaning." While noting that a "sea change" was taking place in oral history, work on memory, they claimed, was only theoretical. They saw the reluctance of oral historians to accent memory as a desire on their part to establish a pedigree for the practice and as contentment with a narrow textual view of memory. What was needed, they continued, were concrete examples of the ways in which memory became history.[136] Whether or not that charge stood up at the time, we will evaluate below. It certainly does not now. Even a swift glance at Portelli's latest work, *The Order Has Been Carried Out*, reveals the depth and insight that oral history interviews, carefully conducted and interpreted, can bring to our understanding of the complicated set of relationships involved in the dialectical tension between memory and history. Frisch, in comments printed on the book's dust jacket, states, "Analytically, meditatively, passionately, and poetically, Portelli explores and documents, as fact and as memory, an episode critical to the history of Italy and World War II and to the postwar world down to the present. . . . [The book] reminds us that oral history matters because it demonstrates how the past and present necessarily, if not comfortably, live together within all of us."[137] In many ways, Portelli's work stands as the culmination of a generation's thinking about the role of memory in oral history and the transformation in ways in which we have conceived our tasks.

Questions of memory have been a part of the discourse on oral history from the early origins of the practice.[138] Definitions and conceptions of memory within that discourse, however, have changed dramatically. Initially, the concern was with the accuracy and reliability of memory or the distinctions between long-term and short-term memory, while memory was seen as a repository from which recollections were brought to consciousness in response to various types of stimuli. One's interest was in the processes and structural coding of memory rather than the convoluted relationship of memory and history, which were seen to be locked in opposition to one another. As insightful as some of this work was, in particular Thompson's discussion in the first edition of *The Voice of the Past* or the speculations of John Neuenschwander in the U.S., it was a world away from later considerations, brought on by a transformation, interestingly enough, traced out by Thompson in a 1994 essay. Ten years earlier, he had noted, oral historians, "saw the main problem as being whether that information within the informant was distorted or contaminated by the passage of time, by remembering, or by reevaluating earlier memories. They were not, in other words, concerned with what we now see as essential mental processes of thinking about experience, of conceiving it in order to express it."[139] Samuel noted that "Memory, so far from being merely a passive receptacle or storage system, an image bank of the past, is rather an active, shaping force: it is dynamic—what it contrives symptomatically to forget is as important as what it remembers—and that is dialectically related to historical thought, rather than being some kind of negative order to it."[140]

Of course, oral historians were not alone in either an interest in memory or in the changing view of the issues and controversies involved in the historical study of memory and their meaning for our understanding of past experience. The literature on the topic is now quite extensive and points to a view of memory as a process dynamically related to history, not as a timeless tradition but as being progressively altered from generation to generation. In this view, memory, narrative, personal and collective identity, and past experience are interwoven in a finely textured and complicated process of historical reconstruction.[141] This has obvious implications for oral historians. The call for concrete examples by Fentress and Wickham, noted above, resonated with a similar but earlier call by Ulrich Neisser for a concentration on the everyday uses of memory.[142]

These critiques of oral history were, however, a bit off base. As far back as the late 1970s and early 1980s, oral historians had presented abundant examples of the role of memory in concrete situations. Passerini had explored issues of memory and political and gender identity in her study of Turin autoworkers. Portelli also had explored social memory in a local and concrete situation in Tierni, Italy. John Bodnar, writing in 1989, had stated explicitly his interest in using oral histories with Studebaker automotive workers in the U.S. for insight into social memories. Joutard in an extended work had documented the social memories of French Protestants. Since that time, Karen Fields, Alistair Thomson, Samuel Schrager, as well as Rogers, Tonkin, and James, just to mention some North American and European writers, have had very interesting and important things to say about social memory. Indeed, a full tally encompassing work in other areas of the world, noting studies by Elizabeth Jelin, Antonio Montenegro, José Carlos Sebe Bom Meihy, and others, as well as a full listing of publications in the U.S. and Europe, would uncover an enormous contribution of oral history to views of social memory in concrete situations, much of which has been ignored by mainstream historiography on memory.[143]

One of the more interesting attempts to understand memory in the oral history process is the work of Howard and Alice Hoffman, described in their essay in this volume. The Hoffmans' work is remarkable for three unrelated reasons: it is one of the few efforts by oral historians to speculate about the process of memory rather than its cultural meaning; it raises the question as to whether it is possible to purposely not remember something, or at least hold memories in abeyance; and it accents the role of research by the interviewee and interviewer prior to the interview.[144]

In his masterly compilation of essays about the relationship between history and memory, Pierre Nora mentions oral history only once, and very briefly in passing, as far as I have been able to determine. Noting the enormous amount of time it takes to process just one hour of tape-recorded conversation, the incredible growth of the number of holdings of interviews, and the fact that these recordings make sense only if listened to in their entirety, Nora wonders what possible purpose they would serve: "Whose will to remember do they ultimately reflect, that of the interviewer or that of the interviewee?" Oral history is, he argues, "a deliberate and calculated compilation of a vanished memory. It adds a secondary and prosthetic memory to actual experience, which is altered by the very fact of being recorded." It is, he concludes, "the clearest expression yet of the 'terroristic' effect of historical memory."[145]

The question of use is incidental to us since our experience has been that interviews are widely used. It is the idea of "secondary" that intrigues. In some sense, all memory is secondary since it is really impossible for us to isolate ourselves from daily reminders and memory jogs about our past experiences. As LaCapra notes, no memory is purely primary.[146] Memory may be selective, but when we tell our stories to others, intervening events and what we have experienced, read, or discussed since the time of the original event under investigation (which, with oral history, may stretch to years) all influence that articulation. In fact, the enhanced story is the one that we as historians now want to tell. Because as oral historians we do not usually go into the field to test memory, we often, especially in archival projects, bring along memory jogs, such as photographs, correspondence, or other documents, or we ask those we interview to review their experiences, consult scrapbooks if available, confer with others, or tour sites. Therefore the memories we collect are refreshed. For these reasons oral history may not have much to tell us about the processes of memory, but it has a great deal to tell us about the dialectical relationship between memory and history, how memory becomes history, and how history becomes memory. For us, memory is not psychology; it is historiography.

In a finely textured and insightful essay on the interplay of history and memory in the creation of the history of the American South and the importance of politics and the poetics of agency and critique, Jacquelyn Dowd Hall makes an interesting point: "We bring to our writing the unfinished business of our own lives and times; moreover, the experience of traveling so long in the country of research *becomes* our past, for our stories grow from a process of remembering and forgetting our encounters with the relics, fragments, whispers of an always already-recollected time. In all these ways, we live both the history we have learned through reading and research and the history we have experienced and inherited, passed down through the groups with which we identify, sedimented in the body, and created through talk."[147]

For the oral historian, that point is central to a discussion of memory because it brings us back to our own historicity. If we accept the proposition that the interview is a joint creation, a shared authority, then we must interrogate the ways in which the memories of the historian/interviewer—our memories—find expression in the interplay of the participants. Every aspect of memory that we attribute to those whom we interview must also be explored in ourselves: the social determinants, such as class, region, background; our professional and research memories; the "relics, fragments, whispers" Hall so eloquently describes. Only in this manner will we be able to assess in what ways memory becomes evidence in the oral history interview.

Assessing the tension between memory and history begins with an examination of the role played by myth. The category of memory in this problematic is collective, social, or popular memory, but what is the definition of myth within this context?[148] Too often *myth* has been used to connote something that is in error, often intentionally so. At other times, such as in Fentress and Wickham, the reference is to legends or deeds of heroes. When I use the term here I am referring to a much broader conception: myth as a narrative that is felt by large numbers of people to be "relatively immune to the distortions of untrustworthy and interested individual reporting"; that is "valued as the most generalized *topos* of socially significant space-time"; and that "sets out the ways in which human activity can be given meaning as episodes in living narrative, as parts of a larger and more encompassing story, a universally salient history."[149] Viewing myth in this sense, it is striking how often the discussion of the tension between memory and history introduces a discussion of myth.

Alistair Thomson notes the clear connection in what he sees as the search for composure in memory and the ways in which myth grants socially acceptable memories, in particular the myths of the nation.[150] Indeed that may be the connection. Many collective memories focus on the ethno and national construction of identity as the universally salient history and thus, as Anthony Smith explores in detail, become open to myths of a special people with a special mission.[151] Thus, like collective, social, or popular memory, myth is by definition a process that subsumes individual insights and explanations of experience. Both memory and myth refer to collectivity, even in the construction of "myth-biographies." In this sense the relationship between myth and history is far more complex than the tension between a correct and an incorrect view of the past.[152] Myths are organizing principles of memory and are crucial to the construction of a collective vision of a past—a history. This dialectic relationship between myth and history has been aptly described by Samuel in *Island Stories*: "Myth and history are not mutually incompatible, but co-exist as complementary and sometimes intersecting modes of representing the past. Myth, so far from being timeless, is subject to a constant process of change. [Myths] accrete their own history, introducing fresh episodes and adding new characters. [Further], historians, however wedded to empirical inquiry, will take on, without knowing it, the deep structures of mythic thought."[153]

In a similar manner, Jonathan Hill notes in an extended essay on the complementarity of mythic and historical consciousness:

> Although not phenomenally separable, myth and history can be analytically distinguished as modes of social consciousness according to the different weightings each gives to the relations between structure and agency. Mythic consciousness gives priority to structure and overriding, transformational principles that can crosscut, contradict, and even negate the sets of relations established through social classifications. . . . If human actors are perceived as having any power to change their conditions, it is because they possess some form of controlled access to the hierarchical structuring of mythic power of liminal, neither-here-nor-there beings [priests/God, communicants/saints—my notes]. Historical consciousness gives greater weighting to agency and social action in the present, which is informed by knowledge of past times that are qualitatively the same as the present. Like the present, the historical past is seen as inhabited by fully human, cultural beings who, although perhaps living in different conditions from those of the present time, had essentially the same powers for making changes as do people living in the present.[154]

The distinction drawn between structure and agency is a fruitful one to keep in mind, as is the fact of complementarity. But it is also important that we not conceive of mythic or historic consciousness as categories of mind but as ways of interpreting social and historical processes. There are several other features of myth that should be noted. First, myths do not rely for their validity upon an appeal to empirical evidence but rather upon the emotive and cognitive participation of the believer in the rites and rituals defining the mythic experience, the ways in which one gains admission into and finds one's place within the hierarchical world of the myth. In some sense, they rely upon the creation of what Passerini in another context has termed a "mythbiography."[155] Rites and rituals are important in the formation of memory, as Paul Connerton reminds us, but they also carry with them access to some form of sacerdotal meaning for their effectiveness.[156] Marching in a commemorative parade not only refreshes the memory of the event being commemorated and the mythic heroes at the center of that event, but it also reaffirms one's position in the hierarchical world in which that commemoration and those heroes have meaning. Often, too, myths point to the special relationship between the collective people and the past by the constructions of narratives of origin.

Comparison of the essays in *The Myths We Live By*, according to James a seminal publication in oral history,[157] with the publications noted above, especially the works of Portelli and James, demonstrates that oral historians have rather consistently submitted the mythic structures of consciousness, as defined above, to the exigencies of concrete instances of human agency. Altogether, these works document through the memories of interviewees the constant creation and reformulation of myths, both personal and communitarian, especially myths surrounding the nation-state, formed sometimes in the face of a contentious history and sometimes, such as in the cases of concentration camps and oppressive regimes, when agency and historical consciousness are impossible. In many of the examples, myths articulated a history that on examination proved to be particularly fraught with violence or, for any number of reasons, great failure. In others, they rationalized the successes of certain types of personalities, ethnic groupings, or classes of people while relegating others to silence or irrelevance. In all cases, they seemed to promise a future of possibility. If, in the words of Alistair Thomson, "memory is a battleground,"[158] the battle is not necessarily between private and public memories but between myth and some form of historical consciousness in both. The key is the particular ways in which the myths dialectically relate to the concrete histories in which they are centered. Something happens to myth on its way to becoming history. It either loses its sacerdotal garment or it becomes its own form of historical consciousness, replacing history with dream and desire.

A problem arises, however, with the conception of historical consciousness. If myth is a fundamental feature of all historical thought, and I think Samuel is correct in that claim, then the analytic categories lose some of their distinctiveness, and historical consciousness seems to simply float, despite disclaimers, beyond the historical processes themselves. History has a history, and when we place historical consciousness within a history—

that is, historicize history—and contextualize what Hill means by historical consciousness, the difference becomes clearer. Without reducing the cultural to the political, I would argue that this historicizing is what sets apart an ideology. And it is the tension between myth and ideology, not between myth and historical consciousness, that distinguishes the construction of the historical narrative created in an oral history interview.[159] As Warren Susman used to tell his students, myth sets the stage; ideology gets the show on the road.

Ideology, as James Scully notes, is a debased term.[160] Historically, the word has been used to describe something that is in error, antiscientific, wrong, full of bias and prejudice, or beyond reasonableness. Also, it has been used to connote a set of ideas that has a strong resonance with a Marxist conception of false consciousness and, furthermore, has been described as a weapon in the class struggle, a symbolic action, a specific type of belief, or the atmosphere indispensable to social respiration.[161] Noting the difficulty of speaking of a politics of interpretation without a working notion of ideology, Gayatri Chakravorty Spivak describes ideology in action as "what a group, as a group, takes to be natural and self-evident" and the subject of ideology as "freely willing and consciously choosing in a world that is seen as battleground."[162] In *Japan's Modern Myths*, Carol Gluck summarizes important works on ideology: "For the anthropologist Clifford Geertz, ideology renders social life significant for those who must live it; . . . [it] provides 'maps of problematic social reality' without which the societal arrangement would seem meaningless. . . . Ideologies . . . reflect and interpret the social realities that sustain them. . . . [They are] what Althusser calls 'the "lived" relation between men and their world.' . . . Since different people construe their world differently, there is always a multiplicity of ideological formations within a society."[163]

If we take the term *historical consciousness* as it appears in the Hill essay quoted above and substitute the term *ideology*, we have an excellent description of the tension between myth and ideology in historical construction. But keep in mind that ideologies are formed in struggle and always exist in tension, if not conflict, alongside other ideologies. While myths promote cohesion and promise the elimination of struggle, ideologies promote division and promise the joy of struggle. Ideologies are also imperial because the classes for which and to whom they speak are imperial. They try to co-opt whatever forms of understanding reality are available to a given group of people at a given time, including scientific categories or myths themselves. Something happens to myths as their adherents attempt to mobilize them in history. Their categories no longer make cohesive sense. They must compete with other myths and other forms of categorization. In short, by putting myths into an ongoing process of change over time they become ideologies.

Ideologies in action exhibit the following characteristics. They contain some more or less empirical description of present social reality and some more or less logical explanation of the origins of (the history of) those social relations. In many cases, given the potency of the myth of scientific explanation in Western culture, often these descriptions will be given in terms open to measurement, such as the percentage of people living in poverty/prosperity or the numbers of slum dwellers. The logical explanations of social conditions will contain a view of the past and also the future. This is how we came to be who we are, and this is what must be done if we are to become who we want to be.

Ideologies are thus always historical narratives, and they always pose some form of future, often stealing visions of utopia as well as rituals and rites from mythic sources. When examined, these narratives inevitably pose the necessity of one group of people and one group alone that has the necessary virtue, intelligence, relation to the world of production, or public trust to carry the mission of the culture, of history, be they the Puritan elect, the proletariat, men of property, men or women, the young or the sages. If one participates in a myth by transcending the present chaos and finding one's place through a transformative experience in a hierarchy (being born again), one participates in an ideology by placing oneself in history through the understanding of the history of one's collectively identified agency.[164] If personal identity is structured collectively through myth it is given agency through ideology.

All of this may seem far afield from our original concern with the evidentiary value of oral history, but the complex understanding of the relationship between myth, memory, ideology, and consciousness provides us with the mediation between culture and politics that was at the center of Richard Cándida Smith's critique and provides the connectedness between individual and collective memory. Through the oral history interview we can marshal the evidence to begin to explore how history is constructed, not through self-conscious literary efforts but through the experience of broad swaths of the people as they struggle to situate themselves in their world and demand their rights to their own understanding of that world. Also, through a careful analysis of interviews, the oral historian is able to marshal evidence of the processes and personal and collective consequences of the active attempts to erase memory—to move beyond a passive conceptualization of forgetting to an analysis of the concerted efforts to obliterate from our past our history of that past.

As Michael Denning notes, "Our moment is not the moment where liberation and culture are the key words. But we have much to learn from a left for whom they were the key words, and as we try to build a newer left, a global left whose symbolic antagonists have been the IMF and the WTO, and the new enclosures that are privatizing the commons . . . we would do well to keep alive the promises and problems of a half century of radical cultural analysis."[165] In the long run, this is what oral history has been and what it continues to promise, with the addendum that oral historians, alone among their peers, by the very fact of what they do, ask a wide variety of people to participate with them in that journey.

Notes

1. Hartewig and Halbach, "History of Oral History." International reports in the 1976 *Oral History Review* included Campbell, "Australia"; Browne, "Brazil"; Meyer, "Mexico and Latin America"; and Lance, "Update from Great Britain."

2. Thompson, "North America"; Grele, "Development, Cultural Peculiarities"; Lance, "Update from Great Britain."

3. A sense of this complexity is evident in the "News from Abroad" section of *Oral History: Journal of the Oral History Society* (hereinafter *Oral History*). See also Meyer, "Recovering, Remembering"; Meihy, "Radicalization"; Passerini, "Oral History in Italy."

4. See Dixon and Mink, *Oral History at Arrowhead*. See also the series of interviews with the association founders published in *Oral History Review*: Treleven, "Jim Mink"; Polsky, "Elizabeth Mason"; Hardy, "Alice Hoffman"; and K'Meyer, "Willa K. Baum." Nevins, "Uses," 27.

5. Treleven, "Jim Mink," 125–27.

6. Polsky, "Elizabeth Mason," 164.

7. Bonfield, "Conversation," 466, quoted in Schlesinger, *Robert Kennedy*, 1: xv.

8. See the commentary of various notable historians in Starr, *Second National Colloquium*.

9. Starr, "Oral History," 7. That this standard has survived until the age of sound archives is seen in Wallot and Fortier, "Archival Science."

10. A typical statement of oral history procedures is Oral History Research Office, Interviewing and Interview Processing, Columbia University, http://www.Columbia.edu/cu/lweb/indiv/oral/interviewing.html (accessed January 31, 2005). For an example of the concern over embarrassing interviewees, see the comments of Philip C. Brooks in Dixon, "Definitions," 7.

11. See Hebrew University of Jerusalem, *Catalogue* 1: 1; Shariff, "Narrating History," 40; Meihy, "Radicalization"; Browne, "Brazil." In 1972, the Ford Foundation sent Charles T. Morrissey, then Oral History Association president, to Indonesia to consult with archivists, particularly at the National Archives of Indonesia, on methods of establishing projects.

12. See the report on the Singapore Oral History Unit under "News and Notes," *International Journal of Oral History* 1, no. 3 (November 1980): 213. Mercedes Vilanova, of Spain, noted her visits to both the Columbia and University of California at Berkeley oral history offices in Vilanova, "Struggle for a History." Likewise, see Neithammer, "United States," and Foronda, "Philippines." A fuller description of the movement in the Philippines is found in Foronda, *Kaysaysayan*.

13. See Thompson, *Voice of the Past*, 2nd ed. A more nuanced description is Samuel, "Local History."

14. Thompson, *Voice of the Past*, 2nd ed., 27–59.

15. See Oral History Society (UK), "Interview in Social History," for reports on a conference on the topic held by the Social Science Research Council, University of Leicester, March 23–25, 1972; La Hausse, "South African Historians"; Popular Memory Group, "Popular Memory"; Lance, "Oral History in Britain." On the concept of "culturalism" in the new social history, see Johnson, "Socialist Humanist History," and Sewell, "Concept(s) of Culture."

16. See special issues of *Oral History*: Vigne, "Family History," and Bornat et al., "Women's History"; also see the journal's "News from Abroad" reports on oral history in Germany, available in Oral History Society (UK), "Europe," and in Australia, available in Oral History Society (UK), "Australasia." See also the various international reports in "Oral History and Regional Studies," Part 5, Dunaway and Baum, *Oral History*, 2nd ed., 341–424.

17. Samuel, "Unofficial Knowledge."

18. The most obvious locus for this view is in the pages of *History Workshop Journal*, but the editors of that journal were not alone in these hopes.

19. See the essays in Thompson and Burchart, *Our Common History*; Lindqvist, "Dig Where You Stand"; Oral History Society (UK), "Finland"; Contini, "Italy"; Meyer, "Recovering, Remembering"; and Andrade, "Mexico." Bozzoli and Delius, "Radical History," and La Hausse, "South African Historians," note oral history's role in keeping alive an oral tradition of resistance to apartheid. A brief bibliography on oral history activism is found in Perks and Thomson, introduction to "Advocacy and Empowerment."

20. Dixon, "Definitions," 6.

21. Thompson, "North America"; Jefferson, "Echoes from the South."

22. Thompson, "North America," was particularly sharp about the expensive processing practices and elitism of the Columbia University Oral History Research Office. Louis Starr, Columbia director, returned the favor in his review of Thompson's work: "In sum, parts of *The Voice of the Past* are more mellifluous than the whole, an exercise in which the right minded are held up to us, and the hell with everyone else." Starr, review of *Voice of the Past*, 68. Delivered in many venues, none published, the most thoroughgoing critique of archival projects belongs to Lawrence Goodwyn, who argued that it was foolish to hire someone else to do one's interviewing, that interviewing should always be done with a definite research agenda in mind, transcribing was a waste of time since no one should be expected to use anyone else's interviews, and the relationship between archivists and their subjects was too close to ever promote a proper adversarial stand between the two.

23. Thompson, "Sharing and Reshaping," describes this process in Great Britain. An excellent example of a publication from an archival project merging the research and interviewing of several authors is Hall et al., *Like a Family*. Community history projects had long blended the collection of interviews and the publication of research results. As examples, see Fee, Shopes, and Zeidman, *Baltimore Book*; National Archives (Singapore), *Kampong Days*; Brecher, Lombardi, and Stackhouse, *Brass Valley*.

24. Grele, "Why Call It Oral History."

25. Sources for the relationship of oral history and community history are too voluminous to reproduce here. The various issues of *Oral History, Oral History Review, History Workshop Journal, Oral History Association of Australia Journal, Canadian Journal of Oral History*, and the *International Journal of Oral History* contain any number of articles or notices of such efforts. In addition, the programs of annual meetings of various national associations and of international meetings are rife with such descriptions. For a discussion of the differences between local and community history and insight into some of the problems with the terms, see Samuel, "Local History."

26. See, for instance, Wood, *Projects in Your Classroom*.

27. See Thompson, "Projects." Jamieson, "Some Aspects," reports on a number of local projects, many long-standing, devoted to various forms of social service and therapy.

28. Thompson, "Achievement." See publications reported in Oral History Research Office, *Oral History: Columbia University* (New York: Oral History Research Office, 1974), 13–15, (1975), 12–15, (1980) 11–14, and (1981), 14–18.

29. See the critique in Fentress and Wickham, *Social Memory*, 89–90.

30. Thompson, "Evidence"; Popular Memory Group, "Popular Memory"; Murphy, "Voice of Memory."

31. Dixon, "Definitions," 7, 8. Brooks, in fact, called interviewees "victims"; ibid., 18. Nevins, "Uses," 28.

32. Hoffman and Hoffman, "Reliability and Validity"; Cutler, "Accuracy"; Moss, "Appreciation." For an indication of the international scope of the empirical view of oral history, see Oral History Association of Australia, "Local History." See also Bozzoli, "Women of Phokeng," 147, which recognizes other uses of the interview but gives primacy to "sources of information."

33. See Nathan, *Critical Choices*; Langlois, *Aural Research*; Moss, *Program Manual*. For an early example of the references to social science literature, see Musto and Benison, "Accuracy." See also Thompson, "Evidence." Lummis, "Structure and Validity," provides a sophisticated version of the argument. The paradoxes of interviewing as a method and the contradiction between the need for rapport in the interview and for an interviewer who is a "passive tool" is brilliantly explored in Merton, Fiske, and Kendall, *Focused Interview*, a work that, interestingly, does not appear in most of the commentary on oral history interviewing.

34. Popular Memory Group, "Popular Memory," 215–16.

35. Yeo, "Community Publications"; Lowenstein, *Weevils in the Flour*; Lynd, "Guerrilla History"; Lynd, "Personal Histories"; Rosen and Rosengarten, "Shoot-Out at Reeltown," 67. But see also J. Green, review of *Rank and File*, which questions the editors' lack of any reference to their editing and selection techniques. Similar are the assumptions, sometimes overt, often unstated, behind the myriad publications of seemingly unedited oral history interviews, ranging from the work of popular historians such as Studs Terkel to Latin American testimonials, to the 1930s U.S. slave narratives, to any number of as-told-to autobiographies. In many ways this was, and remains, the popular view of oral history.

36. Frisch, "Oral History and *Hard Times*" (1979), 76.

37. Ibid., 78.

38. For description and analysis of the complexities of this shift, see La-Capra, "Rethinking Intellectual History."

39. Tonkin, "Implications of Oracy"; Gilb, "Tape Recorded Interviewing"; Benison, "Reflections." Benison was one of the very few American oral historians concerned with the larger questions of sound documentation, and also the mutual creation of the document, which he saw as both the strength and weakness of oral history.

40. Duberman, *Black Mountain*; Grele, "Languages of History."

41. Duberman, *Black Mountain*, 89–90.

42. Conkin, review of *Black Mountain*, 512, called the work "embarrassing," "pretentious," and "the very epitome of bad taste."

43. Samuel, "People's History."

44. Grele, "Anyone over Thirty."

45. Portelli, "Peculiarities," 99–100.

46. Passerini, "Work Ideology and Consensus"; Portelli, "Peculiarities." I cite these two articles instead of the authors' better-known books—Passerini, *Fascism in Popular Memory*, and Portelli, *Death of Luigi Trastulli*—to highlight the fact that both first appeared in *History Workshop Journal*, which was often accused of empiricism and positivism. Also, the time lapse before publication of the English versions of the books obscures the earlier date of the work.

47. Popular Memory Group, "Popular Memory."

48. Grele, "Movement without Aim."

49. Tonkin, "Boundaries of History." Again, the reader is directed to Tonkin's early 1980s articles, which reveal the cumulative thinking behind her later book, *Narrating Our Pasts*. Neithammer and von Plato, *Lebensgeschichte und Sozialkultur*. See Freddy Raphaël's review of these volumes in Raphaël and Breckner, "German Working Class," 201–203. Joutard, *La Legende des Camisards*.

50. *History Workshop Journal*, "Editorial," iii.

51. Both editions of Ritchie, *Doing Oral History*, have extensive discussions of the various ways in which oral history has been and can be used.

52. Passerini, *Fascism in Popular Memory*; Portelli, "What Makes Oral History Different." In Frisch, *Shared Authority*, see particularly "Part II: Interpretative Authority in Oral History: Headnotes," 55–58; "Oral History and the Presentation of Class Consciousness," 59–80; and "Oral History, Documentary, and the Mystification of Power," 159–78. In McMahan and Rogers, *Interactive Oral History Interviewing*, see, in particular, Grele, "Languages of History"; Chase and Bell, "Women's Subjectivity"; and Futrell and Willard, "Intersubjectivity."

53. Portelli, *Battle of Valle Giulia*; Friedlander, *UAW Local*; Yans-McLaughlin, "Metaphors of Self"; Samuel, *East End Underworld*; Hareven and Langenback, *Amoskeag*; Gluck and Patai, *Women's Words*; Alexander, "Women, Class"; Bravo, "Solidarity and Loneliness"; Rocha Lima, "Women in Exile"; Meyer, "Recovering, Remembering"; Benmayor et al., "Stories to Live By."

54. Winter and Sivan, "Setting the Framework," 15.

55. LaCapra, "Holocaust Testimonies." See also Rogers, "Trauma Redeemed," and her longer study, *Righteous Lives*.

56. Samuel and Thompson, introduction to *Myths We Live By*, 2.

57. James, "'Case of María Roldán,'" 122.

58. Essays in Bonnell and Hunt, *Beyond the Cultural Turn*, explore in some detail the varieties and complexity of these shifts. See, in particular, Bonnell and Hunt's introduction; Biernacki, "Method and Metaphor"; and Sewell, "Concept(s) of Culture." Eley, "Is All the World a Text?" outlines the close relationship of the 1960s generation to the cultural turn. Bonnell and Hunt's claim that this turn represented the decline of interest in Marxism is contested by the essays in Nelson and Grossberg, *Marxism*. Denning, *Culture*, is an extraordinarily provocative interpretation of the cultural turn. All three anthologies include little or no mention of oral history despite the obvious complementary nature of the questions asked. Consideration of oral history theory and method would have avoided some embarrassing statements, such as Biernacki, "Method and Metaphor," 78, which claims, "Historical researchers by and large have as evidence of the past only what has been inscribed in static texts or in material

artifacts appropriated as texts." Sadly, this represents the continuing marginality of oral history as much as the myopia of the academy.

59. Geertz, *Interpretation of Cultures*, 452.

60. Thelen, "Memory and American History," 1118–19.

61. Dominique Aron-Schnapper, comments at the Fourth International Conference on Oral History, Aix-en-Provence, France, September 26, 1982. Ironically enough, this was the first international meeting where issues of memory and subjectivity had been broached openly from the perspective of narrative. See also Passerini, "Memory"; Tilly, "People's History"; O'Farrell, "Facts and Fiction," 5–6. I first noted these criticisms in 1985. See Grele, *Envelopes of Sound*, 2nd ed., 282n56.

62. Tilly, "People's History," 7.

63. Tilly, "Tilly's Response," 41, and Grele, "Concluding Comment." I have purposely used quotations from Portelli and Samuel also used by Tilly in her critique so that the reader can see them in two distinctly different contexts.

64. See Thompson et al., "Between Social Scientists," and Tilly, "Tilly's Response."

65. R. C. Smith, "Popular Memory," 106.

66. See, for instance, essays in Dexter, *Specialized Interviewing*. The connection was continued to be viewed as natural, as seen in the currently most useful American oral history handbook, Yow, *Recording Oral History* (1994).

67. Thompson, *Edwardians*.

68. Compare essays in Grele, *International Annual 1990*, to those in Dexter, *Specialized Interviewing*. See also Samuel and Thompson, introduction to *Myths We Live By*, 9–20; Grele, "Surmisable Variety."

69. See the final footnote in Adler, "Politics of Research," 245, wherein Adler answers the argument that "researchers . . . [should] be somewhat aloof from the individuals and organizations they examine, to be freed from the political demands of competing political movements that approve of some categories and not others in their definitions of legitimate politics," by noting, "It's unclear exactly how such distancing can be accomplished, and if it is achieved, whether it provides the interviewer with any better vantage point for addressing these concerns."

70. For a discussion of the complexity of the uses of the concept of "narrative," see Martin, *Recent Theories*.

71. Passerini, *Fascism in Popular Memory*, 8.

72. R. C. Smith, "Popular Memory," 98.

73. Portelli, *Death of Luigi Trastulli*, 48–49.

74. Ibid., ix–xii.

75. See, for example, Portelli, "*Absalom, Absalom!*"; Portelli, "Philosophy and the Facts"; and Portelli, "Oral History as Genre."

76. Connerton, *How Societies Remember*, 19–20.

77. See Grele, "Listen to Their Voices."

78. James, *Doña María's Story*, 228.

79. Tonkin, *Narrating Our Pasts*, 3.

80. Barber, "Interpreting *Oriki*," 15, quoted in Tonkin, *Narrating Our Pasts*, 3.

81. Tonkin, *Narrating Our Pasts*, 6, 109.

82. Murphy, "Voice of Memory," 164.

83. Chamberlain and Thompson, "Genre and Narrative." See also essays in McMahan and Rogers, *Interactive Oral History Interviewing*, in particular, Rogers, "Trauma Redeemed."

84. See Carr, *Time, Narrative, and History*; Bruner, "Narrative Construction of Reality"; Bruner, *Actual Minds, Possible Worlds*; Spence, *Narrative Truth*; Polkinghorne, *Narrative Knowing*.

85. Bonnell and Hunt, *Beyond the Cultural Turn*. See also Nash, *Narrative in Culture*.

86. Carr, *Time, Narrative, and History*, 16.

87. Halttunen, "Cultural History," 171.

88. Polkinghorne, *Narrative Knowing*, 15–17.

89. Bruner, "Life as Narrative," 15.

90. Grele, *Envelopes of Sound*, 2nd ed., 261–68.

91. There are obvious exceptions, especially the telling of narratives of terror, rape, and genocide. For instance, in the case of the Japanese American internment, for many years there was an unwillingness among former internees, out of shame, to discuss the experience. Of course, the fact that a story has been told before does not negate the fact that it can be told anew even to the surprise of the person interviewed: "I never thought of it that way until just now."

92. Ricoeur, *Interpretation Theory*, 92.

93. Portelli, "Death of Luigi Trastulli."

94. Thompson and Burchart, *Our Common History*; Passerini, *Fascism in Popular Memory*; Contini, *La Memoria Divisa*; Talsma and Leydesdorff, "Netherlands"; Botz, "Austria." Literature on oral histories of the Holocaust is quite extensive, but a brief listing of early works is found in Thompson, *Voice of the Past*, 2nd ed., 277. Miller and Miller, "Armenian Survivors"; Sherbakova, "Gulag in Memory"; Kamp, "Three Lives of Saodat"; Kamp, "Restructuring Our Lives"; Schendler, "Post-Communist Discourse"; Bennett, "Forced Settlement"; Dhupelia-Mesthrie, "Dispossession and Memory"; Losi, Passerini, and Salvatici, "Archives of Memory"; Jelin and Kaufman, "Layers of Memory"; Maguire, *Facing Death*; Gluck, "Women's Mass Organizations"; Lutz, Phoenix, and Yuva-Davis, *Crossfires*. For some indication of the complexity of the issues involved, see Torpey, *Politics and the Past*.

95. Tonkin, "Subjective or Objective?" has a particularly useful explanation of these tensions with a focus mostly on the work of Vansina, *Oral Tradition*. See also essays on oral history in *Social Analysis* 4 (Spring 1980), including Rosaldo, "Doing Oral History," which, although not addressed to African studies but to fieldwork in the Philippines, speaks directly to the point. For a description of "oral literature" and its similarity to oral history practice, see Okpewho, *African Oral Literature*, 328–59. Larger issues are explored in Halttunen, "Cultural History"; Meihy, "Radicalization"; and Feierman, "Colonizers." Carr, *Time, Narrative, and History*, 179–85, addresses these issues. See also Faseke, "Nigeria", and Kwang, "China."

96. The term is from Losi, "Beyond the Archives," 6.

97. Schutz, "Common-Sense," 10, quoted in McMahan, *Elite Oral History Discourse*, 97–98.

98. See Gadamer, *Truth and Method*. Jay, "Intellectual History," provides an insightful discussion of the major points of Gadamer's theory of hermeneutics. Clark, Hyde, and McMahan, "Communication" (1980), 30, quoted in McMahan, *Elite Oral History Discourse*, 3.

99. Jay, "Intellectual History," 94.

100. McMahan, *Elite Oral History Discourse*, 3; Jay, "Intellectual History," 97.

101. Clark, Hyde, and McMahan, "Communication" (1980), 30, quoted in McMahan, *Elite Oral History Discourse*, 4.

102. Gadamer, *Truth and Method*, 264, quoted in Jay, "Intellectual History," 95.

103. Portelli, *Death of Luigi Trastulli*, 31.

104. Frisch, *Shared Authority*.

105. Portelli, *Death of Luigi Trastulli*, 31–32.

106. McMahan, *Elite Oral History Discourse*, 98–99, 56.

107. Ibid., 43–44.

108. Grele, "Languages of History."

109. James, "'Case of María Roldán'"; Thomson, "Sharing Authority"; Kerr, "'What the Problem Is'"; Sitzia, "Shared Authority."

110. Adler, "Politics of Research."

111. Polishuk, *Sticking to the Union*, 1–16.

112. Glassie, *Passing the Time*, 620.

113. See LaCapra, "Holocaust Testimonies," 223–25; Roper, "Analysing the Analysed."

114. Capussotti, "Memory," 214.

115. Passerini, "Afterthought," 220.

116. Shores, "Directions," 42; Dixon and Colman, "Objectives and Standards," 78–81.

117. Samuel, "Perils of the Transcript" (1998), 389; Portelli, "What Makes Oral History Different," 46–47.

118. Benison, "Reflections," 76.

119. Treleven, "TAPE System." For one example of digital indexing of recordings, see the work of the Randforce Associates, Amherst, NY, at http://www.randforce.com (accessed January 26, 2005).

120. See, for example, Dunaway, "Radio"; Read, "Different Media."

121. Read, "Different Media," 415–16.

122. The only two noted here are Jackson, *Fieldwork*, and Ward, *Sound Archive Administration*. Both editions of Yow, *Recording Oral History*, and Ritchie, *Doing Oral History*, have fairly extensive bibliographies on these issues.

123. Ong, *Orality and Literacy*; Tannen, *Spoken and Written Language*.

124. Tonkin, *Narrating Our Pasts*, 50–65; Finnegan, *Oral Literature in Africa*.

125. Slim et al., "Ways of Listening"; Anderson and Jack, "Learning to Listen."

126. Tedlock, "Learning to Listen"; Tedlock, *Finding the Center*.

127. See, for instance, Hofmeyr, "Nterata."

128. Read, "Different Media," 416.

129. Reading in this context is more than examining a book. It is reading in the sense of reading a landscape, or a painting, or a city street, or a face.

130. See Applebaum, *Voice*.

131. A point made by Ihde, *Listening and Voice*, 4–5, while discussing the transformation of listening as a result of the electronic communications revolution.

132. Charles Hardy III, "Authoring in Sound: An Eccentric Essay on Aural History, Radio, and Media Convergence" (1999), State University of New York at Albany, spring 2004 course syllabus of Gerald Zahavi, "Producing Historical Documentaries and Features for Radio," http://www.albany.edu/faculty/gz580/documentaryproduction/authoring_in_sound.html (accessed January 31, 2005). On the idea of "soundscape," see Schafer, *Tuning of the World*. An interesting example of an aural essay available online is the collaborative work of Hardy and Portelli, "I Can Almost See the Lights of Home: A Field Trip to Harlan County, Kentucky," http:// www.albany.edu/jmmh/vol2no1/lightssoundessay.html.

133. B. R. Smith, *Acoustic World*, 3.

134. Ihde, *Listening and Voice*, 76–81. Much of Bruce Smith's theoretical presentation is drawn from Ihde's work but, to my mind, is far more comprehensible.

135. B. R. Smith, *Acoustic World*, 9–10; Ihde, *Listening and Voice*, 3–16. For an interesting exploration of the ways in which vision has been privileged and has assumed a totalitarian hold on the Western imagination (all the fault of Descartes), see Levin, *Listening Self*, 29–65.

136. Fentress and Wickham, *Social Memory*, 89. In this essay I follow Fentress and Wickham and use the term *social memory* instead of *collective memory*, partly because I think *social memory* does not carry the baggage of racial or ethnic "spirit" and other dubious constructions. But it must be recognized that *social memory* is subject to reductionism and the argument that memory is the articulation of social position and therefore subject to all the criticisms leveled at social history from a culturalist position.

137. Portelli, *Order Has Been Carried Out*.

138. Almost all the initial reports of the Oral History Association, in the U.S., and the Oral History Society, in Great Britain, were replete with discussions of memory or articles speculating about memory. For the more interesting, see Musto and Benison, "Accuracy"; Storm-Clark, "Miners"; and Thompson, "Problems of Method."

139. Thompson, *Voice of the Past* (1978), 100–108. Neuenschwander, "Remembrance"; Thompson, "Believe It or Not," 3.

140. Samuel, *Theatres of Memory*, 1: x.

141. Some idea of the extent of memory literature is evident in citations in Crane, "Collective Memory." On changing definitions, see Connerton, *How Societies Remember*. On narrative and memory, see Fentress and Wickham, *Social Memory*, 49–59, and Tonkin, *Narrating Our Pasts*, 97–112. The generational image is from Samuel, *Theatres of Memory*, 1: I–xi. Hutton, *Art of Memory*, 1–26. Winter and Sivan, "Setting the Framework." For a less optimistic view, see Maier, "Surfeit of Memory."

142. Neisser, "Important Questions," 12.

143. Passerini, *Fascism in Popular Memory*. Passerini continued exploring memory in *Autobiography of a Generation*. Portelli, *Death of Luigi Trastulli, Battle of Valle Giulia*, and *Order Has Been Carried Out*; Bodnar, "Power and Memory"; Joutard, *La Legende des Camisards*; Fields, "Cannot Remember Mistakenly"; Thomson, *Anzac Memories*, and the earlier Thomson, "Anzac Memories"; Schrager, "What Is Social"; Rogers, *Righteous Lives*; James, "Meatpackers"; Araújo, *Eu Não Sou Cachorro*; Montenegro, *História Oral e Memória*.

144. Hoffman and Hoffman, *Archives of Memory*; a shorter version is Hoffman and Hoffman, "Reliability and Validity."

145. Nora, "Between Memory and History," 1: 10.

146. LaCapra, *History and Memory*, 20–21.

147. Hall, "'Remember This,'" 441.

148. While distinctions between collective, social, and popular memory and the consequences of the use of each of these terms must be recognized, for my purposes here I use the terms indiscriminately.

149. Abercrombie, *Pathways of Memory*, 321. See also Samuel and Thompson, introduction to *Myths We Live By*; Connerton, *How Societies Remember*, 53–61; Maier, "Surfeit of Memory"; Mayer, *Final Solution*, 15–21; A. Smith, *Myths and Memories*.

150. Thomson, "Anzac Legend," 76–78.

151. A. Smith, *Myths and Memories*, 57–123. Bodnar, "Pierre Nora," has much of interest to say about the complementarity of memory studies and the nation-state.

152. This view is at odds with Kammen, *Mystic Chords of Memory*, although Kammen's discussion of the relation between myth and tradition is a vital consideration in the argument for the inherent collectivity of myth.

153. Samuel et al., *Island Stories*, 14. See also Susman, "American Intellectual"; Bidney, "Myth, Symbolism"; Hill, "Myth and History."

154. Hill, "Myth and History," 6. See also the discussion of the transformation of Christ as savior into a historical person in Susman, "American Intellectual," 247.

155. Passerini, "Mythbiography," 59.

156. Connerton, *How Societies Remember*, 41–71; Kirk, *Myth*. See also essays in Dundes, *Sacred Narrative*.

157. James, "'Case of María Roldán,'" 122.

158. Thomson, "Anzac Legend," 73.

159. As early as 1975, I argued that an oral history interview could be understood as a conversational narrative structured linguistically, socially, and cognitively and that the cognitive structure was to be understood through an examination of the tension between myth and ideology revealed in the construction of the history being articulated. See Grele, *Envelopes of Sound* (1975), 139–43. I see no reason to change my mind, and the essays in Samuel and Thompson, *Myths We Live By*, and additional recent works illustrate that tension.

160. Scully, "Defense of Ideology," 9.

161. In Marxist tradition *ideology* has been used in a variety of ways in addition to error. See Eagleton, *Ideology*, and S. B. Smith, *Reading Althusser*, 29–70. Authors who discuss these distinctions are outlined in Boudon, *Analysis of Ideology*, 17–33.

162. Spivak, "Politics of Interpretation," 347.

163. Geertz, "Ideology," 220, and Althusser, *For Marx*, 252, quoted in C. Gluck, *Japan's Modern Myths*, 6–7. See also Burger and Luckman, *Social Construction of Reality*; Eagleton, *Ideology*, 1–31; Althusser, "On Ideology"; and Therborn, *Power of Ideology*.

164. The tension between myth and ideology resonates with similar distinctions made between mythos and logos in Bruner, "Myth and Identity," and between ideology and utopia as used by Jamieson and Hall and described in Denning, *Culture*, 97–104.

165. Denning, *Culture*, 150–51.

II

METHODOLOGY

3

Research Design and Strategies

Mary A. Larson

> A sense of humor is as much a necessity as the flexi-
> bility that allows one to face apparent disaster several
> times a day and somehow keep going.
>
> —Ramon Harris et al., *Practice of Oral History*

Oral historians must have an innate ability to adapt and, as
noted above, flexibility and a sense of humor. To help them
maintain said flexibility and humor, however, a prerequisite is a
good research design. The concept of research design almost by
definition encompasses most aspects of an oral history project,
since it guides work on a project from its inception to its completion. This chapter will of necessity discuss topics that are
treated in more detail in other areas of this reference work. Because of the overarching nature of research design, these issues
must still be addressed under this heading, but the discussion is
primarily limited to how these subjects impact the overall design
and planning of a project.

When researchers begin to think about developing an oral
history project, they almost always have a subject in mind. This
chapter aims to guide researchers through the process of clearly
defining their topic and deciding on the type of oral history they
will be conducting, with whom they will be conducting it, and
which theoretical bases will be guiding it. Once these particulars

have been determined, there are also practical concerns that must be addressed relative to project design, and these are discussed as well.

Structure of the Project

> Every project should be started by determining its objectives.
>
> —Donald Ritchie, *Doing Oral History* (1995)

Genres

One of the first decisions to be made in a project is the type or genre of oral history interview that will be conducted, as that will determine many of the other aspects of the research design. The different genres of oral history could be grouped in many ways (see, for example, Sherna Gluck's division into topical, biographical, and autobiographical).[1] For the purposes of this chapter, however, we will be considering oral histories as categorized into four basic types: subject-oriented histories, life histories, community history, and family history. These divisions have been chosen for this discussion because of the ways in which they point up various aspects of research design. Please note that these groupings are not meant to be mutually exclusive, and some overlap will almost always occur.

Subject-Oriented Oral Histories

The topically based oral history is one of the most common, as this is the type that researchers often turn to when trying to explicate specific questions rather than entering the broader realms defined by life, community, or family histories. Subject-oriented research from the beginning is more focused, with a more clearly conceived agenda and perhaps a stated hypothesis. Even so, at the beginning of the process, investigators need to ask themselves the following questions posed by David Henige: "Is the problem really a significant one whose study will contribute not only to informing its own context but also to illuminating other problems? Has the work been done before? If it has, why does it need to be done again?"[2] It is not enough to just have a topic of interest. There must be a need for the subject to be addressed, or if it has already been addressed, a need for it to be approached differently. The responses to Henige's questions are important, as they will in part guide other considerations of the research design. For example, if previous work has been done and there is not enough information already, then the project must be structured to target the gaps. If earlier attempts at the topic have ignored the voices and experiences of important groups, then these people must be incorporated in the new research.

Oral histories focusing on a specific topic have wide latitude in the choice of research issues.[3] A review of the literature, however, shows that most questions pursued in this manner are based somewhere in the not-so-recent past. This is, of course, partly due to the historical nature of oral history inquiry, even when it is being utilized by anthropologists, sociologists, political scientists, or others. It should be kept in mind, however, that this need not be the case. Growing numbers of projects have been collecting the impressions of interviewees immediately following events of local and national importance. One of the better-known efforts in this vein is the September 11, 2001 Oral History Narrative and Memory Project at Columbia University. Interviewing for that project has taken place across the United States in an attempt to record people's reactions to that day's terrorist attacks in New York City.[4]

Similar research has targeted the documentation of a 1972 flood in Rapid City, South Dakota, and the assassination of Martin Luther King Jr.[5] Work in Mexico City by Elena Poniatowska investigated the immediate aftermath of that city's 1985 earthquake, and the next year, follow-up interviews were begun by the Archivo de la Palabra of the Instituto de Investigaciones to gauge how people's reactions had changed during the intervening time.[6] As Poniatowska noted regarding the immediacy of the first phase of the work, "Documenting our country means writing chronicles and essays about the immediate happenings; writing its real history of the moment. It is important to write down, to rescue; later will come others who will give the interpretation."[7] Following rare campus dissent and demonstrations at the

University of Nevada on Governor's Day 1970 (immediately following the shootings at Kent State), Mary Ellen Glass and her associates conducted interviews with a number of participants on both sides of the dispute. Almost three decades after the fact, Brad Lucas interviewed some of the same individuals to determine how their interpretations of the day's events had evolved.[8]

Projects on the recent past, then, can be seen to be equally valuable as those concerning the more distant past, as they will provide material for researchers in the future. Both types of subject-oriented project will contribute to the array of resources offered by oral history collections.

On a practical note, subject-oriented oral histories can also benefit greatly by having advisory boards composed of individuals who are well versed in a particular topic or who were participants in an event under study. Such boards can help with the identification of possible interviewees and with other advice on how to proceed,[9] and as Ritchie notes, they are often looked upon favorably by funding agencies.[10]

Life History

The life history is also a popular type of oral history because of the possibilities inherent in the genre. It can give us insight into the lives of the famous or can provide a view of a less-celebrated life that could contextualize history. As William Schneider has observed, "The two most common reasons for writing life histories are to portray the events and experiences of an extraordinary person and to emphasize a person whose life illustrates the experiences and history of others in the region."[11]

There are a number of approaches that can be taken when considering the final product of a life history interview, and the choice of which path to take may impact the collection of information. To the extent that this is the case, decisions must be made early in the process. David Dunaway describes three types of life history. The first is similar to a standard biography but includes oral history interviews; the second consists of interviews with a range of people who discuss the subject of the life history; and the third is the "oral memoir," "which features the subject telling his or her own story, with the writer adding explanation and footnotes."[12] (The second and third categories parallel Gluck's biographical and autobiographical categories.)[13] The final form of an oral history, therefore, will influence not only who will need to be interviewed but also how much context building and analysis will be required of the researcher.

Different preparation for life histories should also be considered in research design. As Alessandro Portelli notes, "The life story as a full, coherent oral narrative does not exist in nature; it is a synthetic product of social science—but no less precious for that."[14] But while complete, ordered explications may not spring full blown from the mouths of interviewees, that does not mean that the concept of the life history is necessarily foreign. Margaret Blackman, in discussing her work with Florence Edenshaw Davidson, a Haida woman, observed that whether or not life history per se is an indigenous Haida genre, it is certainly compatible with the Haida emphasis on the individual.[15] This may not always be the case, however, and individuals' comfort with conceptualizing the process of life history documentation, and the ability to do so, may well vary depending upon cultural background or other factors such as gender, race, age, and class. Researchers should remember this while planning their work and be aware that they may need to discuss their understanding of a life history with their interviewee in order for everyone to be on the same page when work begins.

Various groups of individuals may also respond to life history not only in different ways but also with different information, a factor that could be important to the goals of a project. As Nancy Grey Osterud and Lu Ann Jones note, for example, "Some feminist literary critics maintain that women adopt distinctive forms of autobiography. Women often describe themselves in relational terms, constituting themselves through their relationships with significant others; they also tend to construct a fluid self."[16]

Community History

The pursuit of community history is well documented, with such notable works as Laurie Mercier and Madeline Buckendorf's *Using Oral History in Community History Projects*, Willa

Baum's *Oral History for the Local Historical Society*, and Barbara Allen and Lynwood Montell's *From Memory to History*. Although this type of project has been around for some time, there have been spikes of interest in the genre as the result of various events. The Foxfire movement of the mid-1960s, for example, spurred many communities to start recording their own pasts from within, while the United States bicentennial in 1976 (and associated available funds) triggered another rush to documentation in the mid-1970s.[17] And while there has in the past been some disdain toward those researchers focusing on the community level, there seems to be an increasing trend toward such work.[18] The focus of these projects can be on a geographical community (as was the case with the project on Agincourt, Ontario, winner of an Oral History Association award in 2002) or on less physically bounded communities defined by factors such as race, gender, age, class, occupation, or avocation.

From the standpoint of research design, perhaps the most important aspect to emphasize regarding community history is its potential for collaborative work, whether the work is being done by insiders, outsiders, or a combination of both. It is imperative for researchers to meet with the community in question from the very beginning. As Schneider observes, "Without the cooperation, interest, and collaboration of the people, there is no chance to understand what they know and no right to use their information."[19] Schneider's work with Project Jukebox, a series of interactive computer databases of oral history, exemplifies the collaborative approach to this type of research. Most Project Jukebox programs are community based, and from the outset of work, residents are involved in meetings and local liaisons are enlisted to help guide progress and provide input into what is important to them.[20]

Foxfire projects evolved in much the same way (albeit years earlier), with students and teachers presenting their gathered information to interested audiences. At the same time, community members reciprocated with suggestions of interviewees and topics and additional material.[21] As will be discussed later in this chapter, such meetings are often not just courtesy acts demonstrating a cooperative spirit; they may also be required with the community or with local leaders.[22]

Family History

To many, the notion of family history connotes only genealogy or perhaps oral tradition, but serious oral history research
can and has been done in this area. It does not even have to be
the study of one's own family (although that is most common),
but family dynamics, experiences, and interactions can be studied in groups that are not constituted by one's relatives.[23]

Just as there have been catalysts to the study of community
history, so too have there been with family history. In the United
States, groups such as the Daughters of the American Revolution
popularized family history for genealogical purposes around the
turn of the twentieth century, particularly in a reaction to the in-
flux of new immigrants.[24] The 1960s, with their emphasis on
identity as well as on the lives of average people, also boosted
family history's popularity, albeit for different reasons. Linda
Shopes has observed that historians "have paid particular attention to the history of the family since it is so fundamental a social
institution and shapes so much of people's daily lives."[25] Then in
the 1970s, although there has since been controversy over the nature of the material collected by Alex Haley for his *Roots* saga, the
book and associated television miniseries opened popular imagination to the possibilities of such investigations. What seemed
to capture people's attention was not even so much the actual
history presented but rather the research process.[26]

With some exceptions—such as Alex Haley's novel and television miniseries, *Roots: The Saga of an American Family,* and Peter Farquhar's multimedia CD, *The Marjory B. Farquhar Family
History*—family history is often not presented in any sort of public form, but research design for such projects is still important.
A collection of family anecdotes will rarely yield any sort of history that can be interpreted within a larger social or cultural context, so to get beyond that, planning is necessary. A number of
approaches to structuring the projects are available. Linda
Shopes suggests three possible categories of inquiry: "The impact of major historical events and trends; . . . the relationship of
various aspects of social life . . . to individuals within the family;
and the structure and dynamics of family life itself."[27] James
Hoopes, in contrast, discusses investigating the internal versus

external aspects of family life as a way to trace the connections within a family as well as its ties to the outside world.[28]

Theoretical Approaches

Once a researcher has settled on the genre of oral history to be conducted, the next step is deciding upon or becoming aware of the theoretical base informing the interview process for his or her project. Although oral historians make use of multiple theoretical perspectives in their work, a review of the literature indicates that there are three perspectives that stand out in publications: the elite/nonelite dichotomy, critical theory, and grounded theory. Again, as with a number of categories discussed in this chapter, they are not necessarily mutually exclusive, nor should this list be considered exhaustive.

Elite/Nonelite

The debate concerning elite versus nonelite oral histories is, from a theoretical standpoint, mainly one of coverage and who deserves it. Perhaps more ink has been spilt over this topic than almost any other in theoretical and methodological discussions of oral history. Eva McMahan, in detailing James Wilkie's definition of elites and nonelites, describes his view as follows: "The elites . . . are those persons who develop a lore that justifies their attempts to control society. The nonelites, on the other hand, are those persons who create a lore to explain their lack of control."[29] Elite oral history is often considered to be part of the "great white men" school of oral history that was represented by Allan Nevins at Columbia University. It consisted of, as Michael Frisch notes, "the debriefing of the Great Men before they passed on," and began with the inception of the Columbia oral history program in 1948.[30]

Set in opposition to this approach was the interviewing of nonelites—that is, ordinary people—most often described as history "from the bottom up." Early proponents of this idea were British oral historians in the 1950s and 1960s, while researchers in the United States became more heavily invested in this approach in the 1960s (although there were, of course, earlier exceptions).[31]

Both schools have their advocates. In what has become perhaps the most famous (or infamous) defense of elite oral history, Barbara Tuchman once stated that:

> With all sorts of people being invited merely to open their mouths, and ramble effortlessly and endlessly into a tape recorder, prodded daily by acolytes of oral history, a few veins of gold and a vast mass of trash are being preserved which would otherwise have gone to dust. . . . I should hastily add here that among the most useful and scintillating sources I found were two verbal interviews with General Marshall. . . . Marshall, however, was a summit figure worth recording, which is more than can be said for all those shelves and stacks of oral transcripts piling up in recent years.[32]

Similarly, Patrick O'Farrell critiqued the social history being done by Paul Thompson by saying that it only supplied the history of "ordinary" people—something he viewed as inherently uninteresting.[33] And Henige notes the argument of those who believe that, "In their attempt to enshrine the ordinary and the obscure, . . . those who practise oral history are really turning the role of historian on its head. They are modern-day antiquarians, unable to distinguish the fascinating but unimportant aspects of the past from those that really mattered."[34]

Unlike some of these views, however, most of those currently practicing elite oral history do not feel that it needs to be done to the exclusion of nonelite oral history, and they recognize that there is room for both types of interviewing. Alice Hoffman has noted that even Louis Starr, who trained under Nevins and was later director of the Columbia program, thought that both approaches were necessary.[35] It should also be pointed out that elite oral history does not always pertain just to "great white men," but is now seen as relating to those in power, no matter what their racial, ethnic, or gender affiliations. To this end, Blackman in 1982 discussed the fact that most Native American life histories done to that point had been conducted with Native American elites (notably men), although a change in that trend seemed to be occurring.[36] So even underrepresented groups can lay claim to elite/nonelite debates.

On the other end of the continuum (and a gradual continuum is really what it is) are those who strongly advocate for nonelite oral history and its benefits. Some proponents, such as Gary Okihiro, see a nonelite approach as crucial to the identity of oral history, noting that, "Oral history is not only a tool or method for recovering history; it is also a theory of history which maintains that the common folk and the dispossessed have a history and that this history must be written."[37] Echoing this sentiment is Poniatowska, who asserted in 1988 that "in the strictest sense, oral history is almost always related to the vanquished, the defeated, the earth's forsaken ones, that is, the people. Oral history walks side by side with defeat, not victory. Victory is the space of biography."[38] During the revolutions of the 1960s, oral historians around the world became more and more drawn to the idea of capturing the everyday lives of everyday people, or the "inarticulate" and those "hidden from history," as the literature sometimes refers to them.[39] They disappeared from (or really never initially appeared in) the historical record, because they left behind no autobiographies or archived records or were not identifiable by their paper trails.[40]

Much oral history since the 1960s has tried to render these groups visible. In truth, the work of many oral history programs attempts, above all, to record representatively the views of eyewitnesses to history. This work is a combination of interviews with both elites and nonelites as the topics require, and its primary theoretical underpinnings are of appropriate coverage. Despite the merits purported by both camps, the fact that the debate has been ongoing and will probably continue for some time is highlighted by Charles Crawford in his 1974 presidential article in the Oral History Review. He stated that while he thought it overly optimistic to assume that there would be a quick settlement to the controversy, "it has certainly made intelligent comparison more feasible by accumulating extensive quantities of both kinds of data for historical analysis."[41]

The last word on this subject, at least as far as this chapter is concerned, is reserved for Edward "Sandy" Ives, who summed up his perspective on the discussion most succinctly: "Elitism/non-elitism is a ridiculous polarity to begin with. Between the two there is no great gulf fixed. No one is common, and 'great men' are a dime a dozen, and getting cheaper."[42]

Critical Theory

> Reality is complex and many-sided, and it is a primary
> merit of oral history that to a much greater extent than
> most sources it allows the original multiplicity of
> standpoints to be covered.
>
> —Paul Thompson, *Voice of the Past*, 3rd ed.

Critical theory derives initially from the field of literary criticism but has since become part of many of the humanities and social sciences within which oral history is practiced. Although there are many proponents of critical theory in the United States, it would be fair to say that its effect has been even greater in Europe, particularly in Great Britain and Italy, where at least published material would indicate that class concerns (a focus of critical theory) dominate the work of oral historians. Critical theory revolves around the concept of representing the underrepresented and giving voice to their views, particularly as regards gender, class, race, and ethnicity. It is also informed by the theoretical tenets associated with studies of those factors, so each subset may have a slightly different theoretical stance (which will, in turn, bear on the research design of oral history projects).

To some extent, because of its focus on the disenfranchised, critical theory is concerned with the issues of elite versus nonelite coverage, but it can also represent both elite and nonelite members of these communities (per Blackman's discussion on elite interviewing among Native Americans). Also, although members on either side of the elite/nonelite dichotomy can be politically motivated (as with almost any theoretical stance), they are not necessarily so, while most practitioners of critical theory are overt about their politicization. There is also a tendency toward nonbelief in the possibility of (or necessity for) objectivity, and advocacy and empowerment movements have sprung to a large degree from these theoretical underpinnings.

Feminism. Looking primarily at the study (or re-study) of women through oral history, feminist theory has important beliefs relative to a project's research design. On the part of many scholars, there is a repudiation of hierarchy (both in the research and between the interviewer and interviewee), a rejection of the desirability of objectivity, and an embrace of the collaborative effort.[43]

It is seen as juxtaposed not only to elite history but even to the very dichotomy of elite versus nonelite. As Gluck observed: "Not only is the political base of women's oral history different from the Nevins model, but also, and, just as important, the content is special. No matter what women we choose to interview, regardless of how typical or atypical their life experiences have been, there are certain common threads which link all women."[44]

In regaining the voice of women, scholars see a number of benefits for history and other disciplines as well as for women themselves. History derives an advantage not only from the increase in perspectives but also from acquiring the viewpoint of less-practiced respondents. Hoopes described Jean Stein's experience while interviewing individuals for *American Journey: The Times of Robert Kennedy*. Stein noted that "the freshest, most informative material seemed to come less from the public figures than from those for whom being interviewed must have been a novelty, the women particularly."[45] While the husbands, being in the public eye, had pat-and-practiced answers for most questions, their wives had the benefit of knowing the same information and having seen many of the same things, but they were responding to many of these queries for the first time and were not, Hoopes noted, "jaded."[46]

The perceived benefit to women is empowerment on a number of levels. First, and perhaps most basically, a person's self-esteem is increased by the fact that a researcher wants to hear about her life.[47] But second, as projects are completed and results disseminated, the research also allows women to understand the challenges faced by other women and how they coped with their particular situations.[48]

A final cautionary note regards the assumption of homogeneity among women. Although there will be, as Gluck observed, shared experiences between women, Osterud and Jones warn against a belief that there are no distinctions within groups of women: "We must explore the commonalities and differences among women as well as between women and men that flow from class position, race, and ethno-cultural identification."[49]

Class. To a degree, class more than any other critical theory subset is related to the discussion of representation of the nonelite, since so often the "non-elite" and the "working class" are inextricably linked by researchers.[50] The rules of participation, as Staughton Lynd outlined them, are much the same as with feminist theory, with a focus on equality between interviewer and interviewee, collaborative work with a meaningful output for the community, and an assumption of personal involvement on the part of the interviewer (and hence a lack of objectivity).[51]

There is also an explicit emphasis on empowerment, particularly by increasing the awareness of the interviewee through the oral history process. Thompson notes this as a requirement of this theoretical base when he states: "For the historian who wishes to work and write as a socialist, the task must be not simply to celebrate the working class as it is, but to raise its consciousness. There is no point in replacing a conservative myth of upper-class wisdom with a lower-class one. A history is required which leads to action; not to confirm, but to change the world."[52]

Although the degree to which individual projects and researchers reflect such politicization obviously varies, the emphasis on class in oral history research has become commonplace. Henige observed that work done to represent the views of the disenfranchised in Britain, France, and the United States, "has closely reflected this interest, with studies of farmers, miners, and members of the urban working class being featured prominently."[53]

Beyond the empowerment sought through the raising of consciousness and through increasing self-esteem by showing interest in workers' views,[54] there is also another perceived benefit to both the interviewee and his or her community. Alice Hoffman, who spent many years working with steelworkers and unions through oral history and other educational programs, explained the value simply: "Oral history can make it possible for a person to recover, preserve, and interpret his own past, and not have it interpreted for him or imposed upon him."[55]

Race/Ethnicity. Perhaps even more than critical theory, the civil rights movement of the 1960s and the interest in ethnic identity in the 1970s helped to first inform this approach to oral history. Although the projects supported during the United States bicentennial may have celebrated the blending together of ethnic groups and races into an anonymous whole, Tamara

Hareven noted, "The current search for ethnic roots is in itself a rebellion against the concept of the melting pot; it is an effort to salvage what has survived homogenization."[56]

In some regard, many of the studies undertaken under this banner are community histories, although these communities may be culturally rather than geographically bounded. In fact, while many viewed Foxfire as a community history endeavor, one of its proponents, Brian Beun, saw it as ethnic studies, "a powerful formula for helping 'cultural minority students' at home and abroad."[57]

As with many underdocumented groups, a lack of available information was a barrier to creating accurate histories for racial and ethnic communities. Alphine Jefferson observed that, "In order to write a balanced multiracial history, it was felt, new sources had to be located."[58] Oral history interviews supplied that new resource, as projects throughout the United States and elsewhere began to focus their efforts on ethnic–racial topics.[59]

Duke University's oral history program, which existed from 1972 to 1982, was founded specifically for the stated purpose of "training a generation of scholars conversant with oral history methodology as an essential tool in preserving the history of the inarticulate," particularly as it related to blacks and other groups. The program was founded with the support of a Rockefeller Foundation grant, and for ten years it focused primarily on the collection of civil rights material (although other topics were also addressed).[60]

One of the goals of racial and ethnic studies, as noted above, was the balancing of history. As with other critical theory subsets, however, empowerment was also a goal for some adherents to the approach. Gary Okihiro saw such projects as "the first step toward ultimate emancipation," with ethnic groups finally having the ability to break free from colonized history.[61]

Again, there is a caution offered regarding assumptions of homogenization within these types of studies. Arthur Hansen, who has for many years worked with Japanese Americans in southern California, notes the diversity within that community and the way it has impacted his work: "Those of us studying such [racial–ethnic] communities would have to attend to age, generational, class, gender, and ideological divisions within them if we wanted to gain a more complex sense of past reality and avoid the charge of racism."[62]

Grounded Theory

A school of thought first arising out of the discipline of sociology, grounded theory was outlined by Barney Glaser and Anselm Strauss.[63] In its original form, it is an insistence that researchers come to a chosen topic without a hypothesis or preconceived notions. As research continues with a person or group, scholars can form their conclusions or hypotheses by analyzing the data as they gather them and reinterrogating their information to see what insights they can gain. As Strauss and Juliet Corbin note: "A researcher does not begin a project with a preconceived theory in mind (unless his or her purpose is to elaborate and extend existing theory). Rather the researcher begins with an area of study and allows the theory to emerge from the data."[64] Hence the theory derived is *grounded* in the data.

In oral history, this theory has manifested itself in a number of features that have a bearing on research design. Perhaps the most important is that some grounded theorists in oral history believe that the emphasis on a lack of preconceived notions requires that the researcher have no prepared questions or defined problem.[65] Regarding the former, Thompson observes: "The strongest argument for a completely free-flowing interview is when its main purpose is less to seek information than to record a 'narrative interview,' a 'subjective' record of how one man or woman looks back on their life as a whole, or part of it. Just how they speak about it, what they miss out, how they order it, what they emphasize, the words they choose, are important in understanding any interview; but for this purpose they become the essential text which will need to be examined."[66]

Others do not take as extreme a view of the process. Portelli, for example, sees "thick dialogue" as requiring a flexible interview approach, but not to the point of noninterference. His perspective is still in keeping with the revelatory nature of grounded theory in that, as he states, "In thick dialogue, questions arise dialectically from the answers."[67]

Another emphasis of grounded theory that has translated to oral history is the focus not only on the words being spoken by an interviewee but also on awareness of their body language and physical response, although it could be said that oral historians of many theoretical bents try to be cognizant of such things. A final characteristic to note regarding research design is that some oral historians whose work is informed by grounded theory also believe that research into a topic should not be done as a first step in the process since other sources might contaminate their understanding of the issue. Interviews should be begun first, and as themes and potential problems are identified for further investigation, then documentary research can take place.[68]

The project most often referenced as a successful example of what grounded theory can produce is Thompson and Thea Vigne's study *The Edwardians*. They chose a representative sample of British residents that compared occupationally to a 1911 census, and they amassed a daunting number of oral histories, which they then analyzed in order to be able to make observations about Edwardian society. The "thick description" of everyday life by such a large number of individuals provided the data for their analysis.[69]

Planning

While the theoretical and methodological decisions made during the process of structuring the project will have an important impact on the more pragmatic features addressed in this section, it should also be noted that resource availability will also be a decisive factor in the implementation of the research design. By remaining flexible and being constantly aware of the project plan and available resources, however, a balance can be achieved.

Selecting Interviewers

> The key to oral history, be it individual or project, is personnel. The right people must be found to do the interviewing, and the right informants have to be identified.
>
> —Ramon Harris et al., *The Practice of Oral History*

The first step in putting decisions into practice is to select interviewers. The choice of interviewers will be guided partially by the theory informing the process and partially by more practical concerns, including whether or not interviewers should be topical or methodological specialists, insiders or outsiders.

A topical specialist may be particularly appealing to those engaged in subject-oriented projects. An expert in the field under consideration brings to the research a level of background experience that time and resources probably would not permit someone unfamiliar with a topic to develop, so there is that advantage. The ideal situation would be to acquire someone with both subject knowledge and interviewing experience, but as that is not always possible, topical experts can be enlisted to do the work if properly trained in oral history methodology.[70]

Another option would be to find interviewers who are specialists in either interviewing or the historical method more generally. Just as inexperienced interviewers with topical knowledge need to hone interviewing skills, so do experienced interviewers need to acquire a good working knowledge of the subject involved.

Some researchers believe that an interviewer should be a specialist in one of the two above areas.[71] Other oral historians, however, feel differently. For example, Foxfire projects have recovered vast amounts of information for community history projects, but the project has been derided by individual scholars for being the moral equivalent of "pothunting," because research was being done by schoolteachers and students (and not by academics). Along the same line, Gluck asserts that, "Oral history is not, nor should it be, the province of experts. On the contrary, some of the best work today is being done by individuals and groups outside 'the groves of academe.'" She goes on to acknowledge, however, that some reading about the process of interviewing is useful in those cases.[72]

One of the most discussed issues regarding interviewer selection is whether interviewers should be insiders or outsiders relative to the group or individual under consideration. There are both advantages and disadvantages to either choice.

The general sense, at least as reflected in the oral history literature, is that insiders have the benefit of an existing rapport

with interviewees, they know much of the necessary background material (or at least where it is located), and they may
have access to privileged information. However, there is also the
perception that insiders are not seen as neutral (not necessarily a
problem at least as regards critical theory); they may overlook
obvious questions because they take certain things for granted;
and, knowing the rules of engagement in a community, the insider may not want to ask the difficult question. An outsider,
however, may be viewed by interviewees as being more objective, and since the interviewer will not be staying in the community, he or she may be given information that someone
remaining in the community would not be able to elicit.[73]

Researchers have also noted a difference in not only the
amount but also the basic nature of information they have received when they have been an insider versus an outsider.
Alessandro Portelli was an outsider in his work with Kentucky
coal miners, but an insider doing research within his university
in Rome. He observed that, because of his status, "one conse-
quence is that the Kentucky interviews emphasize storytelling
and history-telling, with a great deal of straight information and
narrative, while the Rome interviews read like tentative essays
replete with commentary evaluation and analysis. . . . Narrators
will assume that a 'native' historian already knows the facts, and
will furnish explanations, theories, and judgments, instead."[74]

A simple view of the insider/outsider dichotomy, however,
would be misleading. First, as Schneider notes, there is the
question not only of having an interviewer be an outsider, but
also of the envisioned audience. Whenever an oral history
takes place, there is the immediate audience of the interviewer,
but depending on the intended purpose of the materials, there
is also a second, anticipated audience in those who will be
viewing the final product. Whether that audience is perceived
as being insiders (e.g., for material placed in a local library) or
outsiders (e.g., for a documentary produced for public television) may also make a difference in the types and nature of the
information divulged.[75]

Second, there is the issue of how an insider versus an outsider is defined in a particular community or for a specific individual. This returns to the ongoing discussion of the assumption

of homogeneity that has been raised by Hansen, Osterud and Jones, and others.[76] For example, an interviewer may be a member of a geographical community being studied (as in the case of a neighborhood), but if that person's gender or age are significantly different from that of the interviewees, is that person an insider or an outsider? As Allen and Montell observe, "The researcher's sex and ethnic background can also pose methodological problems and can serve as both an aid and hindrance to local history research."[77] The same might be true of other possible characteristics, including class, race, occupation, and religious affiliation. The point is that even within physically or culturally bounded communities, there is diversity that needs to be considered when planning research.

Selecting Interviewees

> "How do you find these wonderful people?" That is a question I have often been asked, and it implies that "interviewees" are a special kind of animal and that finding them is something like catching nightcrawlers: "You gotta be quick!"
>
> —Edward Ives, *The Tape-Recorded Interview*, 2nd ed.

Finding good interviewees can be a daunting task, but it must be done with care, as it will greatly affect the nature and quality of the information gathered. Perhaps more than anything else, the choices made in this regard will be inextricably tied to the theoretical decisions made earlier.

First, information must be disseminated about a project, and interviewees must be generally recruited. There are a number of ways to accomplish that task. Some researchers advertise on television, radio, or in newspapers, through organizations or newsletters, while others find names through research in local records or in discussions with advisory boards or other interviewees.[78] Ives suggests writing letters to the editor of local papers with an explanation of the project, as that affords one a known identity when first visiting a new location.[79]

There is a danger, however, in mass recruitments for projects, especially if the scope of work will be limited by either resource availability or theoretical concerns. Eliciting more respondents than one can ultimately use may end up causing hard feelings or ill will toward the work, so Ritchie suggests that, "Rather than disappoint people by not interviewing them, projects can limit their initial appeals to informal networks before going public through the media."[80] That approach ultimately gives researchers more control over the process.

Once there is a potential pool of interviewees, selection needs to be done in some manner, usually with an eye toward representative coverage of the groups involved. As Thompson notes, self-selected groups derived from media publicity are rarely representative of the whole, so researchers will probably need to look beyond any initial draws in that regard.[81]

A common way of ensuring adequate coverage for a project is using a matrix. During the research design phase, the topics under consideration can be listed down one axis, while the groups related to those topics can be listed across the top axis. For example, a community oral history project might list as potential topics the Depression, World War II, the 1966 closing of a local mine, the Vietnam War, and the local flood of 1978. Groups needing to be represented could be delineated by occupation (e.g., ranchers, miners, schoolteachers), ethnic or racial groups, or gender, age, or class considerations, in part depending upon the theoretical underpinnings of the research. A grid is then formed that, ideally, would be filled with the names of chroniclers who could address topics from the particular perspectives desired. A similar matrix, called a control chart, is suggested by David Lance, although he mentions it as a way to track what progress has been made in the course of a project rather than utilizing it as a planning tool.[82]

Other means of selecting interviewers include specific types of sampling to ensure proper representation (although this approach can also be used in conjunction with a matrix). Snowball sampling is less statistically based and really refers more to a recruiting tactic. It consists of obtaining suggestions for interviewees from those already interviewed and continuing on in that manner as work progresses. Stratified sampling entails interviewing at all levels of a community or group in order to get equal representation, and purposive sampling is essentially stratified sampling with the additional goal of having all sides represented on controversial or sensitive issues.[83]

Quota sampling reflects an attempt to match the population of a certain place and time with a closely correlated group of interviewees. For example, in Thompson and Vigne's study on Edwardian England noted earlier, they chose a group of interviewees that closely mirrored the demographic proportions listed in the 1911 national census.[84] The various quota categories for sampling—for example, age, gender, race, education, occupation, religion—may vary depending upon the question under study.[85]

And a note in regard to sampling as it pertains to grounded theory: at least as the guidelines for this theory were originally envisioned for sociology, quantitative sampling (i.e., sampling other than that of the snowball variety mentioned above) was seen as unnecessary and perhaps inappropriate to the theoretical goals. Strauss and Corbin noted that, "Researchers are not trying to control variables; rather they are trying to discover them. They are not looking for representativeness or distribution of populations; rather they are looking for how concepts vary dimensionally along their properties. So, although random sampling is possible, it might be detrimental because it could prevent analysts from discovering the variations that they are looking for."[86]

This does not necessarily have to be the case with oral history projects informed by grounded theory, however. One of the most commonly cited examples of successfully implemented grounded theory is Thompson and Vigne's Edwardian study, which is also referenced above as an effective utilization of quota sampling.

When representationally ideal interviewees have been located (however one's theory defines that), there are a few practical considerations that should be addressed as part of the selection process. First, the interviewees must actually be able to participate in the oral history process by being able to communicate their firsthand recollections.[87] That is, not only must they have eyewitness accounts, but their memory must be good enough and they must be sufficiently articulate about their remembrances to be involved in an interview. Second, keep in mind that interviewees do not need to be elderly to have pertinent memories. This is particularly true when projects are addressing current events, but the tendency to work with older chroniclers is so embedded that younger interviewees may be overlooked.[88]

Last, but certainly not least, is the possibility that monetary donations and grants will drive the interviewee selection process. Simply put, this should not happen. As Ritchie asserts, "Economic realities may be inescapable, but oral history projects should include as wide a range of interviews as possible and not be limited to those who can pay for it. Care must be taken not to allow funding sources to inhibit the choice of topics or interviewees."[89]

Determining Scope

The matter of determining the scope of a project will in large part be decided by resources and the availability of interviewees as much as by the research design, and much of this will occur well into the project's progress. To the extent, however, that various aspects are planned for in advance (particularly for proposals to granting agencies or for institutional review board presentations), the following suggestions are presented.

First, the matrix and the control chart discussed earlier are convenient guides both for planning the scope of a project at its outset and for understanding how well the material gathered is meeting the research goals as far as coverage is concerned. These charts are not meant to be carved in stone but can (and should) be adapted as the project evolves.

Second, an interview guide is generally considered a necessity by most oral historians (although not by all grounded theorists). Such a guide can consist of anything from a basic list of topics to a detailed, ordered list of questions, and they are especially useful for projects where there is more than one interviewer, as everyone then goes into the interview with the same goals. Lance suggests making an initial list of subjects to be discussed, then delineating more specific queries under each heading (keeping in mind, of course, what information will be available based on the age and experience of interviewees).[90]

And while this list can be as vague or as detailed as desired, Hoopes cautions against writing out every question verbatim, as that tends to make the conversation seem less spontaneous and detracts from the interactive nature of the interview.[91]

However researchers choose to use interview guides, it should be remembered that they are *just* guides. As Valerie Yow notes, "The guide contains the topics the interviewer will pursue but does not limit the interview to those topics because the narrator will have the freedom to suggest others"[92] (as will the interviewer). Oral history sessions are discussions between two individuals (generally), and they should retain that dialogic nature if they are to be considered oral histories.

Background Preparations

Research

Although there is some disagreement regarding when background research should be done (see the earlier discussion on grounded theory), there is almost complete consensus that scholars should, at some point, conduct extensive research into the subject they are studying.[93] Not only does the advance preparation show proper respect for the interviewee, but it also allows the interviewer to identify inconsistencies in responses and use time with the interviewee to best advantage, for as Hoopes observes, "Having a limited amount of time with the interviewee, you do not want to spend it learning information that you can acquire elsewhere, before the interview."[94]

It is also important to note that background research does not include only investigations of literature on the subject or historical period in question, but should also include research into oral history methodology. Field guides, anthologies, and theoretical works are good places to start.[95]

While most researchers will be able to visit libraries and archives or access materials online, useful sources will not always be available in those locations depending upon the nature of the project. Prominent individuals may be represented by a conspicuous paper trail, but nonelites or those from underdocumented groups may not. In these instances, Gluck suggests consulting sources on the historical era and general living conditions, and Hoopes recommends being creative and using local newspapers (if birth or marriage dates are available) or sources such as high school yearbooks. He further notes that such research is not only possible, but also important, "because one justification usually cited for resistance to studying the history of the poor and minority groups is that the bottom ranks of society supposedly do not leave useful records."[96]

Family histories can also pose a problem in this regard, but if one is researching one's own family, helpful artifacts and documents are often available. Family Bibles and photographs are good resources, and if important dates are known (which is more common within families), public records and newspapers can be valuable sources for information. Shopes suggests that, in doing background research, family historians should compile individual information forms for each family member, adding details as they are uncovered, which provides an easy way to organize material as it is gathered.[97]

Meetings and Clearances

Although community meetings were mentioned earlier as a means of encouraging collaboration, there are also meetings that will be mandatory rather than voluntary and clearances that must be obtained. When entering some communities for research—most notably Native American reservations and other sovereign entities—the approval of certain leadership groups often must be acquired before research can begin. In some instances it will be a tribal or elders' council, while in other cases it will be a different sort of local or regional governmental body, but bear in mind that approval must be obtained before work in some communities can commence.[98] During these meetings, release forms should also be reviewed to ensure that there is no misunderstanding about the nature of the releases or the disposition of materials. If these issues need to be negotiated, it is much easier to do so at the beginning of a project than after a portion of the work has been completed.

Another clearance that must often be obtained, at least in many academic and governmental contexts, is that of the institutional review board (IRB). IRBs and their origins are discussed in more detail in Shopes's chapter elsewhere in this volume, but suffice it to say that one reason for having a clearly defined research design and resolved release form and representation issues is so that a researcher can present his or her plan to an IRB committee with no loose ends. If an IRB review is required at a given institution, a scholar must satisfy the IRB that the project will be conducted in an ethical manner and in accordance with the *Evaluation Guidelines* set forth by the Oral History Association.[99] (Note that following the guidelines and behaving in an ethical fashion are, of course, expected of all oral historians and not just those going before IRB committees, but this is simply mentioned in the context of the IRB review.)

End Products and Availability

These topics are discussed in depth elsewhere in this book, but brief mention will be made of them here to the extent that they impact or are impacted by the research design. For a number of reasons, the planning for all projects needs to take final products into consideration. The first are practical. If the goal of the research is to produce an illustrated book, then photographs should be gathered in the course of work. If a multimedia program is planned, the necessary materials must be collected and the audio must be of a quality so as to be usable. Also, release forms should reflect the possible uses to which the materials can be put.

On a more theoretical level, however, there are other considerations. If interviewees (either on an individual or community scale) trust researchers with their memories and opinions, what do oral historians provide them with in return? What is a researcher's responsibility to interviewees? To a degree, certainly, interviewees may experience an increase in self-esteem or local status because their recollections are viewed as interesting and important, and as mentioned previously, many projects advocate for the empowerment of their participants. But as far as the end products of the oral history go, what do interviewees receive, and if they receive anything, is it of use to them? On this question of restitution, Portelli inquires, "Does the intended audience [for an oral history's final product] include the social circle of the narrators, and what responsibility does the text take on their behalf?"[100]

Oral historians have become more conscious of the need to give something back to interviewees. Many programs provide copies of tapes or transcripts to chroniclers. On a larger, community-wide scale, end products have been designed with local audiences and their needs and wants in mind. Examples include the Web site, "From Here: A Century of Voices from Ohio," produced by The Wallpaper Project, of Auglaize County, Ohio; the museum exhibition, "Agincourt: A Community History," developed by the Multicultural History Society of Ontario at the Scarborough Historical Museum, in Scarborough, Ontario; the video documentaries on Washoe culture, *Rabbit Boss* and *Tah Gum*, produced by the University of Nevada Oral History Program, Reno, Nevada; and various community publishing projects popular in Great Britain.[101] Researchers should take these concerns under consideration when compiling their research design, especially to ensure congruity between the theoretical aims of a project and its final products, as a project that claims empowerment as one of its goals and then returns nothing to the community is contradictory at best and hypocritical at worst.

One way that oral historians attempt to make materials useful to communities is through their placement in local and regional libraries, cultural centers, and museums. This also fulfills researchers' obligations to the academic sphere, by making tapes and transcripts available to other scholars.[102] Perhaps Alice Hoffman best summarized the contribution of such a placement to both researchers and interviewees with the following story: "I remember thanking profusely a steelworker for his time in giving me his memories and his answer was very good. He said, 'Oh hell, Alice, it's better than a tombstone.' He had a better sense than I did that his angle of vision was going to be at Penn State, in the archives for a long time."[103]

This anecdote also highlights the reason that oral historians need to take their research designs and their work seriously. Through the projects they plan, researchers are entrusted with recording and preserving people's memories and ensuring that they will be available and useful "for a long time." That, in itself, is a weighty task.

Notes

1. Gluck, "What's So Special" (1996), 217.

2. Henige, *Oral Historiography*, 23; on selecting previously undocumented topics, see also, Ritchie, *Doing Oral History* (1995), 23.

3. Ritchie, *Doing Oral History* (1995), 24.

4. Oral History Office, September 11, 2001 Oral History Narrative and Memory Project, Columbia University, http://www.columbia.edu/cu/lweb/indiv/oral/sept11.html (accessed January 31, 2005). For a discussion of oral history on current topics, using this project as the focus, see "Images of Sept. 11 Fill Half-Day Session at OHA Conference: 'History Hot' Reveals Complexities Masked in Media Accounts," *Oral History Association Newsletter* 36, no. 3 (Winter 2002): 8–10.

5. Harris et al., *Practice of Oral History*, 51; Crawford, "State of the Profession," 4.

6. Meyer, "Elena Poniatowska," 4; Andrade, "One Year Later," 22.

7. Poniatowska, "Earthquake," 16–17.

8. Governor's Day oral history collection, University of Nevada Oral History Program, Reno.

9. Hardy, "Alice Hoffman," 111.

10. Ritchie, *Doing Oral History* (1995), 30.

11. Schneider, *So They Understand*, 118.

12. Dunaway, "Oral Biography," 257, quoted in Schneider, *So They Understand*, 112.

13. Gluck, "What's So Special" (1996), 217–18.

14. Portelli, *Battle of Valle Giulia*, 4.

15. Blackman, *During My Time*, 14.

16. Osterud and Jones, "'I Must Say So,'" 4.

17. Sitton, "Descendants of *Foxfire*," 20; Hareven, "Generational Memory," 246.

18. Allen and Montell, *Memory to History*, vii–viii, 5.

19. Schneider, *So They Understand*, 20.

20. University of Alaska Fairbanks Oral History Program, Project Jukebox, Elmer E. Rasmuson Library, University of Alaska Fairbanks, http://uaf-db.uaf.edu/Jukebox/PJWeb/pjhome.htm (accessed January 26, 2005).

21. Sitton, "Descendants of *Foxfire*," 29–30.

22. Harris et al., *Practice of Oral History*, 18; Henige, *Oral Historiography*, 25.

23. Hoopes, *Oral History*, 57.

24. Hareven, "Generational Memory," 243.

25. Shopes, "Using Oral History," 232.

26. Hareven, "Generational Memory," 243–44.

27. Shopes, "Using Oral History," 234.

28. Hoopes, *Oral History*, 58.

29. McMahan, *Elite Oral History*, xiv.

30. Frisch, "Oral History and *Hard Times*" (1998), 32; Perks and Thomson, "Critical Developments," 1; Henige, *Oral Historiography,* 107; Hardy, "Alice Hoffman," 109.

31. Perks and Thomson, "Critical Developments," 1; Yow, *Recording Oral History* (1994), 3; Dunaway, "Interdisciplinarity," 8; Shopes, "Using Oral History," 232.

32. Tuchman, "Distinguishing the Significant" (1996), 96.

33. O'Farrell, "Facts and Fiction," 5–6, cited in Grele, *Envelopes of Sound*, 2nd ed., 282n56.

34. Henige, *Oral Historiography*, 109.

35. Hoffman, "Who Are the Elite?" 3–4.

36. Blackman, *During My Time*, 5.

37. Okihiro, "Ethnic History," 42.

38. Poniatowska, "Earthquake," 15.

39. Jefferson, "Echoes from the South," 43–44; Lynd, "Oral History from Below," 1; Perks and Thomson, *Oral History Reader*, ix.

40. Harris et al., *Practice of Oral History*, 4; Perks and Thomson, *Oral History Reader*, ix; Henige, *Oral Historiography*, 17; Jefferson, "Echoes from the South," 46.

41. Crawford, "State of the Profession," 3.

42. Ives, *Tape-Recorded Interview*, 2nd ed., 11.

43. Thompson, *Voice of the Past*, 225; Stacey, "Feminist Ethnography," 112; Osterud and Jones, "'I Must Say So,'" 2.

44. Gluck, "What's So Special" (1996), 217.

45. Stein, *American Journey*, x, quoted in Hoopes, *Oral History*, 26–27.

46. Hoopes, *Oral History*, 27.

47. Gluck, "What's So Special" (1996), 217.

48. Osterud and Jones, "'I Must Say So,'" 3.

49. Ibid.

50. Moss, "Future of Oral History," 14–15; Perks and Thomson, *Oral History Reader*, ix; Perks and Thomson, "Critical Developments," 1; Hardy, "Alice Hoffman," 109.

51. Lynd, "Oral History from Below," 2–5; Portelli, *Battle of Valle Giulia*, xvi–xvii.

52. Thompson, *Voice of the Past*, 3rd ed., 22.

53. Henige, *Oral Historiography*, 107.

54. Perks and Thomson, *Oral History Reader*, ix; Lynd, "Oral History from Below," 1–2.

55. Hoffman, "Who Are the Elite?" 5.

56. Hareven, "Generational Memory," 254.

57. Brian Beun, quoted in Sitton, "Descendents of *Foxfire*," 22–23.

58. Jefferson, "Echoes from the South," 46.

59. For example, the civil rights collections housed at the University of Southern Mississippi's Center for Oral History and Cultural Heritage, Hattiesburg, Mississippi, and at the archives of Tougaloo College, Tougaloo, Mississippi.

60. Jefferson, "Echoes from the South," 43–44.

61. Okihiro, "Ethnic History," 43.

62. Hansen, "Riot of Voices," 136.

63. See Glaser and Strauss, *Grounded Theory*.

64. Strauss and Corbin, *Qualitative Research*, 12.

65. Yow, *Recording Oral History* (1994), 8; Sima Belmar, "For the Record: The Legacy Oral History Project Gets It in Writing," *San Francisco Bay Guardian*, April 30, 2003.

66. Thompson, *Voice of the Past*, 3rd ed., 227.

67. Portelli, *Battle of Valle Giulia*, 11; see also Yow, *Recording Oral History* (1994), 8; Thompson, *Voice of the Past*, 3rd ed., 227.

68. Henige, *Oral Historiography*, 33.

69. Thompson, *Edwardians*, 7; Thompson, *Voice of the Past*, 3rd ed., 146–48; Yow, *Recording Oral History* (1994), 17; Jensen, "Quantification," 15.

70. Ritchie, *Doing Oral History* (1995), 31; Harris et al., *Practice of Oral History*, 10.

71. Harris et al., *Practice of Oral History*, 45.

72. Gluck, "What's So Special" (1996), 219–20.

73. Ritchie, *Doing Oral History* (1995), 31; Allen and Montell, *Memory to History*, 11–12; Gluck, "What's So Special" (1996), 221; Schneider, *So They Understand*, 21; Harris et al., *Practice of Oral History*, 24–25.

74. Portelli, *Battle of Valle Giulia*, 11; Gluck, "What's So Special" (1996), 221.

75. Schneider, *So They Understand*, 21.

76. Hansen, "Riot of Voices," 136; Osterud and Jones, "'I Must Say So,'" 3; Kikumura, "Family Life Histories," 2–3.

77. Allen and Montell, *Memory to History*, 13–14.

78. Ritchie, *Doing Oral History* (1995), 30–31; Green, "Returning History," 54; Yow, *Recording Oral History* (1994), 45; Gluck, "What's So Special" (1996), 220–21.

79. Ives, *Tape-Recorded Interview*, 2nd ed., 26–27.

80. Ritchie, *Doing Oral History* (1995), 30–31.

81. Thompson, *Voice of the Past*, 3rd ed., 22.

82. Lance, "Project Design," 140.

83. Yow, *Recording Oral History* (1994), 45–47; Strauss and Corbin, *Qualitative Research*, 281; Hardy, "Alice Hoffman," 116.

84. Thompson, *Edwardians*, 7; Thompson, *Voice of the Past*, 3rd ed., 146–48; Yow, *Recording Oral History* (1994), 47.

85. Jensen, "Quantification," 19.

86. Strauss and Corbin, *Qualitative Research*, 281.

87. Thompson, *Voice of the Past*, 3rd ed., 212–13.

88. Hoopes, *Oral History*, 28.

89. Ritchie, *Doing Oral History* (1995), 28.

90. Lance, "Project Design," 138.

91. Hoopes, *Oral History*, 80.

92. Yow, *Recording Oral History* (1994), 36.

93. Grele, *Envelopes of Sound*, 2nd ed., 164; Thompson, *Voice of the Past*, 3rd ed., 222; Harris et al., *Practice of Oral History*, 15; Henige, *Oral Historiography*, 24; Jefferson, "Echoes from the South," 52; Yow, *Recording Oral History* (1994), 33; Lance, "Project Design," 136; Hoopes, *Oral History*, 72–73; Okihiro, "Ethnic History," 38.

94. Hoopes, *Oral History*, 72.

95. Grele, *Envelopes of Sound*, 2nd ed., 141; Gluck, "What's So Special" (1996), 220; Okihiro, "Ethnic History," 38.

96. Gluck, "What's So Special" (1996), 223; Hoopes, *Oral History*, 75–76.

97. Shopes, "Using Oral History," 233.

98. Harris et al., *Practice of Oral History*, 18; Henige, *Oral Historiography*, 25.

99. Oral History Association, *Evaluation Guidelines*.

100. Portelli, *Battle of Valle Giulia*, 18–19; see also Lynd, "Oral History from Below," 2.

101. See The Wallpaper Project, From Here: A Century of Voices from Ohio, Ohio Humanities Council, http://www.ohiohumanities.org/current_int/wallpaper/support.htm (accessed January 26, 2005), and University of Nevada Oral History Program, Publications, University of Nevada, http://www.unr.edu/cla/oralhist/ohweb/bestsel.htm (accessed January 26, 2005). On British community history publications, see Bornat, "Two Oral Histories," 78.

102. Ives, *Tape-Recorded Interview*, 2nd ed., 85–86; Ritchie, *Doing Oral History* (1995), 54–55; Thompson, *Voice of the Past*, 3rd ed., 214.

103. Hardy, "Alice Hoffman," 133.

4

Legal and Ethical Issues in Oral History

Linda Shopes

Legal and ethical issues are often discussed sequentially within oral history, with the law understood as defining state-sanctioned rules for specific elements of practice and ethics as setting a higher standard for the right conduct of relationships within the broad context of an interview or project. Although this distinction is not entirely inaccurate, it unnecessarily segregates the two, obscuring their relationship within the overall development of oral history as a mode of historical practice. Thus, in this essay, I will discuss legal and ethical issues within an overall historical framework. I identify three stages in oral history's evolution: its origins as an archival practice, its expansion as a means of democratizing both the historical record and the act of doing history, and its maturation as a complex intellectual and social practice.[1] While these stages have occurred somewhat in succession over the past half century, they also overlap chronologically and conceptually. Discussion of the first stage is heavily weighted toward fundamental legal issues, for they are closely related to oral history's archival origins; discussion of the second and third stages extends to broader ethical concerns.

Oral historians living and working in different nations have codified principles to guide their work according to the legal codes and historical conditions of their various countries. In the United States, the governing document is *Oral History Evaluation*

125

Guidelines, initially developed by the U.S. Oral History Association (OHA) as "Goals and Guidelines" in 1968, amplified as a checklist of "Evaluation Guidelines" in 1979, and then revised in 1989 and again in 2000 to take into account new issues and concerns.[2] The OHA guidelines, as well as other associations' codes, conceptualize legal and ethical principles as a series of rights and responsibilities governing relationships between interviewers and narrators; among interviewers, their various professions and disciplines, and the broader public; and between sponsoring institutions and interviewees, interviewers, the professions, and the public. The challenge for oral historians occurs when responsibilities to one party collide with responsibilities to another, when ethical considerations thus pull in opposite directions. I will discuss some of these conflicts in the body of the essay.

While *Evaluation Guidelines* is a touchstone for any discussion of legal and ethical issues in the U.S. and considerably informs this essay, it is also a historical document, grounded in assumptions about individual and property rights deeply embedded in U.S. laws and culture as well as standards of professional practice that are by definition both exclusionary and protectionist. Recognizing this, Alessandro Portelli has written: "Ultimately, in fact ethical and legal guidelines only make sense if they are the outward manifestation of a broader and deeper sense of personal and political commitment to honesty and to truth. . . . Sticking close to the letter of professional guidelines may not be incompatible with subtler strategies of manipulation and falsification. Ethical guidelines may be, in this case, less a protection of the interviewee from the manipulation of the interviewer than a protection of the interviewer from the claims of the interviewee."[3]

It is important to remember, therefore, that legal and especially ethical issues are at bottom judgment calls. Certainly legal transgressions can have serious consequences for individual researchers and their sponsoring institutions. Ethical lapses not only can harm narrators and burden a researcher, but they can also discredit the work of others. Nonetheless, in my view, individual oral historians need to understand where they stand vis-à-vis accepted practice, act according to their own best judgment, and accept the consequences of their actions.

Law, Ethics, and Oral History as an Archival Practice

Oral history in the U.S. generally dates its origins to the 1940s, with the work of Allan Nevins at Columbia University. Although there were numerous earlier efforts to record firsthand accounts of the past, most notably the life histories gathered by the Great Depression–era Federal Writers' Project, it was Nevins who first initiated a systematic and disciplined effort to record on tape, preserve, and make available for future research recollections deemed of historical significance.[4] Two fundamental ethical issues in oral history are linked to its origins as an archival practice: obtaining the narrator's informed consent for the interview and securing legal release of the interview tape and transcript. The former is linked to the goal of creating as full and accurate account as possible for the permanent record, the latter to issues of copyright and, more broadly, concerns about making interviews both physically and intellectually accessible to potential users.[5] This last point deserves elaboration. Although oral history interviews are by definition intended for permanent preservation, ad hoc projects without the institutional capacity to archive completed interviews and individual scholars conducting interviews for their own work at times neglect to make interviews accessible to others after they have served their immediate purpose. Professional standards enjoin the group or individual to place interviews in a permanent repository where others may have access to them, and in the case of interviews used for scholarly work, so others may interrogate and build upon the work.[6]

Informed Consent

Because a primary goal of oral history is to enhance the extant historical record, good interviewers work with narrators to "speak to history," that is, to create a record worthy of preservation, one that is accurate, expansive, and thoughtful and hence of value not only to scholars but also to society's collective understanding of the past. There are many ways for an interviewer to cultivate a good interview, as discussed elsewhere in this volume. Fundamental, however, is a respect for the person whose story one seeks. Respect, too, can be demonstrated in many ways. Of importance here, however, is the process of informed consent, whereby the interviewer tells the potential narrator everything that person needs to know in order to decide whether or not to participate in an interview and to continue participation once interviewing has begun. Thus potential narrators need to be informed about the purpose, scope, and value of the interview, how it will proceed, and the interviewer's expectations for the interview. Interviewees need to know the intended use of the interview as well as possible future uses; that they will have the opportunity to review and emend the transcript, if project protocols include transcription; and where the interviewer or project intends to place tapes and transcripts for permanent preservation. Narrators must also be informed that they will be asked to sign a copyright release form at the conclusion of the interview, by which they will define the terms according to which the interview can be used, and that the interviewer and the project cannot entirely control the uses to which the interview will be put once it has been made publicly available nor protect it against subpoena. It is also appropriate to discuss any relevant financial considerations, including payment to narrators and disbursement of royalties resulting from publication of the interview. Finally, interviewees need to know that they can refuse to answer any given question during the interview and can terminate the interview at any time with no adverse consequences.

These terms and conditions need thorough review prior to the interview. Unless specific circumstances dictate otherwise, it is also advisable that they be codified in a consent form or memorandum of agreement written in language appropriate to the interviewee and signed by both interviewee and interviewer. Though it can be argued that undue attention to interview protocols and narrator rights prior to the interview can have a chilling effect on the interview itself, in fact quite the opposite can be true. Insofar as securing the narrator's informed consent is approached as more than a pro forma exercise, it can be a means of educating the narrator about the nature and purpose of oral history and can generate enthusiasm for the interview, which in turn helps cultivate a good interview as the narrator is oriented to the interview situation, understands his or her role, and presumably is motivated to create a record of historical value. Moreover, securing informed consent does not end once the form is signed and the tape recorder is turned on. Respect grows—or not—over time, and so consent is negotiated throughout the entire interview as narrators are given the opportunity to tell their story in their own way, as unexpected openings are pursued, as the interviewer both accedes to and presses against constraints imposed by the narrator, as developing trust results in an increasingly frank account or growing mistrust to conversation that is guarded, responses that are perfunctory. In my own interviewing, I have found that once I have assured narrators that they do *not* have to answer questions on any given subject—family finances is often one of these "nervous subjects"—they frequently proceed to talk about precisely that subject in great detail. The point, it seems to me, is that I have demonstrated a respect for the narrators' right to control what they say; and in so doing, I have gained trust and hence the right of access to information not shared casually.

Attention to the process of informed consent also guards against defamation, a particular concern of those conducting interviews for archival purposes. John Neuenschwander, whose *Oral History and the Law* is the single best guide to legal issues in oral history, defines defamation as "a false statement of fact printed or broadcast about a person which tends to injure that person's interest." He goes on to say that "the accepted rule is that anyone who repeats, republishes, or redistributes a defamatory statement made by another can be held liable as well."[7] Thus any interview for the record, that is, any interview made available to others in a public repository and/or reproduced for others in any medium, is potentially liable for defamation. Defamation is a serious charge; it is also one that is not easy to prove. Neuenschwander defines five specific elements that must be present for a statement to be deemed defamatory: the statement itself must be false; it must specifically identify the person claiming injury; it must be communicated to a third person, for example, a researcher listening to the offending interview; the injured party's reputation must have been damaged; and the perpetrator must be at fault, that is, responsible for the injury claimed.[8] Additional constraints also obtain: most states have imposed a statute of limitation on the time between first publication of the offending material and the charge of defamation; the courts have established a much higher bar for proving defamation of public figures as opposed to private individuals; and statements construed as opinion, "nothing more than conjecture and rumor," in the words of one court case, are not considered defamatory—though the line between opinion and fact admittedly can be blurred.[9] Finally, and of particular interest to oral historians, the party claiming injury must be alive—the dead, in other words, cannot be defamed.

This final constraint suggests that the easiest course of action for an oral historian confronted with a potentially defamatory statement is to counsel the narrator to seal that portion of the interview until such time as the person under discussion can reasonably be assumed to be deceased.[10] In addition to this practice, Neuenschwander suggests as alternatives either excising the questionable material from the tape and transcript or deleting the identity of the person in question. Both of these actions, while reasonable, assume that the questionable statements are, in fact, defamatory. But on whose judgment? Perhaps they are accurate. Perhaps the narrator knows something others do not. Hence, an equally reasonable approach may be to try to ascertain the truth or falsity of the statement in question by consulting other sources. If it is true, it is not defamatory.[11]

The larger point in this discussion, however, is that a respectful process of informed consent before and during an interview, by which both interviewer and narrator agree that they are "speaking to history" and not chatting or gossiping informally, can guard against defamatory statements. An interviewee who understands the purpose of the interview, who knows he or she is speaking for the record, can measure comments about another person. A conscientious interviewer can avoid setting up too intimate an exchange, one that nurtures imprudent confidences. If the interviewer/interviewee relationship is trusting enough, they can also engage in a metaconversation about the interview itself while it is going on, that is, decide together within the context of an interview whether or not to pursue a particular line of talk.

The above discussion suggests that informed consent is both universally desirable and possible. Yet a question arises about how much to reveal about the purpose of an interview to a potential narrator, "who," as Jeremy Brecher phrased it some years ago, "if they really understood what we were going to do with the material, would probably not cooperate?"[12] Kathleen Blee further complicates the matter by suggesting that the men and women she interviewed about their participation in the 1920s Ku Klux Klan in Indiana could not give true informed consent to the interviews because they "found it impossible to imagine that I— a native of Indiana and a white person—would not agree, at least secretly, with their racist and bigoted world views."[13] Here, then, is a place where ethical judgments are in order. Typically, oral historians counsel telling a narrator the truth about the subject, purpose, and disposition of an interview but argue that they are under no obligation to inform the narrator of the interpretation they will bring to bear upon an individual's story. But again Brecher raises a provocative question: "What is the nature of our implied contract with our informants, and what limits should that contract place on the way we present them?"[14] In general, too, outright deception is quite rightly considered beyond the bounds of ethical practice. Yet there is the example of filmmaker Claude Lanzmann, who exposed perpetrators of the Nazi Holocaust by filming them with a hidden camera and then included their testimony in his epic film *Shoah*.[15] Does the public's right to hold war criminals accountable trump Lanzmann's failure to secure their consent to the interview? Or not?[16] Standard professional practice, which privileges the rights of narrators, would claim that Lanzmann acted unethically; broader civic and or moral claims would suggest otherwise.

Release Forms and Copyright

Because oral history originated as an archival practice, early practitioners were especially concerned with gaining ownership of completed interviews and transcripts, for without this, they would not have the right to grant others access to this material. This remains an important concern, for put simply, an interview is understood as a creative work owned by the interviewee and hence is subject to the laws of copyright. (The status of the interviewer is less certain, as discussed below.) For an interview to be used by anyone other than the interviewee, the interviewer or the project or institution for which he is working must secure a legal release agreement once the interview is complete, assigning rights to the interview to either the interviewer or to the repository where it will be permanently housed. As Neuenschwander writes, "*Without a legal release, the possessor of the tape or transcript of an oral history interview cannot legally utilize, loan, publish, or make it available to researchers without infringing upon the rights of the interviewee and possibly the interviewer*" (emphasis in original).[17] Rights can be assigned by means of a deed of gift or contract. Both will allow others access to the interview; they will also allow those who retain ownership the rights to use, reproduce, and disseminate the interview, as well as to protect them from its illegal use by others. Both include specific elements, generally phrased in commonly accepted, legally sanctioned language. Although template forms are available, one size does not fit all, and interviewers, projects, and repositories are advised to consult legal counsel to develop a deed of gift or contract appropriate to their project.[18]

Oral historians generally agree that the most important right to secure by means of a legal release is copyright; that is, they seek the transfer of ownership of the creative work that constitutes the interview from the interviewee to the interviewer, project, or repository. Whoever owns the copyright can then reproduce, publish, distribute, and sell the interview and legally prevent others from doing so without explicit permission. However, a narrator does not have to sign over copyright to the interview in order to make it available to others; the narrator can retain the copyright, placing physical custody of the tape and transcript with an individual or archives and permitting limited use or requiring potential users other than the interviewer to secure the narrator's permission if they wish more extensive use. While some oral history programs and archives will thus allow a narrator to retain the copyright to the interview, they usually require that it revert to the institution upon the narrator's death and not transfer to heirs, for repositories cannot track heirs over time. Copyright protection, however, is not maintained in perpetuity. According to the terms of the Copyright Act of 1976, copyright protection for works created on or after January 1, 1978, extends seventy years beyond the life of the author (i.e., interviewee), after which the work enters the public domain. Interviews can also be placed in the public domain at the time of their creation, thereby avoiding the issue of copyright altogether, but this too must be done by means of a legal release.[19]

The status of the interviewer as cocreator and hence joint owner of the copyright to the interview is unclear at this time; it is also related to the interview's position vis-à-vis the sponsoring project or organization. Although the courts have not ruled on the issue, the U.S. Copyright Office recognizes the interviewer as a joint author, "in the absence of an agreement to the contrary."[20] It is generally advised, therefore, that interviewers also sign over copyright when interviews are retained by a project or archives. The one clear exception is an interview conducted by a full-time employee of a given entity as part of his job duties; under such circumstances, termed "work made for hire," the interviewer/employee's rights to the interview are automatically ceded to the employer.[21] However, many interviewers are not full-time employees of the organization or institution sponsoring an oral history project; they are temporary or part-time employees, independent contractors, or volunteers who are not therefore covered by the terms of "work made for hire." Under these circumstances, the sponsoring institution would be wise to secure rights to the interviews at the outset of the project by means of a work for hire or assignment of copyright agreement with the interviewer. Yet it may be appropriate to tailor arrangements to individual circumstances: if, for example, a contract interviewer is interviewing on a subject related to his own research interests or a scholar is conducting interviews without official institutional sponsorship but nonetheless plans to permanently archive the interviews within the institution, he may wish to secure the right to exclusive use of the interviews for a specified period of time.[22]

In addition to addressing the issue of copyright, the legal release also allows the narrator to define the terms according to which the interview can—and cannot—be accessed and used by others. While historians generally prefer releases with no restrictions, an interviewee can protect sensitive material by closing all or portions of the interview for a given number of years. Such a restriction, however, is not inviolate; it can be overruled by court order if the interview is deemed of potential value to a legal proceeding. An interviewee can also forbid users to quote directly from the interview and can require anonymity for a period of time or in perpetuity. This latter situation is especially discouraged by historians, for whom anonymous sources are suspect, but sometimes is requested by a narrator to protect personal safety or privacy.

Regrettably, numerous interviews exist, some of them in public archives, for which no legal release has been obtained. Making these interviews available to others before the expiration of copyright is both illegal and unethical. In these cases, narrators should be recontacted and signed releases for the interviews secured. If a narrator is deceased, efforts should be made to contact heirs to whom copyright has passed and to secure their release of the material. Because the Copyright Office recognizes the interviewer as a joint author, and because copyright law allows a joint author to convey rights to a third party without the approval of the other author, another alternative, if the narrator and his heirs are deceased or cannot be located, is for the interviewer to sign over rights to the interview. Publishers of works that incorporate oral history materials for which no release exists will sometimes accept the institution where the interviews are permanently archived as the de facto owner, who must then indemnify the publisher from any adverse consequences resulting from publication of the interviews.

Explaining release forms and copyright issues to a narrator before an interview can admittedly seem a sterile exercise, one not conducive to the informal collegiality desirable in an interview. Like securing informed consent, however, done in the right spirit, these explanations can affirm the seriousness of the inquiry and the value of the narrator's story. Moreover, while the release and underlying concern about copyright are primarily legal issues, they also confirm a fundamental ethical principle in oral history: that the interviewee is deemed to have a certain authority over what he or she has said in an interview. Some researchers are uncomfortable giving narrators so much control over their stories; journalists, they argue, do not secure releases from their sources, allowing them to define the terms according to which the interview can be used. Historians, however, are not journalists; oral history interviews, unlike most conducted for journalistic purposes, are intended for permanent preservation. Historians also have a higher standard for evidence than journalists; they are enjoined by the canons of the profession to make their sources available to others so they can both interrogate and build upon one another's work. And, unless there is an outstanding reason not to, oral historians simply owe it to their narrators to make their stories known, to include them in the permanent record of the culture. Thus, because oral history interviews are preserved for the record, they are subject to laws of copyright; and the narrator, as original owner of the interview, has the right to define the terms of use.

Other questions arise over issues of confidentiality, that is, the status of information given in an interview that, if revealed, could put the narrator or others at risk of legal sanctions, public embarrassment, or other adverse consequences. Again, a conscientious process of informed consent should alert a narrator to the need for caution in revealing potentially incriminating information, but if the interviewer is about to broach a potentially damaging topic, for example, the narrator's possible involvement in a crime, should he again alert the narrator to the fact that the interview is for the record? Or suppose the narrator, consciously or not, reveals his participation in a crime but fails to request that the material be sealed for a period of time or excised from the interview. Should the interviewer suggest that he do so? Or what if the narrator reveals participation in a crime and requests that the incriminating evidence be closed, but the interviewer, weighing personal protection against the claims of justice or the public's right to know, wonders about the ethics of concealing knowledge of a crime? Should revelations of especially disturbing crimes or crimes with broad social consequences—war crimes or embezzlement of public moneys or domestic violence, for example—enjoy the protection of confidentiality? Or what if the issue is not a crime but behavior one might consider socially reprehensible, for example, prejudicial actions against minorities or women that are not illegal but could, if revealed, prove embarrassing or worse to the narrator? Should the interviewer always retain a neutral stance, refusing to judge—or reveal—an interviewee's incriminating past action?[23]

Evaluation Guidelines states that "interviews should remain confidential until interviewees have given permission for their use" and further affirms narrator privilege to restrict access to the interview.[24] The American Anthropological Association's *Statements on Ethics* emphatically privileges the research subject's right to privacy over other claims: "In research, anthropologists' paramount responsibility is to those they study. When there is a conflict of interest, these individuals must come first. Anthropologists must do everything in their power to protect the physical, social, and psychological welfare and to honor the dignity and privacy of those studied."[25] The American Sociological Association's *Code of Ethics*, however, recognizes that certain circumstances may compromise the protection of confidentiality afforded to research subjects, although its guidelines suggest that the conflict lies not with revealing past actions but with disclosing intended future actions that may be harmful to others: "Sociologists may confront unanticipated circumstances where they become aware of information that is clearly health- or life-threatening to research participants, students, employees, clients, or others. In these cases, sociologists balance the importance of guarantees of confidentiality with other principles in this *Code of Ethics*, standards of conduct, and applicable law."[26]

There are clearly no easy answers to questions about the claims of confidentiality. Neuenschwander notes that while historians, unlike attorneys, clergy, and psychiatrists, do not enjoy client privilege, in fact, few legal sanctions obtain for failure to report knowledge of a crime. He also urges caution in reporting a crime, based on careful consideration of statutes of limitation, potential defamation or claims of defamation, and legal sanctions for breach of confidentiality. In the end, however, professional ethics may conflict with a researcher's perceived civic duty or moral sensibility; researchers must live with themselves and thus decide for themselves how to handle such conflicts.

Oral History and the World Wide Web

The increasing use of the World Wide Web as a means of disseminating oral history interviews has raised additional issues of informed consent and access. If future use of an interview may include posting all or part of it on the Web, an interviewer obviously needs to discuss this with a potential narrator as part of the informed consent process. But the question arises: How can someone unfamiliar with the Web, particularly its potential for making the interview available to millions of people within seconds and permitting little or no control over how it will be used, give informed consent to posting their interview on the Web? At minimum, the interviewer facing this situation should demonstrate the Web and explain its capacities to the interviewee.

Release forms should also include language that allows for—or restricts, if the narrator chooses—placement of interviews and transcripts on the Web. Even if there is no immediate plan to do so, inclusion of such language will allow Web publication in the future. But what about uploading an interview collected in the pre-Web era? If the release includes language governing the future use of the interview that can be interpreted broadly to include dissemination via the Web, project managers can probably do so with impunity. But is this ethical, if the narrator had no knowledge of the Web's capacities when he signed the release? And what about interviews for which the releases include no language that can be construed as supporting Web publication? These issues were much debated in the late 1990s within the Oral History Association. Many felt that if Web publication was desired and an interview release did not include specific language permitting it, the copyright holder was obliged to contact the narrator or his heirs and secure specific permission to do so. Archivists, however, upon whom the burden of this task would fall, understandably balked, arguing that recontacting narrators or their heirs would simply place too great a burden on them. So, the compromise adopted by the association and included in the 2000 iteration of its *Evaluation Guidelines* states, "Good faith efforts should be made to ensure that the uses of recordings and transcripts comply with both the letter and spirit of the interviewee's agreements," implying the need for prudent judgment on the elasticity of existing future use agreements and the advisability of recontacting narrators whose release forms are ambiguous on the issue of Web posting.[27]

The issue is not solely one of narrator agreement, however. Certainly, posting interviews on the Web enhances access enormously. Powerful search engines enable students and other researchers to learn about source material they otherwise would not know existed; and if that material is itself online, the Internet brings it to their computer screen within seconds. But is this sort of uncontrolled and anonymous access always desirable? Opportunities for copyright violation and for misuse of a narrator's words are multiplied a thousandfold, with few of the checks imposed by archives when dealing with patrons face to face.[28] For these reasons, as well as technical and financial considerations, many oral history programs do not post full interviews on their Web sites. Others choose to post audiotapes or transcripts but impose certain constraints, including notifying users of copyright restrictions; requiring permission to quote; and requiring submission of a registration form, stating the purpose for which the user wants to view or listen to the interviews, before access is granted. Yet others, seeking to help users make good sense of the interviews, present them along with contextualizing background information.[29]

Oral History and Federal Regulations Governing Research Involving Human Subjects

Increasingly throughout the 1990s and early 2000s, researchers affiliated with colleges and universities have been required to submit protocols for oral history interviewing projects to their campus Institutional Review Board (IRB) prior to conducting any interviews. IRBs, charged with insuring compliance with federal regulations for the protection of human subjects of research, have claimed authority over oral history because these regulations, codified as Title 45 Public Welfare, Part 46 Protection of Human Subjects (referred to as 45 CFR 46 or the Common Rule), included "interaction" with human subjects as one of the research modes subject to review.[30] However, 45 CFR 46, initially intended to protect research subjects from such unethical practices as those employed in the Tuskegee syphilis study or the Milgram experiments on obedience to authority, defined protection within a framework appropriate to biomedical and behavioral research. As a result, constraints appropriate to these forms of research have been inappropriately applied to oral history:

interviewers have been asked to submit detailed questionnaires in advance of any interview; to maintain narrator anonymity, despite an interviewee's willingness to be identified; and to destroy tapes and transcripts after the research project is completed. Clearly these practices violate fundamental principles of oral history.

Most troublesome, however, has been the concern expressed by some IRBs that interviewers not ask any questions for which, in the language of 45 CFR 46, "any disclosure of the human subjects' responses outside the research could reasonably place the subjects at risk of criminal or civil liability, or be damaging to the subjects' financial standing, employability, or reputation"[31]; or questions that might prove psychologically harmful. While the regulations themselves don't prohibit this sort of research, requiring only that efforts be made to "minimize" risk or harm, some IRBs have interpreted them as constraining challenging or difficult lines of inquiry in an interview. Historians thus have become increasingly concerned that IRB review of oral history is having a chilling effect on legitimate inquiry and indeed impinging upon their academic freedom.[32]

Recognizing these concerns, in 1998 the American Historical Association (AHA) and the Oral History Association initiated contact with what was then the Office for Protection from Research Risks, which was renamed in 2000 the Office of Human Research Protections (OHRP) in the Department of Health and Human Services (HHS), which is the federal office responsible for implementing human subjects regulations, to raise questions about the legitimacy of IRB review of oral history within the existing regulatory framework or, failing that, to secure agreement about a form of review that conforms to the ethical principles of the field. After five years of discussion, in 2003, OHRP concurred with a policy statement developed by the AHA and OHA that "most oral history interviewing projects are not subject to . . . regulations for the protection of human subjects . . . and can be excluded from institutional review board . . . oversight because they do not involve research as defined by HHS regulations." The basis for exclusion hinges on the regulatory definition of research as contributing to "generalizable knowledge." To quote further from the policy statement: "While historians reach for meaning that goes beyond the specific subject of their inquiry, unlike researchers in the biomedical and behavioral sciences they do not reach for generalizable principles of historical or social development, nor do they seek underlying principles or laws of nature that have predictive value and can be applied to other circumstances for the purpose of controlling outcomes."[33] The policy does not imply that oral history is not a legitimate form of research, only that it is not *the type of research* the regulations were designed to cover. Nor does it signal an erosion of concern about high ethical standards for oral history by the AHA or OHA, only that oral historians are free to act in accordance with ethical and legal standards appropriate to oral history, not biomedical or behavioral research.[34]

Local IRBs, however, which enjoy considerable autonomy in interpreting the Common Rule, have generally not accepted the policy of excluding oral history from review; and OHRP itself, subsequent to its concurrence with the AHA/OHA policy statement and in response to queries from local IRBs, issued contrary—and conflicting—guidance, identifying some forms of oral history as in fact subject to review. Challenged by the AHA and OHA on this guidance, OHRP reaffirmed the original policy excluding oral history from review. As of this writing in late 2005, therefore, the matter of IRB review of oral history remains unresolved and indeed quite muddled: IRBs generally claim the authority to review interview protocols; OHRP maintains conflicting points of view; oral historians are obliged to conform to regulatory oversight that, at best, fits awkwardly with the work they do, at worst, constrains it; and professional societies' concerns remain unheeded at the federal level.[35]

Ethics and the Democratic Practice of Oral History

If oral history began as an archival practice in the 1940s, it exploded as a social practice in the 1970s, largely in response to the social and political movements of that era. Social history, that is, the history of social relationships among generally unequal and often competing groups, became the dominant historiographic paradigm, reflecting—and at times attempting to influence—the issues and tensions of contemporary public life. People and groups previously absent or underrepresented in our collective history became the subject of historical inquiry, and these new histories became the occasion for a fundamental rethinking of what properly constitutes historical knowledge. Grassroots groups, frequently in collaboration with local scholars, began to engage with their own history, often motivated by a belief that knowledge of one's past can be empowering in the present. Oral history, as a source of information about the past not available elsewhere, and as a reasonably accessible way of learning about that past for those without advanced training in history, was—and remains—intrinsic to this move to democratize both the content and the practice of history. While oral history in this democratic mode certainly didn't begin in the 1970s—one thinks, for example, of George Ewart Evans's pioneering work in England in the 1950s recording the lifeways of rural people with roots in the nineteenth century—its great efflorescence in the last decades of the twentieth arguably found its impetus in 1970s activism. Yet, for all its value in opening up new areas of inquiry and as a tool for grassroots history, oral history's focus on documenting what have sometimes been termed "the nonelite" also has raised a number of broadly ethical questions. Here I focus on two of the most important: power relationships in oral history and what might be termed the "overidentification" of interviewer with interviewee.

Power Relations in Oral History

As oral historians came to focus interviewing projects on members of various ethnic and racial groups, labor activists and blue-collar workers, and a variety of communities, they became acutely aware that the oral history process, from designing the project to interviewing to using the interviews, often involves a relationship between social unequals, with the oral historian in the dominant position. An interviewer's questions, driven by a particular intellectual agenda, could, it was argued, constrain a narrator from giving a full account of himself, on his own terms; his manner of speech and self-presentation could inhibit a narrator unfamiliar with the codes of middle-class, academic culture; subtle cues, verbal and nonverbal, could unwittingly communicate negative judgments of the narrator's experience; the book or other product resulting from the interviews could objectify complicated individuals as one-dimensional characters, with their words cut and pasted into the work in ways that simply confirm the author's views. Questions were raised about appropriating for personal gain the life stories of those not likely to reap much benefit from having told those stories and about returning something to narrators and their communities in exchange for having extracted their stories.

These questions were not confined to oral history, for the social conditions that gave rise to them reverberated throughout the culture, affecting most intellectual work and having an impact on all field-based research. Anthropologists, for example, considered the implications of their tendency to "study down," and as colonial empires crumbled, questioned their own social role in emerging states. The questions took on a particular urgency for feminists, who, interviewing and writing about women less privileged than they, could all too easily find themselves in the compromised position of reproducing precisely the unequal social relationships they criticized. It's no surprise, then, that issues of power within oral history were raised most pointedly within a feminist frame, most notably in four issues devoted to women's oral history of *Frontiers: A Journal of Women Studies* (appearing in 1977, 1983, and 1998) and in Sherna Berger Gluck and Daphne Patai's 1991 volume, *Women's Words: The Feminist Practice of Oral History*.[36] Collectively, essays in these works argue for both the value of oral history as a means of documenting women's experiences and the need for rigorous self-consciousness about method and modes of presentation.

At times, it must be said, this discussion of power relations has been overwrought and marked by its own kind of hubris. It certainly has underestimated the narrator's power over the interviewer—the power to refuse to talk, to withhold information, even to lie; the power to use an interview to say what the narrator wants to say, whatever the interviewer's questions. It similarly has failed to recognize that narrators too can "get" something from an interview—an opportunity to talk with a sympathetic listener, to gain insight into one's life trajectory, to achieve status within one's own community, and most especially, the satisfaction of having an account of one's experiences included in the collective record of the past. Taken to its extreme, concerns about power inequalities can lead to a paralyzing inaction or the misdirection of attention away from the narrator's story and onto the oral historian's own ethical dilemmas. Yet the dilemmas remain real, and the conscientious oral historian has good reason for an occasional case of the "moral jitters," as Robert Coles has termed the disquiet that arises from an acute sense of one's own privilege in relation to those one is interviewing.[37] How does one negotiate a nonexploitative or nonpatronizing relationship in a situation of social inequality? What do we owe narrators, financially, intellectually, personally? What obligation do we have to return the fruits of our interviewing to the individuals with whom or community with which we have worked?

Once again, *Evaluation Guidelines* defines some general principles and standards to help address these questions. The document cautions interviewers to recognize the effect of social differences on an interview and to keep their own conceptual grid in check: "Interviewers should work to achieve a balance between the objectives of the project and the perspectives of interviewees. They should be sensitive to the diversity of social and cultural experiences and to the implications of race, gender, class, ethnicity, age, religion, and sexual orientation. They should encourage interviewees to respond in their own style and language and to address issues that reflect their concerns." It recognizes the need to treat communities respectfully and to make one's work available to them: "Interviewers should be sensitive to the communities from which they have collected oral histories, taking care not to reinforce thoughtless stereotypes nor to bring undue notoriety to them. Interviewers should take every effort to make the interviews accessible to the communities." And it suggests that narrators are entitled to some return for participating in an oral history project: "Interviewers and oral history programs should conscientiously consider how they might share with interviewees and their communities the rewards and recognition that might result from their work."[38]

Yet these are only guidelines, general statements of principles that must always be worked out in actual practice with *this* interviewee, in *this* community. Nonetheless, it may be helpful to consider good interviewing practice as itself a form of ethical behavior. Taking time to get to know something about who a narrator is before doing the interview; listening carefully to figure out what the narrator is getting at during the interview and then asking the questions that will draw out the narrator; being less concerned with the number of interviews one amasses and more concerned about the quality of relationships that undergird them, whether for an afternoon or a decade—such behavior demonstrates a kind of respect that doesn't obliterate social inequalities but does mitigate them within the fairly bounded social space of an interview. Likewise, establishing a presence in a community before undertaking any interviewing, involving community consultants in the project design, paying attention to diverse social experiences and varying points of view within a single community, recognizing that trust builds over time as trustworthiness is demonstrated can all help establish a respectful relationship between oral historians and the communities in which they work, neutralizing some of the ill effects of a still-present inequality.

Once the interview is over, every interviewee should certainly be given a copy of the interview tape and transcript. Likewise, it is appropriate to place a community-based interview collection in a public repository accessible to community members. In addition, some who have earned royalties for works based on interviews share them with narrators or use a portion of them in ways that benefit narrators' families or communities; others believe their obligation is solely to present narrators' words without misrepresentation. Some oral historians share the fruits of their interviewing in a public forum, allowing narrators, their families, and neighbors the pleasure of hearing their stories, enlarging on them, perhaps correcting the historian's presentation of them, perhaps learning how their individual experiences fit into a broader picture. Others work with local institutions to develop public programs—exhibits, radio shows, increasingly Web sites—to present interviews to broader audiences. All are reasonable responses to questions of equity. Yet as Portelli has reminded oral historians, "returning" to communities what they already know or "giving voice"—as it is sometimes phrased—to people who have no trouble speaking, however well intentioned, can nonetheless be subtly patronizing. He suggests instead that the task is to use the very skills that accompany privilege to bring what one has learned about narrators and their communities into public discourse, to "amplify" narrators' voices so that their experiences and views extend outward to others who otherwise would not hear what they have to say.[39] Acting responsibly in the context of inequality thus has less to do with adherence to professional guidelines than with, on the one hand, poise in negotiating complex social exchanges across lines of difference and, on the other, an understanding of the role of knowledge in society. The issue then becomes how one uses knowledge gained from narrators to advance broadly social goals.

Nonetheless, inequality persists, despite our good intentions and best efforts. Ultimately, as Patai notes, "in an unethical world, we cannot do truly ethical research."[40] Yet some oral historians have begun to press against this "unethical world" in an effort to subvert existing inequalities in generating and interpreting knowledge. They are reimagining their own roles as researchers and scholars and self-consciously cultivating a collaborative relationship with narrators and their communities. Rose T. Diaz and Andrew B. Russell have termed this the "cooperative ideal" and lay out a framework by which oral historians, "functioning as advocates, mediators, and intermediaries," can "bridge existing gaps between academe, public history, and the 'real world.'"[41] Some have expanded upon Michael Frisch's influential notion of "a shared authority" in the interview exchange to work toward "sharing authority" with narrators throughout the entire oral history process.[42] Others, operating within a framework of community development and empowerment, have similarly attempted to adopt a radically democratic practice in doing community history. While much fine work has resulted, all have found that enacting any "ideal" is inevitably messy: tensions and conflicts arise; successes are tempered by breakdowns in communication and failures to complete work as planned; old patterns of professional authority and local deference emerge. In this unethical world, we can expect it to be no different and can only do the best we can.[43]

Overidentification with the Narrator

Many oral historians involved in the effort to democratize the historical record do so from a position of broad sympathy with those whom they interview. They recognize the injustice and indignities narrators and their communities have experienced and respect, often support, narrators' efforts to cope with and change the circumstances of their lives. Some also see their own work as part of a larger cultural project to maintain or restore these lives and struggles in popular memory, to cultivate public appreciation for them, and to present narrators in positive ways. These are worthy sentiments and indeed are frequently sharpened by the particular intimacy that can develop within the interview exchange. Yet they can also veer, with several troubling consequences, toward "liking narrators too much," to paraphrase Valerie Yow.[44] Profoundly painful memories are unwittingly dismissed with ameliorative words because the interviewer cannot bear the dreadful story the narrator is recounting. Cues to information that might shake the interviewer's positive view of a narrator are not heard or are ignored. Hard questions are not asked out of deference or to avoid an awkward conversation.

Coles, reflecting on his years of talking with both black and white families in the American South as he studied the effect of school desegregation on their children, describes with vivid honesty how this "liking too much" affected his own work:

> In the black homes, I went out of my way to give everyone the benefit of the doubt, to notice hospitality, generosity, warmth, liveliness, humility, spirituality—and there was plenty of all that to notice in certain homes. But in other black homes there was a cold distrust and irritability, and even a frank unfriendliness that I also went out of my way to understand, to explain to myself, but not to stress for others, for I was, meanwhile, expressing again and again my unstinting admiration for the obvious bravery of every one of the black children I had met. . . .
>
> I am not saying that I refused any mention of certain unattractive traits in certain families. Rather, I emphasized the attractive and appealing qualities in the families I liked best—to the extent that my descriptive writing, both in professional

journals and for the so-called lay public, drew heavily from my notes taken while working with the children of those families. . . . More and more I downplayed the troubles I encountered in favor of the resiliency I also encountered. . . .

On the white side of the tracks, however, I had considerably less trouble acknowledging the less attractive side of human nature as I spotted it in the families whose children were the first to attend school with black classmates. With those families, I could be relentlessly observant, especially when I heard nasty comments directed at black people. When I heard such comments directed by black people at black people, sometimes within a family, and sometimes with devastating meanness and seriousness, I could only turn my head away, or shake that head with a kind of sad resignation and understanding that I did not feel among my white informants.[45]

As Coles goes on to explain, his sympathies, in fact, had shaped the way he had defined his research problem in the first place, that is, as the way black and white children managed the stresses of school desegregation in the face of massive white racism. Defining the problem as such thus allowed a "'research methodology' that concentrated on certain kinds of 'evidence'" which not incidentally supported Coles's personal abhorrence of racism and concern for its victims.[46]

What a researcher values will always inflect his work; the alternative to "liking too much" is not a naïve neutrality or denial of the fact that an interviewer's posture invariably inflects the interview. Nonetheless, for historians and others engaged in documentary work, there is the ethical problem of, on the one hand, maintaining regard for the people one is interviewing and, on the other, adhering to the disciplinary imperative to tell the truth, not in some essentializing, positivist sense, but by trying to get the whole story, even if following the evidence where it leads undercuts one's sympathies; by probing hesitations, contradictions, and silences in a narrator's account; by getting underneath polite glosses; by asking the hard questions; and by resisting the tendency to create one-dimensional heroes out of the people interviewed, for romanticization is its own form of patronization.

Again, *Evaluation Guidelines* offers a helpful, albeit general ethical principle, stating that "oral history should be conducted in the spirit of critical inquiry" and that "oral historians have a responsibility to maintain the highest professional standards in the conduct of their work, . . . to uphold the standards of the various disciplines and professions with which they are affiliated, . . . [and to] strive to prompt informative dialogue through challenging and perceptive inquiry."[47] And again, the challenge is working this principle out in actual practice. Rapport, after all, can be a fragile thread, easily broken by a mistimed question or insensitive probe. As a way of managing the problems of overidentification with the narrator, Yow suggests a critical reflexivity when interviewing, monitoring one's own emotional reactions to the narrator, challenging one's interests and ideological biases, thinking beyond the questions one intends to ask to consider alternative lines of inquiry.[48] Also important is recognizing that, however highly one regards a narrator, interviewing is always done across lines of difference—otherwise, why interview? And this difference, acting as a counterweight to the very real engagement that can occur in an interview, serves to distance interviewer from narrator, thereby opening up a social space that allows the interviewer to assess and question. Just how much one does so in a given interview is, like much else in oral history, very much a judgment call, one that depends on the specific goals and circumstances of the interviewing project as well, perhaps, as on the temperaments of both interviewer and narrator. Finally, consciously defining the interview as a critical exchange when first discussing protocols with a potential narrator, alerting him or her to the seriousness of historical inquiry, may also pave the way for, in the words of the *Evaluation Guidelines*, "critical inquiry."[49]

Ethics and Oral History's Move to Interpretive Complexity

As oral history matured through the 1980s, its practitioners became increasingly aware that an interview is not a transparent document conveying "new facts" about the past that must simply be assessed as empirically true or false. Rather, an interview came to be understood as a narrative account, an artifact of memory, ideology, language, and the social interaction between interviewee and interviewer, to be interpreted as a text. Certainly the influence of cultural studies upon scholarship during the 1980s and 1990s partially accounts for this growing recognition of the inherent subjectivity of oral narratives. Of equal importance among oral historians was the theoretically inclined *International Journal of Oral History*, published from 1980 to 1990, which routinely included articles that reflected on the unique nature of oral evidence. Perhaps the single most important articulation of a textual approach to oral history is Portelli's often-cited essay, "The Death of Luigi Trastulli: Memory and the Event," in which he writes: "Errors, inventions, and myths [in oral narratives] lead us through and beyond facts to their meanings. . . . They allow us to recognize the interests of the tellers, and the dreams and desires beneath them."[50] The task of the oral historian and others who use interviews for scholarly and creative work thus becomes an interpretive one; the effect is work that moves further and further away from the narratives themselves toward an explication of their meaning. This in turn raises a number of formal concerns about the presentation of narratives that have broadly ethical implications; here I address two: the audience for work in oral history and questions about interpretive authority.

Audience

Oral history narratives can be presented in a variety of media—books, films and videos, radio broadcasts, exhibitions, dramatic presentations, and most recently, Web sites. Whatever the medium, the author or creator must decide how to structure the presentation of narratives within the context of the medium. A book, for example, can take the form of an oral (auto)biography, with minimal commentary by the interviewer/author; it can be a compilation of multiple narratives, organized either thematically or as a succession of individual stories, with editorial commentary to connect and contextualize them; it can integrate quotations from interviews, along with other sources, as part of a broader line of argument developed by the author. Similarly, a film can be structured solely around oral testimony, or it can combine testimony with varying proportions of contemporary accounts and scholarly "talking heads." The approach taken depends on the purpose of work itself; the point here is not to argue one as superior to another or to discuss the relative merits of different modes of presentation.

Whatever the medium, but especially in printed works, as oral historians pursue a more theoretically informed agenda, the interview text tends to be subsumed by its explication, and the work itself is less and less accessible to the kinds of people one has interviewed and about whom one is writing. While *Evaluation Guidelines* focuses on making interviews accessible to others, it also recommends that "all works created from [oral history materials] . . . be available and accessible to the community that participated in the project."[51] Indeed, there is something incongruous about adopting the forms of academic culture to present people's lives when one has learned about those lives through rather ordinary face-to-face interaction with individuals who might reasonably be expected to read what one has to say about them. This incongruity is rooted in a recognition of oral history's value for democratizing the audience for history, as much as the content and the "doing" of history. For while many dismiss formal or scholarly history as "boring," they are nonetheless engaged by personal stories of the past. At their best, works of oral history can be a means of negotiating this paradox, drawing in the reader (or listener or viewer) with a good story, creating sympathy and interest, and then using that to open the reader/listener/viewer to experiences very different from his own, or to help him understand the relationship between personal experience and social life, or to perceive an underlying coherence in a cacophony of voices—to think like a historian, in other words.

Questions of audience are at bottom ethical questions, for by asking for whom one is producing a work, one is ultimately asking why one does what one does. And like all ethical questions, they require judgments—in this case, how to reach the intended audience. The point is not to abandon theoretical explorations, for they enrich oral historians' work enormously; and even work that is ostensibly nontheoretical, that presents interviews without much commentary, nonetheless rests on a substratum of broadly theoretical ideas about the significance of the story being told and appropriate editorial intervention. In fact, some oral historians, ignoring or rejecting the claims of democratic access, choose to produce highly interpretive work for largely academic audiences. However, some choose not to interpret interviews explicitly at all nor to deeply contextualize them, in an effort at broad accessibility, letting the reader/viewer/listener appreciate the story and make of it what he or she will. Others, recognizing the claims of multiple audiences, present their work in different media or write in different voices for different audiences. And yet others, unwilling to segregate interviews from theoretical assessments, and perhaps recognizing that general readers can understand complex ideas if they are presented in clear language, attempt to integrate the two. This last is perhaps the most creative of oral history work, as it seeks new forms of presentation, alternating narrative and analytic chapters in a book, for example; or playing theoretical speculations off of concrete examples quoted from interviews; or moving seamlessly between author's voice and narrator's voice, interlacing one with the other. This work is also perhaps the most respectful of its audience, recognizing the reader/viewer/listener's desire for stories as well as for understanding the meaning of these stories.[52]

Interpretive Authority

As oral history has become more theoretically informed, those who conduct and use interviews have also come to understand more fully how these narratives are social documents, reflecting not only a narrator's individual creativity but also his particular historical position and his relationship with the interviewer, who also participates in the interview from a particular social position. As a result, those who draw upon interviews in a creative work are less likely to let narrators simply have their say; they too claim a voice as interpreter of the interview text. This claim also raises a set of formal questions with broadly ethical implications: Whose voice dominates in such work, the narrator's or the work's putative "creator"? Where does the balance of interpretive authority lie?

While these questions are likely to remain in the background when narrator and creator share the same perspective on the topic at hand, they emerge with particular sharpness when there is a conflict of voices. What does an author do, for example, when he disagrees with a narrator on a given point? Or when his understanding of a matter is fundamentally different from that of the narrator's? Or when he finds out that a narrator is simply wrong, willfully or not? Karen Fields confronted these issues repeatedly as she worked with her grandmother, Mamie Garvin Fields (1888–1987), to produce her oral memoir, *Lemon Swamp and Other Places*, which describes the elder Fields's life as an educated, middle-class black woman in Charleston, South Carolina, through most of the twentieth century. In some places in her story, Mamie Fields wanted to include local details that Karen Fields felt would be meaningless, indeed "tedious," to readers beyond Charleston. At times, Mamie Fields, for whom "matters of race and color are a permanent presence without being [the] principal subject" of her life, criticized Karen Fields for her "angry" preoccupation with them. Like most authors confronting these problems, Karen Fields attempted compromise, but not without battles with her grandmother and not without a residual unease.[53] Sandy Polishuk, writing an oral biography of labor activist Julia Ruutilla based upon interviews she had conducted with her some years earlier, discovered that Ruutilla had falsified certain details of her background, including her racial identity; had obscured other elements of her life; and had overstated her role in various political events. Because Ruutilla had died in the intervening years, Polishuk was unable to ask her to explain discrepancies between her account and the written record, so she appropriately pointed them out to readers, attempted to explain them, and ultimately let most of them remain in the finished work, stating, "Julia must be allowed to speak for herself, but at the same time I had to tell what I knew and believed."[54]

Questions about interpretive authority—or who gets to say what—are especially challenging in community projects and in public history when multiple stakeholders lay claim to a given work: the subjects of the work wish to present a positive view of themselves, the producers wish to adhere to professional standards and maintain a certain intellectual dispassion, the audience wants a good story. Barbara Franco describes the play of these voices in the development of an exhibit about the Winnebago Indian community at the Minnesota Historical Society, a process that echoed the dynamics of many community-based oral history projects: "The exhibit team's curators wanted to examine the history of the Winnebago in Minnesota as a case study that focused on their recent history as an urban Indian community without a reservation land base in the state. The Winnebago [advisory] board, however, was more interested in connecting the current Winnebago community to traditional Winnebago life and in educating outsiders about the early history of the Winnebago and their long connection to Minnesota. . . . Most contemporary issues of urban living were off limits." As the planning process continued, curators muted their voices out of respect for their Winnebago collaborators and in the interests of a continuing relationship with them. "The exhibit that resulted," Franco continued, "was not as interesting to visitors as it might have been. It was very traditional in its approach and didn't connect visitors to the more dynamic contemporary issues in Winnebago culture such as conflicts between urbanization and traditional religion." At issue, she concludes, were "two sets of ethics operating in this exhibit development process—people ethics and historian ethics," or one might reframe it, the ethics of narration and the ethics of interpretation.[55]

For those seeking to present interviews in ways that respect both their own and the narrator's authority, it is perhaps useful to consider negotiating a midcourse between what Frisch has termed the "anti history" approach to oral history, that is, the "view [of] oral historical evidence, because of its immediacy and emotional resonance, as something almost beyond interpretation or accountability, as a direct window on the feelings and, in some senses, on the meaning of past experience," and what Frisch called the "more history" approach, that is, "reducing oral history to simply another kind of evidence to be pushed through the historian's controlling mill."[56] Just *how* to strike a proper balance, of course, remains the challenge. *Evaluation Guidelines* articulates the most fundamental principle for anyone drawing upon interviews in a scholarly or creative work: "Users have a responsibility to retain the integrity of the interviewee's voice, neither misrepresenting the interviewee's words nor taking them out of context."[57] Beyond that, however, *Evaluation Guidelines* remains silent. Nonetheless, just as questions of audience are leading oral historians to seek new forms of presentation, so too is the issue of interpretive authority, resulting in work that explicitly plays with the tension of different, often competing voices. Katherine Borland suggests that we extend "the conversation we initiate while collecting oral narratives to the later stage of interpretation," opening up the possibility of a multilayered account, in which interpretive conflict between interviewee and interviewer, "subject" and author, is presented directly, without an authoritative resolution.[58] In her biography of activist Anne Braden, Catherine Fosl rendered Braden's words in italics, "to retain her voice as clearly distinct from mine, . . . [in order to] allow me a free hand at interpretation without creating a power differential in which [Braden] felt suppressed, particularly at points when our perspectives on her life diverged."[59] Alicia Rouverol, recognizing that interviewees can provide more than a "direct window" on feelings, asked explicitly analytic questions in her interviews with Maine poultry worker Linda Lord. She writes also about restraining her own urges to maintain analytic control over the interview in her published work; of "surrendering to the text" as Lord's words "fought back" against her own interpretive biases about unions and deindustrialization; and of her own efforts to resist imposing a false coherence on Lord's apparently contradictory views on many matters.[60] In these and other ways, oral historians are seeking to represent the dialogue—the open-ended back and forthing—that lies at the heart of the oral history enterprise and to recognize that work resulting from this dialogue is a cocreation of interviewer and narrator.

Conclusion

Legal and ethical considerations permeate the practice of oral history, from initial contact with a potential narrator to final disposition and use of an interview. They are so central because oral history is fundamentally grounded in a relationship between two people, and like all relationships, it is framed by rules, norms, and standards of behavior. It is also a relationship that extends outward to include others—individuals and communities discussed in an interview, users of the interview, the audience for work based on oral history—and they too are included in the web of relationships governed by oral history's legal and ethical standards.

While the legal framework for oral history is rather straightforward—the law permits this, disallows that—ethical concerns, which can sometimes arise in a legal context, are more subjective, requiring, as I have emphasized throughout, judgment on the part of project managers and interviewers. Both, however, as I have also attempted to emphasize, are social constructs, arising in relation to the particular historical circumstances within which oral history has been practiced. They are, accordingly, not fixed, but require the continuing attention of both the field and its individual practitioners. This essay is not, therefore, the last word.

Notes

1. Gluck, "First Generation," 1–9, suggests a similar chronological development.

2. Oral History Association, *Evaluation Guidelines*. In 1967, Dixon and Colman, "Objectives and Standards," became the first record of discussion of professional guidelines in oral history. In 1975, Fry, "Reflections on Ethics," raised the ethical conundrums in the original guidelines. Oral History Association, "Evaluation Guidelines: Wingspread Conference," reported on the development of the evaluation guidelines in 1979. Ethical guidelines from other national oral history organizations include, from the United Kingdom, Alan Ward, "Copyright and Oral History: Is Your Oral History Legal and Ethical?" (Colchester: Oral History Society, 2003), http://www.oralhistory.org.uk/ethics/ (accessed January 26, 2005); National Oral History Association of New Zealand, "Code of Ethical and Technical Practice" (Wellington: National Oral History Association of New Zealand, 2001), http://www.oralhistory.org.nz/Code.htm (accessed January 26, 2005); and Oral History Association of Australia, "OHAA Guidelines of Ethical Practice" (Sydney: Oral History Association of Australia, n.d.), http://cwpp.slq.qld.gov.au/ohaa/Guidelines%20of%20ethical%20practice.htm (accessed January 26, 2005).

3. Portelli, "Tryin' to Gather," 55–56.

4. Starr, "Oral History," describes the origins of the Columbia Oral History Research Office.

5. See Eustis, "Get It in Writing"; Hamilton, "Law of Libel"; Romney, "Legal Considerations"; and Welch, "Lawyer."

6. Oral History Association, *Evaluation Guidelines*, 6, states: "With the permission of interviewees, interviewers should arrange to deposit their interviews in an archival repository that is capable of both preserving the interviews and eventually making them available for general use." The American Historical Association's guideline for interviewing for historical documentation is almost word for word the same as OHA's: "Interviewers should arrange to deposit their interviews in an archival repository that is capable of both preserving the interviews and making them available for general research." American Historical Association, "Statement on Interviewing for Historical Documentation," *Standards of Professional Conduct* (Washington, DC: American Historical Association, 2003), http://www.historians.org/pubs/Free/ProfessionalStandards.htm (accessed January 26, 2005).

7. Neuenschwander, *Oral History and the Law*, 18.

8. Ibid., 19.

9. Ibid., 23.

10. Of course, the question arises: What if the interviewee does not agree to close the statement in question? Elizabeth Millwood described the response of the Southern Oral History Program when this situation arose. The program decided to "bury" the offending interview in its collection by not including it in any finding aids, on the assumption that when someone finally did discover the interview, the offended party would be dead. Millwood herself does not recommend this approach, and in fact, it would seem that a repository, assuming it had legal title to the interview, could act in its own self-interest and close the offending material without the narrator's consent. Millwood, "Oral History Offices."

11. Neuenschwander, *Oral History and the Law*, 18, 23.

12. Brecher, review of *Brothers*, 196.

13. Blee, "Evidence, Empathy, and Ethics," 604.

14. Brecher, review of *Brothers*, 196.

15. Lanzmann, *Shoah: Complete Text*. See also Lanzmann, *Shoah*, DVD.

16. Brecher, review of *Brothers*, 196; Blee, "Evidence, Empathy, and Ethics," 604.

17. Neuenschwander, *Oral History and the Law*, 5.

18. Typically, a narrator assigns rights to both the tape and the intended transcript of it, that is, signs the release form, at the conclusion of the actual interview, before the transcript has been created. Reviewing the transcript or significantly emending it, the narrator could subsequently decide he wishes to change the terms of access to the tape, the transcript, or both, in which case a new release form would need to be negotiated. Assigning rights to the transcript before it is actually produced is somewhat questionable, yet it is standard practice because there is often a considerable time lag between the conduct of the interview and the production of its transcript, during which the narrator may have died or otherwise become unavailable. The narrator may also be disinclined to assign rights to an interview long past or simply be negligent in returning the form. Rights to the tape and to the transcript may be uncoupled, but that would create administrative complexities that are largely unnecessary, insofar as the vast majority of narrators neither question the terms

of their release upon reviewing the transcript nor significantly alter the transcript itself. Project administrators seem to agree that the best practice is to handle specific concerns on a case-by-case basis.

19. U.S. Copyright Office, "Copyright Law of the United States" (Washington, DC: U.S. Copyright Office, 2002), http://www.copyright.gov/title17/ (accessed January 31, 2005).

20. U.S. Copyright Office, Compendium II, Copyright Office Practices, Sec. 317, quoted in Neuenschwander, *Oral History and the Law*, 31.

21. Neuenschwander, *Oral History and the Law*, 32.

22. It should also be noted that colleges and universities are increasingly claiming rights to the intellectual property produced by faculty and staff working within the institution. Scholars working in an academic setting, conducting interviews for their own research, should thus clarify their campus policies regarding ownership of their intellectual work, including interviews.

23. Hall, "Confidentially Speaking," raises many of these and additional questions about confidentiality and suggests—without resolving—several ethically challenging situations.

24. Oral History Association, *Evaluation Guidelines*, 4.

25. Council of the American Anthropological Association, "Relations with Those Studied," *Statements on Ethics: Principles of Professional Responsibility* (Arlington, VA: American Anthropological Association, 1971), http://www.aaanet .org/stmts/ethstmnt.htm (accessed January 26, 2005).

26. American Sociological Association, *Code of Ethics and Policies and Procedures of the ASA Committee on Professional Ethics* (Washington, DC: American Sociological Association, 1999), 10, http://www.asanet.org/members/coe.pdf (accessed January 26, 2005). On reporting a crime, see Neuenschwander, *Oral History and the Law*, 55–57.

27. Oral History Association, *Evaluation Guidelines*, 5; Neuenschwander, *Oral History and the Law*, 43.

28. The decision of the U.S. Supreme Court in *New York Times v. Tasini*, in 2001, has raised particular concerns about transferring copyrighted material from one medium to another without prior permission from the author. The Court ruled that freelance writers who did not explicitly agree to electronic distribution of their work previously published in the *Times* could claim that their copyright agreement was violated, that electronic publication, in other words, constituted a different form of publication. Neuenschwander, *Oral History and the Law*, 43, states that "this decision would seem to strongly support the right of an interviewee to cry foul if and when a program or archive places his or her interview on the Internet without clear or reasonably implied authorization to do so." For further discussion of the copyright issues of Web publication, see Neuenschwander, *Oral History and the Law*, 44–45.

29. For further discussion of the ethics of oral history on the Web, see Mary Ann Larson, "Guarding against Cyberpirates," *Oral History Association Newsletter* 33, no. 3 (Fall 1999): 4–5, and Larson, "Potential, Potential, Potential."

30. Department of Health and Human Services, Office of Human Research Protections, Code of Federal Regulations, Title 45 Public Welfare, Part 46

Protection of Human Subjects, Subpart A, Basic HHS Policy for Protection of Human Research Subjects, http://www.hhs.gov/ohrp/humansubjects/guidance/45cfr46.htm (accessed December 12, 2005). Paragraph 46.102 (f)(1) defines a "human subject" as a "living individual about whom an investigator . . . conducting research obtains data through intervention or *interaction* [emphasis added] with the individual." Interaction is further defined as "includ[ing] communication or interpersonal contact between investigator and subject."

31. Ibid., Paragraph 46.101 (b)(2)(ii).

32. American Association of University Professors, "Protecting Human Beings," offers a thorough discussion of the difficulties of applying regulations developed within a biomedical frame to nonbiomedical research. See also Church, Shopes, and Blanchard, "Common Rule?"; Van den Hoonaard, *Walking the Tightrope*; and Nelson, "Can E. T. Phone Home?"

33. The full text of the policy statement is available from the American Historical Association, Press Releases, http://www.historians.org/PRESS/IRBLetter.pdf (accessed December 12, 2005).

34. Further explication of the policy is available from American Historical Association, Questions Regarding the Policy Statement, http://www.historians.org/PRESS/2003-11-10IRB.htm (accessed December 12, 2005); and American Historical Association, Linda Shopes, Historians and Institutional Review Boards: A Brief Bibliography, http://www.historians.org/PRESS/2003-11-10-IRB-Bib.htm (accessed December 12, 2005).

35. OHRP's reaffirmation of its original policy statement is available from Oral History Association, Linda Shopes and Donald Ritchie, An Update on the Exclusion of Oral History from IRB Review, http://www.dickinson.edu/oha/org_irbupdate.html (accessed December 12, 2005). For a summary of the current state of affairs regarding IRB review of oral history, see Robert Townsend and Meriam Belli, Oral History and IRBs: Caution Urged as Rule Interpretations Vary Widely, *AHA Perspectives Online*, 42, no. 9 (December 2004), http://www.historians.org/perspectives/issues/2004/0412/0412new4.cfm (accessed December 12, 2005). In November 2005, the American Historical Association contacted OHRP, outlining conflicting statements from that office, critiquing its misapprehension of the methods of oral history, and seeking—again—a generalized exclusion of oral history from IRB review; as of this writing, no response had been received. Meanwhile, the AHA's Research Division has developed a guide to the issues for historians: American Historical Association, *Oral History and Institutional Review Boards*. A generalized critique of the ever expansive embrace of IRBs is also developing; see, for example, Hamburger, "New Censorship"; and Center for Advanced Study, University of Illinois, The Illinois White Paper: Improving the System for Protecting Human Subjects: Counteracting IRB "Mission Creep" (November 2005), available at http://www.law.uiuc.edu/conferences/whitepaper/whitepaper.pdf (accessed December 12, 2005). This latter document argues that "most journalism and oral history cannot be appropriately reviewed under the Common Rule" (page 22).

36. *Frontiers* 2, no. 2 (1977); 7, no. 1 (1983); 19, no. 2 (1998); and 19, no. 3 (1998); Gluck and Patai, *Women's Words*. On the issues of power in anthropology, see Clifford and Marcus, *Writing Culture*, and more recently, Jaarsma, *Handle with Care*.

37. Coles, *Doing Documentary Work*, 85.

38. Oral History Association, *Evaluation Guidelines*, 5, 6.

39. Portelli, "Tryin' to Gather," 67–71.

40. Patai, "U.S. Academics," 150.

41. Diaz and Russell, "Oral Historians," 214.

42. Frisch, *Shared Authority*, xxii.

43. Patai, "U.S. Academics," 150; Diaz and Russell, "Oral Historians," 214; Frisch, *Shared Authority*, xx–xxii. For discussions of collaborative oral history work, see Kerr, "What the Problem Is"; Rickard, "Collaborating with Sex Workers"; Rouverol, "Collaborative Oral History"; Sitzia, "Shared Authority"; Shopes, "Commentary"; Frisch, "Commentary, Sharing Authority." For an especially frank discussion of the challenges of community documentation projects, see Hinsdale, Lewis, and Waller, *Comes from the People*.

44. Yow, "Do I Like Them."

45. Coles, *Doing Documentary Work*, 57–58.

46. Ibid., 57–59.

47. Oral History Association, *Evaluation Guidelines*, 4–6.

48. Yow, "Do I Like Them," 79.

49. Oral History Association, *Evaluation Guidelines*, 4.

50. Portelli, "Death of Luigi Trastulli," 2. I am indebted to Ronald J. Grele for formulating the distinction between oral history as document and oral history as text.

51. Oral History Association, *Evaluation Guidelines*, 10.

52. See, for example, Hall et al., *Like a Family*; Nasstrom, *Everybody's Grandmother*; Portelli, *Order Has Been Carried Out*; and Rogers, *Righteous Lives*.

53. Fields, with Fields, *Lemon Swamp*; Fields, "Cannot Remember Mistakenly," 93, 98–99.

54. Polishuk, *Sticking to the Union*, 13.

55. Franco, "Doing History in Public," 8. See also Franco, "Raising the Issues."

56. Frisch, *Shared Authority*, 160.

57. Oral History Association, *Evaluation Guidelines*, 6.

58. Borland, "Not What I Said," 73.

59. Fosl, "When Subjects Talk Back," 7.

60. Chatterley, Rouverol, and Cole, "I Was Content," 124.

5

Oral History Interviews: From Inception to Closure

Charles T. Morrissey

When oral historians assembled at Lake Arrowhead in California in 1966 for their first national meeting, my presentation—outdoors on a gorgeous September morning—was an informal talk about oral history interviewing skills. Since 1962, as oral historian for the Harry S. Truman Library and John F. Kennedy Library Oral History Project, I had been evolving some interviewing "do's and don'ts." In my talk that day, I remarked in an offhand way, "Let me say that very little has been written about techniques of oral history."[1] That gentle comment understated the meagerness of bibliography about the interviewer's role in oral history relationships with memoirists.

Allan Nevins, founder and director of Columbia University's Oral History Research Office (OHRO), showed little interest in question-making processes. As a professor, author, and administrator, his primary quest was to address neglected topics in American history.[2] For us today, it is incredible that the Columbia OHRO did not include an interviewer's questions in preparing the transcripts of its early interviews. Questions were discarded as unimportant.[3]

Moreover, oral history in the U.S. grew from antecedents in the archival profession. As a novice in oral history, from 1962 to 1966, I was instructed by an excellent archivist, James R. Fuchs of the Truman Library, and both of us were employees of the National Archives and Records Service, forerunner of today's National Archives and Records Administration. Now I am astounded to encounter myself giving this tight scope to oral history while speaking to an audience of professional historians in 1964: "Since oral history is usually defined as an effort to fill gaps in written records, it is necessary for an oral historian to know where the gaps are."[4] True, but such constricted vision! Such an obsession with paper! Clearly, I was an anal oral historian. Dare I further admit that I went to Lake Arrowhead advocating that oral historians not organize a separate Oral History Association but instead align with the Society of American Archivists?

The "gaps" have grown, but Ronald J. Grele has ably summarized the broadening of the scope of oral history from the 1966 Lake Arrowhead colloquium to the present: "Originating in many areas as a way to fill in the gaps in the written record, either as archival practice or because that written record simply ignored so much of the daily life of so many people, oral history has outgrown its roots in the search for data and has become an activity seeking to understand all forms of subjectivity: memory, ideology, myth, discourse systems, speech acts, silences, perceptions, and consciousness in all its multiple meanings."[5]

My thinking about oral history, almost forty years after James V. Mink of the University of California at Los Angeles brought us together at Lake Arrowhead, continues to evolve. As you read this personalized assortment of "do's and don'ts," please ponder shrewd advice from William Warner Moss, one of my successors as head of the Kennedy Library Oral History Project. Moss points out, wisely, "Just as no two interviewees are alike, so no two interviewers are alike, and success depends to a great extent on the capability and interest of the people involved rather than a structured application of designed questions."[6] Question-asking in oral history interviews is an art, individualized, and even intuitive. The oral history bibliography still lacks a volume titled "The Historian as Interviewer," but here is one person's approach, grounded in practical experience, to asking informants to share their memories.

I

First, ask questions of yourself before asking questions of the memoirists you hope to interview. By answering your own questions thoughtfully before your interviews are scheduled, you raise the likelihood that your questions in actual interviews will stimulate informative answers.

Before each interview, I think carefully about how each prospective interviewee in an oral history project should be invited to participate. Should the initiative come from me? Or is it wiser for the chief officer of the institution whose history I am documenting by recording oral history interviews to extend the invitation? The latter has the imprimatur of authority.

Usually, you are seeking collaboration from strangers you hope will agree to cocreate a historical document consisting of their answers to your questions. Building rapport with these persons is crucial because oral history is a mutual endeavor.[7] Moreover, it is a voluntary activity. Prospective memoirists are free to demur from being interviewed. The invitation is not a subpoena to testify by court order in a legal dispute. They may lament that time has eroded their memories of names, dates, and details of events. They may view a historian's queries as irrelevant in today's workaday world with its frenetic pace of decision making. Oral historians in the United States must bear in mind that they function in a media-dominated culture that is present minded and future oriented, where historical amnesia is a national flaw. They may recall unpleasantly the boring history courses they endured as students and the mind-numbing textbooks they had to memorize. Colloquially, they may echo Carl Sandburg's disdainful "The past is a bucket of ashes" ("Prairie," *Cornhuskers*, 1918) or Henry Wadsworth Longfellow's "Let the dead Past bury its dead!" ("A Psalm of Life," *Knickerbocker Magazine*, 1838). They may even view you, the oral historian, as the next-to-last person they will encounter in their lifetimes, the final one being the mortician who will come to fetch the corpse. To you they may insist they never did anything of historical importance, and you will have to convince them, tactfully, that indeed they did.

Oral historians are exactly that—historians—and they interview about the past. Specialists from other disciplines function as historians when doing oral history. Accordingly, most oral sources are older rather than younger occupants of the demographic life charts. It is best to contact these sources initially by mail, with the invitation coming directly from the person most appropriate to issue it. Letterheads and job titles signify the official auspices of the sponsoring institution. But think carefully about stationery that lists trustees or other supporters in a vertical column along the left-hand or right-hand margins. If these names represent a cohort of like-minded advocates uniformly positioned on the political spectrum, they will not engender cooperation with your project from their political opponents. Their endorsement will also raise concerns about your professional objectivity; you may be dismissed contemptuously as merely a court historian, a hired gun, not an open-minded inquirer. If your sponsors are all rich white men who live in one section of town, their names will not induce cooperation from laboring African American women who live in a different part of town.

Ideally, this initial mailing should ask and answer six basic questions; below you will read how every oral history interview is configured by asking the same six basic questions. Limiting your letter to two pages at most, explain *who* (you) will do *what* (record an oral history interview), *where* and *when* (a place and time convenient for the recipient), and *how* (by recording the exchange of questions and answers, transcribing the conversation, allowing the respondent to edit the transcript, depositing the finalized transcript in a suitable archive, and devising a legal agreement governing ownership, access, and dissemination). All of this is difficult to communicate and may raise apprehensions among people who are skittish about having their voices recorded if they fear they will expose to posterity their truncated educations or halting use of English as a second language (or even as a first language, despite an elite education at Andover, Yale, and the Harvard Business School). Or they may be fearful of any interaction entailing legal commitments in a litigious society overpopulated with lawyers. (In more ways than one are lawyers the enemies of historians; see below.) And you still need to answer the most important and most difficult of the six basic questions: the *why* question. The recipient of this letter will ask, Why does this oral history project want to interview me? Your answer: because the prospective respondent has memories of historical significance worth preserving.

Each letter concludes by explaining that the oral historian—you—will telephone a few days after the prospective memoirist has received this mailing to explore any concerns about the "basic six" and discuss the *when* and *where* questions so scheduling can be arranged. In this phone conversation, I review the procedures outlined succinctly in the letter, often emphasizing that this collaboration will not be a media interview for tonight's newscast or tomorrow's newspaper; instead it will be a history interview for archival deposit. Journalists rank near lawyers as hazards if prospects view oral historians as similar practitioners; many have woeful tales of journalists distorting what they were told.[8] I routinely refer to the respondent's opportunity for editorial review so that the ultimate transcript will convey the memoirist's intended narrative. But I assure all that minimal editing is preferred to retain the oral character of our session together, and I may pointedly assure academics they won't be expected to revise their transcripts into the stilted formal language of professional publications in their specialties. As graduate students, many scholars were taught never to use the first-person singular in professional papers, but in oral history narratives the first-person singular is unavoidable. I repeat assurances about devising a legal agreement as a safeguard against abuse of the interview's content, but do so gently to avoid rousing the specter of legal complications. If a memoirist is willing to exchange candor for confidentiality by agreeing to give an interview with the proviso it be legally closed for a stipulated length of time, I concede to this preference. Ideally, in the world of oral history it is best that as much as possible of oral history reminiscences be opened to public access as soon as possible, but the arguments for temporary restrictions have compelling logic, too. It is better to obtain oral history memoirs and have to wait to use them than never to procure those memories at all.

In this phone conversation, I ask the respondent if he/she can recommend any materials I should consult in order to prepare myself as interviewer. As examples, I mention scrapbooks, diaries, letters, annual reports, yearbooks, class reunion books, press coverage, even photo albums. Every active physician in academic medicine has an up-to-date curriculum vitae, and grant applications to funding agencies are informative depictions of their past achievements and clear aspirations when their grant proposals were submitted. I tell them a truism about oral history: the more the interviewer—you—knows *before* an interview, the more you will learn *in* the interview. Preparation is essential. When prospective interviewees suggest sources I should consult as preparation, I assiduously do homework in these materials.

Before asking interviewees about sources I should consult, I have tried to learn all I can in other independent sources. In libraries, I read all I can find about my interviewees—written by them, about them, and about their locales, work, lifestyles, and the like. Usually, I forge working relationships with archivists who can provide me with institutional records—minutes of trustees' meetings, official correspondence, in-house newspapers or employee bulletins, files of press releases, accreditation reports, and so forth. Oral history can be defined as recorded interviews that preserve historically significant memories for future use, but an oral historian can be defined as a person who uses all kinds of materials, in addition to recording spoken memories, to document and explain the past. Bear in mind the sage advice of Leopold von Ranke, the nineteenth-century German historian at the University of Berlin, who proclaimed that the best historical sources are those created contemporaneously with events.[9] Closer is better. Memory can be distant and is continually reconfigured over time, causing some memories to fade into disappearance, others to balloon into exaggeration, and still others to get constantly revised. Oral historians cannot deny the fragility of memory and must acknowledge it is supple and pliant. Nor can oral historians deny that von Ranke got it right. Oral history is best done in conjunction with traditional archival research. My former students have heard me preach this gospel, and one of them, John A. Kayser of the Graduate School of Social Work at the University of Denver, is fond of quoting my stricture: "Paper trail first, memory trail second."[10]

Rewards for doing prior research are numerous.[11] Consider these:

- Following the paper trail first helps you to determine who was where when and thus should be interviewed about specific topics. Some people have dropped out of historical consciousness but can be retrieved by studying the paper trail and then interviewed on the memory trail. Others have mythic reputations for accomplishments falsely attributed to them, and you can deduce that early.[12] Although Americans deny that they live in a class-segmented society, and anonymous people who were decisive role players are obscured in popular memory by prominent people claiming more credit than justifiably warranted, you can identify those who are historically knowledgeable and select them as interviewees, deflating the bloviators.
- Research on the paper trail can identify those gaps that your interviewees can fill by speaking their memories. Decisions made by long-distance telephone negotiations may leave no paper trails beyond monthly bills for numbers called on specific dates and lengths of conversations. E-mail messages can be erased. Jet aircraft speed conference participants to a central meeting place, and after returning them swiftly home leave no paper trail remnants except for airline ticket receipts. Lawyers advise businessmen not to make records of meetings that federal regulators could subpoena in search of antitrust or other violations. In academe, tenure review committees are cautioned not to keep minutes of their deliberations; disgruntled candidates refused promotions can get access to them if litigation ensues. Presidential selection committees are told to camouflage candidates with code names and confer orally among themselves; minutes and memoranda may get leaked to the curious media. Forthright letters in which professors are asked to evaluate their students are no longer written. Diaries get destroyed, journals get junked, files get filched. While researching the paper trail, you can deduce what is absent from the array before you ask about the missing links.

If this litany of transgressions—the defilement of files—is disturbing to you, bear in mind that photocopying machines often restoreth to knowledge what other forms of electronic communication and aircraft taketh away. Perusing more than one paper trail can provide you with data missing from the first one you examined.

- Researching archival collections for questions to ask prospective interviewees is much quicker and simpler than researching paper-trail sources to answer historical questions. Issues in American history through the nineteenth century must be answered solely by archival research; no Civil War soldiers still survive as veterans to interview. But researching for questions to ask, as distinct from answers to give, can move rapidly. Applying the basic six, the paper trail often divulges who (the poet you will interview), did what (won a Pulitzer Prize), when (year of award, reported in newspapers), how (by writing praised verses), where (in a cabin in the woods), but not why (the motivation that spurred her creativity). Your research can isolate the *why* question, important to ask in your interview. You may learn that creativity sprang from angst in the personal life of the poet in unresolved mother–daughter tensions and other psychological issues, revealed through psychotherapy. How to ask about such intimate probings? Read on!

- If you wonder if your respondents will lie to you or slyly try to mislead you, the answer is "no" as soon as they realize you have thoroughly done your homework. They wouldn't dare distort the factuality of a situation lest they get caught as deceivers. Occasionally, a respondent mumbles, "You probably know more about this than I do." Smile; you're being complimented for your preparation. But don't gloat. Rapport does not thrive on one-upmanship.

- Thorough preparation will impress your interviewee that you are seriously committed to good interviewing and will encourage full, detailed answers to your questions, not short, casual responses that barely scratch the surface of the memoirist's deeper knowledge.

- At the outset of every oral history project, the questions you are asked about it are entirely quantitative: How many people are you going to interview? How many tapes or pages of transcript will you obtain? (Be wary of these queries; tapes vary in length and pages can be single-spaced or double-spaced.) How long will your project continue? How much will it cost? When the project is completed, however, the questions shift from quantitative to qualitative: Just how good is all that stuff you taped? Ask the qualitative question at the outset, because it will be the ultimate criterion by which your project will be measured for its value. Preparation germinates quality.
- Preparation can help you to decide what sequence is best for scheduling your interviews. I plot my prospective memoirists onto an oval diagram, much like the round target Vermont hunters might emplace on a tree when shooting their guns during rifle practice before deer season begins. Into the bull's eye go the handful of names of most important memoirists. In concentric circles go the other names, with importance declining within each band farther from the center. On the outer rim go the names of the least important prospects. Sequentially, I start interviewing people named on the outer rim, moving in a circular route toward the prime occupants of the bull's eye. My theory is that you want to be best prepared—at the top of your game—when you aim for the bull's eye, and interviewing others on outer peripheries will heighten your marksmanship. You want to do your best with your best. Moreover, if the denizens of your bull's eye are busy people who might give you one session but not two, you need to do your best within the single opportunity afforded to you. Planning interviews sequentially also allows you to link your preparation with the experiences of your prospects. You can proceed colleague by colleague, thereby isolating reluctant interviewees by pointing out, diplomatically, that they are the last holdouts and that others may question their stubborn resistance.
- During your preparation, you can identify and photocopy particular documents you can carry to the interview and

share with respondents. This can prompt memories evoked by looking at photographs or reading texts. This can clarify items with muddled meanings. Be sure to key your "props" so that the words spoken on tape are directly linked to the items being discussed.[13]

Before each interview, I sit quietly and cogitate on questions such as these:

- How can I make this interview useful for others? For instance, what questions could I ask this person to help a genealogist, a local historian of the town where this person came of age, an architectural historian interested in the spaces this person has inhabited, a historian of this person's religious sect, a public historian wanting to incorporate spoken recollections into the audio interpretation of museum artifacts, or someone such as Jeff Friedman, interested in artistic outcomes?
- I visualize a college campus and ask myself what a political scientist, a sociologist, a folklorist, or students of public administration or educational practices and policies would ask in an interview like this one. Academe divides the world of learning into discreet compartments called departments, but real life in the real world is not arranged like a university. Oral history is multidisciplinary; this is one of its glories. Oral historians have to think outside the boxes.
- I mull on what divides me from my interviewee in terms of numerous social factors: age, gender, race, class, ethnicity, education, regional dialects, political outlook. The list goes on and on: I am a New Englander in Texas, a humanist among physicians, a flatlander (born out of state) among woodchucks (native-born Vermonters), a technophobe interviewing computer nerds in biomedical informatics. I try to identify each difference between me and my interviewee and formulate verbal strategies for surmounting those differences. The good news is that differences often contribute to dispassionate clinical relationships that make interviews flourish. A stranger interacting

with a stranger can produce candid answers to probing questions.[14] Clinical relationships are professional encounters. With forethought, I try to capitalize on differences to clasp clinical relationships.[15]

- I also mull on what unites me with my interviewee in ways that may help cultivate rapport, but likewise may pose problems in terms of professional competition, or shared family myths, or professional courtesies, or reluctance to speak critically of our common alma mater or other "home institutions." The bad news is that similarities often contribute to emotionally laden relationships that make interviews awkward. An intimate interacting with another intimate—members of the same family, say—can produce squeamish answers to resented questions. Intimate relationships are not clinical and not professional. Grandchildren hoping to interview grandparents may think insider status is an advantage, and surely they may be right, especially when it comes to gaining access, but being an insider poses its own set of problems.[16] This oral historian prefers clinical relationships.

- Reviewing my interviewee's life, probable knowledge, and hopefully retentive memory, I ask myself beforehand: What can he/she speak from experience that could possibly be most helpful for enlarging understanding, providing explanations, resolving perplexities, and in other ways contributing to my project?

- What might be the most surprising disclosures I might hear from my interviewee?

- What sensitivities should I anticipate? This is not easy to foresee because some people will surprise you by being skittish about questions you assume innocently are free of tension and by not being uncomfortable when asked questions you figure will touch raw nerves. Sensitivities are subjective; they vary from person to person.

- If the time allotted for my interview is unexpectedly shortened, what are the most important questions I need to ask? My scheduled forty-five minutes with U.S. Senator Jacob Javitz, longtime Republican from New York, evaporated to fifteen minutes as he talked on his office phone, his back turned to me seated across his desk. Concluding his conversation and placing the phone on its cradle, he whirled in his chair to face me and tersely said, narrowing his eyes, "You have fifteen minutes." Revising my agenda, I asked the most important questions, realizing that the delay had stolen most of those I had prepared.

- I don't memorize questions before an interview, but I do choose carefully the wording for questions that may be viewed as sensitive or difficult to answer. The most sensitive questions in America today are not about sex but about money. Instead of querying a politician about how he/she funded a campaign by bluntly asking, "Where did you get the money?"—which might prompt a defiant "None of your business!"—I use milder words for money, such as *wherewithal* or *support*. I anticipate which questions may need to be objectified or framed in a two-sentence format (see below).

- This sounds elementary, but be sure to know mundane logistics about getting to your interviewees: route directions, ample driving time, parking perplexities. You don't want to interrupt an interview to feed a parking meter and find your pockets don't contain enough coins. If you need to cool your heels before an interview, you can productively use these moments to review your notes one final time. Be prepared for hassles; the security officers at the Hughes Aircraft Company in southern California would not let me pass the reception desk carrying a tape recorder, even though my interviewee was in charge of security for the company and earlier had handled security for Howard Hughes.

- Dress? I adhere to what I foresee to be prevailing practices in the place I will enter: no neckties for union carpenters in Vermont. Once, however, dressed like an executive when I went to interview DuPont's retired chief executive officer, Irving Shapiro, in Wilmington, Delaware, I was surprised to find him sporting golf clothes. "I've got a golf game after we get done," he explained. For the second interview session the next morning I arrived at his office dressed casually, but he was attired in a blue business suit.

"I've got an important business lunch when we get done," he explained.

- With respect to equipment, I put in my briefcase more cassette tapes than I expect to need, each one capable of recording sixty minutes (thirty minutes on two tracks, or sides). I carry an extension cord. My microphone and power cords are already inserted into the recorder. Likewise, on a cassette already inserted into the recorder, I first dub identifying information: the interviewee's name, the date and place of the upcoming interview, the project's title, and my name. That cassette is ready to record as soon as the recorder is activated at the place of the interview. I carry batteries if I'm uncertain about plug-in power, which I strongly prefer. Batteries run down.[17]

Now I'm ready to head toward the interview site, my rendezvous with destiny, feeling prepared, but knowing each interview is different from every other interview. The British diplomatic historian H. A. L. Fisher was right when he said that a historian "should recognize in the development of human destinies the play of the contingent and the unforeseen."[18] Oral historians know that each oral history interview also entails of "the play of the contingent and the unforeseen."

II

Before you interview, think long and hard about logistical situations. To augment rapport, I readily agree to interview people where they are most comfortable. This means I go to their homes, which in turn means, if I have not been there before, I must find the route and get there early. It also means I am entering an unfamiliar place with unanticipated recording hazards. Train your eyes to look for power outlets you can use for plugs. Avoid kitchens—ice-making refrigerators can be surprisingly noisy, and even shake floors. Avoid woodstoves—logs crackle. In your mind's eye, try to visualize how you can shift furniture quickly and easily to put two chairs near an outlet, with a table for positioning your tape recorder. Try to place the microphone on a separate surface and on a plastic holder or a soft cushion such as a pocket-size package of facial tissues. Be prudent; if you, as a stranger who is invited inside a domicile as a guest, try to rearrange the furniture brashly and abruptly, your rapport may plummet.

I glance at the dining room and often suggest we sit across the corner of the table, using a third chair for placing the tape recorder where I can see it easily, but my respondent cannot. For interviewees, this follows the time-worn adage "Out of sight, out of mind." Respondents are less likely to be nervous about a tape recorder in the room if they can't see it. But never tape surreptitiously. That is unethical. You can signal casually with your fingers as you calmly say, "I'll turn this on now, if you're ready."

In office environments, I ask beforehand if there is a conference room we can use, with telephones rendered mute so incoming calls won't tinkle. Beware of heating pipes that can bang noisily in winter and air conditioning ducts that drone in the summer. Tape recorders do not distinguish between human voices and other sounds; they record what is dominant. If your respondent agrees to come to your home turf for the interview, you have a great advantage that eases your stress. In the huge Texas Medical Center in Houston, I identified several conference rooms with excellent acoustic qualities, and thanks to helpful office managers, I have reserved these for interviewing, set up my tape recorder and microphone beforehand, walked to the office of my interviewee and walked him or her back to the interview site. (Even old-timers can be confused by veering hospital corridors heading toward *terra incognita*.) I sit my companion in the designated chair for the interviewee and seat myself in the chair designated for me, with notepad and pen already at hand. Still, in the best of circumstances noise will intrude. Doctors practice near hospitals, to which emergency vehicles rush the ill and injured, sirens screaming. Neighbors mow their lawns, and evangelists seeking souls to save—yours and mine—do come knocking at the door, causing interruptions. Trash collectors in trucks that repeatedly blare beep-beep warnings will know that you are inside, trying to record an interview. This is not paranoia; flight controllers at nearby airports will alter landing and takeoff patterns so noisy airplanes will bedevil you. Once, while

I was recording an interview in Monument, Colorado, two Siamese cats discovered I had invaded their living room. One climbed the draperies, demonstrating it could outdo monkeys in the zoo. The other saw my plug-in cord flex slightly and leaped at it, hoping to swing from it, exhibiting agility worthy of stardom with a traveling circus, but instead this nimble but naughty feline caused—pardon the pun—catastrophe.

You will have a logistical problem if you set out to interview one person but find two, or more, are ready to greet you when you arrive. In general, I advocate one-on-one, that is, one interviewer and one respondent, alone together in a quiet room, as best. Group interviewing has undeniable advantages: economically, you accomplish more by interviewing several people at one sitting, and one person's recollections can spark otherwise forgotten memories in another person's mind. But a hierarchy of deference may quickly emerge, with the person with senior status (due to age, wealth, authority, or accomplishments) dominating the discussion, and others reluctant to diverge from the consensus being established. Males may dominate, or a single blowhard may declaim, and the timid may be mum.[19] Respondents lined up like panelists on a talk show may start conversations among themselves while one is answering a question, creating a cacophonic array of voices layered like a thick deli sandwich for the transcriber to spend tedious and protracted time trying to decipher. Economy doesn't serve to fulfill the qualitative aims for your project, and with careful preparation, an interviewer can stimulate the memory prompts that might have occurred in a group interview. Mature historical judgments recognize the nuances of analysis, and group interviews don't cultivate nuances. Before an interview, you may have to stipulate that one-on-one is the practice of your project and do so diplomatically to avoid jeopardizing rapport. Nonetheless, you may find one mate hovering to protect the other. In San Leandro, California, I found the second husband kibitzing on how his spouse and her first husband raised their children during the "hard times" of the Depression of the 1930s and the war years that followed, even though he was not part of that domestic scene. I was asking her to document the household dynamics before he later entered her life as her second husband. His comments lacked historicity, but I could not get him out of the room. (By speaking during the interview, he became part of it, and accordingly a party to the legal agreement.)

You and other oral historians may decide you will together interview a single respondent. Two on one is acceptable if you both have specialized knowledge you can bring to interviewing persons with the same types of knowledge. But before the interview, you and your partner need to agree on three matters: who will solely be in charge of the recording machine, who will pursue which lines of questioning, and that neither will interrupt the other. In the interview itself, you should sit so the respondent can see you sitting together, chair by chair. Don't put the respondent between you, forcing him or her to turn left and right, trying to involve you both as conversationalists and fearing maybe one is being neglected due to unintended discourtesy.

III

Across the doorstep, into my interviewee's home, I do not unclasp my briefcase. Instead, I try to make cordial conversation with my host/hostess, showing that an oral historian can be an affable Irish American, disarming any trepidation about the reason I am there: to conduct the upcoming interview. My immediate task is to solidify rapport. Gently, I try to locate ourselves physically where the interview can be conducted. I review again the procedures of the oral history project, mentioning safeguards. When the person starts to reminisce about a topic relevant to my mission, I say perkily, "This is exactly what I am hoping you will share with me today, and to spare you the trouble of repeating yourself let me turn on this tape recorder." Swiftly into the outlet goes the power cord, in front of the memoirist goes the microphone, onto a separate surface (but visible to me) goes the recorder. With spools spinning, I say, "You were just saying about—," identifying the topic, and the respondent joins on cue by saying, "Yes—," and the recorded interview is underway.

When I explain this procedure to students during oral history workshops, they often express surprise. You don't start at the beginning? they ask. No, I don't start with, What is your name? What is your birth date? I don't want interviewees to sense this is a legal deposition or a visit by a census taker or inquisitive, government-employed gumshoe investigating fraud. Nor do I dictate that preliminary information on the tape in their presence. Nor do I want them to stiffen uncomfortably when the technology brought across their doorstep is made to function. I am not a dentist with a drill making house calls. I want to swing into the interview as smoothly as possible. Starting by recording a story the respondent has offered to tell means we're starting in an upbeat, voluntary way. Rapport is the keystone of every oral history interview you will ever conduct.[20]

Now that you have surmounted that huge hurdle of getting the actual interview underway:

- Ask one question at a time. If you bunch several questions together, your respondent will choose one in preference to the others, and the others—all worth asking—may get neglected.
- Make your questions open ended, inviting your interviewee to speak his/her story in self-chosen words, constituting an autobiographical narrative. Don't ask respondents to verify your preconceptions; your version may be wrong. Don't pose either/or alternatives, forcing your respondent to fit remembered life experiences to your imposed framework. Instead of asking, "Why did you locate your business in Springfield instead of Pittsfield?" ask "How did you decide where to locate your business?" There may have been alternatives beyond the two you juxtaposed from your pre-interview research.[21]
- Express your questions in lay language. Professional jargon does not cross the doorstep. Make your questions so crystal clear there can be no doubt about understanding them. Some answers I've read in transcripts, I fear, are actually responses of puzzlement about the essence of the question.
- Speak up and speak slowly in the presence of elderly folks. Ears age more rapidly than other body parts. When you have asked a question, you can remind yourself to

shut your mouth and bite your tongue. Learn to live with silences that seem like eternities; actually they are surprisingly short.[22] Wordless vacuums are awkward in social conversations, but in oral history interviews they provide interviewees with unfettered moments to organize their thoughts, possibly about topics they haven't contemplated for decades. Pauses induce quality responses. If you feel impelled to fill a verbal vacuum by attaching an example to the question you just asked, your respondent may address your example, not your question. Don't complicate questions. Emulate Henry David Thoreau, the hermit of Walden Pond: "Simplify! Simplify!" ("Where I Lived and What I Lived For," *Walden, Or a Life in the Woods,* 1854.)

- Listen carefully to what you hear. Don't tune out. Time after time, your next question will most likely emerge from what your respondent is saying. Remember your question to be sure your memoirist is dealing with it. Remember your question also in case your companion asks you to repeat it. If you bungle this reasonable request, you are admitting you are not paying minimal attention to the interview you are conducting. Your rapport will sink.

- Don't argue, for the same reason: you don't want to lose your rapport. Ask for elaborations, clarifications, explanations. Be a student in the presence of a teacher, not a lawyer cross-examining a witness for the opposition.

- Go with the flow. If your interviewee makes abrupt transitions, from chronology to topics to players, from past to present and back to disjointed segments of the past, follow the course as set for you. Dr. Sigmund Freud alerted us more than a century ago to the idea that free association reveals a person's patterns of thought and emotion even if a verbalized stream of consciousness seems random.[23] Make notes about points you want to return to. Transcripts of my interviews often show I am passive during the first one quarter or one third of an interview, gradually becoming more active, concluding aggressively in the last quarter. If good rapport is persistently maintained, this shift can occur seamlessly.

Proceeding on the assumption that some topics are likely to be sensitive and might threaten the rapport carefully cultivated, I deliberately defer these difficult questions until the interview is well beyond its onset. Moreover, I try not to ask about sensitive matters in immediate or close succession. Instead, I try to intersperse them among queries I assume the respondent will enjoy addressing. However, if a respondent voluntarily alludes to an issue deemed sensitive by my previous reckoning, I use that allusion to pursue the subject he/she has helpfully introduced into our dialogue. William Emerson Brock III, as an example, was elected in 1970 in Tennessee to the U.S. Senate as a Republican, a remarkable political achievement in an era when Tennessee was still predominantly a Democratic state in its voting behavior. But as the incumbent senator running for a second term in 1976, he lost his seat to James Sasser, his Democratic opponent. Pre-interview research in an obvious and widely available resource, *The New York Times Index*, alerted me that in October 1976, shortly before election day, Sasser was criticizing Brock for raising campaign funds illegally. Thus I had two sensitivities regarding Brock's senatorial career: the money issue and the fact that he lost his bid to stay in the Senate. No politician is happy talking about defeats. Indeed, some even delete lost campaigns from their self-authored entries in *Who's Who in America*, thus demonstrating how paper trails can contain deliberate omissions. All politicians enjoy talking about victories. My interview with William E. Brock started with his 1970 success, and his cool blue eyes sparkled with evident pleasure as he told the story. Casually, he mentioned he faced some charges of fiscal malfeasance in that campaign similar to accusations he had confronted six years later. His allusion allowed me, in my next question, to pursue the 1976 allegations. Using the same simple words he had just spoken, I framed my question this way: "You say you faced some charges in 1970 that you faced again in 1976." With an affirmative head nod he agreed. "With respect to the 1976 campaign, how did you deal with those charges?"

Notice how this question to Brock consists of two sentences. The first is a confirmation that he had just said something of historical interest. The second, based on the first, pursues the historical significance of what he has said.

Regularly, I deploy this two-sentence format whenever I sense an interviewee needs to hear why I think a forthcoming question requires a justification as part of our interview.[24] The first sentence establishes the relevance of a line of upcoming questions, attempts to defuse the topic emotionally, or suggests why it merits our attention. The second sentence is the question, rationalized by its predecessor, and always ends with a question mark. In effect, the first sentence says, I need to ask you this, and the second sentence says, Here is what I need to ask you.

Sometimes I rationalize questions I need to ask by citing major figures in the scholarly professions, past and present. Frederick Jackson Turner, the famous progenitor of the Frontier Thesis about the development of America's democratic ethos, emphatically urged his students at the University of Wisconsin, and later at Harvard University, when they were doing research in primary sources to ask an epistemological question about the creator of the documents they were analyzing: What was "the opportunity of a witness to know?"[25] I borrow Turner's advice and apply it when respondents make statements, and I wonder how they know what they claim to know. This is especially worrisome when from prior research I know they were not in the room when a particular decision was made by others. Evidentially, how much historicity lies in their assertions? How much weight can a future researcher give to their testimony? The first sentence of my two-sentence format would be: "The famous historian of the American frontier, Frederick Jackson Turner, urged his students, when they studied the papers of a historically significant figure, to ask, What was his opportunity to know this?" The second sentence, always a question, would be, "What was *your* opportunity to know this?" The answer would clarify for you the historicity of his claim to knowledge. Consider the possibilities (but don't verbalize them): he could hear voices through a transom; a secretary in the room taking stenographic notes told him about the decision-making process a few minutes after the meeting ended; he heard gossip about it two days later in the faculty lounge; he read about it in the newspaper (possibly reported by a journalist also not in the room). If I blurted out, "How do you know this?" my respondent might interpret my bluntly worded probe as imprudently suggesting I doubted his/her veracity. Implying your interviewee is a liar or deceiver doesn't enhance rapport.

In similar fashion, I sometimes escort an invisible colleague to my interviews and involve him in the question-asking process. His name is Harvey, so named after the six-foot invisible rabbit also named Harvey in the 1944 play and the 1950 movie titled *Harvey*. Jimmy Stewart was the star actor in the Hollywood version—not that I fantasize myself as the Jimmy Stewart of the oral history profession. Harvey is a future historian, and I mobilize him as an ally. "Imagine if a future historian sat here in this room with us now, participating in this interview," I say to a reluctant interviewee (phrasing my question in the two-sentence format). "This future historian would likely speak up now and say he needs to ask the obvious question: How did you deal with that issue?" Or, varying the language while tangling with the same problem: "A future historian would be grateful to you for hearing how this difficulty was confronted." Or: "A future historian reading the transcript of this interview would at this point expect me to ask you—." Or: "A future historian would rank me as remiss for not now giving you the opportunity to answer this important question." Then I pop the tough one. Harvey smiles—invisibly, of course.[26]

A longtime chemist at Procter and Gamble (P&G) in Cincinnati, Ohio, remarked casually in his interview that when he was a young employee in the 1920s it was company policy not to hire Roman Catholics on the management side of that large producer of household products. Inwardly, I bristled at this comment— my Irish was stirred—but outwardly I tried to sustain an unflinching professional composure. I did not interrupt him; I did not quarrel with this revelation (to me) of bigotry. But when the time quickly arrived for my next question, I said: "A future historian would fault me for not asking you to elaborate about the company employment policies you just mentioned were practiced in the 1920s." Sentence two: "Why were Catholics not hired on the management side of the company?" He had raised this topic; I tried to validate its pursuit by appealing to the needs of the future. This strategy worked. I sat quietly, not volunteering possible explanations I could conjure in my imagination, such as the Ku Klux Klan threatened a consumers' boycott if P&G hired

Catholics. His answer? The company's blue-collar workforce was heavily unionized. Many workers were Roman Catholics of German ancestry, since Cincinnati was ethnically a heavily German city. Corporate leaders feared Catholics on the management side would be spies for the union's leaders. After hearing this explanation, Harvey figuratively reached over and patted my shoulder, murmuring in my ear, "It's a good thing you didn't accuse him of being in cahoots with the Ku Klux Klan. He would have tossed both of us out of this room."

While every oral history interview asks six basic questions, the most important of the six is the *why* question. Here you are asking for motivation, inspiration, aspiration, objectives, ideals, maybe visceral stimuli that might not be known unless you ask respondents to articulate them. Likewise, paper trail records may answer five of the basic six and neglect the why explanation. Consider an example similar to the one you read above, about our Pulitzer Prize–winning poet. In this instance, four of the basic six are known, the fifth is partly known, and the sixth is totally unknown. Or in a different instance: who (a board of trustees), did what (authorized a new policy), when and where (the date and place specified in the minutes of the meeting), how (by approving a resolution), why (reasons unstated). The minutes may simply read: "It was moved, seconded, and voted to——." By interviewing a trustee who attended the meeting, you can ask if there is more information that answers the *why* question. Did the passing vote follow intensive premeeting negotiations that were off the record and involved trade-offs, such as, "I'll vote for your resolution if you vote for mine"? From this trustee, you can get answers from a witness for the unaddressed *why* question in the minutes. Always assume people are motivated by more than one reason, so ask for reasons. Also assume that many decisions are close calls and that people cogitated gravely over what course to follow. As discussed below, "the art of contrary interviewing" may impel you to reverse the *why* question and ask *why not*, revealing why a different course of action did not ensue.

Be mindful that the *why* question can threaten rapport because it presumes people are dispassionate about rational decisions. Some people may squirm uncomfortably if unable to rationalize intuitive compulsions. Some may fear you are a psychiatrist in the guise of an oral historian. Some may feel you are trespassing across an invisible line separating a person's public life from personal life, and you may find it wise to preface your *why* question with an explanation of why you're asking it. Remember our Pulitzer Prize–winning poet whose verses were rooted in mother–daughter tensions and other psychological hang-ups? When interviewing her, you need to justify your *why* question about the emotional seedbed from which her verses flowered. Feminist scholars emphasize that the personal is political in the lives of women, but this generalization applies to males as well as females, although males may be reluctant to concede this point is valid.

Generalizations are the curse of oral history memoirs, and specifics are often the nuggets that make them glitter. Asking the basic six questions may spawn generalized answers, throwing the burden on you to ask follow-up questions. This burden is obligatory. Welcome it; follow-up questions can transform a mediocre interview about generalities into a superior interview that is meaty. Go from generalities to specifics, asking for as many particulars as you can possibly glean. Invite each respondent to give an example of each point he/she makes. After listening to the example to be sure it is drawn from your respondent's experiences, ask for a second example. Hearing two, ask for three. This is called postholing. Your mantra is alliterative: Dig for details, probe for particulars, scour for specifics.[27] Liberate yourself from the orthodoxy of America's mass media, where reportage surveys huge subjects in brief overviews and miniscule sound bytes are candy capsules for the public mind. Delving for details helps us to deal with a reality of all historical subjects: they are more complex than they initially appear.

Just as *why* questions may trouble some respondents, so your probe for particulars may strike them as irksome because they cannot recall the details you request. If respondents say with visible frustration, "I can't remember the date of that meeting," you can say, "Don't worry; just tell me what happened at that meeting." Or you hear, "I can't remember the address of that house on Spruce Street in Berkeley where my landlady was

Mrs. Rinne from Finland." I say, "Don't let that bother you; I can look it up in an old city directory or phone directory." If the search for particulars is difficult for respondents (undeniably, the aging process does thin the chemical synapses in human minds), I simply ask, "What is foremost in your memory when you were a graduate student renting a room in Mrs. Rinne's house on Spruce Street?"

Oral history interviews are superb opportunities for documenting matters of historical significance that are not documented elsewhere. Whenever you sense your respondent is knowledgeable about something for which you suspect little or no independent paper trails or other sources exist, ask eagerly about these holes your interviewee can fill. Childhood is one such area in every lifespan; for many families, the only surviving documents are photographs, the snapshots having already been weeded by fond parents to show their little darlings as bright and charming progeny. Courtship is another, if the amorous couple lived within easy distance of each other and did not write letters, as soldiers and sweethearts did during World War II. Unlawful activities are secretive to avoid the creation of incriminating evidence, and if your informant has childhood memories of the bootlegging of illegal liquor in the Prohibition Era of 1920–1933, you can obtain those verbalized recollections to fill that void. Whenever a respondent refers to the unwritten rules of a workplace, I am immediately alerted that I confront an inviting opportunity to hear documentation of guidelines not formalized in any paper trail record. How gay culture operated in the era before gays could publicly affirm their sexual orientations can be documented through spoken memories. Whenever people tell me how they beat the system—by hiding Holocaust survivors, or circumventing government rationing during World War II or the military draft during the Vietnam War, or smashing the glass ceiling restraining talented women—I ask how they beat the system.

When paper trails presumably do exist but for privacy reasons are not available to you, lack of access can be at least partly skirted by asking informants to speak about the unattainable data. For example, unless you are an official federal investigator, librarians cannot ethically or legally disclose to you which patrons borrowed which books. So if you are not a government gumshoe but are doing an individual's oral biography, you can ask your interviewee what books he or she found useful at libraries.

Just as oral history interviews can document the otherwise undocumented, so these interviews are opportunities to ask about and obtain documents that can be filed with the tapes of your interview or appended to the transcript. Even when people tell me during my pre-interview preparation phase that they were not diary keepers, I will ask, after they have recounted an interesting episode, if they made a record of that occasion. A letter the Peace Corps volunteer wrote home? A report to superiors, or a memo for the file? Did the campus newspaper publish a report of that campus unrest? Did someone with a camera snap photographs? Conducting oral history interviews and acquiring manuscript materials are tandem activities.

Furthermore, in oral history interviews you can ask informants to evaluate the scope and reliability of independent sources bearing on your respondent's recollections. Did the student newspaper accurately reflect student opinion? Did the letters home omit unsavory details? Did the office files mask realities instead of exposing them? Did institutional culture discourage any negative comments in written communications? Oral history interviews allow the interplay of memory and other materials as you and others confront a basic research question about all documents of all kinds: How can you believe your sources are credible?

Like *credibility*, another important word in my oral history lexicon is *evocations*. I invite respondents to evoke past occasions and personalities that had great personal meaning for them. Questions as examples: "Would you evoke for me what it was like for you when you first learned the Supreme Court had outlawed segregated schools in *Brown v. Board of Education?*" "—when you heard John F. Kennedy had been shot in Dallas?" "—when you heard the doctor say your child had polio?" Or, if a person has just explained how a particular teacher was a tremendously important life-shaping model, I will ask, "Please evoke for me how this teacher was for you a powerful presence?" (Don't add "in the classroom" but leave your question

open-ended in case the influence was exerted outside the classroom.) Evocations can provide insightful descriptions of the personal chemistry between individuals or the drama of tense
situations or the humor of ludicrous situations. Ask about the
cultural texture of times and places. Evocations are word pic-
tures arising from invitations to provide the type of material that
novelists skillfully compose about their fictional figures, but oral
historians don't fictionalize. In oral history, we can hear genuine
tales of real people in real situations. Paper trail accounts of emotive occurrences are often dry-as-dust documents, but oral histories can convey affective meanings. Encourage these evocations
of the span of human feelings, from horror to elation.

Some interviewees are so present minded that their answers
convey their current thinking about your history-centered questions, not their verbalized memories of what you asked about.
Grele warns oral historians to consider "how the now informs
the discussion of the then."[28] Try to persuade your respondents
to depict themselves in the context of the times you are asking
about. Here again I mobilize the two-sentence format as my
technique. Suppose you are interviewing a person, such as Senator John F. Kerry, who was a critic of America's war in Vietnam,
1965–1975. To establish the relevance of my questions, I start
with today's first draft of history, the daily newspaper, and move
to yesterday's concern, which is the historical issue I want spoken memories to document. The first sentence is: "There is much
discussion today about America's military presence abroad."
The second sentence is: "Going back to the 1960s, at that time
how did you view the escalation of America's presence in Vietnam?" History textbooks narrate the American story from past
to present, but oral historians reverse this sequence and justify
questions by going from the present to the past.

Outcome determines recollection: this is another problem
confronting historians who solicit spoken memories and reckon
their validity. Electoral campaigns are remembered through victories or defeats; a marriage that ends in divorce is not warmly
remembered in images of the gaiety of the wedding reception
but is remembered as tribulations that led to divorce court. You
can encourage respondents to avoid filtering their memories
through outcomes by using the two-sentence format to position

them in the context existing before outcomes were known. When people recount their lives as a series of sequences that in retrospect seem natural, even inevitable, I might ask, "Go back to your senior year in high school." Sentence two: "At that time, how did you view your future choices?" This invites them to slow down a narrative that leaps from high school to a particular college to a particular graduate school with a particular career in mind. Life as lived is a constant process of making choices among alternatives; life as remembered in oral history interviews allows respondents to explain choice-making in their lives, thus enriching the texture of how they traveled from past to present. Paper trails tend to document choices that were made. Oral history can retrieve choices that were pondered.

Oral historians also practice "the art of contrary interviewing." While listening carefully to what respondents say, they also listen for what is unsaid, and later ask about the omissions. If, when reminiscing about childhood on a family farm, a respondent gives only warm weather examples of rural life, I'll subsequently ask about the farm in winter. If memories of influential figures in adolescence center on the father, I'll ask about the mother. If memories of schooling are classroom scenes, I'll ask about the playground, getting to school, and after-school activities. When I ask about childhood in a particular town and hear about stores, schools, and churches, I'll ask about unmentioned institutions, such as the library, the movie theater, and disreputable places such as pool halls or the hobo jungle near the railroad tracks. If accounts feature rich people who lived in spacious houses on the hill, I'll ask about poor people who lived below in rookeries in the flats. If the town is portrayed as the abode of white people, I'll ask about the town's African American population, and how in the age of virulent Jim Crow segregation race was managed in the social system.

While oral historians are listening, they also are visualizing how life was lived by the person giving a first-person account of it. The ability to imagine how others have lived is a valuable resource for oral historians. The spoken memories we hear spark visual images on the movie screen I argue exist in everybody's mind. (Admittedly, my biomedical colleagues at Baylor College of Medicine in Houston disputed this neurological claim about brain components.) Onto this movie screen, we project images that translate into our own lived experiences what others are saying, and herein lies a danger. Hearing a respondent tell about elementary school experiences causes me to visualize him/her walking inside the red brick walls of the Pierce Grammar School on Chestnut Street in West Newton, Massachusetts, where I started kindergarten in 1938 and continued through sixth grade. When my informant talks about an influential sixth-grade teacher, I see *my* sixth-grade teacher, Miss Ruth O'Donnell, encouraging my aspirations to be a writer and lamenting my doltish ineptness with arithmetic. The lesson for oral historians is clear: don't suppose you understand another person's story without hearing it spoken. Ask, don't assume. One of the worst blunders we can make is to blurt out a sudden, "I know exactly what you mean!" Restraint, careful listening, and interrogation may produce a narrative different from your own but nonetheless authentic in terms of representing genuinely the life as lived by the person reminiscing about it.

When an informant tells a story that clearly holds strong emotional content—you can tell by tone of voice, facial grimness, and similar body language—but I don't hear explanations of why this episode is vividly recalled, I often ask the *meanings* question. Specifically: "What meanings has that experience carried for you since it happened?" Or if a person laughs lightly now about an experience that could have been painful when it happened, I'll ask, "Has the meaning of that episode varied over time during your life?" Whenever I'm uncertain about the meanings people apply to the memories they recount, I ask them to express the meanings themselves. I don't want to guess about them afterward or force users of my transcripts to conjecture about them.

If you sense your informant is rambling, be tolerant of the ramble. You may be discrediting a monologue as irrelevant to the purposes of your interview, only to learn your interviewee is taking a circuitous discursive approach to the essence of your question. Relevance and rambling are subjective judgments on our parts, and we may be wrong about their pertinence to memories of historical significance. One person's dismissal of a commentary as blather unhitched to the focus of the interview may be another person's arrow to the heart of a researcher's topic. For linguists, the research value of oral history memoirs is how words are pronounced and linked, not exclusively how they convey meaning. Oral historians in Idaho recorded an interview they subsequently lamented had no likely usefulness for any researcher who might visit their library. But an architectural historian was delighted to learn, from reading the transcript, how the interviewee described her childhood home as an adobe structure on the Idaho High Desert, the farthest north this particular style had migrated from the American Southwest. The researcher was ecstatic on discovering the location of this migratory specimen of the architectural style she was studying.

An interviewee may respond to one of your keen questions by saying something such as: "That is an interesting question. Would you please turn off your tape recorder?" When this happens, try earnestly *not* to turn off your tape recorder. Once it is off, you may have difficulty getting it back on. Hearing a respondent off tape poses a problem: if you define the interview as what you both say on tape, what do you do with this unrecorded information? If you and the interviewee discuss the relevance or sensitivity of the answer to your question and agree it belongs on the tape, the second telling, after the tape recorder is activated, will always be a shortened paraphrase of the off-tape version you just heard. Try to keep the tape recorder functioning by saying, "I'll save you time; if you decide it doesn't belong on tape, you won't have to repeat it." Or: "You'll be getting a transcript of this interview to edit, and maybe that is the suitable time for deciding if it should be part of the interview." Or: "We find in oral history interviewing that people tend to abbreviate their stories when they repeat them." But you may lose these valiant battles to get the bothersome story initially on tape, and to maintain rapport you may resort to the diplomatic alternative: reluctantly, you turn off your recording machine.

During an interview, your partner may casually ask you what you think about challenges and choices in his/her life that you hear in the narrative being recorded. Beware of suddenly but subtly being asked to answer questions instead of asking them. Once the roles are reversed and you are being queried by the person you came to interview, it may be difficult to get the relationship back on its bearings. Try gently but firmly to avoid the pitfalls of becoming a respondent instead of an interrogator by saying, "It is better that I hear you express your knowledge of these topics than we hear my ignorance of them," or, "You were there; I was not." "You're my teacher; I'm your student," or, "Let's defer my opinions of these matters to our postinterview conversation rather than clutter the interview with them now."

Some people want me to concur with their judgments in controversial issues. "It was okay," says a Caucasian Californian, expectantly, "to relocate those Japanese American spies soon after the Pearl Harbor bombing, right?" I avoid swallowing the bait and getting hooked on their line. Rapport is threatened if I blurt out my own personal belief: "Wrong; internment of Japanese Americans was totally unwarranted for security reasons and unjust for constitutional reasons." Diplomatic alternatives? "I was a youngster eight years old and three thousand miles east of the Pacific Coast when internment happened; you were here and saw it happen." To this, in a second sentence, I add a question, or I add a tactic that worked perfectly for me in an interview recorded high in the Berkeley hills: "I've never understood why Japanese Americans were interned but Italian Americans were not, and in World War II we were fighting Italy as well as Japan." That unleashed a panegyric about Italian Americans in the San Francisco region, ranging fondly from Joe DiMaggio's upbringing in the North Beach neighborhood to iconic Napa Valley wine makers. Oral history interviewing is one of the very few activities in life in which you can mobilize your ignorance as an asset.

Be prepared also for a respondent to ask, either innocently or deviously, what another participant in your project has said about the controversies being recounted. All oral history memoirs are considered confidential until signed legal agreements make them open. They continue to be confidential if legal agreements stipulate closure of all or segments of transcripts. To refuse to answer your respondent's inquiry, "What did Harry say about this when you interviewed him?" may fracture your rapport. You can respond by saying, "In oral history we treat all materials being processed as confidential until legal agreements make them open." You might add that your role is akin to a doctor's professional ethic requiring protection of patients' records. If my respondent looks skeptical, I might add, "I can't tell you what Harry said because I won't tell Harry what you're saying now." Most nod their heads affirmatively when hearing this assurance.

When your interviewee voices an interpretation about a past event that you (silently) sense does not fit the consensus of opinion about what actually happened, ask your informant to mention other people who were present as participants or witnesses. If you need to obtain further testimonies about this particular occasion, you will now know whom to approach.

Oral historians are listening and watching intently during interviews, but their tape recorders are only listening.[29] Humans have eyes and ears; tape recorders have only ears. I watch the nonverbal behavior of my interviewees attentively. Visually, I can detect clues to how they feel about my questions, varying from joyful welcome to derisive disdain to vexing discomfort. These clues help me decide the choice and wording of upcoming questions. Also, if memoirists communicate by nonverbal references, I can either make notes for the transcript or put into words what was conveyed but unsaid. "In spring that stream was about as wide as that lawn," says the interviewee, pointing through a glass window to her yard. "About fifty feet wide?" ask I. "Yes," says she, and thus the future knows what she signaled but did not speak.

Videotapes record more than audiotapes hear, of course, but before lugging lights and cameras across an interviewee's doorstep, think long and hard about technology as a menace to rapport between individuals. With some people, the simple act of turning on a tape recorder can be a thorny transition. From experience, I have learned to separate videotaping as a second step after audiotaping as a first step. The initial goal is to get the entire interview recorded on audiotape. Later, the second goal is to pose the informant where selected portions of the transcribed audiotape are best repeated for telling to a video camera.

Listeners to your tapes—your transcriber, especially—will be grateful to you if you keep your own voice hushed except to ask questions. Even though spontaneous vocal rejoinders such as "uh-huh" and "hmmmm" show you are listening attentively and buttress rapport, these so-called phatic sounds on tapes interfere with the much more important words your narrator is speaking. I try to clamp my mouth shut (not an easy task) and respond to what I hear with facial and other visual signs of comprehension. Interviews are not occasions to hear myself talk beyond asking questions. But even this self-imposed gag rule can have ironic consequences. Proud of myself for being a tight-lipped listener during an interview with a Baylor-trained physician, I didn't realize he was attentive to my nonverbal responses. After the interview concluded, he remarked, "You know, you dilate your eyes a lot."

One exception to this self-imposed gag rule does routinely occur when one side or track of a cassette is about to expire or a cassette is nearly full and needs to be replaced by a fresh one. When flipping a tape, I speak in order to prevent the memoirist from talking while the machine is not recording. I don't want to lose that unrecorded segment. With practice, you can flip a cassette or switch cassettes in about two seconds of deft handling while uttering words as trite as, "I'm certainly enjoying this interview and appreciate your contribution to our project." If your fingers fumble clumsily, you can add, "You're kind to share your memories, and others will appreciate your kindness, too." When starting with a fresh side or track or new cassette, you can repeat an abbreviated summation of your narrator's words just before the transition caused an interruption: "You were just saying—." These words also cover the blank tape at the outset of each reel. By the time your narrator affirms your brief reiteration, the transition is a smooth linkage. Then lean away from your recorder and even pivot toward your narrator, signaling that all is well with the third pair of ears in the interviewing room and the conversation can genially continue without attention to the electronic equipment.

IV

Every interview can be ended by asking two questions.

First, "Are there any questions I've failed to ask you which you would like to raise?" Respondents almost always reply with a hearty no, sometimes telling you they're surprised you had so many questions to ask. Sometimes you will be complimented for your preparation and knowledge of the interview subject. Hearing this, you now know how dead people feel when St. Peter invites them to step forward and enter heaven's pearly gates.

Second, "Are there any topics you would like to return to and say more about?" Maybe half of all respondents will pause, ponder, and say yes, elaborating on a point made earlier, or clarifying it, or emphasizing it.

Then I say, "Thank you." I want these words on tape because they deserve to be part of the official record. Back to basics: oral history doesn't happen if memory-rich respondents don't voluntarily allow us to make it happen.

Then I turn off the tape recorder. But I do not pull the cord from the outlet, nor do I move the microphone. Together we sit, and I usually mention something about the interview that is positive about its usefulness. For example, "What you said about college girls providing farm labor during World War II will be helpful to historians because there is nothing in the historical society's archives about that topic, except male farmers complaining about farmhands being drafted at harvest time." Or: "Your account of the library board's refusing to fire the librarian accused of being a pinko during the McCarthyism hysteria of the early 1950s is helpful because the library's records are silent on that issue." In a surprised voice you may hear, "Is that right?" Note how this second example enforces the value of speaking candidly about sensitive subjects in a community's history. The more I reckon a respondent is downcast about the interview— memories had faded, names and dates did not instantly come to mind—the more I cite remembered vignettes as beneficial testimony. If a person has summarized ninety years of life in ninety minutes of reminiscing, I don't want to leave her feeling glum about the worthiness of it. Our role is not to create depression in the mindsets of the elderly, but to leave them feeling good about how they have been good to us and others. Moreover, their willingness to edit the transcript you'll be sending will be higher if they share your upbeat outlook. Depressed people procrastinate.

The postinterview session is when you ask your respondent to spell proper names, explain obtuse professional nomenclature or shorthand, demystify place-names and acronyms, and the like. On my notepad I have jotted these phonetically during the interview. But rather than twirling and shoving my notepad toward the respondent, asking him/her to spell my guesses correctly, I do the asking and the writing because some people—physicians especially—have such poor handwriting you have to decipher their scrawl, which can be as perplexing as the words you heard when uttered in the interview. Be prepared for a truncated postinterview session. Doctors will rise telling you they have patients waiting. Befriend secretaries. Ask, "Does the doctor's daughter spell her name Leslie or Lesley?" "Is Kelly Boyd a son or daughter?" Ask if you can phone if you have questions to answer, in order to simplify the task upcoming for your transcriber. Ask if your transcriber can phone.

In the postinterview session, I ask the respondent if I may phone if, while reviewing the transcript, one or a handful of questions arise that I should have asked during the interview but failed to do so. Asking questions by phone and integrating them into the transcript, clearly identified and dated as to provenance, saves you the time and expense of scheduling another interview session. Don't tape a telephone conversation without first asking and receiving permission to do so.

More shoptalk can center on scheduling another session or outlining what lies ahead: transcription, editing, negotiating the legal agreement. I tell informants I will enclose a sample (i.e., boilerplate) legal form with the transcript mailed for review and phone a few days later to ask if they have any questions about either. This creates the risk of the interview being condemned to limbo if your interviewee should die before signing a release and you have to deal with the executor of his/her estate. But ethically I prefer not to discuss ownership issues and assignment of legal rights until the respondent knows fully and exactly what product our labors have mutually created.

After interviews have ended, I may ask for advice about who else might be considered for this project. If I sense a person who should be interviewed may be averse to being approached and I know my current interviewee was, or is, friendly with my reluctant prospect, I ask if I may mention to my prospect that we have recorded this memoir. "By all means," is what I hope to hear, with an added, "Tell her she should give you an interview. Your project won't be complete without her."

If at any time during this postinterview conversation a respondent suddenly exclaims, "Oh, I forgot to tell you about—," I promptly say, "We can remedy that easily. I'll just turn on the recorder again." Then, signaling with two fingers as I do so, I say, "You want to add about—." By not moving the microphone or pulling the plug, we have allowed an addendum to enrich the interview. Once again, I say, "Thank you." Once again, I don't tinker with the microphone or plug in case a second recollection abruptly occurs and we need to tape it.

The postinterview session is time for the social conversation you wanted to pursue in the interview, when instead you bit your tongue and deferred it. "You mentioned you went to Oberlin College; my daughter, Susan, is an Oberlin graduate." "Oh," comes the rejoinder, "when was she there?" Off you go bopping on the Oberlin odyssey. If you were offered a liquid libation before or during the interview and discreetly declined, you can now accept it and make as much noise as you like with spoons and crockery or cascading ice cubes in a tall glass. You can summon sullen family members you exiled to far corners of the house and engage them in friendly conversation so they no longer feel like social pariahs. You can laugh or chortle. You can talk about yourself. You can be the social animal you know you are. Oral historians are extroverts.

Finally, when I stand up to leave, I pull the plug and bundle all my equipment into my satchel, thanking everybody profusely while heading to the doorway and back across the doorstep. Yes, your plug has been pulled on your interview, but the plug has not been pulled on the interview process. Your rendezvous with destiny entails more work. Duplicating tapes and then transcription lie ahead. Other tasks will follow. Real work—dare I say reel work?—beckons you forward. You and Harvey chuckle at your pun—reel work—as the door clicks behind you.

Notes

1. Schippers, "Techniques," 54.
2. Fetner, *Immersed in Great Affairs*, 65.

3. Saul Benison, in charge of OHRO interviews on the history of medicine, 1955–1960, wrote, "I shall be plain; it has been my experience that many oral historians are less than meticulous in their research, that they do not include their questions in the memoirs, that they care little for the niceties of bibliography and care less for coping with historical problems." Benison, "Reflections," 73–74.

4. Morrissey, "Truman," 55. This article was given first as a paper during the annual meeting of the Mississippi Valley Historical Association (subsequently, the Organization of American Historians), in Cleveland, Ohio, on April 30, 1964.

5. Grele, "Oral History," 2: 881.

6. Moss, *Program Manual*, 45.

7. Mutual interviewer–interviewee responsibilities are detailed in Oral History Association, *Evaluation Guidelines*.

8. On the differences in interviewer–interviewee relationships between journalism and oral history, see Feldstein, "Kissing Cousins," 14–17.

9. Krieger, *Ranke*, 2.

10. Kayser and Morrissey, "Historically Significant Memories," 62.

11. See, for example, Ritchie, *Doing Oral History*, 2nd ed., 85–86.

12. On mythmaking, see Morrissey, "Mythmakers." On mythmaking by creation of paper-trail documents, see Morrissey, "Stories of Memory."

13. For more on use of props and other devices to aid memory recall, see Slim et al., "Ways of Listening," 119–25.

14. Ives, *Tape-Recorded Interview* (1980), 38, discusses "stranger value."

15. See also Yow's chapter on "Interpersonal Relations in the Interview," in *Recording Oral History* (1994), 116–42.

16. Ibid., 199–202, discusses family dynamics in historical research.

17. Concerning the purposes of the recorded introduction, see Sommer and Quinlan, *Oral History Manual*, 67. On the matter of avoiding batteries, Ritchie, *Doing Oral History*, 2nd ed., 58, agrees with me, but Yow, *Recording Oral History* (1994), 51, disagrees.

18. Fisher, *History of Europe*, v.

19. For more on group interviews, see Slim et al., "Ways of Listening," 118–19.

20. Yow, *Recording Oral History* (1994), 60–66, discusses behaviors that either build or hinder rapport.

21. For more on questioning technique, see McGuire, "'Existential' Interviewing," 58–69.

22. On listening, see Anderson and Jack, "Learning to Listen," 169–70, and on silences, see White, "Marking Absences," 173–78.

23. For a full definition of free association, see *The Freud Encyclopedia: Theory, Therapy, and Culture*, ed. Edward Erwin (New York: Routledge, 2002), s. v. "Free Association." Peter Gay recounts Freud's development of free association in *Freud*, 73, 297–98, but note that on 127 free association is misnamed because the spoken sequences "are invisibly but indissolubly welded together." The similarities and differences between oral history interviewing

and psychiatric interviewing are examined by James W. Lomax, a psychiatrist, and me in Lomax and Morrissey, "Interview as Inquiry." For more on oral history interviewing and the psychology of autobiographical memory, see my remarks in Morrissey, foreword, which appears in Hoffman and Hoffman, *Archives of Memory*.

24. I introduced the two-sentence format in 1966 at the first national meeting of oral historians. See Schippers, "Techniques," 53. Twenty years later, the practice was automatic for me. See Morrissey, "Two-Sentence Format," 44.

25. As recalled by Herbert Eugene Bolton in an undated letter in the fall of 1951 to Wilbur R. Jacobs, in Jacobs, *On Turner's Trail*, 265.

26. Charles T. Morrissey, "Asking Hard Questions: Harvey the Historian as Colleague," *Oral History Association Newsletter* 38, no. 2 (2004): 8.

27. Charlton, *Oral History for Texans*, 2nd ed., 27–28, lists seven specific probing techniques, including nonverbal ones.

28. Grele, "Anyone over Thirty," 43.

29. On the "aesthetics" of tape recording interviews, see Dunaway, "Field Recording," 32–36.

6

Oral History and Archives: Documenting Context

James E. Fogerty

Oral history is a unique form of documentation in that it does not exist in a defined form before it is created through the interaction of an interviewer with a narrator. Despite the occasional reference to "collecting" oral history, the interviews represented in any oral history collection had to be created before they could be deposited in a library or archives. The existing resources of the narrator's memory, drawn upon and undoubtedly formed in part by the interviewer's inquiry, are thus used to create a new resource.

It is the long and often laborious process of creation that we address in this chapter. Too often, oral historians, caught up in the pleasure and excitement of the interview and the personal interaction it offers, forget that the interview itself is neither the beginning nor the end of the process of creating oral history. It begins, in fact, with the conception of an interview or series of interviews and continues through research, narrator selection, and the interviews to transcription, editing, publication, and finally, public use in a variety of formats. At each stage of the process, context is created that becomes an important part of the interview and its meaning.

One of oral history's greatest benefits—the fact that nearly anyone, properly directed, can create it—has also proven one of its occasional drawbacks. The seeming ease with which oral history can be created—an interviewer appears to need only a recorder, some tape, and a narrator willing to talk—has fostered the illusion that oral history is a simple undertaking. This misunderstanding of the realities of oral history creation has spawned an abundance of poorly planned and executed interviews that have little residual value for research.

If lack of planning and poor execution often limit the uses for interviews, lack of attention to context is the greater problem, as pointed out by Canadian archivists Jean-Pierre Wallot and Normand Fortier. Even skilled oral historians may ignore the fact that "the circumstances surrounding the interview—the *context*—and the way the interview is conducted" are critical elements to the end users of oral history.[1] The reality of context, and its documentation, are not new to archives, though contextual reality has been applied infrequently in dealing with nontraditional archival materials such as oral history. Canadian theoretician and educator Hugh A. Taylor instructed archivists that this "contextual approach is concerned in the first instance with acquiring knowledge of the context in which information is recorded rather than knowledge of the information contents of records."[2]

Documenting Context

Few oral historians are archivists, however, and thus few of them begin the process of creating oral history with documentation of the process, as well as the narrator's memory, in mind. Archivists and curators of many different collections refer to the history of an item as its "provenance," referring to the what, when, where, how, and why of its creation. Insofar as possible, for instance, an art curator will want to document where, how, with what materials, and by whom a work of art was created, as well as the record of its ownership through the years. Other information will be sought as well, such as the inspiration for the work, the setting in which it was created, and the identity of the subject.

Such information is equally important for oral history interviews, for it establishes the context within which each interview was conceived and created, thus establishing an important frame of reference. Wallot and Fortier explain, "Oral sources depend on the relationship established between the interviewer and interviewee: a complete appreciation of the result therefore depends on a knowledge of the interview and its context (place, presence of third party, relationship between interviewer and subject, and so on)."[3] This information is critical to a user's ability to interpret the information contained in each oral history interview.

Since oral histories do not exist until created by an interviewer, the opportunity to create a record of provenance is clearly there. An interview should never become a "found object," stripped of the story of its creation and without any record of its context except that intuited by an eventual cataloger or user.

It is useful to note the confusion that can be engendered by terminology—especially when a widely used term is misapplied in some instances.

> With reference to oral history, the term "collect" is frequently employed—as in "We're collecting oral history." Still worse is the term "gather"—as in "We're gathering oral history to supplement our collections." Both terms, but particularly the often-used "collect," are inaccurate when applied to oral history. "Collect" implies that oral history, like a manuscript collection, exits and is only waiting to be found and acquired. While the data that becomes oral history is present in the minds of potential narrators, it does not exist in any organized, collectible form. It must, rather, be created—and not alone, but through the interaction of an interviewer with the narrator. Existing resources are thus used to create, not collect, a new resource.[4]

There are two main avenues by which oral history may enter an archives, library, or other repository. The most proactive is direct creation, through which the repository staff participates in every aspect of interview creation, from conception through narrator selection, interviewing, and preparation for research use. While this approach is increasingly common in many institutions, it may also be viewed as an expensive alternative to a more passive role.

The second avenue is to collect actively, or simply to accept, interviews created by others. This is the path followed by a great many institutions as they build collections and provide permanent housing and access for oral history created without direct linkage to a repository. While the acceptance of previously created oral history may spare a repository the expense of conception and creation, it is hardly without cost. Indeed the costs may be excessive if the interviews have been created without care and attention to context. Donation of interviews to a repository is often an afterthought on the part of the creator whose work is complete and who wishes simply to ensure a permanent home for the interview tapes. As Wallot and Fortier indicate, the act of "the depositing in archives of recordings without appropriate documentation makes evaluation of the recordings very costly, and, consequently, proper use of the recordings very difficult."[5]

Appraisal of potential accessions is a key component of collection building in any institution. Oral histories that lack such essentials as adequate documentation of the process of their creation, transcripts for each interview, narrator contracts, and other important elements can seldom be considered viable candidates for acquisition. The cost of acquiring such interviews is enormous, and the potential for their eventual use too uncertain to allow most institutions to consider adding them to existing collections. The expense of re-creating context where no record exists is far too great.

Individual Interviews versus the Project

While each oral history interview is indeed "individual" in that it deals with a single person, there are significant differences between what might be termed "solo" interviews and those created as part of a larger project. Both have context that must be documented, but the context for the project interviews will be much larger and more complex. Life histories, for instance, derive their value from the experiences of a single individual whose views are documented without reference to similar or competing views of others. Interviews created as part of a defined project, however, derive special value from their relationship to one another. If carefully selected, these narrators will both corroborate and differ from the views of others, thus providing highly valuable perspectives on the issues that are the subject of the project.

There are many examples of oral history projects; for illustration, I will refer to several that have been undertaken by the Minnesota Historical Society's Oral History Office. Projects on environmental issues, the farm economy, the resort industry, the controversial construction of a high-voltage power line across farmland, and a number of immigrant communities all exemplify the rationale for constructing a project with complementary interviews rather than a series of unrelated individual interviews.[6] The environmental issues project, for instance, allowed selection of narrators with widely differing views on public use of protected recreation areas and on levels of protection afforded shoreline set aside under the Wild and Scenic Rivers Act. The resort industry project included operators of large facilities with multiple entertainment options and mom-and-pop resorts that relied principally on fishing. It also included resort operators from two quite different areas of the state, allowing documentation of the contrast between the businesses and their guests. Protesters, supporters, and those caught in the middle were interviewed for the power-line construction project, and projects documenting new immigrants also draw on narrators whose perspectives display differences as well as similarities. The first project, dealing with Minnesota's Asian Indian community, for instance, was carefully structured to include Hindus, Sikhs, Muslims, Jains, and others, as well as people from many geographic areas of the vast Indian subcontinent. Subsequent projects in the India series include generational variety as well.

The reality of creating such oral history projects must be carefully documented as part of the process. The work of creating focus, selecting narrators, maintaining balance, and articulating issues for discussion during the interviews is critical to their understanding and interpretation. It is important for oral historians to understand that documentation of oral history begins with the conception of each interview, whether it is the life history of a single narrator or one of a series of interviews that form part of a project. The ways in which project goals are defined, topics for discussion chosen, and narrators selected should be reflected in documents created as the project progresses. It is also important to document who participated in those discussions, since they will have played major roles in shaping the project and its context.

These examples of the considerations necessary to the proper documentation of oral history lead us to discussion of the products of that creative process.

The Products of Oral History

The creation of even the simplest oral history interview, if it is to be of archival quality, requires the assembly or creation of a good many documents. I have chosen to list them by category below, with a discussion of each and specific examples of the documents that might become part of such a collection. The list is extensive, and competent oral historians will recognize that they already create or gather these documents as part of their work in creating interviews. The task at hand is simply to recognize that these documents are all critical components of each interview's context and establish its provenance and thus its credibility.

A key consideration in the building of background files is the reality that institutional memories are short and uncertain. The departure of project staff familiar with specific interviews may render materials difficult to use without adequate identification.

Research Files

The assembly of items to provide background information for an oral history project will begin before the project is even launched. The information gathered will help project development in such areas as the definition of scope, selection of narrators, and development of topics for discussion. Research files may become quite bulky and are usually maintained separately from the files of individual narrators. A distinction should be made between information gathered to be of use in overall project development and the narrator-specific, biographical information that may be placed in each narrator's file.

Projects will differ, of course, in the level and extent of documentation gathered as part of background research. The Minnesota Powerline Construction Oral History Project, for instance, came to include several large storage boxes of material gathered to document the complex issues and the individuals and organizations involved. Among the materials are reports on the conception, development, and construction of the power-generating plant and power line; reports detailing all aspects of health issues believed to be associated with the power line; press releases from the line's builders, the governor's office, and other organizations; flyers and broadsides announcing community meetings and other events; federal government reports on the line; maps, local news articles, newsletters issued by groups formed to protest construction; and photographs. Additional materials include an excellent paper on the controversy prepared by a graduate student at the University of Minnesota, Morris, and the procedures manual prepared to guide the oral history project's staff. This collection has become a key resource for researchers using the power line oral history interviews. The newsletters issued by local protest groups, for instance, were informally produced and ephemeral; those at the Minnesota Historical Society form the only comprehensive collection now in existence. And while some of the other documents may exist in other places, their inclusion in a single collection at a central location associated with the oral history collection is a major boon to research.

Unfortunately, many items of this sort do not survive the completion of oral history projects. While collected to aid research and facilitate the development of interview discussion topics, the project organizers frequently fail to recognize that the background documents are also valuable to researchers. Whenever practical, they should be brought together to form a collection, catalogued and made available for use. The electronic cataloging now in use in virtually every institution provides great ease in linking the oral history interviews to the associated collection of project research materials.

Project Files/Narrator Files

Every oral history project will generate communications common to more than one narrator or aimed at those who offer support for, or interest in, the project as a whole. Those items should be filed together for ease of access and to prevent the needless duplication of generating additional copies of these items for each narrator file. There is no need, for instance, to make copies for individual narrator files of project information sheets, invitations to project events, or project press releases. Those items need to be included in the project archives, and the creation of project-level files obviates the necessity to make multiple copies.

Communication with individual narrators should be separated into files dedicated to each person interviewed. In that file are placed copies of correspondence with that person, the person's photograph, a copy of the completed donor contract, and any background research material relating specifically to that individual.

By creating these separate series of files, information on the project is organized for rapid retrieval.

Correspondence/Communication

Copies of all correspondence with narrators should be filed with all of the material relating to that individual interview. *Include e-mail!* Print out relevant e-mail communications with narrators and others relating to the project or interview. Printing out the e-mail may seem like duplication of effort, but it ensures that a permanent record of all communication with that individual will be filed in one place and available for reference in the future. Retaining the e-mail as a computer file does not ensure its permanence and definitely does not ensure its availability for future reference. Since important issues regarding an interview may well be resolved through the exchange of e-mail, it is critical to retain this record as part of the permanent file.

Donor Contract

The contract concluded with each narrator, assigning rights for use, copyright, and ownership to the institution sponsoring the project, is perhaps the most important piece of paper in the project files. Without written transfer of interview ownership to the institution, the tapes cannot be transcribed or used in any way by anyone and are thus without value. The donor contract should be signed at the conclusion of the taped interview. If more than one interview session is held with a single narrator, the contract should be signed at the conclusion of the final taping session. It should clearly state the narrator's intent to transfer ownership and copyright to the institution. If any restrictions are imposed on use, they should also be spelled out clearly in the contract, with a specific date given for expiration of the restriction. Interviews should never be accepted with permanent restrictions on use, and the expiration of restriction should never be stated as the narrator's death. No institution possesses the resources to track hundreds of narrators throughout their lives in order to establish specific dates of death.

Oral history is created to be used. Restrictions on use should be discouraged and, when inevitable, kept to a minimum. There are certainly instances in which candor cannot be ensured without the imposition of restrictions on immediate use of the interview. But the number of interviews restricted should be minimized by attention to narrator concerns and by the interviewer's clear explanation of the influence of the passage of time on sensitive information. Restrictions of more than a decade after the date of the interview should be the exception, not the rule.

Contracts should be created in duplicate, with both copies signed by the narrator at the conclusion of the interview or interview series. If the contract covers a series of interviews, the dates of each interview must be listed in the contract. One copy of the signed contract remains with the narrator; the other returns to the institution where it is copied immediately. The copy is filed in the narrator file; the original is filed with others from that project in a secure location where its permanence can be assured.

Photographs

An important ingredient in many oral history interviews is a photograph of the narrator. Nearly all interview transcripts at the Minnesota Historical Society include a photograph of the narrator, since we have found that virtually all users enjoy seeing the narrators as well as reading their comments. Inclusion of a photograph also personalizes the interview transcript and increases its value to many narrators and their families.

A photograph of the narrator may be augmented by more photographs, depending on the project and its goals, funding, and the desires of its sponsors. Interviews documenting the history of a corporation, for instance, might include photographs of former officers, company products, company logos as they evolved through the years, and company facilities. The illustrations will usually depend upon the content of the interviews and on the availability of suitable images. An interview with a prominent churchman in Minneapolis, for instance, included not only a photograph of him taken near the time of the interview, but also an additional photograph of him as a younger man, as well as photographs of his church at various points in its history, previous pastors mentioned in the text, and even one of the city, locating the church within the wider context of its surroundings.

Copies of every photograph included should be retained in the narrator's file or in a file devoted to project photography. Since only a scanned image of the photograph is used in the final document, retention of the original or copy is a simple undertaking. Each photograph should be clearly identified on the reverse using a soft 6B drawing pencil that is available in art supply shops. Identification will obviously facilitate use of the files for research and also for future institutional use should the interviews be reprinted.

Interview Transcripts

Every interview should be transcribed. While transcription is a labor-intensive and protracted process, it is necessary to a main goal of creating oral history—its use. In this day of declining consumer patience and an Internet-fueled demand for instant gratification, production of interviews that cannot be accessed without listening to an audiotape is a waste of resources.

The availability of word processing has greatly decreased the expense of producing transcripts, but unless one has access to low-cost or volunteer transcribers and editors, it remains somewhat costly. The benefits, however, far outweigh the costs. With word processing, one creates a document that can be edited, updated, corrected, and reprinted with far less effort and expense than was true only fifteen years ago. And the electronic document thus created can allow a user to conduct word and subject searches across an entire project of related interviews, thus greatly increasing their potential utility to a wide variety of audiences.

All transcripts should be retained in both electronic and paper files. The electronic file will serve as the principal copy for generating replacement copies of the transcript as needed. Electronic copies of all of a project's interview transcripts can be gathered into a single file and presented to users as a unit, thus allowing the term searches noted above. Electronic files should be located on a secure server to prevent the unintended damage that can occur to documents stored on a computer's hard drive.

Editing of oral history transcripts is done to prepare them for public use, eliminating elements (such as repetitive false starts and misstatement of names and locations) that are part and parcel of any conversation. False starts, for instance, may be understandable when listening to the spoken word but confusing and misleading when reduced to a page of printed words. Editing is usually accomplished on paper copies of the transcript to allow the editor (usually the interviewer) to have a sense of the appearance of the printed document that will eventually become the published version available for public use. The edits are then transferred to the electronic record.

There will be several printed copies in existence by the time the editing process is complete, each bearing evidence of alterations that will define the interview's transformation from spoken to printed document. Several of those paper edit copies will become important components of the archival record of each interview's creation.

The archival record of the oral history project should be structured to include three copies of each interview transcript. They are:

- the initial edit—usually performed by the interviewer
- the narrator's edit
- the final edit, contained in a copy of the printed/published transcript

Although the transcript may be subject to many other full and partial edits, the three listed above are the only ones necessary to retain in the permanent project file.

It is important to retain the initial edit because it records changes made in the original interview. This may include the removal of some false starts, repetitions, conversational idiosyncrasies ("you know"), and the insertion of a word here and there to clarify the narrator's intent. The record of the initial edit is thus a critical document, for it clearly delineates the ways in which the transcript has been altered for use.

The narrator's edit is equally important, for it reflects the interview subject's own clarifications, additions, spelling corrections, and other preferences. Retention of this document ensures that narrators' possible future concerns over transcript content can be matched directly with their written instructions.

Oral history project managers should bring some imagination to the work of producing finished transcripts, since they are often the most tangible, visible products of the interviews. Oral historians should never forget that, while they may be focused on gathering information and assembling it for use, each interview represents part of the narrator's life and experience. It thus becomes a highly personal document and one worthy of careful attention to its production.

At the Minnesota Historical Society, we regard transcripts as key products of each interview and every project. They are handsomely bound not only for permanence and to increase utility to users, but also as presentation copies to narrators and sponsors. The pleasure with which these are received on every occasion leaves no doubt of their importance in promoting the value of oral history and its significance. I well recall the family whose grandfather I interviewed about his experiences in business. Though the interview was no life history, it was a well-illustrated and articulate look at an aspect of his life less well known to family members. Shortly after he received a presentation copy, we received a request for one hundred additional copies for distribution to family members at Christmas. The scale of the order was a bit unusual, but not the intent. It was a reminder of the power of oral history to its subjects, a reality often overlooked by oral historians.

Video Log

If the project includes a video component, a video log should be compiled for all of the videotape footage. A video log is a scene-by-scene index to the videotape, without which its use is difficult. Video footage without a log is rather like audiotape without a transcript. It can only be accessed by those users willing to watch hours of tape in the hope of finding relevant images. If they do locate usable footage, they are then faced with the necessity of creating their own video logs to relocate footage they have already viewed.

Video footage will often have two components—an interview with a narrator and background footage filmed to illustrate or accompany the oral history interview. Options that should be considered in the creation of video oral history are covered in a separate section below.

The narrator's interview on video should be transcribed without editing. Users of the footage will need to know as closely as possible what is said. Even the dreaded "conversational idiosyncrasies" must be included, for this transcription is intended to facilitate use of videotape, not for research use.

The background footage will be logged scene by scene, with whatever detail is appropriate to guide users to the images they need. The log should briefly describe the scenes as they unfold but without overly involved description that will only confuse the users. A printout of the video log should be filed in the project file; the electronic copy should become part of the project documentation, stored safely on a central server.

Funding Proposal Text and Budget

If the oral history project received funding from outside the sponsoring institution, a copy of the funding proposal and budget should be retained in the project files. The proposal will include the project rationale, supporting data, a plan of work, time schedule, list of personnel, and information on the budget and its allocation. While the budget information may not be public, it and the proposal text are key documents that establish both purpose and procedure for the project. In doing so, they provide important evidence of the goals and objectives of the project interviews.

In addition to the funding proposal, periodic reports prepared as part of the project should also be included in the permanent files. These reports trace the realities of project operation, documenting plans that succeeded as well as those that were altered. The final report is of special importance, since it will summarize the work accomplished and evaluate, to some extent, success in achieving project goals.

Project Introduction

Every transcript in every project should include the same introduction, written to place that interview in the context of the project as a whole. It is critical that users understand that while project interviews stand as individual entities, they were created as part of a larger undertaking. That knowledge will help to explain the interview's focus on specific topics to the exclusion of others and the size and scope of the complete project. Regardless of which interview in a project is first accessed by a user, it should clearly communicate a sense of the project and its intent. A copy of the final introduction should be placed in the project file for future reference. Even though an electronic copy of the document will, of course, be retained on a secure server, the file copy will alert future users to its existence and provide against the possibility of damage to the electronic version.

Publicity

Many oral history projects will merit publicity on conclusion—and perhaps during their progress. Oral history is a popular form of documentation, and its immediate connection to real people creates numerous opportunities to present the project and its products to the public. Whether the publicity is a notice published in the scholarly press, a news article in a local newspaper, or a public event held to honor narrators and their families, all publicity should be retained for the project files. Such files would include the inevitable newspaper clippings, with the name of the publication and date carefully noted for posterity and hopefully copied to a medium more permanent than newsprint.

Promotional announcements, time schedules for public programs, news releases, and photographs will help to document events held to celebrate the completion of a project. At the Minnesota Historical Society, events held to celebrate the completion of projects are routinely photographed, with the images kept in the project files and used in reports, publicity, and public presentations.

Videotape as a Component of Oral History

The decision to include videotape in the production of oral history interviews brings additional considerations to the planning mix. From documentation of context to cataloging of both audio and videotapes to issues of preservation and use, video adds more than images to an oral history project.

The question of whether to videotape oral history interviews or not is debated during the planning stages of many oral history projects. The ubiquitous presence of video technology—and its rapid descent in both price and complexity—has made its relationship to oral history a major issue. Context is an especially important factor in the production of oral history with a video component, and preservation of an archival quality master tape is also a critical consideration.

Most oral history interviews do not contain a video component, despite the availability of equipment and the ease of its use. The majority of oral history interviews created today are recorded the old-fashioned way—on some tape medium, be it analog or digital. More about that debate a little later. Regardless of that fact, videotape has become the medium of choice for an increasing number of oral history interviews. Given that reality, it is useful to review the options available in its use.

Videotape is variously employed in oral history, sometimes to tape entire interviews as an adjunct to audiotaping, sometimes to incorporate illustration of a narrator's descriptions. Video provides significant opportunities and also has several drawbacks. Here is a brief discussion of both.

Pros

Video offers the viewer the opportunity to see the places or processes a narrator describes in an interview. For example, the use of video in the Minnesota Resort Industry Oral History Project allows users to virtually walk through the famous Bay Lake Lodge resort, admiring the panorama of water, trees, and wildlife as they go. When lodge owner Jack Ruttger describes the view of the lake and its effect on guests, researchers can see and admire it, too. And when another resort owner describes the new swimming pool that has become a major amenity, one can see and assess it through the medium of videotape. Video also offers increased opportunities for postinterview use of the visual images, which may be used alone or in concert with other images. Agricultural landscapes that form part of the Minnesota Farm Economy Oral History Project, for instance, have seen service in a variety of television productions.

Video also offers a tremendous advantage when interviewing craftspeople, for instance, whose work and the conditions under which it is produced are part of the story. Thomas L. Charlton explained: "Oral history interviewees who are, or have been, craftsmen find video recording to be far superior to audio recording when they are asked to tell of their life experiences."[7] Videotape is integral to an understanding of such Minnesota craftspeople as Ojibwe elder and beadworker Batiste Sam or the eminent carver of fish decoys John Jensen. It can also illuminate the work of such people as architects. The value of the Minnesota Historical Society's interview series with Vienna-born architect Elizabeth Close is greatly increased by video footage of some of the buildings designed by Close and her husband.

Cons

Video is expensive, both in terms of equipment and personnel. Moreover, videotape itself makes poor archival material because it is not permanent and it cannot be easily transcribed. Audiotapes must be dubbed from the videotape or recorded simultaneously and used for creating the transcript.

Video is also intrusive. Despite reduction in the size of video cameras, they remain much larger than audio recording equipment. And the presence of a videographer and a sound engineer, in addition to the interviewer, does not contribute a sense of intimacy to the interview. There is also the issue of quality. While handheld video cameras are readily available to consumers, few of them create images of the quality necessary to merit permanent preservation. Light and sound quality are key components of video oral history, and both require much more than the services of a single amateur armed with the best the local electronics outlet store has to offer. That best may be fine for recording family events, but it is seldom adequate for the permanent record oral history becomes. And it is almost never adequate to the multitude of uses to which oral history videotape may be put by future users. The major "cons" of videotaping may thus be summed up as expense and intrusion.

The legal realities of videotape must also be considered. As Charlton stated, "It may not be enough for oral historians to rest their cases on U.S. copyright law. Video recordings—with images that can be distorted, deliberately or inadvertently, and a potential for tape editing vastly more complex than that normally associated with audiotapes—may lead to legal proceedings fraught with danger for oral historians."[8] Quotation from an audiotape transcript is one thing; a narrator's video image, flashing across thousands of television screens in an instant, presents a distinctly different set of considerations.

Why Use Video in Oral History?

As with every other component of oral history, the use of video should be carefully reasoned and based upon the value it adds to the final product. Too often, video is adopted because it is there, rather than because it actually adds much information to the underlying oral history interviews.

Video is visual! That rather obvious fact is overlooked in the planning of many oral history projects that employ videotape. If the video footage offers little addition to the narrator's information, which can be captured perfectly well on audiotape, then video should not be employed. Endless footage of a narrator seated in a chair against a static background offers hardly any information or context that cannot be contained in several good photographs taken on the day of the interview.

Taking everything into account, the use of video should be undertaken only when it brings something unique to the project. The most thoughtful and appropriate process for creating video history is one I have dubbed the "Perlis Plan" in tribute to Vivian Perlis of Yale University. A pioneer in defining the use of video in oral history, Perlis discarded the idea of simply turning the camera on a seated narrator and letting the tape run. Instead, she correctly noted that what users wanted was to see the things the narrator described, or better still, to see the narrator doing something rather than talking about it. Video footage of a farmer using his land and showing the accommodations he has made to balance production and ecology, for example, offers a great deal of visual information to supplement the interview text.

A critical consideration in the production of video oral history is the fact that, especially with background or illustrative material, one is creating raw footage for possible future use. Unlike the details of audio- and videotape in which the narrator appears directly, background footage is created largely on the speculation that it will prove valuable to future users. It should be *informed* speculation, of course, based upon a genuine understanding of how such material is likely to be used in television and film production. If carefully produced, background footage may have residual value that outweighs that from the associated interviews. The Minnesota Historical Society has found that footage of dawn breaking over a northern lake, people settling in to campsites, and children playing in the headwaters of the Mississippi River have definite value to television production companies for whom the choice of sending a crew to create such images is far more expensive than licensing existing material.

These considerations are highly important when assessing both the value videotape may add to oral history and the archival and preservation realities that will be faced when the videotape—as well as the audiotape—finds its way into the permanent collection. Any video oral history program should be based upon a clearly defined statement of purpose, including principles such as:

1. To add a visual dimension to selected oral history interviews, with emphasis on providing visual information that enhances an audio interview with the same narrator.
2. To provide visual context for narrators and the subjects they discuss.
3. To build an archive of broadcast-quality videotape interviews and cover footage for research use.
4. To develop teaching aids from both interview and cover videotape footage that will provide instruction to participants in the society's oral history workshops and seminars.
5. To develop edited videotape segments that will heighten understanding of the oral history program by both the general public and potential funding agencies.

Before committing the resources necessary to produce high-quality video oral history, and the accompanying documentation, an oral history program director should answer the following questions:

1. What is the purpose of the video interview?
   a. Will it be part of a finished "program"?
   b. Will it mainly be for research and reference and typically viewed in its entirety?
   c. Why do you need moving images and visual elements?
   d. How does the purpose support the goals and objectives of your project or organization?
2. What is your budget? How can you make the most of it? Do you want to emphasize technical quality (best camera, best format) and good editing, or do you want to create the greatest number of interviews you can afford?
3. Who is the audience?
4. Where and how will the video be used? Where will the master be preserved?
5. Is video the correct medium (as opposed to slide/tape program or audio only interview)?

6. What visuals will add information and interest to the interview?
7. Where will the interview be taped (studio, home, office, outdoors)?
8. How will the video interview be made known and distributed?

Oral History and Preservation

No one wants to invest in oral history only to find that the chosen medium of the collection cannot be preserved for future use. An important goal of a project director is to ensure that the products of oral history, which represent the hard work of many people, are of archival quality, with both master and user copies stored suitably for long-term preservation and for public access. As Wallot and Fortier warn, "Over and above the requirements with respect to the environment and the handling of the tape . . . one must take into account the variety of recording formats, which are usually incompatible, and rapid technological change, particularly in the case of video recordings. Consequently, archives [may] have to constantly recopy documents in a common format, since it is hardly possible to maintain a complete inventory of playback and copying equipment."[9]

The permanent preservation of nearly any media presents a complex array of issues. The ways in which these issues are addressed are topics debated at great length among conservators, users, tape manufacturers, and those—like archivists—concerned with the realities of maintaining fragile media for the longest possible period of time.

Preservation of oral history media is also complicated by the continuing development of new and different recording media. Digital audiotape (DAT), recordable compact discs (CD-Rs), and minidiscs are only a few of the "new" media challenging oral historians and archivists. As always, newer is inevitably better to some, including to some oral historians whose greatest interest is in the immediate public use of tape recordings, rather than in long-term preservation. Since use can always be made of oral history interviews recorded on media suitable for preservation, that is the focus of the discussion in this chapter.

While the basics of tape preservation may be summarized for wide application, the nuances are complex, indeed, and subject to widely varying interpretations. This chapter cannot include an extended discussion of these nuances; it includes only a summary that will guide the producers and holders of oral history collections toward best practice.[10] Here, then, is a brief discussion of the basic considerations involved in the preservation of audio- and videotape.

Audiotape

Audiotape remains the most widely used medium for recording oral history interviews. Even when interviews are recorded on videotape, an audiotape recording of the interview should be made for preservation.

Format

Most oral history is recorded on analog audiotape. The taped interview represents the core product of every oral history interview. While the transcript, edited, bound, and attractively presented for public use, may be far more heavily used than the tape, it is the tape itself that represents the interview in its purest form. The master tapes must be carefully preserved, for they are the most faithful record of the interview as it happened.

That said, the interview must be conducted using the best audiotape available. As in many other aspects of real life, "best" does not always mean "most expensive." In fact, the more expensive high-bias audiotape developed for use in recording music does not offer any appreciable advantage over basic professional-grade audiotape.

The cassette tape with sixty minutes of recording time (thirty minutes on each side of the tape) is the standard recording and preservation medium. Master recordings on reel-to-reel tape should be retained in that format, with use copies provided on cassette tape.

The increasing popularity of DAT, CD-R, and other formats has created another challenge for oral historians and archivists. Despite the interest in these formats and their utility in certain instances, neither has supplanted professional-grade analog audiotape as the medium of choice for long-term preservation. And, given the reality that digital copies can easily be made from analog masters, there is no reason to gamble future preservation on formats without proven viability for the long term. Those charged with making the substantial investment necessary to create oral history interviews must take the safest route possible to ensure they exist in usable form in the future.

Storage

It does little good to use the best possible materials in the creation of oral history if the resulting tapes are stored in less than suitable conditions. Audiotape is susceptible to damage from such environmental problems as dirt, light, and excessive heat and humidity. Audiotape masters should be stored in a secure location, each standing upright on its edge and enclosed in an archival-quality box for safety and ease in shelving. Master storage should be in temperatures calibrated to a steady forty to fifty degrees Fahrenheit, with humidity maintained in the range of 20–30 percent. Audiotape copies intended for ready use should be stored on edge in containers, with temperatures of sixty-five to seventy degrees Fahrenheit and a humidity of 45–50 percent. Master copies should never be used except to strike further use copies if those are damaged.

Videotape

The attraction of videotape in the production of oral history has grown rapidly in recent years. As video recording equipment has become less awkward and space consuming, and as the image quality has improved, the opportunity to create moving images as part of oral history has been taken by many oral historians. While hardly appropriate for all interviews, videotape does offer downstream user values that may balance its considerable cost, storage requirements, and difficulties as a preservation medium.

Format

Most oral history videotape is created using analog tape in one of the variations of VHS or in Betacam-SP. VHS is by far the most widely utilized, though it is not appropriate for long-term preservation. If it must be used in creating the master tape, the S-VHS format is preferable to lower-quality VHS varieties. It should be kept in mind, however, that VHS was not developed with preservation in mind. It is a highly flexible and widely viewable format for dissemination of images for public use, but it is not designed for archival use.

The major investment in creating video oral history, however, is best made in the highest archival-quality videotape available. Betacam-SP continues to fill that place despite fears that it, like so many other formats, will be superseded by others. It remains widely available, though the recording equipment necessary to produce the finest product is both expensive and complex. The video history program of the Minnesota Historical Society's Oral History Office has used Betacam-SP since its inception in 1984. The use of contract videographers ensures that the recording equipment used is of very high quality, without the necessity of an institutional commitment to acquire and continually upgrade such equipment. In addition to its value as an important analog video format of archival quality, Betacam-SP has other advantages. Its excellent quality ensures that duplicate copies made for public use on VHS tape will have far greater visual quality than copies made from VHS masters. Commercial use of video oral history is also far more likely when users find they can edit from a duplicate Beta-SP master.

Digital videotape is also available, of course, and may be preferred by users who fear the obsolescence of analog tape or who believe a digital format offers them more production options. Not all digital videotape is of archival quality, however, and tape created using the process known as compression is never of archival quality for long-term preservation.

Storage

As with audiotape, videotape is susceptible to damage from dirt, light, and excessive heat and humidity. Long-term storage conditions should be stabilized at around fifty degrees Fahrenheit and 20–50 percent relative humidity. Tapes should be housed in protective casings (they are usually purchased in plastic or paper cases) and shelved on edge.

Preparing Oral History for Use

As has been stated many times, oral history is created for use. Whether and how it is used is in part dependent upon the way in which access to the interviews is created. For years, oral history has been catalogued as a library material, though without the guidelines that standardize access to books, serials, photographs, and other documents. The result is a perplexing variety of cataloging conventions, often jerry-built by librarians and archivists trying to fit oral history into classification systems ill suited to its particular needs.

The difficulties evident in finding and using oral history interviews have been noted for years. In part, this situation has been exacerbated by the fact, identified by Bruce Bruemmer, that "oral historians are producers, not curators. Most of their work is developed as a means to a final product, whether it be a book, an article, a motion picture, or a public-relations device. Understandably, when the final product is completed, there is little incentive to follow-up interviews with tedious editing, abstracting, and cataloging."[11] The problem was also deepened by the fact that to many of those archivists and librarians who control the cataloging—and thus the access—to material in their collections, oral history seemed, as Bruemmer states it, rather like "the occasional odd-sized document that is left on the accession shelf because it is difficult to catalog."[12]

For years, much oral history languished in limbo—uncataloged and thus unfindable, or forced into cataloging conventions that obscured its content and value. This reality attracted only sporadic attention from oral historians, who often seemed unaware of the problem and indifferent to its solution. In 1990, however, a concerted effort was mounted by a small group of oral historians, archivists, and librarians aware of the dangers of continued inattention to the issue of public access. The effort received further impetus at the 1991 annual meeting of the Society of American Archivists, when this group met and issued a public call for action. Shortly thereafter, led by former Oral History Association presidents Lila Goff, Dale Treleven, and Kim Lady Smith, they acquired a grant from the National Historical Publications and Records Commission to address the issue of access to oral history by creating a cataloging system anyone could use.

The result of this effort was the groundbreaking *Oral History Cataloging Manual*, published in 1995 by the Society of American Archivists. It has become the basic reference in the field and has instituted an oral history cataloging standard that has greatly increased the visibility and accessibility of oral history wherever it is used. The manual's principal author, Marion Matters, expressed quite clearly the thought behind the successful construction of a framework for the cataloging of oral history: "Because of the affinities between oral history materials and archival records, this manual is based heavily on the archival approach to cataloging. Archival cataloging is characterized by its focus on the context in which materials were created (their provenance) as much as on their content or physical characteristics. It is also characterized by collective description; that is, the description of groups of materials related by provenance. Archival (and oral history) descriptions are created by supplying information extracted from various sources, rather than transcribing information from a chief source of information such as a title page, label, or screen."[13]

While the *Oral History Cataloging Manual* has made it possible for oral histories to be presented for public use in a standardized fashion, the basics of preparing them for cataloging remain. Interviews must still be assigned accession and catalog numbers, labeled (both master tapes and public-use copies), and shelved. In addition, the transcripts must also be prepared and cataloged, since they are likely to receive far more use than the tapes ever will.

Oral History and the Internet

To anyone concerned about the use of oral history, the Internet offers a dazzling array of possibilities. Access is worldwide and virtually immediate, connecting users to resources with only a few clicks of a computer mouse or touch pad. The standardized cataloging formats provided by the *Oral History Cataloging Manual* are especially important in this environment, for they standardize the appearance and terminology so important to the search engines (such as Google and Yahoo) that deliver resources to users through the World Wide Web.

The increasing use of Web site access to the catalogs of libraries and archives has sealed the fate of published catalogs of oral history collections. While some may still be printed for the purpose of promoting a particular collection to its immediate community and supporters, published catalogs are virtually irrelevant to the Internet generation. Printed catalogs are usually out of date before they are printed, and the number of users they can deliver to library and archival resources is miniscule compared to the international audience available through the Internet.

Nothing Is Perfect: Internet Concerns for Oral Historians

While Internet access offers remarkable opportunities to increase the visibility and use of oral history interviews, those opportunities are not without parallel concerns. Chief among these are the twin issues of copyright and privacy.

Copyright

Copyright in most oral history interviews is held by the institution that sponsored them. As noted earlier, copyright is formally dealt with in the contract between the narrator and the institution that establishes the legal status of each interview.

While access to the information contained in oral histories is a key objective of their creators, absolute access cannot be created without assessing its consequences. Internet access to most oral history interviews consists of access to the catalog summary of interviews and projects created during the cataloging process. The summaries contain contextual information on projects and individual interviews, describing the objectives for which they were created and listing the narrators by name. Each interview may also be summarized to create another level of information.

The full text of oral history interview transcripts can easily be made available. Most interviews created in the last fifteen years have been transcribed using one or another word processing program (such as Microsoft Word or WordPerfect), and are thus already in electronic format. Despite this fact, most oral history transcripts are not available through Internet access to the catalog Web sites of libraries and archives. The admittedly great opportunity to create worldwide access to individual oral history transcripts has largely been rejected for reasons of control and copyright.

In subscribing to these concerns, the administrators of most oral history collections have adopted the stance of book publishers in refusing to make their products available without the certainty of copyright protection. While this concern is likely to be addressed in the future, reluctance to place the full text of interview transcripts on Web sites accessible to anyone at any time is likely to inhibit any such move by the institutions holding the largest and most important oral history collections. Control of a resource created at considerable expense and with painstaking care is not something relinquished with much ease.

Privacy

Linked to issues involving copyright are those concerning privacy. Oral history interviews represent close and personal relationships between interviewers, narrators, and sponsoring institutions. This relationship is taken seriously by all parties. Interviewers feel a sense of obligation to the people who have allowed them to create a record of their feelings and perspectives. Narrators feel an inevitable connection to stories that are very much their own. Institutions have a vested interest in ensuring the maintenance of good relations with those who trust them with the responsible management of the interviews they create.

The interlocking interests shared by interviewers, narrators, and institutions inevitably affect the use of oral history interviews. Many institutions do not allow unrestricted copying of either tapes or complete transcripts, and thus the uninhibited use of transcript text possible through the Internet is not always attractive. The concept of worldwide access to text is alluring; the reality offers pause for consideration. It is one thing to make transcripts available to researchers who must appear in a library or archives, or request interlibrary loan, to gain access. It is quite another thing to make full text of those same interviews available without restriction to distant, faceless users who may be anywhere, at any time.

Privacy concerns extend even to the personal information on narrators provided as part of the summary data in catalog records. Once limited to on-site use in controlled situations, the magic of the Internet makes this information available to a wide audience that may contain far more curiosity seekers and commercial users than traditional researchers. In an age beset by increasing concerns over identity theft and Internet snooping, institutions providing public access to their collections via the Internet must be aware of the realities they confront. These considerations have already led many institutions to limit the personal information provided in interview summaries. To be "Google-stalked," as one narrator phrased it, is not a pleasant experience, nor can an institution escape responsibility for providing personal information without carefully considering the risks involved.

Solution

The ability to use the Internet to make oral history transcripts (and sound and images) available worldwide is already at hand. Oral historians, archivists, and librarians continue to be frustrated by issues of copyright and privacy that remain obstacles to harnessing that potential. Sooner rather than later, it will surely be possible to make full text of oral history transcripts available through institutional Web sites without the risks of unauthorized use. Once these risks can be controlled, the remarkable reality of full-text word searching across a whole project of interview transcripts will be realized. Then the value of investments in oral history will be much more apparent as wide public use results from greatly increased access.

Conclusion

The lasting value of oral history interviews can be realized only if they are carefully preserved, made available for wide and easy use, and supported by records that faithfully document the context within which they were created. The costs of creating oral history have frequently been exaggerated, but they are real and considerable. Those costs can only be justified if the resulting product is treated with the same care and respect accorded other records of permanent value.

Treating oral history tapes and transcripts as documents with enduring value also ensures that the narrators—without whom there would be no oral history—are treated with similar respect. The power of oral history is often noted by proponents; that power is only evident in interviews that can be found and used.

The more widely oral history is known and used, the more important will be the record of its creation. Ensuring that such records are created and maintained is a key responsibility of every oral historian.

Notes

1. Wallot and Fortier, "Archival Science," 371.
2. Nesmith, "Taylor's Contextual Idea," 16.
3. Wallot and Fortier, "Archival Science," 372.
4. Fogerty, "Filling the Gap," 151.
5. Wallot and Fortier, "Archival Science," 371.
6. For more on these projects, see Minnesota Historical Society, Oral History Collection, http://www.mnhs.org/collections/oralhistory/oralhistory.htm (accessed January 30, 2005).
7. Charlton, "Videotaped Oral Histories," 232.
8. Ibid., 235.
9. Wallot and Fortier, "Archival Science," 373.
10. For more information on this topic, see, in addition to other references cited in this article, Child, *Information Sources*; Fogerty, "Oral History as a Tool"; Ritchie, *Doing Oral History*; and Van Bogart, *Magnetic Tape*. Several Web sites contain excellent summary information on audiotape and videotape preservation and provide links to other sources. See, for example, Association of Moving Image Archivists, http://www.amianet.org (accessed February 1, 2005);

Stanford University Libraries, Preservation Department, Cool: Conservation OnLine, Resources for Conservation Professionals, http://palimpsest.Stanford .edu (accessed February 1, 2005); and Library of Congress, "Cylinder, Disc and Tape Care in a Nutshell," http://www.lcweb.loc.gov/preserv/care/record .html (accessed February 1, 2005).

11. Bruemmer, "Access," 495.

12. Ibid.

13. Matters, *Cataloging Manual*, 1.

7

The Uneasy Page: Transcribing and Editing Oral History

Elinor A. Mazé

Speech is the best show man puts on.

—Benjamin Whorf

Speech is somatic, a bodily function, and it is accompanied by physical inflections—tone of voice, winks, smiles, raised eyebrows, hand gestures—that are not reproducible in writing. Spoken language is repetitive, fragmentary, contradictory, limited in vocabulary, loaded down with space holders. . . . And yet people can generally make themselves understood right away. As a medium, writing is a million times weaker than speech. It's a hieroglyph competing with a symphony.

—Louis Menand, *New Yorker*

The transcript has been a part of oral history practice in the United States from the beginning. In the beginning, the transcript was the only record of an interview to survive, to be archived, preserved, and made accessible for study. Of Allan Nevins's inaugural program, launched in 1948 as the Oral History Research Office at Columbia University, Alice Kessler-Harris wrote, "Except for a small fragment of the original interview, intended to illustrate the subject's voice and style, tapes of the interviews were erased. The written transcript was considered sufficient information."[1] Nevins's first interviews, in fact, were done without benefit of an electronic recording device, according to Louis Starr, Nevins's successor at Columbia; a graduate student sat by taking notes as Nevins and his interviewees conversed.[2] These transcripts, rough drafts typed from the student's handwritten notes, are what remains of what many consider to be the beginning of modern oral history.

Created before the advent of accessible recording technology, the antecedents of oral history were, necessarily, written transcripts. Among these early antecedents are the extensive interviews with former slaves conducted and transcribed by John B. Cade at Southern University and Prairie View State College and by Ophelia Settle at Fisk University, beginning in 1929.[3] The Federal Writers' Project continued this work during the 1930s, transcribing interviews with thousands of "ordinary" representatives of everyday America. This early work was not called oral history, but the transcribed interviews—deposited in the Library of Congress and now accessible via the World Wide Web[4]—are considered by many oral historians to be the most important twentieth-century antecedents of modern oral history.

Earlier examples of verbatim transcripts of interviews for historical purposes are the "Dictations" of Hubert Howe Bancroft. Transcriptions of hundreds of interviews with pioneers in the American West are now in the archives of the Bancroft Library at the University of California at Berkeley.[5] Bancroft—or members of his staff—conducted most of the interviews in the late 1880s. A few years earlier, Lyman Copeland Draper, secretary of the Wisconsin Historical Society, labored hard to transcribe his interviews with individuals he considered to be of historical importance, among them Daniel Boone's son, Nathan.[6] These early practitioners considered it worthwhile to record more or less verbatim, as best they could with pen, paper, and memory, the words of their informants. The choices they made as they created their transcripts, choices concerning transcription of idiolect and dialect, choices of omission and inclusion, choices of style and historical or contextual comment, were not yet matters of scholarly debate. When recording interviews for historiographic purposes became the discipline of oral history,

whether and how to transcribe the recordings becam
perennial concern.

Should oral history interviews be transcribed
practical point of view, for most historians, the argument is top
sidedly in favor of creating transcripts whenever possible. In
2001, Carl Wilmsen wrote, "Interview tapes are transcribed for
three major reasons: to enhance the ease of use of the interview,
to render it more readily accessible to a variety of audiences, and
since paper has a longer shelf life than magnetic and digital media, to increase its longevity in an archive."[7] By 1977, Starr had
already declared the debate to be nearly over, "because of the
overwhelming preference of users for transcripts, calls for which
exceed calls for tape in some of the larger oral history collections
by ratios of a thousand to one and higher. . . . Tapes, no matter
how carefully indexed, are awkward to use."[8] A year later, David
Lance wrote, "Given that the average speed of reading is about
three times as fast as the average rate of speaking . . . the value
and importance of the transcript obviously lies in the convenience of access it permits."[9] In 1997, Tracy K'Meyer asked oral
historian Willa K. Baum, "What would you say if someone asked
the question, 'Why not just leave things in tape form?'" Baum
replied, "It's an easy answer. Nobody would use them."[10] Donald Ritchie has reiterated the point in the 2003 edition of his comprehensive guide to oral history: "Given a choice, researchers
invariably prefer transcripts over tapes. Eyes can read easier
than ears can hear. . . . Archivists note that very few researchers
ask to listen to the tapes if transcripts are available."[11]

Manuals of oral history practice have likewise generally ad-
vocated transcription whenever resources permit.[12] The convenience of the printed page and its relatively unmediated
accessibility—for literate researchers, at least—are the reasons
most often cited. There are other reasons, as well. David Henige
wrote, "Whenever the historian transcribes oral materials the
very act of transcription enhances his grasp of their content."[13]
Dennis Tedlock also made this point, adding, "It should be done
while the interview is still fresh in [the interviewer's] mind so
that he can provide such details as might not be clear from the
tape alone, such as gestures."[14] Henige and Tedlock both urged
interviewers to do the transcription themselves, a practice that

may actually be uncommon, at least in larger institutional oral history programs. Nonetheless, Henige's advice, if extended to include a careful reading of the transcript, is still sound in the opinion of many: "Whenever possible, and every effort should be made to render it possible, each interview or small group of interviews should be transcribed almost as soon as (and certainly within a few days [of when]) they have been conducted. The variable and dynamic aspects of oral research—the living sources—make this procedure absolutely imperative because it is really the only way the historian can detect new areas of discussion or different points of view, as well as anomalies, contradictions, and textual uncertainties that he will need to follow up."[15] Thad Sitton, George Mehaffy, and O. L. Davis wrote concerning oral history projects for young students that "the majority of projects require interviewers to transcribe their own tapes. Students who listen to their own interviews will naturally become more proficient interviewers; the evidence is clear on that." Further, they pointed out, the benefits of transcribing cut across the curriculum: "The student must transcribe the material and struggle with the problem of ordering the oral testimony by punctuation and paragraph. A better inquiry lesson into the practical usefulness of such formal structures can scarcely be devised!"[16] A recent posting to the H-Oralhist discussion echoed this point: "It always astounds me how much richer the interview is when listening to it piece by piece in the transcription process. It's impossible to 'hear' all the subtleties when doing the actual interview, when we interviewers are so focused on questions, keeping the process moving along, monitoring equipment, etc."[17] Separate, then, from the question of the value and meaning of the transcript as an archived text is the notion that the act of transcribing is valuable as it forces close, attentive listening to the recording. From such careful listening should come better scholarship and written or performed works more faithful in understanding and interpretation to the original oral dialogue.

Even when recordings remain the main object of study, the transcript can provide a very helpful guide to the audio record. On the Library of Congress Web site announcing the availability of recordings of interviews with former slaves, it is noted that "those recordings that suffer from poor audio quality have gaps in their transcriptions, but even in those cases, the transcriptions are a useful tool for following and understanding the interviews."[18]

Oral historians in the United States have insisted on transcription, and many consider the transcript to be a primary source, equal for research purposes to the audio recording from which it was made. Canadians, among others, have taken a different view. Writing about the source of differences between Canadian and U.S. practice in oral history, Richard Lochead cited the Canadian Broadcasting Company (CBC) as a major determining force. The CBC had, after World War II, a "cultural mandate to try to seek out and find the Canadian identity and express it wherever it was found."[19] The CBC collected untranscribed tapes and deposited them in Canada's national archives, and Lochead attributed Canadian oral historians' insistence on the primacy of the audio recording to that which became Canadian national archival practice. The Canadian Oral History Association states the matter on its Web site: "Oral history, therefore, refers to recorded interviews with individuals about the past, or first-person reminiscences. The primary form of the oral history document is the recorded human voice. This document, in turn, may be applied as informational source material or directly in sound or transcribed form."[20] Likewise, a browse through the online catalog of oral histories at the British Library Sound Archive[21] suggests that, in that collection at least, the sound recordings are preeminent. When they exist, transcripts are noted in the catalog records as "documentation," suggesting that the transcripts are considered to be guides to the primary audio source.

Oral history practice with respect to transcription thus varies around the world, and debate about it continues. The debate extends beyond practical matters of processing and managing oral histories. It engages historians in questions about the theoretical foundations of oral historiography, the ethics of accessibility, and standards of preservation.

The question at once most vexing and most interesting is, What becomes of the spoken word when it is written down? The question has been considered from several points of view and within various disciplines. Linguists, psychologists, ethnographers, and philosophers have all studied the consequences of literacy, and oral historians have used research from these fields as they formulated their own theories and practices. The relationship between the oral history interview—the interpersonal event itself—and the printed transcription of it has been scrutinized and debated in every decade since the 1940s. There has evolved no consensus that "the transcript is nothing more and nothing less than the whole truth of what was spoken during that interview."[22]

In a 1984 commentary in the *Oral History Review*, David Dunaway wrote, "What do we do when we transcribe? 'Turn tape into type' is one uncomplicated answer. But even verbatim transcription (if possible) and careful notes cannot re-create the history-telling interview. . . . The oral interview is a multilayered communicative event, which a transcript only palely reflects."[23] The point has been made by many oral historians. In *The Death of Luigi Trastulli and Other Stories*, Alessandro Portelli wrote, "Even if we tried to print interviews in their entirety, we would end up with lengthy and almost unreadable texts (in which the mechanical fidelity of transcriptions thinly veils the qualitative betrayal of turning beautiful speech into unreadable writing); and we would be turning oral into written discourse anyway, which is no minor interference."[24]

In his 1994 book, *The World on Paper: The Conceptual and Cognitive Implications of Writing and Reading*, David Olson put the matter this way:

> No writing system, including the alphabet, brings all aspects of what is said into awareness. . . . Even scripts such as the alphabet, which may be taken as representing the verbal form of an expression, fail to provide an explicit representation for the illocutionary force of an utterance. To the extent that they transcribe *what* was said, they fail to transcribe *how* it was said, and with it the indicators of how the speaker intended for the listener to take what was said. What is lost in the act of transcription is precisely what is so difficult to recover in the act of reading, namely, how the expression is to be taken. . . . Even modern readers and writers have difficulty recognizing that texts, no matter how well written, never provide more than an indication of a speaker's or writer's audience-directed intention. Alphabetic scripts represent verbal form, what was

said, not the attitude of the speaker to that verbal form, what was meant by it.[25]

Olson has been taken to task for his "unfalsifiable idealizing of spoken discourse" and his implicit assumption that there is "some magical nonspoken access" to a speaker's meanings.[26] It is certainly true that divining authorial intention is viewed as a murky and fruitless venture by many modern critics. Olson's point about the "illocutionary force" of spoken language is important, nonetheless. An interviewee's innermost intentions—certainly complex and perhaps at least partly nonverbal—may not be accessible to either listeners or readers, but the former have more to go on in their interpretive efforts. The oral history interview begins not as a composed text but as an interpersonal event, a conversation, a dual performance, created not only with spoken words but with gesture, silence, intonation, rhythm, volume, accent, and dozens of other elements of expression that convey meaning during the event but that are utterly lost—"locked out," in Dunaway's words[27]—in the transcript, and that even an audio recording is inadequate to preserve. Beyond the dozens of ways in which words can be said, each way conveying a different meaning, there are the interpersonal and situational currents that shape the speaking, currents that are palpable to those present, even to those seeing a video or hearing an audio recording, but completely missing from the printed page. "Spoken words," wrote Walter Ong, "are always modifications of a total situation which is more than verbal."[28] How much more, then, is the transcript a modification of the more-than-verbal "situation" of the oral history interview. Elizabeth Tonkin warned that researchers "have not been taught to consider that interviews are oral genres." Considering the many illocutionary aspects of speaking, Tonkin concluded, "Transcription of oral accounts . . . is not just a problem, it is, properly speaking, impossible."[29] The difficulty for oral historians lies in the fact that transcriptions of spoken words and texts that begin life as writing, deliberately composed and intended to be read, are fundamentally different genres, but the production of a printed text in the end in both cases blurs the distinction. Writing in 1970, Gould Colman was sanguine about the communicative power of the transcript when he argued, "What we are engaged in is the most valid form of historical documentation that exists. . . . What are we documenting? . . . Of course, what we are documenting is the interaction that occurs between interviewer and respondent. Our document is a record of that interaction. If we keep the tape recorder going, and if we don't mess it up by editing, we can turn out a verbatim transcript which is far more valid than other primary source material."[30] Such optimism about the transcript is probably shared by few oral historians today, even though transcribing is standard practice in most projects and reliance on transcripts for research is still widespread.

For methods of writing transcripts to preserve more of what is lost, oral historians have turned to scholars in other fields. Linguists, anthropologists, ethnographers, and others have invented orthographic systems to represent the nonverbal aspects of speech—the many kinds of laughter, facial expressions, and intonation, for example—that can make such a critical difference between what a speaker conveys as he or she speaks and what a reader understands. Workers in the field of discourse analysis have developed several schemes of notation to serve a wide range of research and therapeutic endeavors.[31] Reflecting on the possible usefulness of discourse analysis methods for transcribing oral history interviews, Michael Agar wrote, "Discourse analysis is a powerful analytic tool for the transcribed interview, as useful to oral historians and ethnographers as it is to any other group with an interest in texts."[32] The transcription methods used in discourse analysis include various symbols and coding systems to represent inflection, intonation, pauses, and other aspects of communication not represented by typing out spoken words alone. Oral historian Dennis Tedlock developed a simpler system of notation to convey more of the nonlexical, nonsyntactical aspects of speech, more of what he considered the poetical qualities of oral history. Tedlock's system used ordinary typographical features such as boldface fonts, capitalization, indentation, and line spacing to represent variations in volume, rhythm, and other aspects of speech.[33] Reviewing Tedlock's work, Tonkin noted that "even this visually suggestive transposition does not of itself render pronunciation features, such as the 'accent' which in Britain is such a socially significant part of speech performance."[34]

Tedlock and Agar may be right that using specialized ortho-graphic systems would be useful to oral historians. But many oral historians have been wary of these systems. Portelli demon-strated the effect of typographic style on the meaning of a tran-scribed passage. Centered on the page, each line with an initial capital, his sample text "hesitates between historical statement, epic poem, and monument; the way readers understand it de-pends to a large extent on the historian's decision to transcribe it, respectively, as linear prose, verse, or epigraph."[35] The complex-ities and dangers of special transcription lead many oral histori-ans to espouse a view expressed by Francis Good. "In the end," wrote Good, "those wishing to move over the border into disci-plines involving such elements as conversational analysis would be wise to go back to the sound record. It is simply unrealistic to believe it is possible to capture much of the important informa-tion conveyed in speech mannerisms that is missing in conven-tional print transcripts."[36] Specialized orthographic systems are tools for research and analysis, not primary documents, mostly because they remove the transcription to a rarified realm acces-sible only to a very small number of specially trained researchers, among whom number few oral historians or inter-viewees. It would, in other words, do the opposite of what many oral historians intend to do, which is to make of oral history an account that belongs to the people, to the tellers and their peers, an account as accessible and meaningful to them as to scholars piecing together wider contexts.[37]

Another problem presented by transcription is that in some cultures—especially but not exclusively in literate and bureau-cratic ones—the creation of a printed document can convey an au-thority upon a narrative that it does not possess in spoken form. In a passage often quoted by proponents of oral history tran-scription, Ong wrote, "Nothing is more evanescent than sound, which has its being only while it is in process of perishing. *Verba Volant, scripta manent.* If sound is metamorphosed or reduced to spatial equivalents by writing, the resulting product has, if not eternal duration, at least a repose which suggests imperishable-ness."[38] As Portelli put it, "Especially after being transcribed—thus acquiring the supposed objectivity of 'documents'—words can be detached from their context and used independently of the original intention."[39] Ong's comments about the permanence of writing overlook the importance of audio and video recording, of course, which can offer an equal illusion of imperishability to sound and sight. There is no doubt, however, that the oral history interview, metamorphosed into a written transcript, a printed text, bound, deposited in a library or archive, and cataloged, acquires an aura of imperishable authority that the extemporaneous interview event did not have.

One way of understanding the difference in significance between the spoken and printed words of an interview is viewing it as a matter not only of how the transcript is written, but also of how it is read. As Olson put it, "Conceptual implications arise from the *ways of reading*, for it is the art of reading which allows a text to be taken as a model for verbal form, that is, for 'what is said.' These models of what is said, whether as sounds, words or sentences, are always incomplete, giving rise to problems of interpretation."[40] It is important to remember, then, that transcripts are created for many kinds of readers. Oral historians, interviewees and their families and community members, and scholars from many academic disciplines, all differ in their interpretive sophistication and critical experience, their attitudes toward printed texts, and their ability and willingness, Olson argued, "to infer those aspects of meaning which are not represented graphically at all" in those texts.[41] Generalizing the implications of these differences is hazardous at best, and the hazards give rise to continuing debate about what oral history is and what form it should take.

Another of the important aspects of a written text is its authorship. As Michel Foucault pointed out, for Western literate culture, attribution of authorship is crucial to how texts are read; authorship imposes a "principle of thrift in the proliferation of meaning."[42] If transcription conveys permanence and authority upon an oral history memoir, the question of authorship acquires even greater importance. Whose name goes on the title page of an oral history transcript? Whose name is the main heading for the transcript in a library catalog? Kathryn Marie Dudley wrote, "The production of oral testimony is always a collaborative, dialogic, jointly orchestrated affair. Out of this social interaction emerges a document of which it can rightly be said that the author function is up for grabs. . . . What gives the author function its critical edge in oral history and ethnography is the fact that no one 'authors' the texts we produce, yet the truth conditions of our discourse require that *someone* step forward to claim that authorship, with all the legal, political and moral ramifications it entails."[43] If the interview is most productively understood as a dialogic event, formed by the narrative strategies of both the interviewer and the interviewee, then any archived representation of that event must somehow grant equal authorship to those on all sides of the microphone. A hardbound transcript, with author and title lettered on the spine and a set of entries in a library catalog, grants immutable stature to the version of the text between the covers and to the authorship attribution required for conventional archival handling.

The question is, therefore, how different is this acquired immutability—if not authority—for the transcriptions compared to the audio or video recordings? Hayden White wrote, summarizing Foucault, "Any given mode of discourse is identifiable, then, not by what it permits consciousness to *say* about the world, but by what it prohibits it from saying, the area of experience that the linguistic act itself cuts off from representation in language."[44] Is it possible that the immensely fuller record of the interview afforded by audio or video media, which capture so much more of the communicative gestures of body and voice that the transcript omits, preserves more of what Foucault claims the linguistic act represses? It might be argued that the linguistic act alone—the words alone, spoken or written—has repressive power that can be loosened to some extent by preservation of more of the performance features of that linguistic act through audio and visual media. If so, the transcript is not adequate. But the preference for it will persist, certainly as long as historical inquiry and the universe of scholarship exists primarily in print. There is no sign that this will soon change. Scholars may claim that the worlds of thought and culture themselves are radically changed by the ubiquity of audio and visual media; the cases for these claims are still made and critiqued in writing.

Explorers, missionaries, anthropologists, ethnographers, and folklorists have long been engaged in the documenting, preserving, and understanding of oral traditions and cultures of people whose most important narratives are not written. In recent decades, oral historians have been involved in these activities as well, and there have been many discussions about the appropriateness of oral history techniques—including transcription—for those tasks. Consideration of the survival of meaning in oral traditions—storytelling, ritual, narrative performances—when they are committed to written texts also informs the debate about the nature and validity of any transcription of speech, including that of the highly literate.

As Tonkin stated, "Features of delivery—voice quality, chanting or singing, accompanying music or dancing, the type of occasion on which a performance occurs and the place, the status of the performer and the nature of the audience itself—all these can be criterial features of an oral genre, as they prepare the audience to respond in certain ways. The oral conditions of performance mean too that oral genres are actively 'dialogic': they are social activities in real time."[45] Tonkin's work examines oral narratives and demonstrates how they blur distinctions between performance, ritual, art, history, and literature. They are oral, and they may recount a people's notion about the past, but the occasion of their telling is a complex matter, crucial to their meaning. These stories are bound to be misconstrued if they are not somehow transmitted inseparably with the facts of that occasion. William Schneider put the matter this way:

> Years ago, Alan Dundes (1964) pointed out that stories contain at least three elements: text—what the story is about; texture—the way the story is told; and context—the circumstances surrounding the telling. . . . These considerations have become basic to our understanding of oral literature and the verbal arts, terms which are often used interchangeably but carry slightly different emphases. . . . Taken together, the terms point to the hallmarks of oral tradition. It is creative and personal, but it is also structured and experienced by a group of people who share a basic understanding of the way stories are told and how to comprehend their meaning.
>
> This tension between structure, creativity, and meaning is easily lost in oral recordings, which are made at one point in time and passed on to an audience of people who don't know the speaker or his or her culture. This dilemma challenges us

to ask: What have we captured on tape and what eludes us on the machine but is integral to the telling?[46]

If, as Schneider contended, much that is crucial to understanding is missing from audio (or video) recordings, certainly much more is missing from the transcription. Can a transcription convey anything reliably meaningful about what happens in an oral performance? From studies among Alaskan and Yukon cultures, Schneider and fellow researcher Phyllis Morrow deduced, "Oral tradition is negotiated, performative, and interpretive. It cannot be captured." Furthermore, they concluded:

> Oral tradition is less about tellers and texts than about relationships. . . . It is people's relationships with each other and their experiences that prompt all telling, remembering, and hearing. Because oral traditions live when they are told, preserving texts on paper . . . does nothing to maintain the relationships through which the cultural processes we term traditions are enacted. Because oral traditions are only told when they live, as the relationships among the people that tell and hear them change, so do the symbolic forms with which they make meaning. . . . There are no meanings without meaning makers. . . . What we can reconstruct or infer from their structure at best lacks warmth and subtlety and at worst gives us a false sense of accomplishment.[47]

How to transmit occasion is the challenge for scholars—oral historians, among others—who wish to preserve these oral events for present and future study. In Schneider's view, "Oral history is both the act of recording and the record that is produced."[48] Concerning storytelling performance, anthropologist Ruth Finnegan wrote, "Oral literature is by definition dependent on a performer who formulates it in words on a specific occasion."[49] This can inform our understanding of present-day oral cultures, cultures where the meaning of stories told depends upon the familial or tribal relationships of tellers and listeners and the occasions of their telling. A story meant for ritual recounting, a performance by an authorized person in a traditional context, becomes a different thing when recorded by an outsider and even stranger a thing when it is transcribed and deposited in an archive. Oral historians must ask, then, what the transcript means to the story-teller and to readers removed in time and location from the telling. Can a scholar retrieve from it anything useful for an understanding of the people from whom it was taken?

Many have grappled with the problem of understanding the role of literacy in predominantly oral cultures. Even at the outset of such considerations, defining literacy is problematic. "On the most simple level," wrote Isabel Hofmeyr, "reading and writing . . . do not automatically go together and each can be disaggregated into a range of subsidiary skills and activities."[50] All varieties of literacy influence in various ways an interviewee's way of speaking and attitude toward the occasion and toward the transcript, the written record of that speaking. Echoing the opinion of Ruth Finnegan, Hofmeyr noted that "universal claims about the cognitive consequences of writing . . . rarely hold true for a variety of contexts. . . . Instead, . . . one should be as specific as possible by spelling out the effects of literacy on orality in particular situations."[51] Deborah Tannen argued for acknowledgment that "orality and literacy are not mutually exclusive. Rather, they are complex and intertwined dimensions, the understanding of which enriches and enables our understanding of language." Tannen based her view in part on a "close analysis of tape-recorded, transcribed casual conversations" among New York Jewish speakers, a group her study found to be both highly oral and highly literate.[52] Greg Sarris, reflecting on his experiences with American Indian storytellers, wrote, "In oral discourse the context of orality covers the personal territory of those involved in the exchange, and because the territory is so wide . . . no single party has access to the whole of the exchange. One party may write a story, but one party's story is no more the whole story than a cup of water is the river."[53] The context, the audience, and the occasion are everything in traditional oral recitations. In the role of archive creator, the oral historian faces the challenge to preserve the sources in their most original form and to place these on public deposit. The role of transcription, and often of translation, is important if the world beyond narrow borders is to know something of what has been gathered, but the possibilities of misinterpretation are many when the performance is committed to the printed page.

Another of the challenges of transcribing is how—or whether—to render speakers' dialect, idiolect, or both on the printed page. In a 1937 note to interviewers in the Federal Writers' Project, Sterling A. Brown, the project's editor for Negro affairs, instructed, "Simplicity in recording the dialect is to be desired in order to hold the interest and attention of the readers. It seems to me that readers are repelled by pages sprinkled with misspellings, commas and apostrophes. . . . Truth to idiom is more important, I believe, than truth to pronunciation. . . . In order to make this volume of slave narratives more appealing and less difficult for the average reader, I recommend that truth to idiom be paramount, and exact truth to pronunciation secondary."[54] Brown further suggested a number of specific spellings for what he judged to be common features of the "Negro dialect," and in so doing obviously made many assumptions about who would be reading and judging the transcripts and what uses they would be put to by his own and future generations. None of his assumptions would withstand scrutiny today. As noted on the Library of Congress's Born in Slavery Web site,

> The interviewers were writers, not professionals trained in the phonetic transcription of speech. And the instructions they received were not altogether clear. . . . [Brown] urged that "words that definitely have a notably different pronunciation from the usual should be recorded as heard," evidently assuming that "the usual" was self-evident.
>
> In fact, the situation was far more problematic than the instructions from project leaders recognized. All the informants were of course black, most interviewers were white, and by the 1930s, when the interviews took place, white representations of black speech already had an ugly history of entrenched stereotype dating back at least to the early nineteenth century. What most interviewers assumed to be "the usual" patterns of their informants' speech was unavoidably influenced by preconceptions and stereotypes.[55]

In her essay on the WPA slave narrative transcriptions, Lori Ann Garner wrote, "Because of the contextual change from a speaker and audience to a printed page and silent reader, it is important to recognize the issues that those attempting to make this shift must confront. . . . In the case of the WPA narratives, the new performance arena of the printed page is a context in which dialect features convey much more than objectively transcribed speech patterns and are charged with associative values."[56] Any transcription of dialect draws attention to itself, especially in a scholarly—printed and archived—context. The normative conventions of writing are pervasive, even among people whose dialect differs markedly from those conventions. As Keith Gilyard pointed out, "People don't read solely the way they speak. Nor do they write the way they speak unless they draw only upon native oral resources." Gilyard echoed the view of many linguists, maintaining that the dialects of ethnic minorities are "linguistically equal and . . . the fact that they are not equal in society is a matter of society, not linguistics."[57] This social inequality makes transcription of dialect a political issue that cannot be ignored. It is not a simple issue, however. Garner was critical of historian C. Van Woodward, who saw uniform racial bias in the WPA slave narratives and concluded that less attempt to transcribe dialect meant less racial bias. "First," wrote Garner, "this theory mistakenly equates transcription of 'thick dialect' unequivocally with implied racial slurs, denying the multiple associative meanings dialect can adopt in an author's or transcriber's work." Garner, citing cases in which dialect was transcribed by black interviewers and served various roles in the narratives when employed by both white and black transcribers, observed, "All seem to be employing selectively techniques of literary dialect to distinguish their own voices from those of their subjects."[58] As the discipline of oral history has evolved, most transcribers have eschewed renderings of the phonetic aspects of dialect in transcripts, while leaving intact the morphological, syntactical, and lexical variations that also distinguish most dialects. The extent to which this renders the transcript unreliable as a historical document is a matter still debated.

As noted above in the discussion of traditionally or predominantly oral cultures, many kinds of spoken language live uneasily at best on the printed page. This is true in some predominantly literate cultures as well. Russian Mat, the highly obscene street language firmly suppressed in imperial and Soviet Russia, is a particularly interesting example. Since the collapse of the Communist regime, Mat has partly emerged from suppression; it is no longer exclusively the language of working-class men, and it now appears in print in literary as well as popular genres. But there are still governmental efforts to suppress it, and it remains a language charged with political and cultural tensions.[59] Oral history must certainly deal with such popular oral forms of language; one of the challenges is conveying the context of its utterance in transcripts. Even interviewees who speak a "standard" variety of language, one that closely resembles standard written language, may utter obscenities in an interview but do so by mouthing the words soundlessly or accompanying them with gesture and expression that pull the punch in ways lost in the transcription. The recent brouhaha among H-Net discussion list editors over a conference announcement that included an obscenity further illustrates the great difficulty—not to say impossibility—of contextualizing some kinds of language in scholarly texts. In spite of a great deal of learned and reasoned writing by both those who were offended and those who were not, the offending gerund continued to appear peculiar and off register in the forum's postings and discussion logs.[60] A squeamishness about committing obscenity to written text forces us to face the incongruities of transferring the oral history interview from a spoken to a written genre. It is an expansion of the point made by Gilyard, cited above, that linguistically equal dialects are not socially or politically equal. The inequality is reflected in the unease that characterizes some forms of spoken language appearing in print.

Critical theorist Mikhail Bakhtin saw it as a matter of style: "Any style is inseparably related to the utterance and to typical forms of utterances, that is, speech genres."[61] Although Bakhtin's point of departure was the critical understanding of literary texts, his views are not irrelevant to the understanding of other narrative texts, including transcripts. As Sherna Gluck and Daphne Patai pointed out, "Contemporary literary theory—challenging the older historian's tendency to see oral history as a transparent representation of experience—made us aware that the typical product of an interview is a text, not a reproduction of reality, and that models of textual analysis were therefore needed."[62] Thus are Bakhtin's further observations relevant:

"Where there is style there is genre. The transfer of style from one genre to another not only alters the way a style sounds, under conditions of a genre unnatural to it, but also violates or renews the given genre."[63] There may indeed be a potential for renewal of the transcript genre—even, perhaps, for composed, literary genres—in each instance of transcribing speech that does not usually appear in print. It is perhaps this potential that continues to inspire oral historians to pursue their craft and create works of scholarship and performance based on their recordings and transcriptions. It is what Portelli termed the "creative complexity of oral narrative."[64]

Oral historians have been increasingly concerned with empowerment, especially of minorities and of those whose voices have not been heard or considered in mainstream scholarship. The transcript and its processing and uses are part of this concern. As Eric Peterson and Kristin Langellier stated, "Transcribing is a decontextualizing (from performance) and textualizing (to print) movement that locates cultural conventions and social structures of the personal and of narrative. Transcription is not simply a problem of representation, of choosing the 'best' technique among multiple models. Rather, transcription constitutes text and context in ways that are not just partial but political, implicating narrator, interviewee, and researcher(s) alike within a system of power relations."[65] Gluck and Patai, in their book about gender issues in oral history practice, made the point that "a story or statement that, in its oral form, is 'by' the speaker very often reaches the public in the form of a text 'by' the scholar, whether as a life history or as excerpts used by a scholar to illustrate a line of argument."[66] Many feel that this transfer of genre and authorship constitutes a betrayal of the democratizing and empowering potential of oral history, and the edited transcript is implicated in the process. As Staughton Lynd put the matter in 1993, "Transcription of the interview for use in the historian's written presentations to an academic audience is not the only purpose of an interview, and perhaps not the most important." Some years earlier, Lynd and co-author Alice Lynd had written in the preface to *Rank and File: Personal Histories by Working-Class Organizers*, "The purpose of the interviews . . . was emphatically not to provide raw material for conventional academic history by ourselves or anyone else. Instead, the idea was to get beyond a situation in which one group of people (workers) experience history and another group of people (professional historians) interprets the experiences for them." The Lynds intended the occasions of recounting—community forums, workshops, as well as interviews—to be opportunities in which "young people in the community could receive an oral tradition."[67] And yet recordings of the Lynds' oral history occasions—and transcripts as guides to the content of those recordings—surely have great value for succeeding generations of activists as well as historians. This does not run counter to the Lynds' activist motivation to generate occasions for oral recounting; it would seem rather to support it and to contribute to the longevity of their work.

Accessibility of the products of oral history interviews is also a matter of concern, a matter related to the issues of empowerment. In its statement of principles and standards for oral historians, the Oral History Association makes clear the importance of accessibility: "In recognition of the importance of oral history to an understanding of the past and of the cost and effort involved, interviewers and interviewees should mutually strive to record candid information of lasting value and to make that information accessible. . . . Interviewers should make every effort to make the interviews accessible to the communities."[68] But many questions have been raised on this point: Accessible in what form, and to whom, and on what terms, and in whose judgment? As Portelli wrote, "On the one hand, museums and archives are not always accessible and friendly to nonprofessional users; on the other, what do we do with the precious informant who does not know how to read the transcript or does not own a cassette player or VCR to play back the tapes?"[69] Decisions about the form, preservation, and availability of the transcript have far-reaching implications for what oral history is or should be. Printed text is accessible—to the literate—and relatively unmediated, but arrangements for preservation and access usually interpose barriers that, to some memoirists and their communities, can be formidable if not insurmountable. An oral history transcript handled as an archival manuscript, for example, available for reading only on formal request, is in no practical sense accessible to many of the people whose stories it is oral history's unique mission to collect. Access and archival practice are considered at length elsewhere in this volume; the point here is that those matters intersect with issues concerning the authenticity and appropriateness of transcripts.

Oral history transcripts always require editing of some sort, and there are many questions to consider regarding editorial practice for these documents. Important among these issues are, first, the right of the interviewee to review and edit the transcript and, second, oral historians' practices in preparing transcripts for preservation and access.

Oral historians remain divided on the question of whether interviewees should have the opportunity to review transcripts of their interviews. Some have argued that the transcript gains authenticity when the interviewee has had a chance to correct, amplify, even censor the written account of what he or she said. Writing for the *Oral History Review* in 2004, Rebecca Jones stated, "It is only at the time of the review, when the narrator sees a manuscript that might be published, that he or she considers the story as a public text. This encourages them to reflect on the story they have told and modify, add, or subtract information."[70] Others have argued that only the unedited, verbatim transcript is the true account. In this view, the value of the interview is its spontaneity, the opportunity it provides to catch the unguarded and uncensored comment, even in spite of the interviewee's intentions. This view is hard to defend, however, since as Thomas Charlton has pointed out, *"The very act of transcribing . . . is a major editorial step"* (emphasis in original).[71] The current trend, sensitive to matters of empowerment, seems to be in favor of allowing interviewees to possess their texts, to review and edit them as they wish. This does not solve the problem of fairly representing in editable text the words of interviewees who do not feel at ease with reading and editing, who may not even recognize their speech in texts rendered in standard spelling and typographical conventions. According to Portelli, "The conventions of grammar, punctuation, and typographic style, unavoidable in the rendering of spoken narrative into printed text, impose an arbitrary and alien rhythm upon that narrative."[72] Nor is this discomfort with the transcript limited to the less literate. "Strange, isn't it, how less-than-literate a writer is when he only talks," lamented an interviewee in a letter that accompanied his heavily edited transcript, sent back to the oral history office—the Baylor University Institute for Oral History—for final processing. The institute's policy in preparing transcripts for the archives is to incorporate interviewees' editorial changes.[73] In this case, the changes will result in a document that is much more a written autobiographical memoir than a transcript of an interview, a nearly complete shift of genre. In the institute's view, it is interviewees' prerogative to do this. However, if interviewees in no way restrict access to the recordings of their interviews, a note in the front matter of the edited and deposited transcripts may inform readers that the transcript differs significantly from those recordings.

Many oral historians continue to make the case that transcribing itself, and certainly all editing, constitutes creation of a new text that cannot be viewed as merely a replica of the oral interview. Even the application of punctuation to the verbatim transcript can effect a powerful transformation—not to say deformation—of the original spoken narrative. "The function of most punctuation," wrote Louis Menand, "is to help organize the relationships among the parts of a sentence. Its role is semantic: to add precision and complexity to meaning."[74] Oral history transcribers and editors punctuating transcripts are thus adding precision and complexity and thereby creating meanings that are not those of the speaker. As Anthony Pym put it, "Writing may do far more than fail to represent nonwriting."[75] That the new text is not a replica of the oral interview does not necessarily invalidate it. Many have felt that the new text is more authentic as a record of the interviewee's intended meanings, if not of the words she or he spoke. Edward Ives wrote, "If what you do is to transcribe the interview and then send the transcription to the informant for correction or amplification, and if the informant does in fact make alterations—deleting passages, adding fuller explanations, correcting sentence structure and the like—then the resultant manuscript becomes the primary document, the tape and transcript merely rough drafts. In this situation, if you want to find out what the informant 'said' about something, you would not go to the tape but to the corrected transcript."[76] This is problematic because of the dialogic nature of the oral history process. Meanings, intentions, memories all change over time, even the relatively short time between interview and review. The interview itself, questioning and prompting by the interviewer, the time for reflection and reconsideration afterward, further research in memorabilia, an innumerable variety of events and influences can make one day's account of historical memories seem inaccurate, inappropriate, in need of revision. Interpersonal power dynamics may be at work, too. As Wilmsen pointed out, "The fact that narrators have varying experience with the written word, the world of publishing, research archives, libraries, et cetera, affects what editing decisions are made, who makes them, and why." He argued, "If the power differential is viewed as large, . . . narrators may be less inclined to challenge editing decisions of interviewers/editors, or may be more timid about making editorial decisions themselves. . . . On the other hand, narrators who are highly experienced with the written word may also defer to the interviewer/editor and the 'expert' in oral history as to how the interview should proceed and what editorial decisions should be made." Privileged narrators, he explained, "may be well versed in getting a point across in written text. . . . They will thus shape their responses to the questions in the interview for this audience as well as to achieve whatever other purpose they may have in consenting to the interview." In contrast, Wilmsen wrote, "in the case of non-privileged people . . . many have limited experience with the production of written texts for broad audiences. . . . They thus could be more candid. . . . On the other hand, such narrators may be quite skilled in the use of the spoken word. They may thus seek to control the interview itself rather than rely on the editing process to refine the text."[77]

Michael Frisch argued in favor of correcting the transcribed speech of "common people or the working class" as an attempt to redress the imbalance between them and "people of position or power," whose statements are "routinely printed with correct syntax and spelling," whose news media interviews are "selectively edited so that articles or reports always contain coherent statements."[78] These views make it clear that review by the interviewee, granting the interviewee editorial prerogative, does not settle the issue of the transcript's validity as a representation of the interviewee's story.[79] Perhaps the best one can say is that all versions of the recounted story are artifacts, useful to someone who wishes to scrutinize them and the circumstances of their creation. Arguments about what is the primary text and what is not are perhaps beside the point. What is called for simply is full and careful attention to the processes and circumstances that bring an oral history into existence.

Oral historians also remain deeply divided on how to handle the "ums" and "ers," the false starts and midsentence changes of direction, the constant repetitions of "like" and "you know" with which oral speech is often filled. In another recent case, an interviewer penciled across the top of a transcript, "Please take out all the 'you-knows.' [The interviewee] would want that; he is highly educated and articulate." More than one issue is raised by this example. First, of course, is the fact that the interviewer was asserting what the interviewee would want, a judgment that may be correct and perceptive, but may not. Secondly, it raises the issue of the editorial handling of the oral speech. Some advocate extensive editing. Frisch wrote, "To transcribe each pause or false start or tic would make an otherwise clear tape absolutely unreadable on paper, inevitably suggesting to readers an inarticulateness anything but characteristic of the speaker-as-heard. On the other hand, to eliminate them all arbitrarily might risk a distortion of a different kind. . . . When one knows an interview intimately, it is possible to sense how many 'you knows' are needed in print to give the feel of a speaker's rhythm and style without distorting how their voice 'reads.'" Frisch proclaimed, "The integrity of a transcript is best protected, in documentary use, by an aggressive editorial approach that does not shrink from substantial manipulation of the text."[80]

Others feel strongly that verbatim transcribing, including the "ums" and "ers," is the only way to make a faithful, reliable account of the interview. Allen claimed,

Because of the nature of the oral history interview and its potential value as a spontaneous expression of a person's opinions or recollections, in oral history transcribing we retain the broken-off sentences, the stops and starts, even parts of words uttered and checked. These pieces of conversation form a matrix which may be clear to no one at the moment, but they may have a particular or a cumulative value for some researcher in the time to come. . . . Our care in the handling of the tape and the transcript is the only thing that the future researcher can trust if he is to trust in the validity of oral history at all.[81]

As Phaswane Mpe has pointed out, "There is often such a stress on getting to the point . . . that the point, expressed as it sometimes is in small details, gets missed altogether."[82] In a similar vein, Jeff Friedman wrote, "Theoreticians have noted that a 'break-down' of the narrative is often a cue for the inability of an asymmetrical power relation between narrator and interviewer to continue. This is often a result of interview situations which call for an 'official' narrative given in 'official language' which suppresses a narrator's actual subject position. Once that stretch between subject positions is too much to sustain, the narrative breaks down into fragments and crutch words." Eliminating the fragments and crutch words, Friedman contended, removes crucial evidence of interpersonal power dynamics from the transcript.[83] Thus the question again can be seen as a matter of democratization—empowerment, in effect; editors must always ask themselves whose ends they are serving by their editorial decisions, whose version of the story they are crafting and preserving. Portelli summarized the matter this way: "There is no all-purpose transcript. . . . The same applies to editing: Is it intended to reproduce as carefully as possible the actual sounds of the spoken word or to make the spoken word accessible to readers through the written medium?"[84] Wilmsen concluded that "transcribing and editing are integral parts of the interview process and the same social forces which shape meaning in the interview come to bear on the editing process."[85]

Most would agree, perhaps, that editing requires the utmost sensitivity; the uses of the interview, the diverse interests of the present and future audiences for it, cannot be foreseen, and as few assumptions as possible should be made about how to serve those interests. There may be few today who share Allen's optimism: "The comforting thing about editing a transcript is that according to standard grammatical rules there does exist a logical and correct way to punctuate anything."[86] In 1971, Raphael Samuel called for transcription standards that are little closer to realization today than then when he wrote, "It would be helpful if historians could be dissuaded from transcribing speech according to the conventions and constrictions of written prose, if they could make some attempt to convey the cadences of speech as well as its content, even if they do not aim to be phonetically exact. There is no reason why sentences should make an orderly progression from beginning to end, with verbs and adjectives and nouns each in their grammatically allotted place."[87]

Many oral historians share with enthusiasm the view expressed by Linda Shopes and Bret Enyon, among others, concerning the potential of electronic media and the Internet "for restoring orality to oral history."[88] These advocates contend that the advantages of electronic publication extend to the transcript as well as to the audio recording. As Shopes put it on a Web site for teachers, "Electronic technologies are democratizing access to extant oral history collections by on-line publication of both actual interview recordings and written transcripts of them." Shopes continued, "Web publication of interviews has numerous advantages beyond mere access. Electronic search engines enable users to identify material relevant to their own interests easily and quickly, without listening to hours of tape or plowing through pages of transcript. Hypertext linkages of excerpted or footnoted interviews to full transcripts allow a reader to more fully contextualize a given quote or idea; to assess how carefully an author has retained the integrity of a narrator's voice in the material quoted; and to more fully evaluate an author's interpretive gloss on a narrator's account."[89] Furthermore, as Mary Larson pointed out, the capacity of the Web to bring together in a single point of access information in many media and from many physical sources can "give a researcher a much more solid background, . . . particularly important in cross-cultural settings where chroniclers are concerned that their words or images will be misinterpreted by people who know nothing about their community."[90]

Not all oral historians agree that hypertext Web forms contribute to the understanding of transcripts, however. The concerns of those who disagree are similar to concerns described earlier with regard to the significance of differences between oral and written genres. These theorists contend that as narrative is linear, hypertext markup of a transcript cannot accurately convey the process by which the narrative developed and its meanings were conveyed.[91] Jay David Bolter, however, cautioned against oversimplification in analyzing hypertext: "It is often said that a printed text is linear, whereas a hypertext is nonlinear, but this is not quite accurate. Our experience of reading takes place in time, and in that sense any particular instantiation of a hypertext, like any particular reading of a printed work, is linear. Hypertexts are not non linear, but rather multilinear." He goes on to point out that it is possible to make print media multilinear—newspapers, magazines, and dictionaries are examples—and to make hypertext linear, with the links serving merely to move the reader from the end of one section to the beginning of the next.[92] Indeed, even the simple index or table of contents appended to a transcript makes it possible to read—and hence interpret, wisely or not—in an order other than that in which the speech it records occurred. Transcribing is an editorial act and a transformation of genre; in some ways, use of a nonprint medium is no more radical a transformation than the initial transcription. In any case, there is danger of both overestimating and oversimplifying the implications for meaning when a narrative is transported to different media.

Other writers have expressed concerns about the distracting and superficial qualities of electronic media. Advice to Web-page builders always emphasizes the importance of fast downloads, attention-grabbing design, and condensation of essential content to fit on a single screen. As Paul Thompson observed, "The fascination is in flicking from one sort of information to another, rather than in exploring anything in depth. . . . Hence, while multimedia can store life stories, it is designed for a form of use which is fundamentally inimical to any sustained narrative or authorial argument. In other words, it depends on what its users make of it."[93] But Thompson also recognized the great potential for preserving precisely those crucially meaningful aspects of oral histories that the written transcript jettisons and that audio and video recording can help preserve. He wrote, "In principle it would be possible to organize an archive so that you could read a transcript, and then at will switch over and hear the sound of the same passage, and see the expressions of the speaker: which would represent an enormous advance in the accuracy and potential interpretative insights of researchers using interviews."[94]

Democratization of access is another advantage claimed for Web versions of transcripts. The claim is valid for many researchers, readers, and communities, but it is not universally so. The so-called digital divide still exists; many people still do not have access to computers or networks, especially in rural and sparsely populated regions. For these people, the issue of accessibility—so-called repatriation—of the oral history is still unresolved.

Including transcription in oral history processing is expensive; in fact, the cost of transcription is perhaps chief among its practical drawbacks. That cost is chiefly labor cost. Many hours of skilled work are required to transcribe oral histories and to prepare the transcripts for access and preservation. The time required for creating and processing transcripts is always many times a multiple of the hours of interview recorded. Published estimates of how long it takes to transcribe, audit, correct, and edit an oral history interview vary from ten to twenty to over forty hours per hour of recording.[95] The higher estimates usually include time for indexing, abstracting, and preparing for archival deposit, and practices vary with respect to these final processes. In any case, transcription procedures and costs, practical matters of budget and management, bear directly upon the matter of access to the final product. On the issue of accessibility, practical and theoretical concerns converge. Again, notwithstanding these issues, transcribing continues.

The technology of transcribing has evolved with the media of audio recording, although the greatest hope—voice recognition software that can reliably, efficiently, and entirely automate the transcription process—remains unrealized. Systems now exist, however, for manual transcribing of both digital and analog audio recordings of interviews. The most convenient of the systems include headphones and foot pedals to facilitate close listening and replaying of short segments. Word processing software is obviously a great boon to easy and efficient production of transcripts, although the usual caveats apply: reliance on the autocorrection functions of such programs as Microsoft Word can produce highly undesirable results, especially when dealing with the idiosyncrasies of spoken language.

Many have recognized the value of the interviewer doing the transcribing. It is likely that this is relatively rare, however, at least in larger oral history organizations. Some interviewers do provide word lists or other background materials to help transcribers with names and terms peculiar to the interview. Editorial policies and practices vary concerning what becomes of the verbatim transcript before it is turned over to the archives or the public; many of the issues involved have been discussed at length above. But whatever editing is done, the beginning point is the verbatim transcript in which every word is committed to the page. The next step is usually a so-called audit check, best done by someone other than the transcriber. The audit checker listens to the recording while reading the verbatim transcript and notes any discrepancies between what was transcribed and what was spoken. Once any transcribing errors have been corrected, the editing process continues with corrections to spelling and punctuation and verification of proper names, unfamiliar terms, and such. Again, policies vary with respect to the extent of editorial changes allowable at this stage. It is best to adopt a set of reference guides for editors' use, including a style manual and dictionaries for general and specialized or regional vocabularies. Some oral history organizations have developed their own style guides that adapt standard ones to the specialized demands of oral history. The important thing in any case is to make editorial policies explicit and to apply them consistently.

Once the transcript has been created, audit-checked, and edited—usually very lightly—it is given sometimes to the interviewer to review, and almost always to the interviewee. Interviewees are usually invited to make whatever corrections, additions, clarifications, or other emendations they wish to the transcript; it is not uncommon, however, to send a cover letter urging the interviewee to accept the unpolished quality of transcribed speech and to concentrate instead on supplying missing names and clarifying anything poorly heard or wrongly transcribed. Instructions to interviewees usually also include a time limit, a statement that after a specified length of time the transcript will be considered complete, whether or not the interviewee's edited version has been received. Oral history organizations are usually generous in these terms and willing to extend deadlines on request. Deadlines, even flexible ones, are necessary to avoid having transcripts languish in processing limbo.

Transcripts prepared for deposit in archives or for other public uses usually include front matter of some kind that provides necessary and helpful additional information. In addition to the full names of interviewees, interviewers, the date and location of the interview, the sponsoring organization, and the copyright date—typical title page information—this front matter also often includes details about editorial policy, processing steps, legal status, names of people who worked on the volume, and a statement about the legal status of the volume. Many oral history programs also include other information to help contextualize the oral memoir. Biographical information about the participants in the interviews, a description of the project of which the interview was a part, its sources of funding, and its organizational context may be included. Statements about the relationship between the transcript and the audio or video recording can also be included. Oral history archivist Francis Good provides an example: "My transcripts bear a detailed 'Note to reader' which includes the warning that users should listen to the original sound recording, at least in part and particularly for any aspect that is critical for the reader; and I include a short attempt at explaining the principles used to interpret words from sound to print."[96]

Another common addition to oral history transcripts is an index. This may be simply an index of names and concepts in the transcript itself, or it may be a list of or include references to timed locations in the audio recordings. The latter sort of references are greatly enhanced in digital media, of course; digitization allows nearly instant linkage between transcript and audio, as well as access through the Web, on local networks, on compact disc, or through any number of other digital means.

The processing of oral history interviews for the archives and public access generates a sizeable number of documents— letters, deeds of gift or statements of copyright or other legal restrictions, and perhaps most significantly, versions of the transcripts edited in the hands of the interviewees, the so-called autograph copies of transcripts. These are often documents that researchers would find extremely interesting, especially if the interviewee has restricted access to the recordings or transcripts or has heavily emended the transcripts. Their great potential interest notwithstanding, these materials must be kept in safety and in confidence; it devolves upon oral history organizations or their archivists to ensure the preservation of these materials as well as adherence to the stated wishes of interview participants.

The editing of transcripts, verifying proper names and terms and indexing concepts, creates a large body of information that some oral history organizations have attempted to preserve as a research aid in itself, either for internal use by editors or for end users of completed transcripts. This body of information, comprising indexes, word lists, abstracts, and other such matter, can be stored in a data management system and made accessible through a more or less sophisticated search engine, depending on the resources available to build and maintain the system.[97]

"The historian creates history and makes sense of it," David Faris wrote, stating simply a view with a long pedigree in philosophy and historiography. He continued, "Events themselves, at least insofar as they can be considered historically, have meaning only as pasts of stories."[98] The transcriber and the editor, in creating printed documents from what was itself an event of more or less historical importance, create a new narrative; they impose a new story line on the recounted human events. The crucial question for oral history practice is how to represent the genre accurately, how to capture it for present and future study. The interview itself is a complicated social event, understood differently by each participant. In the end, the possible scenarios of interpretation are as varied and individual as the people who participate. It may be that there is little value in trying to create a comprehensive taxonomy of psychological, social, political, and other forces and currents that shape the record—transcript and recording—of a particular oral history interview. Analyzing and interpreting the record insightfully simply requires the best of a researcher—the widest knowledge, the deepest experience, the greatest sensitivity, the most acute self-awareness. More than this, we ask that the record be accessible to the most diverse population of readers possible, that diverse wisdom be brought to bear in the analysis and interpretation, in the creation of historical meaning in diverse contexts.

The words of Raphael Samuel, first written in 1971 when oral history was a young discipline, remain relevant: "Research can never be a once-and-for-all affair, nor is there ever a single use to which evidence can be put. Historians in the future will bring fresh interests to bear upon the materials we collect; they will be asking different questions and seeking different answers."[99]

Notes

1. Kessler-Harris, introduction to *Envelopes of Sound* (1975), 2.
2. Starr, "Oral History," 8–9.
3. Norman R. Yetman, "An Introduction to the WPA Slave Narratives: Collections That Led the Way," Born in Slavery: Slave Narratives from the Federal Writers' Project, 1936–1938, American Memory Collections, Library of Congress, http://memory.loc.gov/ammem/snhtml/snintro06.html (accessed January 4, 2005).
4. "American Life Histories: Manuscripts from the Federal Writers' Project, 1936–1940," American Memory Collections, Library of Congress, http://lcweb2.loc.gov/ammem/wpaintro/wpahome.html (accessed January 4, 2005).
5. Bancroft Library, "Bancroft Collection of Western and Latin Americana," University of California at Berkeley, http://bancroft.berkeley.edu/collections/bancroft.html (accessed January 4, 2005).
6. See Conaway, "Lyman Copeland Draper."
7. Wilmsen, "For the Record," 69–70.
8. Starr, "Oral History," 7.
9. Lance, *Archive Approach*, 20.
10. K'Meyer, "Willa K. Baum," 101.
11. Ritchie, *Doing Oral History*, 2nd ed., 64.
12. See, for example, Sommer and Quinlan, *Oral History Manual*, 75; Davis, Back, and MacLean, *From Tape to Type*, 34; Deering and Pomeroy, *Transcribing without Tears*, 1; Yow, *Recording Oral History* (1994), 227; Hoopes, *Oral History*, 114; Baum, *Transcribing and Editing*, 14–15; Henige, *Oral Historiography*, 63; Ives, *Tape-Recorded Interview* (1980), 88; and Lance, *Archive Approach*, 20.
13. Henige, *Oral Historiography*, 63.
14. Tedlock, "Learning to Listen," 122–23.
15. Henige, *Oral Historiography*, 63.
16. Sitton, Mehaffy, and Davis, *Oral History*, 81, 18.

17. Millie Rahn, "Deed of Gift Issues," posting to H-Net: Humanities and Social Sciences Online, H-Oralhist Discussion Network, October 28, 2004, http://www.h-net.org (accessed January 4, 2005).

18. Library of Congress, American Memory Collections, "Voices from the Days of Slavery: Former Slaves Tell Their Stories," About This Collection, http://memory.loc.gov/ammem/collections/voices/vfsabout.html (accessed January 4, 2005).

19. Lochead, "Oral History in Canada," 5.

20. Canadian Oral History Association, "What Is Oral History," http://oral-history.ncf.ca/index.html (accessed January 4, 2005).

21. British Library, "British Library Sound Archive," http://www.bl.uk/collections/sound-archive/cat.html (accessed January 4, 2005).

22. Allen, "Editorial Ego," 36.

23. Dunaway, "Transcription," 115–16.

24. Portelli, *Death of Luigi Trastulli*, 76. Similarly, Michael Frisch wrote that "speech that sounds articulate and coherent to the ear tends to read, when too-literally transcribed in print, like inarticulate stage mumbling; such transcription becomes an obstacle to hearing what the person in the interview is trying to say." Frisch, *Shared Authority*, 45. Likewise, Paul Thompson noted, "We have already had to learn how different an interview is on audio tape from a typed transcript with words only. The typed form can never convey more than a hint of the tones, accents and emotions in the spoken word, and the irregular pauses of speech necessarily disappear behind the logical sequence of grammatical punctuation." Thompson, "Sharing and Reshaping," 178. Gould Colman put the matter this way: "Even with the most skilled and conscientious transcribers, part of the interview will be lost in transcription, the extent of the loss being related to the speaker's use of inflection and other untranscribable elements of language." Colman, "More Systematic Procedures," 82.

25. Olson, *World on Paper*, 260–61.

26. Pym, review, 134.

27. Dunaway, "Transcription," 116.

28. Ong, *Orality and Literacy*, 100.

29. Tonkin, *Narrating Our Pasts*, 54, 75.

30. See Reingold, "Critic Looks at Oral History," 223–24.

31. For a comprehensive review of these notational techniques, see Edwards and Lampert, *Talking Data*. A basic reference in the field of discourse analysis is Schiffrin, Tannen, and Hamilton, *Handbook of Discourse Analysis*.

32. Agar, "Transcript Handling," 219.

33. Tedlock, "Learning to Listen."

34. Tonkin, *Narrating Our Pasts*, 75.

35. Portelli, "Oral History As Genre," 40.

36. Good, "Voice, Ear and Text," 104.

37. See Oral History Association, *Evaluation Guidelines*, which explicitly promotes making oral history accessible.

38. Ong, "Grammar Today," 402.

39. Portelli, *Death of Luigi Trastulli*, 260.

40. Olson, *World on Paper*, 18–19.

41. Ibid., 272.

42. Foucault, "What Is an Author?" 159.

43. Dudley, "In the Archive," 165.

44. White, "Foucault Decoded," 32.

45. Tonkin, *Narrating Our Pasts*, 51–52.

46. Schneider, "Lessons from Alaska Natives," 186. Schneider refers to Dundes, "Texture, Text, and Context."

47. Morrow and Schneider, *When Our Words Return*, 224–25.

48. Schneider, *So They Understand*, 62.

49. Finnegan, *Oral Literature in Africa*, 2.

50. Hofmeyr, "Jonah," 640.

51. Ibid., 653.

52. Tannen, "Commingling of Orality and Literacy," 42.

53. Sarris, "Mabel McKay's Stories," 176.

54. Sterling A. Brown, "Notes by an Editor on Dialect Usage in Accounts by Interviews with Ex-slaves," Federal Writers' Project, 1936–1938, Work Projects Administration for the District of Columbia, *Slave Narratives: A Folk History of Slavery in the United States from Interviews with Former Slaves* (Washington, DC, 1941), xxviii, in Library of Congress, "Born in Slavery: Slave Narratives from the Federal Writers' Project, 1936–1938," American Memory Collections, http://memory.loc.gov/cgi-bin/ampage?collId=mesn&fileName=001/mesn001.db&recNum=26 (accessed February 9, 2005).

55. Library of Congress, "A Note on the Language of the Narratives," "Born in Slavery: Slave Narratives from the Federal Writers' Project, 1936–1938," American Memory Collections, http://memory.loc.gov/ammem/snhtml/snlang.html (accessed February 9, 2005).

56. Garner, "Representations of Speech," 216.

57. Gilyard, *Let's Flip the Script*, 70.

58. Garner, "Representations of Speech," 226, 228.

59. See Smith, S. A., "Social Meanings"; Erofeyev, "Dirty Words."

60. See the call for papers for "Performing Excess," special issue of *Women and Performance*, submitted to H-Announce on July 2, 2004, announcement ID no. 139498, http://www.h-net.msu.edu/announce/show.cgi?ID=139498 (accessed February 15, 2005). Discussion of the language of the announcement occurred on HNET-STAFF, the private, internal policy discussion list for H-Net editors and administrators.

61. Bakhtin, *Speech Genres*, 63.

62. Gluck and Patai, introduction to *Women's Words*, 3.

63. Bakhtin, *Speech Genres*, 66.

64. Portelli, "Oral History as Genre," 40.

65. Peterson and Langellier, "Personal Narrative Methodology," 144.

66. Gluck and Patai, introduction to *Women's Words*, 2.

67. Lynd, "Oral History from Below," 3.

68. Oral History Association, *Evaluation Guidelines*, 5–6.

69. Portelli, *Battle of Valle Giulia*, 68.

70. Jones, "*Blended Voices*," 35.

71. Charlton, *Oral History for Texans*, 2nd ed., 51.

72. Portelli, *Death of Luigi Trastulli*, 47–48. Others who have made this point include Raphael Samuel, who wrote in 1971: "The imposition of grammatical forms, when it is attempted, creates its own rhythms and cadences, and they have little in common with those of the human tongue. People do not usually speak in paragraphs, and what they have to say does not usually follow an ordered sequence of comma, semi-colon, and full stop; yet very often this is the way in which their speech is reproduced." Samuel, "Perils of the Transcript" (1971): 19.

73. There are a few exceptions to this policy. Spelling and punctuation changes are not incorporated if they are inconsistent with the institute's adopted guides: the latest edition of the *Chicago Manual of Style*, an in-house style guide covering special and frequently encountered cases, and the most recent edition of *Merriam-Webster's Collegiate Dictionary*.

74. Menand, "Bad Comma."

75. Pym, review, 134.

76. Ives, *Tape-Recorded Interview* (1980), 87–88.

77. Wilmsen, "For the Record," 76.

78. Frisch, *Shared Authority*, 86.

79. Gluck and Patai, introduction to *Women's Words*, 2, expressed doubt that giving interviewees one single chance to review their transcripts makes them "true partners in the process."

80. Frisch, *Shared Authority*, 83, 45.

81. Allen, "Editorial Ego," 41.

82. Mpe, "Orality and Literacy," 83.

83. Jeff Friedman, "Re: Ums uhs ers etc. in Transcript," posting to H-Net: Humanities and Social Sciences Online, H-Oralhist Discussion Network, November 10, 2004, http://h-net.org (accessed November 18, 2004). Friedman refers readers to Rosenwald and Ochberg, *Storied Lives*, for more information.

84. Portelli, *Battle of Valle Giulia*, 15.

85. Wilmsen, "For the Record," 69.

86. Allen, "Editorial Ego," 45.

87. Samuel, "Perils of the Transcript" (1971): 21.

88. Linda Shopes, History Matters: Making Sense of Evidence, "Making Sense of Oral History," George Mason University, http://historymatters.gmu.edu/mse/oral/online.html (accessed December 3, 2004). See also Enyon, "New Century," 17.

89. Shopes, Oral History Online (see note 90).

90. Larson, "Keeping Our Words."

91. See, for example, the careful comparison of printed and Web text versions of oral interviews with Holocaust survivors in Schiffrin, "Linguistics and History."

92. Bolter, "Hypertext," 5.

93. Thompson, "Sharing and Reshaping," 179.

94. Ibid., 177.

95. Ives, *Tape-Recorded Interview* (1980), 88; Ritchie, *Doing Oral History* (1995), 42; Baum, *Transcribing and Editing*, 18–19.

96. Francis Good, "Editing Confusion," posting to H-Net: Humanities and Social Sciences Online, H-Oralhist Discussion Network, September 12, 2004, http://h-net.org (accessed January 5, 2005).

97. See, for example, the description of the research aids developed at the Northern Territories Archive Service in Darwin, Australia, in Francis Good, "Interview Summaries," posting to H-Net: Humanities and Social Sciences Online, H-Oralhist Discussion Network, September 16, 2004, http://h-net.org (accessed December 14, 2004).

98. Faris, "Narrative Form," 168–69.

99. Samuel, "Perils of the Transcript" (1971): 22.

References

Abbott, Lawrence. *I Stand in the Center of the Good: Interviews with Contemporary Native American Artists*. Lincoln: University of Nebraska Press, 1994.

Abercrombie, Thomas A. *Pathways of Memory and Power: Ethnography and History among an Andean People*. Madison: University of Wisconsin Press, 1998.

Acker, Joan, Kate Barry, and Joke Essevelt. "Objectivity and Truth: Problems in Doing Feminist Research." *Women's Studies International Forum* 6 (1983): 423–35.

Adam, Barbara. *Timewatch: The Social Analysis of Time*. Cambridge: Polity, 1995.

Adams, Noah, Bill D. Moyers, Robert Jay Lifton, Philip G. Zimbardo, Ishmael Reed, James Reston, and Deborah Amos. *Father Cares: The Last of Jonestown*. Washington, DC: National Public Radio, 1981. 2 audiocassettes.

Adler, Glen. "The Politics of Research during a Liberation Struggle: Interviewing Black Workers in South Africa." In Grele, ed., *International Annual 1990*, 229–45.

Agar, Michael. "Transcript Handling: An Ethnographic Strategy." *Oral History Review* 15 (Spring 1987): 209–19.

Albright, Daniel. "Literary and Psychological Models of the Self." In Neisser and Fivush, eds., *Remembering Self*, 19–40.

Alexander, Sally. *Becoming a Woman: And Other Essays in 19th and 20th Century Feminist History*. London: Verso, 1995.

———. "Women, Class, and Sexual Difference." *History Workshop* 17 (Spring 1984): 125–49.

Allen, Barbara, and William Lynwood Montell. *From Memory to History: Using Oral Sources in Local Historical Research*. Nashville, TN: American Association for State and Local History, 1981.

Allen, Susan Emily. "Resisting the Editorial Ego: Editing Oral History." *Oral History Review* 10 (1982): 33–45.

Alpern, Sara, Joyce Antler, Elisabeth Israels Perry, and Ingrid Winther Scobie, eds. *The Challenge of Feminist Biography.* Chicago: University of Illinois Press, 1992.

Althusser, Louis. *For Marx.* Translated by Ben Brewster. London: New Left, 1969.

———. "On Ideology." In *Lenin and Philosophy, and Other Essays*, 158–86. New York: Verso, 1971.

American Association of University Professors. "Protecting Human Beings: Institutional Review Boards and Social Science Research." *Academe* 87, no. 3 (May–June 2001): 55–67.

Anderson, Kathryn, and Dana C. Jack. "Learning to Listen: Interview Techniques and Analysis." In Perks and Thomson, eds., *Oral History Reader*, 157–71.

Anderson, Nels. *The Hobo: The Sociology of the Homeless Man.* Chicago: University of Chicago Press, 1923.

Andrade, Eva Salgado. "Epilogue: One Year Later." *Oral History Review* 16, no. 1 (Spring 1988): 21–31.

———. "Oral History in Mexico." *International Journal of Oral History* 9, no. 3 (November 1988): 215–20.

Andrews, Molly, Shelley Day Sclater, Corinne Squire, and Amal Treacher, eds. *Lines of Narrative: Psychosocial Perspectives.* London: Routledge, 2000.

Antler, Joyce. "Having It all, Almost: Confronting the Legacy of Lucy Sprague Mitchell." In Alpern et al., eds., *The Challenge of Feminist Biography*, 97–115.

Applebaum, David. *Voice.* Albany: State University of New York Press, 1990.

Araújo, Paulo Cesar de. *Eu Não Sou Cachorro, Não: Música Popular Cafona e Ditadura Militar.* Rio de Janeiro: Editoria Record, 2002.

Armitage, Susan H. "Introduction." *Frontiers: Journal of Women Studies* 19, no. 3 (1993): iii–iv.

———. "The Next Step." *Frontiers: Journal of Women Studies* 7, no. 1 (1983): 3–8.

Armitage, Susan H., and Sherna Berger Gluck. "Reflections on Women's Oral History: An Exchange." *Frontiers: Journal of Women Studies* 19, no. 3 (1998): 1–11.

Armitage, Susan H., Patricia Hart, and Karen Weathermon, eds. *Women's Oral History: The Frontiers Reader.* Lincoln: University of Nebraska Press, 2002.

Ashplant, Timothy G. "Anecdote as Narrative Resource in Working-Class Life Stories: Parody, Dramatization, and Sequence." In Chamberlain and Thompson, eds., *Narrative and Genre*, 99–113.

Atkinson, J. Maxwell. "Displaying Neutrality: Formal Aspects of Informal Court Proceedings." In Drew and Heritage, eds., *Talk at Work*, 199–211.

Atkinson, R. *The Life Story Interview.* London: Sage, 1998.

Austin-Broos, Diane, and Raymond T. Smith. *Jamaica Genesis.* Chicago: University of Chicago Press, 1997.

Baddeley, Alan D. *Your Memory: A User's Guide.* New York: Macmillan, 1982.

Bailey, Chris Howard. "*Precious Blood*: Encountering Inter-Ethnic Issues in Oral History Research, Reconstruction, and Representation." *Oral History Review* 18, no. 2 (Fall 1990): 61–108.

Bakan, David. "Some Reflections about Narrative Research and Hurt and Harm." In Josselson, ed., *Ethics and Process in the Narrative Study of Lives*, 1–8.

Baker, James T. *Studs Terkel*. New York: Twayne, 1992.

Bakhtin, Mikhail M. *The Dialogic Imagination: Four Essays*. Edited by M. Holquist. Translated by C. Emerson and M. Holquist. Austin: University of Texas Press, 1981.

———. *Speech Genres and Other Late Essays*. Translated by Vern W. McGee. Austin: University of Texas Press, 1986.

Banks, Ann, ed. *First Person America*. New York: Random House, 1980.

———. *First Person America: Voices from the Thirties*. Washington, DC: National Public Radio, 1980. 3 audiocassettes.

Barber, Karin. "Interpreting *Oriki* as History and as Literature." In *Discourse and Its Disguises: The Interpretation of African Oral Texts*, edited by Karin Barber and P. F. de Moraes Farias, 13–23. Birmingham: University of Birmingham Centre of West African Studies, 1989.

Barnouw, Erik. *Documentary: A History of the Non-fiction Film*. 2nd rev. ed. Oxford: Oxford University Press, 1993.

———. *The Golden Web*. Vol. 2, *A History of Broadcasting in the United States*. New York: Oxford University Press, 1968.

———. *The Sponsor: Notes on a Modern Potentate*. New York: Oxford University Press, 1978.

———. *A Tower in Babel*. Vol. 1, *A History of Broadcasting in the United States*. New York: Oxford University Press, 1966.

Bar-On, Dan. "Ethical Issues in Biographical Interviews and Analysis." In Josselson, ed., *Ethics and Process in the Narrative Study of Lives*, 9–21.

Baron, Samuel. "My Life with Plekhanov." In Baron and Pletsch, eds. *Introspection in Biography*, 191–208.

———. "Psychological Dimensions of the Biographical Process." In Baron and Pletsch, eds., *Introspection in Biography*, 1–32.

Baron, Samuel, and Carl Pletsch, eds. *Introspection in Biography: The Biographer's Quest for Self-Awareness*. Hillsdale, NJ: Erlbaum, 1985.

Barthes, Roland. "The Death of the Author." In *Image–Music–Text*, 42–48. Translated by Stephen Heath. New York: Hill and Wang, 1977.

Bartlett, Frederic C. *Remembering: A Study in Experimental and Social Psychology*. 1932. Reprint; Cambridge: Cambridge University Press, 1967.

Baudrillard, Jean. *For a Critique of the Political Economy of Signs*. Translated by C. Levin. St. Louis: Telos, 1981.

Baum, Willa. *Oral History for the Local Historical Society*. Stockton: Conference of California Historical Societies, 1969.

———. *Oral History for the Local Historical Society*. 3rd ed. American Association of State and Local History Book Series. Walnut Creek, CA: AltaMira, 1995.

———. *Transcribing and Editing Oral History*. Walnut Creek, CA: AltaMira, 1991.

Bauman, Richard. *Story, Performance, and Event: Contextual Studies of Oral Narrative*. Cambridge: Cambridge University Press, 1986.

Bell, Beverly. *Walking on Fire: Haitian Women's Stories of Survival and Resistance*. Ithaca, NY: Cornell University Press, 2001.

BenEzer, Gadi. *The Ethiopian Jewish Exodus: Narratives of the Migration Journey to Israel 1977–1985*. London: Routledge, 2002.

Benison, Saul. "Reflections on Oral History." *American Archivist* 28, no. 1 (January 1965): 71–77.

Benjamin, Walter. "A Berlin Chronicle." In *One-Way Street and Other Writings*. London: Verso, 1997.

Benmayor, Rina, Ana Juarbe, Blanca Vazquez Erazo, and Celia Alvarez. "Stories to Live By: Continuity and Change in Three Generations of Puerto Rican Women." *Oral History Review* 16, no. 2 (Fall 1988): 1–46.

Bennett, Olivia. "The Real Costs of Forced Settlement." *Oral History: Journal of the Oral History Society* 27, no. 1 (Spring 1999): 35–46.

Benson, Susan Porter. "Screening Labor Militancy." *Oral History Review* 24, no. 2 (Winter 1997): 95–100.

Berger, Arthur Asa. *Narratives in Popular Culture: Media and Everyday Life*. London: Sage, 1997.

Bergmann, Jorg R. "Veiled Morality: Notes on Discretion in Psychiatry." In Drew and Heritage, eds., *Talk at Work*, 137–62.

Berlin, Ira, Marc Favreau, and Steven F. Miller. *Remembering Slavery: African Americans Talk about Their Personal Experiences of Slavery and Freedom*. New York: New Press, 1998. Book and 2 audiocassettes.

Berliner, Alan. *The Family Album: A Film*. New York: Milestone Films, 1986. Videocassette.

———. *Intimate Stranger*. New York: Milestone Film and Video, 1991. Videocassette.

Berliner, Alan, and Oscar Berliner. *Nobody's Business*. New York: Milestone Film and Video, 1996. Videocassette.

Berman, Morris. *The Twilight of American Culture*. New York: Norton, 2002.

Bernhardt, Debra. *New Yorkers at Work: Oral Histories of Life, Labor, and Industry*. New York: Robert F. Wagner Archives, New York University, 1981. Audiocassette.

Berube, Allan. *Coming Out under Fire: The History of Gay Men and Women in World War Two*. New York: Free Press, 1990.

Bidney, David. "Myth, Symbolism, and Truth." In *Myth: A Symposium*, edited by Thomas A. Seboeck, 3–24. Bloomington: Indiana University Press, 1988.

Biel, Michael J. "The Making and Use of Recordings in Broadcast before 1936." Ph.D. diss., Northwestern University, 1977.

Biernacki, Richard. "Method and Metaphor after the New Cultural History." In Bonnell and Hunt, eds., *Beyond the Cultural Turn*, 62–94.

Biocca, Frank. "The Pursuit of Sound: Radio, Perception, and Utopia in the Early Twentieth Century." *Media, Culture, and Society* 10 (1988): 61–79.

Birren, James E., Gary M. Kenyon, Jan-Erik Ruth, Johannes J. F. Schroots, and Torbjorn Svenson, eds. *Aging and Biography: Explorations in Adult Development*. New York: Springer, 1996.

Bjorklund, Diane. *Interpreting the Self: Two Hundred Years of American Autobiography*. Chicago: University of Chicago Press, 1998.

Blackman, Margaret. *During My Time: Florence Edenshaw Davidson, a Haida Woman*. Seattle: University of Washington Press, 1982.

Blakely, Robert J. *To Serve the Public Interest: Educational Broadcasting in the United States*. Syracuse, NY: Syracuse University Press, 1979.

Blatti, Jo. "Toward a Complex Sense of Reality." *Oral History Review* 13 (1985): 123–29.

Blee, Kathleen M. "Evidence, Empathy, and Ethics: Lessons from Oral Histories of the Klan." *Journal of American History* 80 (1993): 596–606.

Bloom, Lynne Z. "Listen! Women Speaking." *Frontiers: Journal of Women Studies* 2, no. 2 (Summer 1977): 1–3.

Bluem, A. William. "Radio: The Forgotten Art." In *Documentary in American Television: Form, Function, Method*, chap. 3. New York: Hastings House, 1965.

Boatright, Mody C., and William A. Owens. *Tales from the Derrick Floor: A People's History of the Oil Industry*. Garden City, NY: Doubleday, 1970.

Bodnar, John. "Pierre Nora, National Memory, and Democracy: A Review." *Journal of American History* 87, no. 3 (December 2000): 951–63.

———. "Power and Memory in Oral History: Workers and Managers at Studebaker." *Journal of American History* 75, no. 4 (March 1989): 1201–21.

———. *Remaking America: Public Memory, Commemoration, and Patriotism in the Twentieth Century*. Princeton, NJ: Princeton University Press, 1992.

Bolter, Jay David. "Hypertext and the Question of Visual Literacy." In *Handbook of Literacy and Technology: Transformations in a Post-Typographic World*, edited by David Reinking, Michael C. McKenna, Linda D. Labbo, and Ronald D. Kieffer, 3–14. Mahwah, NJ: Erlbaum, 1998.

Bolton, Charles C. Review of *Will the Circle Be Unbroken?* by George King (Atlanta: Southern Regional Council, 1997). *Oral History Review* 27, no. 2 (Summer–Fall 2000): 183–85.

Bonfield, Lynn A. "Conversation with Arthur M. Schlesinger, Jr.: The Use of Oral History." *American Archivist* 43, no. 4 (Fall 1980): 461–72.

Bonnell, Victoria E., and Lynn Hunt, eds. *Beyond the Cultural Turn: New Directions in the Study of Society and Culture*. Berkeley: University of California Press, 1999.

———. Introduction. In *Beyond the Cultural Turn*, 1–32.

Borland, Katherine. "'That's Not What I Said': Interpretive Conflict in Oral Narrative Research." In Gluck and Patai, eds., *Women's Words*, 63–75.

Bornat, Joanna. "Two Oral Histories: Valuing Our Differences." *Oral History Review* 21, no. 1 (Spring 1993): 78–95.

Bornat, Joanna, Eve Hostettler, Jill Liddington, Paul Thompson, and Thea Vigne. "Women's History." Special issue, *Oral History: Journal of the Oral History Society* 5, no. 2 (Autumn 1977).

Botkin, B. A. *Lay My Burden Down: A Folk History of Slavery*. Chicago: University of Chicago Press, 1945.

Botz, Gerhard. "Oral History in Austria." In Hartewig and Halbach, eds., "History of Oral History," 97–106.

Boudon, Raymond. *The Analysis of Ideology*. Translated by Malcolm Slater. Chicago: University of Chicago Press, 1989.

Bozzoli, Belinda. "Interviewing the Women of Phokeng." In Perks and Thomson, eds., *Oral History Reader*, 145–56.

Bozzoli, Belinda, and Peter Delius. "Radical History and South African Society." *Radical History Review* 46/47 (January 1990): 13–46.

Bravo, Anna. "Solidarity and Loneliness: Piedmontese Peasant Women at the Turn of the Century." *International Journal of Oral History* 3, no. 2 (June 1982): 76–91.

Brecher, Jeremy. Review of *Brothers: Male Dominance and Technological Change*, by Cynthia Cockburn. *International Journal of Oral History* 5, no. 3 (November 1984): 194–97.

Brecher, Jeremy, Jerry Lombardi, and Jan Stackhouse, eds. *Brass Valley: The Story of Working People's Lives and Struggles in an American Industrial Region*. Philadelphia: Temple University Press, 1982.

Briggs, Charles L. *Learning How to Ask: A Sociolinguistic Appraisal of the Role of the Interview in Social Science Research*. Cambridge: Cambridge University Press, 1986.

Brooks, Michael. "'Long, Long Ago': Recipe for a Middle School Oral History Program." *OHA Magazine of History* 11, no. 3 (Spring 1997): 32–35.

Browne, George P. "Oral History in Brazil off to an Encouraging Start." *Oral History Review* 4 (1976): 53–55.

Browne, Vincent J. "Oral History and the Civil Rights Documentation Project." In *Selections from the Fifth and Sixth National Colloquia on Oral History*, compiled by Peter D. Olch and Forrest C. Pogue, 90–95. New York: Oral History Association, 1972.

Bruemmer, Bruce H. "Access to Oral History: A National Agenda." *American Archivist* 54, no. 4 (Fall 1991): 494–501.

Bruner, Jerome. *Actual Minds, Possible Worlds*. Cambridge, MA: Harvard University Press, 1986.

———. "Life as Narrative." *Social Research* 54, no. 1 (1987): 11–32.

———. "Myth and Identity." In *On Knowing: Essays for the Left Hand*, 127–86. Cambridge, MA: Harvard University Press, 1971.

———. "The Narrative Construction of Reality." *Critical Inquiry* 18, no. 1 (Autumn 1991): 1–21.

Bryant, Byron. "Interview with Ammon Hennacy." In McKinney, ed., *Exacting Ear*, 43–61.

Bryant, Clora, Buddy Collette, William Green, Steve Isoardi, Jack Kelson, Horace Tapscott, Gerald Wilson, and Marl Young, eds. *Central Avenue Sounds: Jazz in Los Angeles*. Berkeley: University of California Press, 1998.

Bugnard, Pierre-Philippe. "Les Retrouvailles de la Biographie et de la Nouvelle Histoire." *Schweizerische Zeitschrift fur Geschichte, Revue suisse d'Histoire* 45, no. 2 (1995): 236–54.

Bull, Peter. "On Identifying Questions, Replies, and Non-replies in Political Interviews." *Journal of Language and Social Psychology* 13, no. 2 (1994): 115–31.

Burger, Peter L., and Thomas Luckman. *The Social Construction of Reality: A Treatise in the Sociology of Knowledge*. New York: Anchor, 1966.

Butler, Judith. *Gender Trouble: Feminism and the Subversion of Identity*. London: Routledge, 1990.

Button, Graham. "Answers as Interactional Products: Two Sequential Practices Used in Job Interviews." In Drew and Heritage, eds., *Talk at Work*, 212–31.

Campbell, Joan. "Developments in Oral History in Australia." *Oral History Review* 4 (1976): 49–52.

Capussotti, Enrica. "Memory: A Complex Battlefield." In Losi, Passerini, and Silvia, eds., "Archives of Memory," 194–218.

Carleton, Jill. "Embodying Autobiography: A Lesbian Performance of Gay Male Performance Arts." *Women and Performance: A Journal of Feminist Theory* 10, nos. 19–20 (1999): 73–83.

Carr, David. *Time, Narrative, and History*. Bloomington: University of Indiana Press, 1986.

Carr, Edward Hallett. *What Is History?* London: Macmillan, 1961.

Carroll, John B. *Language, Thought, and Reality: Selected Writings of Benjamin Lee Whorf*. Cambridge: Technology Press of Massachusetts Institute of Technology, 1956.

Cash, Joseph H., and Herbert T. Hoover. *To Be an Indian: An Oral History*. New York: Holt, Rinehart and Winston, 1971.

Cavarero, Adriana. *Relating Narratives: Storytelling and Selfhood*. Translated by Paul A. Kottman. London: Routledge, 2000.

Chafe, William Henry, Raymond Gavins, and Robert Rogers Korstad. *Remembering Jim Crow: African Americans Tell about Life in the Segregated South*. New York: New Press, 2001.

Chamberlain, Mary. "Gender and Memory: Oral History and Women's History." In *Engendering History: Caribbean Women in Historical Perspective*, edited by Verene Shepherd, Bridget Brereton, and Barbara Bailey, 94–110. New York: St. Martin's, 1995.

———. *Narratives of Exile and Return*. New York: St. Martin's, 1997.

———. "'Praise Songs' of the Family: Lineage and Kinship in the Caribbean Diaspora." *History Workshop Journal* 50 (Autumn 2000): 114–28.

Chamberlain, Mary, and Paul Thompson. "Genre and Narrative in Life Stories." In Chamberlain and Thompson, eds., *Narrative and Genre*, 1–22.

———, eds. *Narrative and Genre*. Routledge Studies in Memory and Narrative. London: Routledge, 1998.

Chamberlain, Mary, Paul Thompson, Selma Leydesdorff, and Kim Lacy Rogers, eds. "Introduction to the Series." In Chamberlain and Thompson, eds., *Narrative and Genre*, xiii–xv.

Chamberlayne, Prue, Joanna Bornat, and Tom Wengraf, eds. *The Turn to Biographical Methods in Social Science: Comparative Issues and Examples*. London: Routledge, 2000.

Chanfrault-Duchet, Marie-Françoise. "Narrative Structures, Social Models, and Symbolic Representation in the Life Story." In Gluck and Patai, eds., *Women's Words*, 77–92.

———. "Textualisation of the Self and Gender Identity in the Life Story." In Cosslett, Lury, and Summerfield, eds., *Feminism and Autobiography*, 61–75.

Charlton, Thomas L. *Oral History for Texans*. Austin: Texas Historical Commission, 1981.

———. *Oral History for Texans*. 2nd ed. Austin: Texas Historical Commission, 1985.

———. "Videotaped Oral Histories: Problems and Prospects." *American Archivist* 47, no. 3 (Summer 1984): 228–36.

Chartier, Roger. "Texts, Printing, Readings." In *The New Cultural History*, edited by Lynn Hunt, 154–75. Berkeley: University of California Press, 1989.

Chase, Susan E., and Colleen S. Bell. "Interpreting the Complexity of Women's Subjectivity." In McMahan and Rogers, eds., *Interactive Oral History Interviewing*, 63–81.

Chatterley, Cedric N., Alicia J. Rouverol, and Stephen A. Cole. *"I Was Content and Not Content": The Story of Linda Lord and the Closing of Penobscot Poultry*. Carbondale: Southern Illinois University Press, 2000.

Chevalier, Tracy. *Girl with a Pearl Earring*. New York: Dutton, 1999.

Child, Margaret S., comp. *Directory of Information Sources on Scientific Research Related to the Preservation of Sound Recordings, Still and Moving Images, and Magnetic Tape*. Washington, DC: Commission on Preservation and Access, 1993.

Christie, J. R. R., and Fred Orton. "Writing on a Text of the Life." *Art History* 11, no. 4 (December 1988): 545–62.

Church, Jonathan T., Linda Shopes, and Margaret A. Blanchard. "Should All Disciplines Be Subject to the Common Rule?" *Academe* 88, no. 3 (May–June 2002): 62–69.

Clark, E. Culpepper, Michael J. Hyde, and Eva M. McMahan. "Communication in the Oral History Interview: Investigating Problems of Interpreting Oral Data." Paper presented at the annual meeting of the Speech Communication Association, Minneapolis, November 5, 1978.

———. "Communication in the Oral History Interview: Investigating Problems of Interpreting Oral Data." *International Journal of Oral History* 1 (February 1980): 28–40.

Clayman, Steven E. "Answers and Evasions." *Language in Society* 30 (2001): 403–42.

———. "Displaying Neutrality in Television News Interviews." *Social Problems* 35, no. 4 (1988): 474–92.

———. "Footing in the Achievement of Neutrality: The Case of News-Interview Discourse." In Drew and Heritage, eds., *Talk at Work*, 163–98.

———. "News Interview Openings: Aspects of Sequential Organization." In *Broadcast Talk*, edited by Paddy Scannell, 48–75. London: Sage, 1991.

———. "Reformulating the Question: A Device for Answering/Not Answering Questions in News Interviews and Press Conferences." *Text* 13, no. 2 (1993): 159–88.

Clifford, James. *From Puzzles to Portraits: Problems of a Literary Biographer*. Chapel Hill: University of North Carolina Press, 1970.

Clifford, James, and George E. Marcus, eds. *Writing Culture: The Poetics and Politics of Ethnography*. Berkeley: University of California Press, 1986.

Cobb, James C. *"The Most Southern Place on Earth": The Mississippi Delta and the Roots of Regional Identity.* New York: Oxford University Press, 1992.

Cobley, Paul. *Narrative.* London: Routledge, 2001.

Cohen, Gillian. "The Effects of Aging on Autobiographical Memory." In Thompson, ed., *Autobiographical Memory,* 105–24.

Coles, Robert. *Doing Documentary Work.* New York: New York Public Library/Oxford University Press, 1997.

Collins, Mary. *National Public Radio: The Cast of Characters.* Washington, DC: Seven Locks, 1993.

Colman, Gould P., ed. *The Fourth National Colloquium on Oral History.* New York: Oral History Association, 1970.

———. "Oral History—An Appeal for More Systematic Procedures." *American Archivist* 28, no. 1 (January 1965): 79–83.

———. "Where to Now?" In Colman, ed., *Fourth National Colloquium,* 1–3.

Conaway, Charles William. "Lyman Copeland Draper, Father of American Oral History." *Journal of Library History* 1, no. 4 (1966): 234–41.

Conkin, Paul. Review of *Black Mountain,* by Martin Duberman. *Journal of American History* 60, no. 3 (September 1973): 512.

Connerton, Paul. *How Societies Remember.* Cambridge: Cambridge University Press, 1989.

Conquergood, Dwight. "Performing as a Moral Act: Ethical Dimensions of the Ethnography of Performance." *Literature in Performance* 5, no. 2 (April 1985): 1–13.

Contini, Giovanni. *La Memoria Divisa.* Milano: Rizzoli, 1997.

———. "Toward a Story of Oral History in Italy." In Hartewig and Halbach, eds., "History of Oral History," 57–69.

Cory, Mark E. "Soundplay: The Polyphonous Tradition of German Radio Art." In Kahn and Whitehead, eds., *Wireless Imagination,* 331–72.

Cosslett, Tess, Celia Lury, and Penny Summerfield, eds. *Feminism and Autobiography: Texts, Theories, Methods.* London: Routledge, 2000.

Cottle, Thomas J. *Private Lives and Public Accounts.* Amherst: University of Massachusetts Press, 1977.

Couch, William Terry. Preface to *These Are Our Lives.* Chapel Hill: University of North Carolina Press, 1939.

Crane, Susan A. "Writing the Individual Back into Collective Memory." *American Historical Review* 102, no. 5 (December 1997): 1372–85.

Crawford, Charles W. "Oral History—The State of the Profession." *Oral History Review* 2 (1974): 1–9.

Curry, Constance. *Silver Rights.* Chapel Hill, NC: Algonquin, 1999.

Cutler, William, III. "Accuracy in Oral History Interviewing." In Dunaway and Baum, eds., *Oral History,* 2nd ed., 99–106.

Daley, Caroline. "'He Would Know, But I Just Have a Feeling': Gender and Oral History." *Women's History Review* 7, no. 3 (1998): 343–59.

Davis, Cullom, Kathryn Back, and Kay MacLean. *Oral History: From Tape to Type.* Chicago: American Library Association, 1977.

Davis, David Brion. "Recent Directions in American Cultural History." *American Historical Review* 73, no. 3 (February 1968): 696–707.

Dawson, Graham. *Soldier Heroes: British Adventure, Empire, and the Imagining of Masculinities*. London: Routledge, 1994.

Dearling, Robert, and Celia Dearling. "Tape Recording." Section 5 in *The Guinness Book of Recorded Sound*. London: Guinness, 1984.

Deering, Mary Jo, and Barbara Pomeroy. *Transcribing without Tears: A Guide to Transcribing and Editing Oral History Interviews*. Washington, DC: George Washington University, 1976.

de Graaf, John, and Alan Harris Stein. "The Guerrilla Journalist as Oral Historian: An Interview with Louis 'Studs' Terkel." *Oral History Review* 29, no. 1 (Winter/Spring 2002): 87–107.

Denning, Michael. *Culture in the Age of Three Worlds*. New York: Verso, 2004.

Denzin, Norman K. *Interpretive Biography*. Thousand Oaks, CA: Sage, 1989.

DeVault, Marjorie. *Liberating Method: Feminism and Social Research*. Philadelphia: Temple University Press, 1999.

Dexter, Lewis Anthony. *Elite and Specialized Interviewing*. Evanston, IL: Northwestern University Press, 1970.

Dhupelia-Mesthrie, Uma. "Dispossession and Memory: The Black River Community in Cape Town." *Oral History: Journal of the Oral History Society* 28, no. 2 (Autumn 2000): 35–43.

Dickins, Dorothy. "Nutrition Investigation of Negro Tenants in the Yazoo Mississippi Delta." *Mississippi Agricultural Experiment Station Bulletin* 254: 30–33, 47.

Diaz, Rose T., and Andrew B. Russell. "Oral Historians: Community Oral History and the Cooperative Ideal." In *Public History: Essays from the Field*, edited by James B. Gardner and Peter S. LaPaglia, 203–16. Malabar, FL: Kreiger, 1999.

Dittmer, John. *Local People: The Struggle for Civil Rights in Mississippi*. Urbana: University of Illinois Press, 1994.

Dixon, Elizabeth I. "Definitions of Oral History." In Dixon and Mink, eds., *Oral History at Arrowhead*, 4–24.

Dixon, Elizabeth I., and Gould P. Colman. "Objectives and Standards." In Dixon and Mink, eds., *Oral History at Arrowhead*, 69–89.

Dixon, Elizabeth I., and James V. Mink, eds. *Oral History at Arrowhead: The Proceedings of the First National Colloquium on Oral History*. Los Angeles: Oral History Association, 1967.

Dollard, John. *Criteria for the Life History*. New Haven: Yale University Press, 1935.

Dosse, François. *History of Structuralism. Vol. 1. The Rising Sign, 1945–1966*. Translated by Deborah Glassman. Minneapolis: University of Minnesota Press, 1977.

Drew, Paul, and John Heritage. "Analyzing Talk at Work: An Introduction." In Drew and Heritage, eds., *Talk at Work*, 3–65.

———, eds. *Talk at Work: Interaction in Institutional Settings*. Cambridge: Cambridge University Press, 1992.

Duberman, Martin. *Black Mountain: An Exploration in Community*. New York: E. P. Dutton, 1972.

Dudley, Kathryn Marie. "In the Archive, in the Field: What Kind of Document Is an 'Oral History'?" In Chamberlain and Thompson, eds., *Narrative and Genre*, 160–66.

Dunaway, David King. "Field Recording Oral History." *Oral History Review* 15, no. 1 (Spring 1987): 21–42.

———. "The Interdisciplinarity of Oral History." In Dunaway and Baum, eds., *Oral History*, 2nd ed., 7–22.

———. "The Oral Biography." *Biography* 4, no. 3 (1991): 256–66.

———. "Radio and the Public Use of Oral History." In Dunaway and Baum, eds., *Oral History* (1984), 333–46.

———. "Radio and the Public Use of Oral History." In Dunaway and Baum, eds., *Oral History*, 2nd ed., 306–20.

———. "Transcription: Shadow or Reality?" *Oral History Review* 12 (1984): 113–17.

Dunaway, David K., and Willa K. Baum, eds. *Oral History: An Interdisciplinary Anthology*. Nashville, TN: American Association for State and Local History, 1984.

———. *Oral History: An Interdisciplinary Anthology*. 2nd ed. American Association for State and Local History Book Series. Walnut Creek, CA: AltaMira, 1996.

Dundes, Alan, ed. *Sacred Narrative: Readings in the Theory of Myth*. Berkeley: University of California Press, 1984.

———. "Texture, Text, and Context." *Southern Folklore Quarterly* 28 (1964): 251–65.

Eagleton, Terry. *Ideology: An Introduction*. London: Verso, 1991.

Ebbinghaus, Hermann. *Memory: A Contribution to Experimental Psychology*. Translated by Henry A. Ruger and Clara E. Bussenius. 1913. Reprint; New York: Dover, 1987.

Edel, Leon. "Figure under the Carpet." In *Telling Lives*, 16–34.

———. *Literary Biography*. London: R. Hart Davis, 1957.

———. *Telling Lives: The Biographer's Art*. Edited by Marc Pachter. Washington, DC: New Republic Books, 1979.

Edwards, Jane A., and Marin D. Lampert, eds. *Talking Data: Transcription and Coding in Discourse Research*. Hillsdale, NJ: Erlbaum, 1993.

Elder, Glen H., Jr. *Children of the Great Depression: Social Change in Life Experience*. Chicago: University of Chicago Press, 1974.

———. *Children of the Great Depression: Social Change in Life Experience*. 25th Anniversary ed. Boulder, CO: Westview, 1999.

———. "The Life Course and Human Development." In *Handbook of Child Psychology*, edited by William Damon, 5th ed., Vol. 1, *Theoretical Models of Human Development*, edited by Richard M. Lerner, 939–91. New York: Wiley, 1998.

———, ed. *Life Course Dynamics: Trajectories and Transitions, 1968–1980*. Ithaca, NY: Cornell University Press, 1985.

———. "Time, Human Agency, and Perspectives on the Life Course." *Social Psychology Quarterly* 57 (1994): 4–15.

Eley, Geoff. "Is All the World a Text? From Social History of Society to the History of Society Two Decades Later." In *The Historic Turn in the Social Sciences,* edited by Terrence McDonald, 193–244. Ann Arbor: University of Michigan Press, 1996.

Elias, Norbert. "On Human Beings and Their Emotions: A Process Sociological Essay." In *The Body: Social Process and Cultural Theory,* edited by Mike Featherstone, Mike Hepworth, and Bryan S. Turner, 103–25. London: Sage, 1991.

Ellmann, Richard. *Literary Biography.* Oxford: Clarendon, 1971.

Elms, Alan C. *Uncovering Lives: The Uneasy Alliance of Biography and Psychology.* New York: Oxford University Press, 1994.

Ely, Richard, and Allyssa McCabe. "Gender Differences in Memories for Speech." In Leydesdorff, Passerini, and Thompson, eds., *Gender and Memory,* 17–30.

Erikson, Erik. *Childhood and Society.* New York: Norton, 1950.

Erofeyev, Victor. "Dirty Words." *New Yorker,* September 15, 2003, 42–48.

Etter-Lewis, Gwendolyn. "Black Women's Life Stories: Reclaiming Self in Narrative Texts." In Gluck and Patai, eds., *Women's Words,* 43–58.

Eustis, Truman W., III. "Get It in Writing: Oral History and the Law." *Oral History Review* 4 (1976): 6–18.

Evans, George Ewart. *Where Beards Wag All: The Relevance of Oral Tradition.* London: Faber, 1970.

Everett, Stephen E. *Oral History Techniques and Procedures.* Washington, DC: Center of Military History, U.S. Army, 1992.

Eynon, Bret. "Oral History and the New Century," *Oral History Review* 26, no. 2 (Summer/Fall 1999): 16–27.

Fabian, Johannes. *Power and Performance: Ethnographic Exploration through Proverbial Wisdom and Theater in Shaba, Zaire.* Madison: University of Wisconsin Press, 1990.

Faderman, Lillian. *Odd Girls and Twilight Lovers: A History of Lesbian Life in Twentieth-Century America.* New York: Columbia University Press, 1991.

Faires, Nora. "The Great Flint Sit-Down Strike as Theater." *Radical History Review* 43 (1989): 121–35.

Faris, David E. "Narrative Form and Oral History: Some Problems and Possibilities." *International Journal of Oral History* 1, no. 3 (November 1980): 159–80.

Farmer, Paul. "On Suffering and Structural Violence: A View from Below." In *Social Suffering,* edited by Arthur Kleinman, Veena Das, and Margaret Lock, 261–84. Berkeley: University of California Press, 1997.

Farquhar, Peter, and Marjorie Bridge Farquhar. *MBF Marjory B. Farquhar: A Family History.* Berkeley: University of California, Berkeley, Regional Oral History Office, 1996. CD-ROM.

Faseke, Modupeola M. "Oral History in Nigeria: Issues, Problems, and Prospects." *Oral History Review* 18, no. 1 (Spring 1990): 77–91.

Fee, Elizabeth, Linda Shopes, and Linda Zeidman, eds. *The Baltimore Book: New Views of Local History.* Philadelphia: Temple University Press, 1991.

Feierman, Steven. "Colonizers, Scholars, and the Creation of Invisible Histories." In Bonnell and Hunt, eds., *Beyond the Cultural Turn,* 182–216.

Feinstein, David, Stanley Krippner, and Dennis Granger. "Mythmaking and Human Development." *Journal of Humanistic Psychology* 28, no. 3 (1988): 23–50.

Feldman, Allen. *Formations of Violence: The Narrative of the Body and Political Terror in Northern Ireland.* Chicago: University of Chicago Press, 1991.

Feldstein, Mark. "Kissing Cousins: Journalism and Oral History." *Oral History Review* 31, no. 1 (Winter/Spring 2004): 1–22.

Fentress, James, and Chris Wickham. *Social Memory.* Oxford: Blackwell, 1992.

Fetner, Gerald L. *Immersed in Great Affairs: Allan Nevins and the Heroic Age of American History.* Albany: State University of New York Press, 2004.

Feuchtwang, Stephan. "Distant Homes, Our Genre: Recognizing Chinese Lives as an Anthropologist." In Chamberlain and Thompson, eds., *Narrative and Genre,* 126–41.

Feynman, Richard P. *What Do You Care What Other People Think? Further Adventures of a Curious Character.* New York: Norton, 1988.

Fields, Karen E. "What One Cannot Remember Mistakenly." In Jeffrey and Edwall, eds., *Memory and History,* 89–104.

Fields, Mamie Garvin, with Karen Fields. *Lemon Swamp and Other Places: A Carolina Memoir.* New York: Free Press, 1983.

Fine, Elizabeth C. *The Folklore Text: From Performance to Print.* Bloomington: Indiana University Press, 1984.

Finnegan, Ruth. *Oral Literature in Africa.* Nairobi: Oxford University Press, 1970.

Fisher, H. A. L. *A History of Europe.* Complete edition in one volume. 1936. Reprint; London: Edward Arnold, 1941.

Fogerty, James E. "Filling the Gap: Oral History in the Archives." *American Archivist* 46, no. 2 (Spring 1983): 148–57.

———. "Oral History as a Tool in Archival Development." *Comma: International Journal on Archives* 1–2 (2002): 207–10.

Fonow, Mary Margaret, and Judith A. Cook. *Beyond Methodology: Feminist Scholarship as Lived Research.* Bloomington: Indiana University Press, 1991.

Fontana, Andrea, and James H. Frey. "The Interview: From Structured Questions to Negotiated Text." In *Handbook of Qualitative Research,* 2nd ed., edited by N. K. Denzin and Y. S. Lincoln, 645–72. Thousand Oaks, CA: Sage, 2000.

Fornatale, Peter, and Joshua E. Mills. *Radio in the Television Age.* Woodstock, NY: Overlook, 1980.

Foronda, Marcelino A., Jr. *Kaysaysayan: Studies on Local and Oral History.* Manila: De La Salle University Press, 1991.

———. "Oral History in the Philippines." *International Journal of Oral History* 2, no. 1 (February 1981): 13–25.

Fosl, Catherine. "When Subjects Talk Back: Writing Anne Braden's Life-in-Progress." Paper presented at the annual meeting of the Oral History Association, Bethesda, MD, October 10, 2003.

Foucault, Michel. "What Is an Author?" In *Textual Strategies: Perspectives in Post-Structuralist Criticism,* edited by Josué V. Harari, 141–60. Ithaca, NY: Cornell University Press, 1979.

Fox, Nicols. "NPR Grows Up." *Washington Journalism Review* 13, no. 7 (September 1991): 30–37.

Franco, Barbara. "Doing History in Public: Balancing Historical Fact with Public Meaning." *AHA Perspectives* 33, no. 5 (May–June 1995): 5–8.

———. "Raising the Issues." Paper presented at Raising Our Sites conference, Pennsylvania Humanities Council, Philadelphia, February 2000.

Frank, Gelya. "'Becoming the Other': Empathy and Biographical Interpretation." *Biography* 8, no. 3 (1985): 189–210.

Frankel, Richard. "Talking in Interviews: A Dispreference for Patient-Initiated Questions in Physician-Patient Encounters." In *Everyday Language Studies in Ethnomethodology*, edited by G. Psathas, 231–62. Lanham, MD: University Press of America, 1979.

Frantz, Joe. "Video-Taping Notable U.S. Historians." In *Third National Colloquium on Oral History*, edited by Gould P. Colman. New York: Oral History Association, 1969.

Frattaroli, Elio. "Healing the Soul: Why Medication for Anxiety and Depression Is Not Enough." Paper presented to the North Carolina Psychoanalytic Foundation, Research Triangle Park, March 1, 2003.

Friedlander, Peter. *The Emergence of a UAW Local, 1936–1939: A Study in Class and Culture*. Pittsburgh, PA: University of Pittsburgh Press, 1975.

Friedman, Jeff. "Muscle Memory: Performing Embodied Knowledge." In *The Art and Performance of Memory: Sounds and Gestures of Recollection*, edited by Richard Cándida Smith, 156–80. London: Routledge, 2003.

———. "'Wave When You Pass': Presented by the StreetSigns Center for Literature and Performance." *Oral History Review* 28, no. 1 (Winter–Spring 2001): 127–32.

Friedman, W. J., and P. A. deWinstanley, "Changes in the Subjective Properties of Autobiographical Memories with the Passage of Time." *Memory* 6 (1998): 367–81.

Frisch, Michael. "Commentary, Sharing Authority: Oral History and the Collaborative Process." *Oral History Review* 30, no. 1 (Winter–Spring 2003): 111–14.

———. "Editor's Introduction." *Oral History Review* 18, no. 2 (Fall 1990).

———. "Oral History and *Hard Times*: A Review Essay." *Oral History Review* (1979): 70–79.

———. "Oral History and *Hard Times*: A Review Essay." In *Shared Authority* (1990), 5–13.

———. "Oral History and *Hard Times*: A Review Essay." In Perks and Thomson, eds., *Oral History Reader* (1998), 29–37.

———. "Preparing Interview Transcripts for Documentary Publication: A Line-by-Line Illustration of the Editing Process." In *Shared Authority*, 81–146.

———. *A Shared Authority: Essays on the Craft and Meaning of Oral and Public History*. Albany: State University of New York Press, 1990.

Frisch, Michael, and Linda Shopes. "Introduction." *Journal of American History* 81 (1994): 592–93.

Frontiers: A Journal of Women Studies 2, no. 2 (Summer 1977).

Frontiers: A Journal of Women Studies 7, no. 1 (1983).

Frontiers: A Journal of Women Studies 19, no. 2 (1998).

Frontiers: A Journal of Women Studies 19, no. 3 (1998).

Fry, Amelia R. "Reflections on Ethics." *Oral History Review* 3 (1975): 17–28.

Fukuyama, Francis. *The End of History and the Last Man.* Harmondsworth: Penguin, 1992.

Futrell, Allan W., and Charles A. Willard. "Intersubjectivity and Interviewing." In McMahan and Rogers, eds., *Interactive Oral History Interviewing,* 83–105.

Gadamer, Hans-Georg. *Truth and Method.* Edited by Garrett Barden and John Cumming. New York: Seabury, 1975.

Gaines, Kevin. *Uplifting the Race: Black Leadership, Politics, and Culture in the Twentieth Century.* Chapel Hill: University of North Carolina Press, 1996.

Gallacher, Cathryn A., and Dale Treleven. "Developing an Online Database and Printed Directory and Subject Guide to Oral History Collections." *Oral History Review* 16 (1988): 33–68.

Garcia, Mario T. *Memories of Chicano History: The Life and Narrative of Bert Corona.* Berkeley: University of California Press, 1994.

Garner, Lori Ann. "Representations of Speech in the WPA Slave Narratives of Florida and the Writings of Zora Neale Hurston." *Western Folklore* 59, no. 3/4 (Summer/Fall 2000): 215–31.

Gay, Peter. *Freud: A Life for Our Time.* New York: Norton, 1988.

Geer, Richard Owen. "Out of Control in Colquitt: Swamp Gravy Makes Stone Soup." *Drama Review* 40, no. 2 (Summer 1996): 103–30.

Geertz, Clifford. "Ideology as a Cultural System." In *Interpretation of Cultures,* 193–233.

——. *The Interpretation of Cultures.* New York: Basic, 1973.

Geiger, Susan. "What's So Feminist about Women's Oral History?" *Journal of Women's History* 2, no. 1 (1990): 169–82.

Gellner, Ernst. *Thought and Change.* London: Weidenfeld and Nicolson, 1964.

Georges, Robert A. "Toward an Understanding of Storytelling Events." *Journal of American Folklore* 82 (1969): 313–28.

Giddens, D. John Anthony. *Modernity and Self-Identity: Self and Society in the Late Modern Age.* Cambridge: Polity, 1991.

Giele, Janet Z., and Glen H. Elder Jr., eds. *Methods of Life Course Research: Qualitative and Quantitative Approaches.* Thousand Oaks, CA: Sage, 1998.

Gilb, Corrine L. "Tape Recorded Interviewing: Some Thoughts from California." *American Archivist* 20 (October 1957): 335–44.

Gilligan, Carol. *In a Different Voice.* Cambridge, MA: Harvard University Press, 1982.

Gilligan, Carol, and Lyn Mikel Brown. *Meeting at the Crossroads: Women's Psychology and Girls' Development.* Cambridge, MA: Harvard University Press, 1992.

Gilyard, Keith. *Let's Flip the Script: An African American Discourse on Language, Literature, and Learning.* Detroit: Wayne State University Press, 1996.

Glaser, Barney, and Anselm Strauss. *The Discovery of Grounded Theory: Strategies for Qualitative Research.* Chicago: Aldine, 1967.

Glassie, Henry. *Passing the Time in Ballymenone: Culture and History of an Ulster Community*. Philadelphia: University of Pennsylvania Press, 1982.

Gluck, Carol. *Japan's Modern Myths: Ideology in the Late Meiji Period*. Princeton, NJ: Princeton University Press, 1989.

Gluck, Sherna Berger. "Advocacy Oral History: Palestinian Women in Resistance." In Gluck and Patai, eds., *Women's Words*, 205–19.

——. *An American Feminist in Palestine: The Intifada Years*. Philadelphia: Temple University Press, 1994.

——. "From First Generation Oral Historian to Fourth and Beyond." *Oral History Review* 26, no. 2 (Summer–Fall 1999): 1–9.

——, ed. *From Parlor to Prison: Five American Suffragists Talk about Their Lives*. New York: Random House, 1977.

——. "'We Will Not Be Another Algeria'; Women's Mass Organizations, Changing Consciousness, and the Potential for Women's Liberation in a Future Palestine State." In Grele, ed., *International Annual 1990*, 211–28.

——. "What's So Special about Women? Women's Oral History." *Frontiers: Journal of Women Studies* 2, no. 1 (Summer 1977): 3–13.

——. "What's So Special about Women? Women's Oral History." In Dunaway and Baum, eds., *Oral History* (1984), 221–37.

——. "What's So Special about Women? Women's Oral History." In Dunaway and Baum, eds., *Oral History*, 2nd ed. (1996), 215–30.

Gluck, Sherna Berger, and Daphne Patai. Afterword. In *Women's Words*, 221–23.

——. Introduction. In *Women's Words*, 1–5.

——. "The Memory of Politics and the Politics of Memory: Palestinian Women's Narratives." Paper presented for Middle East Studies Association, San Francisco, 1997.

——, eds. *Women's Words: The Feminist Practice of Oral History*. London: Routledge, 1991.

Gluck, Sherna Berger, Donald A. Ritchie, and Bret Eynon. "Reflections on Oral History in the New Millennium: Roundtable Comments." *Oral History Review* 26 (Summer–Fall 1999): 1–28.

Goffman, Erving. *Behavior in Public Places: Notes on the Social Organization of Gatherings*. New York: Free Press of Glencoe, 1963.

——. *Forms of Talk*. Philadelphia: University of Pennsylvania Press, 1981.

——. *The Presentation of Self in Everyday Life*. Garden City, NY: Doubleday Anchor, 1959.

Goldberg, Stanley. "The Manhattan Project Series." In Schorzman, ed., *Introduction to Videohistory*, 83–100.

Good, Francis. "Voice, Ear and Text: Words & Meaning." *Oral History Association of Australia Journal* 22 (2000): 104.

Gordon, Lyndall. "Women's Lives: The Unmapped Country." In *The Art of Literary Biography*, edited by John Batchelor, 87–98. Oxford: Clarendon, 1995.

Gorfein, David S., and Robert R. Hoffman. *Memory and Learning: The Ebbinghaus Centennial Conference 1985*. Hillsdale, NJ: Erlbaum, 1987.

Gould, Glenn. *Glenn Gould's Solitude Triology: Three Sound Documentaries*. Toronto: CBC Records, 1992. 3 compact discs.

Govoni, Paolo. "Biography: A Critical Tool to Bridge the History of Science and the History of Women in Science." *Nuncius* 15, no. 1 (2000): 399–409.

Greatbach, David. "Aspects of Topical Organization in News Interviews: The Use of Agenda-Shifting Procedures by Interviewees." *Media, Culture, and Society* 8 (1986): 441–55.

———. "On the Management of Disagreement between News Interviewees." In Drew and Heritage, eds., *Talk at Work*, 268–301.

———. "Some Standard Uses of Supplementary Questions in News Interviews." In *Belfast Working Papers in Language and Linguistics*, edited by J. Wilson and B. W. Crow, 86–123. Belfast: University of Ulster, 1986.

Green, Anna. "Returning History to the Community: Oral History in a Museum Setting." *Oral History Review* 24, no. 2 (Winter 1997): 53–72.

Green, Jim. Review of *Rank and File: Personal Histories of Working Class Organizers*, edited by Alice Lynd and Staughton Lynd. *History Workshop* 4 (Autumn 1977): 223–25.

Greenspan, Miriam. *Healing through the Dark Emotions: The Wisdom of Grief, Fear, and Despair.* Boston: Shambhala, 2003.

Greenwood, Dorothy F. "Radio's Part in Adult Education." In Marx, ed., *Television and Radio*, 147–52.

Grele, Ronald J. "Can Anyone over Thirty Be Trusted?: A Friendly Critique of Oral History." *Oral History Review* (1978): 36–44.

———. "Concluding Comment." *International Journal of Oral History* 6, no. 1 (February 1985): 42–46.

———. "The Development, Cultural Peculiarities and State of Oral History in the United States." In Hartewig and Halbach, eds., "History of Oral History," 3–15.

———. "Editorial." *International Journal of Oral History* 1, no. 1 (February 1980): 2–3.

———, ed. *Envelopes of Sound: Six Practitioners Discuss the Method, Theory, and Practice of Oral History and Oral Testimony.* Chicago: Precedent, 1975.

———, ed. *Envelopes of Sound: The Art of Oral History.* 2nd ed. New York: Praeger, 1991.

———. "History and the Languages of History in the Oral History Interview: Who Answers Whose Questions and Why?" In McMahan and Rogers, eds., *Interactive Oral History Interviewing*, 1–18.

———, ed. *International Annual of Oral History 1990: Subjectivity and Multiculturalism in Oral History.* London: Greenwood, 1992.

———. Introduction. *The UCLA Oral History Program: Catalog of the Collection*, compiled by Constance S. Bullock with the assistance of Saundra Taylor. Los Angeles: University of California, 1982.

———. "Listen to Their Voices: Two Case Studies in the Interpretation of Oral History Interviews." In *Envelopes of Sound*, 2nd ed., 212–36.

———. "Movement without Aim: Methodological and Theoretical Problems in Oral History." In *Envelopes of Sound*, 2nd ed., 126–54.

———. "Oral History." In *Encyclopedia of Historians and Historical Writing*, edited by Kelly Boyd. 2 vols. Chicago: Fitzroy Dearborn, 1999.

———. "Riffs and Improvisations: An Interview with Studs Terkel." In *Envelopes of Sound*, 2nd ed., 10–49.

———. "A Surmisable Variety: Interdisciplinarity and Oral Testimony." In *Envelopes of Sound*, 2nd ed., 156–95.

———. "Why Call It Oral History: Some Ruminations from the Field." *Pennsylvania History* 60, no. 4 (October 1993): 506–9.

Greven, Philip. *Four Generations: Population, Land, and Family in Colonial Andover, Massachusetts*. Ithaca, NY: Cornell University Press, 1970.

Gugelberger, George M., ed. *The Real Thing: Testimonial Discourse and Latin America*. Durham, NC: Duke University Press, 1996.

Hagestad, Gunhild O. "Social Perspectives on the Life Course." In *Handbook of Aging and the Social Sciences*, 3rd ed., edited by Robert H. Binstock and Linda K. George, 151–68. San Diego: Academic, 1990.

Halbwachs, Maurice. *On Collective Memory*. New York: Harper and Row, 1980.

Hale, Sondra. "Feminist Method, Process, and Self-Criticism: Interviewing Sudanese Women." In Gluck and Patai, eds., *Women's Words*, 121–36.

Haley, Alex. "Black History, Oral History, and Genealogy." *Oral History Review* 1 (1973): 1–25.

———. *Roots: The Saga of an American Family*. Garden City, NY: Doubleday, 1976.

Hall, Jacquelyn Dowd. "'You Must Remember This': Autobiography as Social Critique." *Journal of American History* 85, no. 2 (September 1998): 439–65.

Hall, Jacquelyn Dowd, James Leloudis, Robert Korstad, Mary Murphy, Lu Ann Jones, and Christopher B. Daly. Foreword by Michael Frisch. *Like a Family: The Making of a Southern Cotton Mill World*. 2nd ed. Chapel Hill: University of North Carolina Press, 2000.

Hall, Lesley. "Confidentially Speaking: Ethics in an Interview Situation." *Oral History in New Zealand* 11 (1999): 19–22.

Halttunen, Karen. "Cultural History and the Challenge of Narrativity." In Bonnell and Hunt, eds., *Beyond the Cultural Turn*, 165–81.

Hamilton, E. Douglas. "Oral History and the Law of Libel." In Starr, *Second National Colloquium on Oral History*, 41–56.

Hanke, Lewis. "American Historians and the World Today: Responsibilities and Opportunities." *American Historical Review* 80 (1975): 1–20.

Hankins, Thomas L. "In Defence of Biography: The Use of Biography in the History of Science." *History of Science* 17 (1979): 1–16.

Hankiss, Agnes. "Ontologies of the Self: On the Mythological Rearranging of One's Own Life History." In *Biology and Society: The Life History Approach in the Social Sciences*, edited by Daniel Bertaux, 203–9. Beverly Hills, CA: Sage, 1981.

Hansen, Arthur. "A Riot of Voices: Racial and Ethnic Variables in Interactive Oral History Interviewing." In McMahan and Rogers, *Interactive Oral History Interviewing*, 107–39.

Haraway, Donna. *Primate Visions*. London: Routledge, 1989.

Hardy, Charles, III. "Authoring in Sound: An Eccentric Essay on Aural History, Radio, and Media Convergence." Unpublished manuscript.

———. "An Interview with Alice Hoffman." *Oral History Review* 28, no. 2 (Summer–Fall 2001): 101–35.

———. "Prodigal Sons, Trap Doors, and Painted Women: Reflections on Life Stories, Urban Legends, and Aural History." *Oral History: Journal of the Oral History Society* 29, no. 1 (Spring 2001): 98–105.

Hareven, Tamara K. *Aging and Generational Relations: Life-Course and Cross-Cultural Perspectives.* New York: Aldine de Gruyter, 1996.

———. "The Search for Generational Memory." In Dunaway and Baum, eds., *Oral History*, 2nd ed., 241–56.

Hareven, Tamara K., and Randolph Langenbach. *Amoskeag: Life and Work in an American Factory-City.* New York: Pantheon, 1978.

Hareven, Tamara, and Andrejs Plakans. *Family History at the Crossroads.* Princeton, NJ: Princeton University Press, 1987.

Harris, J. William. *Deep Souths: Delta, Piedmont, and Sea Island Society in the Age of Segregation.* Baltimore, MD: Johns Hopkins University Press, 2001.

Harris, Ramon, Joseph Cash, Herbert Hoover, and Stephen Ward. *The Practice of Oral History: A Handbook.* Glen Rock, NJ: Microfilming Corporation of America, 1975.

Hart, James D. Foreword. *Catalogue of the Regional Oral History Office 1954–1979*, edited by Suzanne B. Riess and Willa K. Baum. Berkeley: Bancroft Library, University of California, 1980.

Hartewig, Karin, and Wulf R. Halbach, eds. "The History of Oral History: Development, Present State, and Future Prospects." Special issue, *BIOS: Zeitschrift für Biographieforschung und Oral History*, 1990.

Hay, Harry. *Radically Gay: Gay Liberation in the Words of Its Founder.* Edited by Will Roscoe. Boston: Beacon, 1996.

Healey, Dorothy. *Dorothy Healey Remembers: A Life in the American Communist Party.* Edited by Maurice Isserman. New York: Oxford University Press, 1990.

Heath, Christian. "The Delivery and Reception of Diagnosis in the General Practice Consultation." In Drew and Heritage, eds., *Talk at Work*, 235–67.

Hebrew University of Jerusalem, Institute of Contemporary Jewry, Oral History Division. *Catalogue 1.* Jerusalem: The Division, 1963.

Heilbrun, Carolyn G. *Writing a Woman's Life.* New York: Ballantine, 1989.

Henige, David. *Oral Historiography.* New York: Longman, 1988.

Heritage, John, and Andrew Roth. "Grammar and Institution: Questions and Questioning in the Broadcast News Interview." *Research in Language and Social Interaction* 28, no. 1 (1995): 1–60.

Hewins, Angela. *The Dillen: Memories of a Man of Stratford-upon-Avon.* Oxford: Oxford University Press, 1981.

Hill, Jonathan D. "Myth and History." In *Rethinking History and Myth: Indigenous South American Perspectives on the Past*, 1–18. Chicago: University of Illinois Press, 1988.

Hill, Ruth Edmonds, ed. *Women of Courage: An Exhibition of Photographs by Judith Sedwick.* Cambridge, MA: Radcliffe College, 1984.

Hiltermann, Joost R. *Behind the Intifada: Labor and Women's Movements in the Occupied Territories.* Princeton, NJ: Princeton University Press, 1991.

Hinsdale, Mary Ann, Helen M. Lewis, and S. Maxine Waller. *It Comes from the People: Community Development and Local Theology.* Philadelphia: Temple University Press, 1995.

Hirsch, Jerrold. *Portrait of America: A Cultural History of the Federal Writers' Project.* Chapel Hill: University of North Carolina Press, 2003.

History Workshop Journal. "Editorial: Oral History." *History Workshop Journal* 8 (Autumn 1979): i–iii.

Hodgkin, Katherine, and Susannah Radstone, eds. *Contested Pasts: The Politics of Memory.* London: Routledge, 2003.

———. *Regimes of Memory.* London: Routledge, 2003.

Hoffman, Alice. "Reliability and Validity in Oral History." In Dunaway and Baum, eds., *Oral History* (1984), 67–73.

———. "Reliability and Validity in Oral History." In Dunaway and Baum, eds., *Oral History*, 2nd ed. (1996), 87–93.

———. "Who Are the Elite, and What Is a Non-Elitist?" *Oral History Review* 4 (1976): 1–5.

Hoffman, Alice M., and Howard S. Hoffman. *Archives of Memory: A Soldier Recalls World War II.* Lexington: University Press of Kentucky, 1990.

———. "Reliability and Validity in Oral History: The Case for Memory." In Jeffrey and Edwall, eds., *Memory and History*, 107–30.

Hofmeyr, Isabel. "Jonah and the Swallowing Monster: Orality and Literacy on a Berlin Mission Station in the Transvaal." *Journal of Southern African Studies* 17, no. 4 (December 1991): 633–53.

———. "'Nterata'/'The Wire': Fences, Boundaries, Orality, Literacy." In Grele, ed., *International Annual 1990*, 69–92.

Holman, Barbara D. *Oral History Collection of the Forest History Society: An Annotated Guide.* Guides to Forest and Conservation History of North American, no. 1. Santa Cruz, CA: Forest History Society, 1976.

Holstein, James A., and Jaber F. Gubrium. *The Self We Live By: Narrative Identity in a Postmodern World.* New York: Oxford University Press, 2000.

Honig, Emily. "Getting to the Source: Striking Lives, Oral History, and the Politics of Memory." *Journal of Women's History* 9, no. 1 (1997): 139–57.

Hoopes, James. *Oral History: An Introduction for Students.* Chapel Hill: University of North Carolina Press, 1979.

Hopper, Robert. "Conversational Dramatism and Everyday Life Performance." *Text and Performance Quarterly* 13, no. 2 (April 1993): 181–83.

Horowitz, Robert F. "History Comes to Life and *You Are There.*" In O'Connor, ed., *American History, American Television*, 79–94.

Howe, Michael A. *Introduction to Human Memory: A Psychological Approach.* New York: Harper and Row, 1970.

Hutchby, Ian, and Robin Wooffitt. *Conversation Analysis.* Cambridge: Polity, 1998.

Hutton, Patrick. *History as an Art of Memory.* Hanover, NH: University Press of New England, 1993.

Hyde, Michael J. "Paradox: Toward a Prescriptive Theory of Communication." Ph.D. diss., Purdue University, 1977.

Hymes, Dell. "Folklore's Nature and the Sun's Myths." *Journal of American Folklore* 84 (1975): 345–69.

Ihde, Don. *Listening and Voice: A Phenomenology of Sound.* Athens: University of Ohio Press, 1976.

Ives, Edward D. *The Tape-Recorded Interview: A Manual for Field Workers in Folklore and Oral History.* Rev. and enl. ed. Knoxville: University of Tennessee Press, 1980.

———. *The Tape-Recorded Interview: A Manual for Field Workers in Folklore and Oral History.* 2nd ed. Knoxville: University of Tennessee Press, 1995.

Jaarsma, Sjoerd R., ed. *Handle with Care: Ownership and Control of Ethnographic Materials.* Pittsburgh, PA: University of Pittsburgh Press, 2002.

Jackson, Bruce. *Fieldwork.* Urbana: University of Illinois Press, 1987.

Jacobs, Wilbur R. *On Turner's Trail: 100 Years of Writing Western History.* Lawrence: University Press of Kansas, 1994.

James, Daniel. "'The Case of María Roldán and the Señora with Money Is Very Clear, It's a Fable': Stories, Anecdotes, and Other Performances in Doña María's Testimony." In *Doña María's Story*, 120–56.

———. *Doña María's Story: Life History, Memory, and Political Identity.* Durham, NC: Duke University Press, 2000.

———. "Meatpackers, Peronists, and Collective Memory: A View from the South." *American Historical Review* 102, no. 5 (December 1997): 1404–12.

———. "'Tales Told Out on the Borderlands': Reading Doña María's Story for Gender." In *Doña María's Story*, 213–43.

James, William. *Psychology.* Cleveland: World Publishing, 1948.

Jamieson, Ronda. "Some Aspects of Oral History in New Zealand, the United States of America and the United Kingdom." *Report for the Winston Churchill Memorial Trust of Australia.* Melbourne: Oral History Association of Australia, 1992.

Jay, Martin. "Should Intellectual History Take a Linguistic Turn? Reflections on the Habermas-Gadamer Debate." In LaCapra and Kaplan, eds., *Modern European Intellectual History*, 86–110.

Jefferson, Alphine. "Echoes from the South: The History and Methodology of the Duke University Oral History Program, 1972–1982." *Oral History Review* 12 (1984): 43–62.

Jeffrey, Jaclyn, and Glenace Edwall, eds. *Memory and History: Essays on Recalling and Interpreting Experience.* Lanham, MD: University Press of America, 1994.

Jelin, Elizabeth, and Susana C. Kaufman. "Layers of Memory: Twenty Years after in Argentina." In *The Politics of War: Memory and Commemoration*, edited by T. G. Ashplant, Graham Dawson, and Michael Roper, 87–110. London: Routledge, 2000.

Jensen, Richard. "Oral History, Quantification, and the New Social History." *Oral History Review* 9 (1981): 13–25.

Johnson, Richard. "Edward Thompson and Eugene Genovese and Socialist Humanist History." *History Workshop* 6 (Autumn 1978): 79–100.

Jones, LeAlan, Lloyd Newman, and David Isay. *Ghetto Life 101; Remorse: The Fourteen Stories of Eric Morse*. New York: Sound Portraits Productions, 1997. Compact disc.

———. *Our America: Life and Death on the South Side of Chicago*. New York: Scribner, 1997.

Jones, Rebecca. "*Blended Voices*: Crafting a Narrative from Oral History Interviews." *Oral History Review* 31, no. 1 (Winter/Spring 2004): 23–42.

Jorgensen, Beth Ellen. *The Writing of Elena Poniatowska: Engaging Dialogues*. Austin: University of Texas Press, 1994.

Josselson, Ruthellen, ed. *Ethics and Process in the Narrative Study of Lives*. Thousand Oaks, CA: Sage, 1996.

Joutard, Phillipe. *La Legende des Camisards: une Sensibilite au Passé*. Paris: Gallimard, 1977.

Joyce, Rosemary O. *A Woman's Place: The Life History of a Rural Ohio Grandmother*. Columbus: Ohio State University Press, 1983.

Jung, Carl. *Man and His Symbols*. Garden City, NY: Doubleday, 1964.

———. *Memories, Dreams, Reflections*. Edited by Aniela Jaffe. Translated by Richard and Clara Winston. New York: Random House, 1961.

———. "The Relations between the Ego and the Unconscious. Part Two: Individuation." In *The Basic Writings of C. G. Jung*, edited by Violet Staub de Laszlo, 181–229. New York: Modern Library, 1993.

Kahn, Douglas, and Gregory Whitehead, eds. *Wireless Imagination: Sound, Radio, and the Avant-Garde*. Cambridge, MA: MIT Press, 1992.

Kahn, Robert L., and Toni C. Antonucci. "Convoys of Social Support: A Life-Course Approach." In *Aging: Social Change*, edited by Sara B. Kiesler, James N. Morgan, and Valerie Kincade Oppenheimer, 383–405. New York: Academic, 1981.

Kammen, Michael. *Mystic Chords of Memory: The Transformation of Tradition in American Culture*. New York: Knopf, 1991.

Kamp, Marianne R. "Theme Articles: Restructuring Our Lives: National Unification and German Biographies." *Oral History Review* 21, no. 2 (Winter 1993): 1–81.

———. "Three Lives of Saodat: Communist, Uzbek, Survivor." *Oral History Review* 28, no. 2 (Summer–Fall 2001): 21–58.

Kaufman, Moisés, and Leigh Fondahouski. *The Laramie Project*. New York: Dramatists Play Service, 2001.

Kay, H. "Learning and Retaining Verbal Material." *British Journal of Psychology* 46 (1955): 81–100.

Kayser, John A., and Charles T. Morrissey. "Historically Significant Memories in Social Work: Two Perspectives on Oral History Research and the Helping Professions." *Reflections: Narratives of Professional Helping* 4, no. 4 (Fall 1998): 61–66.

Kendall, Paul Murray. "Walking the Boundaries." In Oates, ed., *Biography as High Adventure*, 32–49.

Kennedy, Elizabeth Lapovsky, and Madeline D. Davis. *Boots of Leather, Slippers of Gold: The History of a Lesbian Community*. New York: Routledge, 1993.

Kern, Stephen. *The Culture of Time and Space, 1880–1918*. Cambridge, MA: Harvard University Press, 1983.

Kerr, Daniel. "'We Know What the Problem Is': Using Oral History to Develop a Collaborate Analysis of Homelessness from the Bottom Up." *Oral History Review* 30, no. 1 (Winter–Spring 2003): 27–46.

Kessler-Harris, Alice. Introduction. In Grele, *Envelopes of Sound* (1975), 1–9.

———. "Social History." In *The New American History, Revised and Expanded Edition*, edited by Eric Foner, 231–55. Philadelphia: Temple University Press, 1997.

Kikumura, Akemi. "Family Life Histories: A Collaborative Venture." *Oral History Review* 14 (1986): 1–7.

Kirk, G. S. *Myth: Its Meaning and Functions in Ancient and Other Cultures*. Cambridge: Cambridge University Press, 1970.

Kirsch, Gesa E. *Ethical Dilemmas in Feminist Research: The Politics of Location, Interpretation, and Publication*. Albany: State University of New York Press, 1999.

Kleinman, Arthur. "The Violences of Everyday Life: The Multiple Forms and Dynamics of Social Violence." In *Violence and Subjectivity*, edited by Veena Das, Arthur Kleinman, Mamphela Ramphele, and Pamela Reynolds, 226–41. Berkeley: University of California Press, 2000.

K'Meyer, Tracy E. "An Interview with Willa K. Baum: A Career at the Regional Oral History Office." *Oral History Review* 24, no. 1 (Summer 1997): 91–112.

Koch, Chris. "On Working at Pacifica." In McKinney, ed., *Exacting Ear*, 35–39.

Kohli, Martin. "The World We Forgot: A Historical Review of the Life Course." In Marshall, ed., *Later Life*, 271–303.

Kopijn, Yvette. "The Oral History Interview in a Cross-Cultural Setting: An Analysis of Its Linguistic, Social and Ideological Structures." In Chamberlain and Thompson, eds., *Narrative and Genre*, 142–59.

Koppes, Clayton R. "The Social Destiny of Radio: Hope and Disillusionment in the 1920s." *South Atlantic Quarterly* 68 (1969): 363–76.

Krieger, Leonard. *Ranke: The Meaning of History*. Chicago: University of Chicago Press, 1977.

Kuhn, Clifford M., Harlon E. Joye, and E. Bernard West. *Living Atlanta: An Oral History of the City, 1914–1948*. Athens: University of Georgia Press, 1990.

Kuhn, Thomas. *The Structure of Scientific Revolutions*. Chicago: University of Chicago Press, 1970.

Kvale, Steiner. *Interviews: An Introduction to Qualitative Research Interviewing*. Thousand Oaks, CA: Sage, 1996.

Kwang, Luke S. K. "Oral History in China: A Preliminary Review." *Oral History Review* 20, no. 1–2 (Spring–Fall 1992): 23–50.

LaCapra, Dominick. *History and Memory after Auschwitz*. Ithaca, NY: Cornell University Press, 1998.

———. "Holocaust Testimonies: Attending to the Victim's Voice." In *Catastrophe and Meaning: The Holocaust and the Twentieth Century*, edited by Moishe Postone and Eric Santer, 209–31. Chicago: University of Chicago Press, 2003.

———. "Rethinking Intellectual History and Reading Texts." In LaCapra and Kaplan, eds., *Modern European Intellectual History*, 47–85.

LaCapra, Dominick, and Steven L. Kaplan, eds. *Modern European Intellectual History: Reappraisals and New Perspectives*. Ithaca, NY: Cornell University Press, 1982.

La Hausse, Paul. "Oral History and South African Historians." *Radical History Review* 46/47 (January 1990): 346–56.

Lance, David. *An Archive Approach to Oral History*. London: Imperial War Museum, 1978.

———. "Oral History in Britain." *Oral History Review* 2 (1974): 64–76.

———. "Oral History Project Design." In Dunaway and Baum, eds., *Oral History*, 2nd ed., 135–42.

———. "An Update from Great Britain." *Oral History Review* 4 (1976): 62–64.

Langellier, Kristin. "Personal Narratives: Perspectives on Theory and Research." *Text and Performance Quarterly* 9, no. 4 (October 1989): 243–76.

Langer, William. "The Next Assignment." *American Historical Review* 63 (1958): 283–304.

Langlois, W. J., ed. *Guide to Aural Research*. Victoria: Provincial Archives of British Columbia, 1976.

———. "Soundscapes: Interview with Imbert Orchard." In Dunaway and Baum, eds., *Oral History* (1984): 407–14.

Langness, Lewis L., and Gelya Frank. *Lives: An Anthropological Approach to Biography*. Novato, CA: Chandler and Sharp, 1981.

Lanzmann, Claude. *Shoah*. New York: New Yorker Films Video, 2003. DVD.

———. *Shoah, an Oral History of the Holocaust: The Complete Text of the Film*. New York: Pantheon, 1985.

Larson, Mary Ann. "Keeping Our Words as Keepers of Words." Paper presented at the annual meeting of the Society of American Archivists, Orlando, FL, September 1998.

Larson, Mary Ann. "Potential, Potential, Potential: The Marriage of Oral History and the World Wide Web." *Journal of American History* 88, no. 2 (September 2001): 596–607.

Lasch, Christopher. *The Culture of Narcissism: American Life in an Age of Diminishing Expectations*. New York: Norton, 1979.

Laslett, Peter. "Necessary Knowledge: Age and Aging in the Societies of the Past." In *Aging in the Past: Demography, Society, and Old Age*, edited by David I. Kertzer and Peter Laslett, 3–77. Berkeley: University of California Press, 1995.

———. *The World We Have Lost*. New York: Scribners, 1966.

Lazarus, Richard S. "Hope: An Emotion and a Vital Coping Resource against Despair." *Social Research* 66, no. 2 (Summer 1999): 653–79.

Leab, Daniel J. "*See It Now*: A Legend Reassessed." In O'Connor, ed., *American History, American Television*: 1–32.

Lebeaux, Richard. "Thoreau's Lives, Lebeaux's Lives." In Baron and Pletsch, eds., *Introspection in Biography*, 225–48.

Lee, Chana Kai. *For Freedom's Sake: The Life of Fannie Lou Hamer*. Urbana: University of Illinois Press, 1999.

Leonard, Linda. *Witness to the Fire: Creativity and the Veil of Addiction*. Boston: Shambhala, 1989.

Levin, David Michael. *The Listening Self: Personal Growth, Social Change and the Closure of Metaphysics*. London: Routledge, 1989.

Levinson, Daniel. *The Seasons of a Woman's Life*. In collaboration with Judy Levinson. New York: Knopf, 1996.

Levinson, Daniel, Charlotte N. Darrow, Edward B. Klein, Maria H. Levinson, and Braxton McKee, eds. *The Seasons of a Man's Life*. New York: Knopf, 1978.

Lewin, Rhoda. *Witnesses to the Holocaust: An Oral History*. Boston: Twayne, 1990.

Lewis, Oscar. *The Children of Sanchez: Autobiography of a Mexican Family*. London: Penguin, 1970.

Lewis, Robert A. "Emotional Intimacy among Men." *Journal of Social Issues* 34, no. 1 (1978): 108–21.

Leydesdorff, Selma. "The Screen of Nostalgia: Oral History and the Ordeal of Working Class Jews in Amsterdam." *International Journal of Oral History* 7, no. 2 (June 1986): 109–15.

Leydesdorff, Selma, Luisa Passerini, and Paul Thompson, eds. *Gender and Memory*. New York: Oxford University Press, 1996.

Lichty, Lawrence, and Thomas Bohn. "Radio's 'March of Time': Dramatized News." *Journalism Quarterly* 51, no. 3 (Autumn 1974): 458–62.

Linde, Charlotte. "Explanatory Systems in Oral Life Stories." In *Cultural Models in Language and Thought*, edited by Dorothy Holland and Naomi Quinn, 343–66. Cambridge: Cambridge University Press, 1987.

———. *Life Stories: The Creation of Coherence*. Oxford: Oxford University Press, 1993.

Lindlof, Thomas R. *Qualitative Communication Research Methods*. Thousand Oaks, CA: Sage, 1995.

Lindqvist, Sven. "Dig Where You Stand." *Oral History: Journal of the Oral History Society* 7, no. 2 (Autumn 1979): 24–30.

Linton, Marigold. "Transformations of Memory in Everyday Life." In Neisser, ed., *Memory Observed*, 77–91.

Lochead, Richard. "Directions in Oral History in Canada." *Canadian Oral History Association Journal* 6 (1983): 5.

Loftus, Elizabeth F., and John C. Palmer. "Reconstruction of Automobile Destruction." In Neisser, ed., *Memory Observed*, 109–15.

Lomax, Alan. *Mister Jelly Roll: The Fortunes of Jelly Roll Morton, New Orleans Creole and "Inventor of Jazz."* Berkeley : University of California Press, 2001.

Lomax, James W., and Charles T. Morrissey. "The Interview as Inquiry for Psychiatrists and Oral Historians: Convergence and Divergence in Skills and Goals." *Public Historian* 11, no. 1 (Winter 1989): 17–24.

Lopes, José Sérgio Leite, and Rosilene Alvim. "A Brazilian Worker's Autobiography in an Unexpected Form." In Chamberlain and Thompson, eds., *Narrative and Genre*, 63–80.

Losi, Natale. "Beyond the Archives of Memory." In Losi, Passerini, and Salvatici, eds., "Archives of Memory," 5–14.

Losi, Natale, Luisa Passerini, and Silvia Salvatici, eds. "Archives of Memory: Supporting Traumatized Communities through Narration and Remembrance." *Psychosocial Notebook* 2 (October 2001).

Lowenstein, Wendy. *Weevils in the Flour: An Oral Record of the 1930s Depression in Australia*. Melbourne: Hyland House, 1978.

Lummis, Trevor. "Structure and Validity in Oral Evidence." *International Journal of Oral History* 2, no. 2 (June 1983): 109–20.

Lutz, Helma, Ann Phoenix, and Nira Yuva-Davis, eds. *Crossfires: Nationalism, Racism and Gender in Europe*. London: Pluto, 1993.

Lynd, Alice, and Staughton Lynd. *Rank and File: Personal Histories by Working-Class Organizers*. Boston: Beacon, 1973.

Lynd, Staughton. "Guerrilla History in Gary." *Liberation* 14 (October 1969): 17–20.

———. "Oral History from Below." *Oral History Review* 21, no. 1 (Spring 1993): 1–8.

———. "Personal Histories of the Early CIO." *Radical America* 5, no. 3 (May–June 1971): 50–51.

Lyotard, Jean-François. *The Postmodern Condition: A Report on Knowledge*. Translated by Geoff Bennington and Brian Massumi. Manchester, England: Manchester University Press, 1984.

MacDonald, J. Fred. "The Development of Broadcast Journalism." In *Don't Touch That Dial: Radio Programming in American Life from 1920 to 1960*, chap. 6. Chicago: Nelson-Hall, 1979.

Mader, Wilhelm. "Emotionality and Continuity in Biographical Contexts." In Birren et al., eds., *Aging and Biography*, 39–60.

Maguire, Peter. *Facing Death*. New York: Columbia University Press, 2005.

Maier, Charles. "A Surfeit of Memory? Reflections on History, Melancholy and Denial." *History and Memory* 5 (1993): 136–51.

Manchester, William. *The Death of a President, November 22–November 25, 1963*. New York: Harper and Row, 1967.

Mandelbaum, Ken. *A Chorus Line and the Musicals of Michael Bennett*. New York: St. Martin's, 1989.

Mann, Nancy D., comp. "Directory of Women's Oral History Projects and Collections." *Frontiers: Journal of Women Studies* 7, no 1 (1983): 114–21.

Marshall, Victor W., ed. *Later Life: The Social Psychology of Aging*. Beverly Hills, CA: Sage, 1986.

———. "A Sociological Perspective on Aging and Dying." In Marshall, ed., *Later Life*, 125–46.

Martin, Wallace. *Recent Theories of Narrative*. Ithaca, NY: Cornell University Press, 1986.

Marx, Herbert L., Jr., ed. *Television and Radio in American Life*. New York: H. W. Wilson, 1953.

Massey, Ellen Gray, ed. *Bittersweet Country*. Garden City, NY: Doubleday, 1978.

Matters, Marion. *Oral History Cataloging Manual*. Chicago: Society of American Archivists, 1995.

Mayer, Arno. *Why the Heavens Did Not Darken?: The "Final Solution" in History*. New York: Pantheon, 1988.

Mayhew, Henry. *London Labour and the London Poor: A Cyclopaedia of the Condition and Earnings of Those That Will Work, Those That Cannot*. London: G. Woodfall, 1851.

McAdams, Dan P. "Narrating the Self in Adulthood." In Birren et al., eds., *Aging and Biography*, 131–48.

———. *The Stories We Live By: Personal Myths and the Making of the Self*. New York: William Morrow, 1993.

McAdams, Dan, Ruthellen Josselson, and Amia Lieblich, eds. Introduction. In *Turns in the Road: Narrative Studies of Lives in Transition*. Washington DC: American Psychological Association, 2001.

McChesney, Robert W. *Telecommunications, Mass Media, and Democracy: The Battle for the Control of U.S. Broadcasting, 1928–1935*. New York: Oxford University Press, 1993.

McFadzean, Andrew. "Interviews with Robert Bowie: The Use of Oral Testimony." *Oral History Review* 26, no. 2 (Summer–Fall 1999): 29–46.

McGuire, Susan Allen. "Expanding Information Sets by Means of 'Existential' Interviewing." *Oral History Review* 15, no. 1 (1987): 55–70.

McKinney, Eleanor, ed. *The Exacting Ear: The Story of Listener-Sponsored Radio, and an Anthology of Programs from KPFA, KPFK, and WBAI*. New York: Pantheon, 1966.

McMahan, Eva M. *Elite Oral History Discourse: A Study of Cooperation and Coherence*. Tuscaloosa: University of Alabama Press, 1989.

McMahan, Eva M., and Kim Lacy Rogers, eds. *Interactive Oral History Interviewing*. Hillsdale, NJ: Erlbaum, 1994.

McMillen, Neil R. *Dark Journey: Black Mississippians and the Age of Segregation*. Urbana: University of Illinois Press, 1989.

McRobbie, Angela. "Jackie: An Ideology of Adolescent Femininity." In *Popular Culture: Past and Present: A Reader*, edited by Bernard Waites, Tony Bennett, and Graham Martin, 263–83. London: Taylor and Francis, 1982.

Menand, Louis. "Bad Comma: Lynne Truss's Strange Grammar." *New Yorker*, June 28, 2004.

Meihy, José Carlos Sebe Bom. "The Radicalization of Oral History." *Words and Silences* New Series 2, no. 1 (June 2003): 31–41.

Menchú, Rigoberta. *I, Rigoberta Menchú: An Indian Woman in Guatemala*. Edited and introduced by Elisabeth Burgos-Debray. London: Verso, 1984.

Mercier, Laurie, and Madeline Buckendorf. *Using Oral History in Community History Projects*. Los Angeles: Oral History Association, 1992.

Merton, Robert K., Marjorie Fiske, and Patricia L. Kendall. *The Focused Interview: A Manual of Problems and Procedures*. 2nd ed. New York: Free Press, 1956.

Meyer, Eugenia. "Elena Poniatowska, Task and Commitment." *Oral History Review* 16, no. 1 (1988): 1–5.

———. "Oral History in Mexico and Latin America." *Oral History Review* 4 (1976): 56–61.

———. "Recovering, Remembering, Denouncing: Keeping Memory of the Past Updated: Oral History in Latin American and the Caribbean." In Hartewig and Halbach, eds., "History of Oral History," 17–25.

Miller, Donald, and Lorna Touryan Miller. "Armenian Survivors: A Typological Analysis of Victim Response." *Oral History Review* 10 (1982): 47–72.

Millwood, Elizabeth. "How Oral History Offices Deal with Legal Challenges." Plenary panel presentation, annual meeting of the Oral History Association. Bethesda, MD, October 12, 2003.

Minister, Kristina. "A Feminist Frame for the Oral History Interview." In Gluck and Patai, eds., *Women's Words*, 27–42.

Minor, Dale. "Freedom Now!" In McKinney, ed., *Exacting Ear*, 163–85.

Mintz, Sidney. *Worker in the Cane: A Puerto Rican Life History*. New Haven, CT: Yale University Press, 1960.

Mishler, Eliot G. *Research Interviewing: Context and Narrative*. Cambridge, MA: Harvard University Press, 1986.

Modell, John. *Into One's Own: From Youth to Adulthood in the United States, 1920–1975*. Berkeley: University of California Press, 1989.

Moerman, Michael. *Talking Culture: Ethnography and Conversation Analysis*. Philadelphia: University of Pennsylvania Press, 1988.

Montell, Lynwood. *The Saga of Coe Ridge: A Study in Oral History*. Knoxville: University of Tennessee Press, 1970.

Montenegro, Antonio Torres, ed. *História Oral e Memória: Cultura Popular Revisitada*. Sao Paulo: Contexto, 1994.

Morrissey, Charles T. Foreword. In Hoffman and Hoffman, *Archives of Memory*, xii–xv.

———. "On Oral History Interviewing." In Dexter, *Elite and Specialized Interviewing*, 109–18.

———. "Oral History and the Mythmakers." *Historic Preservation* 16 (November–December 1964): 232–37.

———. "Stories of Memory, Myth, and Contrivance: The Oral Historian as Skeptic." *Sound Historian: Journal of the Texas Oral History Association* 6, no. 1 (2000): 1–8.

———. "Truman and the Presidency: Records and Oral Recollections." *American Archivist* 28, no. 1 (January 1965): 53–61.

———. "The Two-Sentence Format as an Interviewing Technique in Oral History Fieldwork." *Oral History Review* 15, no. 1 (Spring 1987): 43–54.

Morrow, Phyllis, and William Schneider, eds. *When Our Words Return: Writing, Hearing, and Remembering Oral Traditions of Alaska and the Yukon*. Logan: Utah State University Press, 1995.

Moss, William. "The Future of Oral History." *Oral History Review* 3 (1975): 5–15.

———. "Oral History: An Appreciation." In Dunaway and Baum, *Oral History*, 2nd ed., 107–20.

———. *Oral History Program Manual*. New York: Praeger, 1974.

———. "Oral History: What Is It and Where Did It Come From?" In Stricklin and Sharpless, eds., *Past Meets the Present*, 5–14.

Moye, Joseph Todd. "'Sick and Tired of Being Sick and Tired': Social Origins and Consequences of the Black Freedom Struggle in Sunflower County, Mississippi, 1954–1986." Ph.D. diss., University of Texas, 1999.

Mpe, Phaswane. "Orality and Literacy in an Electronic Era." *South African Archives Journal* 40 (1998): 80–86.

Murphy, John. "The Voice of Memory: History, Autobiography and Oral History." *Historical Studies* 22 (1986): 157–75.

Musto, David F., and Saul Benison. "Studies in the Accuracy of Oral Interviews." In Colman, ed., *Fourth National Colloquium*, 167–81.

Nash, Christopher. *Narrative in Culture: The Uses of Story Telling in the Sciences, Philosophy and Literature*. London: Routledge, 1990.

Nasstrom, Kathryn L. *Everybody's Grandmother and Nobody's Fool: Frances Freeborn Pauley and the Struggle for Social Justice*. Ithaca, NY: Cornell University Press, 2000.

Nathan, Harriet. *Critical Choices in Interviews: Conduct, Use, and Research Role*. Berkeley: University of California Institute of Governmental Studies, 1986.

National Archives (Singapore). *Kampong Days: Village Life and Times in Singapore Revisited*. Singapore: National Archives, 1993.

National Public Radio. *The Golden Cradle Series: Immigrant Women in the United States*. Washington, DC: National Public Radio, 1984. 5 audiocassettes.

Nesse, Rudolph M. "The Evolution of Hope and Despair." *Social Research* 66, no. 2 (Summer 1999): 429–70.

Neisser, Ulric, ed. *Memory Observed: Remembering in Natural Contexts*. San Francisco: Freeman, 1982.

———. "Memory: What Are the Important Questions?" In Neisser, ed., *Memory Observed*, 3–19.

———. "Self-Narratives: True and False." In Neisser and Fivush, eds., *Remembering Self*, 1–18.

Neisser, Ulric, and Robyn Fivush, eds. *The Remembering Self: Construction and Accuracy in the Self-Narrative*. Cambridge: Cambridge University Press, 1994.

Neithammer, Lutz. "Oral History in the United States: *Zur Entwicklung und Problematic Daichroner Befragungen*." *Archive für Sozialgeschichte* 18 (1978): 457–501.

Neithammer, Lutz, and Alexander von Plato, eds. *Lebensgeschichte und Sozialkultur im Ruhrgebiet 1930–1960*. 3 vols. Bonn: Dietz, 1989.

Nelson, Cary. "Can E. T. Phone Home? The Brave New World of University Surveillance." *Academe* 89 (September–October 2003): 30–35.

Nelson, Cary, and Laurence Grossberg, eds. *Marxism and the Interpretation of Culture*. Urbana: University of Illinois Press, 1988.

Nesmith, Tom. "Hugh Taylor's Contextual Idea for Archives and the Foundation of Graduate Education in Archival Studies." In *The Archival Imagination: Essays in Honour of Hugh A. Taylor*, edited by Barbara Lazenby Craig, 13–37. Ottawa: Association of Canadian Archivists, 1992.

Nethercott, Shaun S., and Neil O. Leighton. "Memory, Process, and Performance." *Oral History Review* 18, no. 2 (Fall 1990): 37–60.

———. "Out of the Archives and onto the Stage." In Perks and Thomson, eds., *Oral History Reader*, 457–64.

Neuenschwander, John A. *Oral History and the Law*. 3rd ed. Carlisle, PA: Oral History Association, 2002.

———. "Remembrance of Things Past: Oral Historians and Long Term Memory." *Oral History Review* 6 (1978): 45–53.

Nevins, Allan. *The Gateway to History*. New York: D. Appleton-Century, 1938.

———. "Oral History: How and Why It Was Born." In Dunaway and Baum, eds., *Oral History* (1984), 31–32.

———. "The Uses of Oral History." In Dixon and Mink, eds., *Oral History at Arrowhead*, 25–37.

Nora, Pierre. "Between Memory and History." In *Realms of Memory: Rethinking the French Past*. Vol. 1. *Conflicts and Divisions*, 1–20. Translated by Arthur Goldhammer. New York: Columbia University Press, 1996.

Oakley, Ann. "Interviewing Women: A Contradiction in Terms." In *Doing Feminist Research*, edited by Helen Roberts, 30–61. London: Routledge, Kegan and Paul, 1981.

Oates, Stephen B., ed. *Biography as High Adventure: Life-Writers Speak on Their Art*. Amherst: University of Massachusetts Press, 1986.

O'Connor, John E., ed. *American History, American Television: Interpreting the Video Past*. New York: Frederick Ungar, 1983.

Odom, Howard. *Southern Regions of the United States*. Chapel Hill: University of North Carolina Press, 1936.

O'Farrell, Patrick. "Oral History: Facts and Fiction." *Quadrant* (November 1979): 3–9.

Okihiro, Gary. "Oral History and the Writing of Ethnic History: A Reconnaissance into Method and Theory." *Oral History Review* 9 (1981): 27–46.

Okpewho, Isidore. *African Oral Literature: Backgrounds, Character, and Continuity*. Bloomington: Indiana University Press, 1992.

Olson, David R. *The World on Paper: The Conceptual and Cognitive Implications of Writing and Reading*. Cambridge: Cambridge University Press, 1994.

Ong, Walter J. "Grammar Today: 'Structure' in a Vocal World." *Quarterly Journal of Speech* 43, no. 4 (December 1957): 399–407.

———. *Orality and Literacy: The Technologizing of the Word*. New York: Routledge, 2002.

Oral History Association. *Oral History Evaluation Guidelines*. Adopted 1989. Revised 2000. Carlisle, PA: Oral History Association, 2001. Also available online at http://www.dickinson.edu/oha/pub_eg.html (accessed February 1, 2005).

———. "Oral History: Evaluation Guidelines: The Wingspread Conference." *Oral History Review* 8 (1980): 6–19.

Oral History Association of Australia. "Local History, Family History, and Oral History." Special issue, *Oral History Association of Australia Journal*, 4 (1981–1982).

Oral History in the United States: A Report from the Oral History Research Office of Columbia University. New York: Columbia University Oral History Research Office, 1965.

Oral History Index: An International Directory of Oral History Interviews. Westport, CT: Meckler, 1990.

Oral History Society (UK). "The Interview in Social History." Special issue, *Oral History: Journal of the Oral History Society* 1, no. 4 (1972).

———. "News from Abroad: Australasia." *Oral History: Journal of the Oral History Society* 8, no. 1 (Spring 1980): 12–13.

———. "News from Abroad: Europe." *Oral History, Journal of the Oral History Society* 13, no. 1 (Spring 1985): 17–18.

———. "News from Abroad: Finland." *Oral History, Journal of the Oral History Society* 25, no. 2 (Autumn 1997): 19.

Osterud, Nancy Grey, and Lu Ann Jones. "'If I Must Say So Myself': Oral Histories of Rural Women." *Oral History Review* 17, no. 2 (Fall 1989): 1–23.

Parke, Catherine N. *Biography: Writing Lives.* New York: Twayne, 1996.

Passerini, Luisa. "An Afterthought on a Work in Progress and a Forethought towards Its Future." In Losi, Passerini, and Salvatici, eds., "Archives of Memory," 219–26.

———. *Autobiography of a Generation: Italy 1968.* Hanover, NH: Wesleyan University Press, 1996.

———. *Fascism in Popular Memory: The Cultural Experience of the Turin Working Class.* Translated by Robert Lumley and Jude Bloomfield. Cambridge: Cambridge University Press, 1987.

———. "Italian Working Class Culture between the Wars: Consensus to Fascism and Work Ideology." *International Journal of Oral History* 1 (1980): 1–27.

———, ed. *Memory and Totalitarianism.* Oxford: Oxford University Press, 1992.

———. "Memory: Resume of the Final Session of the International Conference on Oral History in Aix-en-Provence." *History Workshop* 15 (Spring 1983): 195–96.

———. "Mythbiography in Oral History." In Samuel and Thompson, eds., *Myths We Live By,* 49–69.

———. "Oral History in Italy after the Second World War: From Populism to Subjectivity." *International Journal of Oral History* 9, no. 2 (June 1988): 114–24.

———. "Work Ideology and Consensus under Italian Fascism." *History Workshop Journal* 8 (Autumn 1979): 82–108.

Patai, Daphne. "Ethical Problems of Personal Narratives, or, Who Should Eat the Last Piece of Cake?" *International Journal of Oral History* 8, no. 1 (1987): 5–27.

———. "U.S. Academics and Third World Women: Is Ethical Research Possible?" In Gluck and Patai, eds., *Women's Words,* 137–53.

Pearson, Carol S. *The Hero Within: Six Archetypes We Live By.* New York: Harper, 1989.

Perdue, Theda. *Nations Remembered: An Oral History of the Cherokee, Chickasaws, Choctaws, Creeks, and Seminoles.* Norman: University of Oklahoma Press, 1993.

Perks, Robert, and Alistair Thomson. "Critical Developments." In Perks and Thomson, eds., *Oral History Reader,* 1–8.

———. Introduction to Part III, "Advocacy and Empowerment." In Perks and Thomson, eds., *Oral History Reader,* 183–88.

———, eds. *The Oral History Reader.* London: Routledge, 1998.

Personal Narratives Group, eds. *Interpreting Women's Lives: Feminist Theory and Personal Narrative.* Bloomington: Indiana University Press, 1989.

Peter, John. *The Oral History of Modern Architecture: Interviews with the Greatest Architects of the Twentieth Century.* New York: Abrams, 1994.

Peterson, Eric E., and Kristin M. Langellier. "The Politics of Personal Narrative Methodology." *Text and Performance Quarterly* 17, no. 2 (April 1997): 135–52.

Piketty, Guillaume. "La Biographie Comme Genre Historique." *Vingtieme Siecle* 63 (1999): 119–26.

Pillemer, David B. *Momentous Events, Vivid Memories.* Cambridge, MA: Harvard University Press, 2000.

Pillemer, David B., A. B. Desrochers, and C. M. Ebanks. "Remembering the Past in the Present: Verb Tense Shifts in Autobiographical Memory Narratives." In Thompson, ed., *Autobiographical Memory*, 145–62.

Piscitelli, Adriana. "Love and Ambition: Gender, Memory, and Stories from Brazilian Coffee Plantation Families." In Leydesdorff, Passerini, and Thompson, eds., *Gender and Memory*, 89–103.

Plummer, Ken. *Documents of Life: An Introduction to the Problems and Literature of a Humanistic Method.* London: George Allen and Unwin, 1983.

———. *Documents of Life 2.* London: Sage, 2001.

Pogue, Forrest C. *George C. Marshall.* New York: Viking, 1963.

———. *Pogue's War: Diaries of a WWII Combat Historian.* Lexington: University Press of Kentucky, 2001.

Polishuk, Sandy. *Sticking to the Union: An Oral History of the Life and Times of Julia Ruuttila.* New York: Palgrave Macmillan, 2003.

Polkinghorne, Donald E. *Narrative Knowing and the Human Sciences.* Albany: State University of New York Press, 1988.

Pollock, Della. "Making History Go." In *Exceptional Spaces: Essays in Performance and History*, edited by Della Pollock, 1–45. Chapel Hill: University of North Carolina Press, 1998.

———. "Telling the Told: Performing Like a Family." *Oral History Review* 18, no. 2 (Fall 1990): 1–36.

Polsky, Richard. "An Interview with Elizabeth Mason." *Oral History Review* 27, no. 2 (Summer–Fall 2000): 157–79.

Poniatowska, Elena. "The Earthquake." *Oral History Review* 16, no. 1 (Spring 1988): 7–20.

———. *Hasta No Verte, Jesús Mío.* México: Editiones Era, 1969.

———. *Nothing, Nobody: The Voices of the Mexico City Earthquake.* Translated by Aurora Camacho de Schmidt and Arthur Schmidt. Philadelphia: Temple University Press, 1995.

Popular Memory Group. "Popular Memory: Theory, Politics, Memory." In *Making Histories: Studies in History-Writing and Politics*, edited by Richard Johnson, Gregor McLennan, Bill Schwarz, and David Sutton, 205–52. London: Hutchinson, 1982.

Portelli, Alessandro. "*Absalom, Absalom!*: Oral History and Literature." In *Death of Luigi Trastulli*, 270–82.

———. *The Battle of Valle Giulia: Oral History and the Art of Dialogue.* Madison: University of Wisconsin Press, 1997.

———. *The Death of Luigi Trastulli and Other Stories: Form and Meaning in Oral History.* Albany: State University of New York Press, 1991.

———. "The Death of Luigi Trastulli: Memory and the Event." In *Death of Luigi Trastulli*, 1–26.

——. "Oral History as Genre." In Chamberlain and Thompson, eds., *Narrative and Genre*, 23–45.

——. *The Order Has Been Carried Out: History, Memory, and Meaning of a Nazi Massacre in Rome*. New York: Palgrave Macmillan, 2003.

——. "The Peculiarities of Oral History." *History Workshop Journal* 12 (Autumn 1981): 96–107.

——. "Philosophy and the Facts: Subjectivity and Narrative Form in Autobiography and Oral History." In *Battle of Valle Giulia*, 79–90.

——. "The Time of My Life: Functions of Time in Oral History." *International Journal of Oral History* 2 (1981): 162–80.

——. "Tryin' to Gather a Little Knowledge: Some Thoughts on the Ethics of Oral History." In *Battle of Valle Giulia*, 55–71.

——. "Uchronic Dreams: Working-Class Memory and Possible Worlds." In Samuel and Thompson, eds., *Myths We Live By*, 143–60.

——. "What Makes Oral History Different." In *Death of Luigi Trastulli*, 45–58.

Porter, Bruce. "Has Success Spoiled NPR?" *Columbia Journalism Review* 29, no. 3 (September–October 1990): 26–32.

Powell, James M. Introduction. In *Leopold von Ranke and the Shaping of the Historical Discipline*, edited by Georg G. Iggers and James M. Powell, xiii–xxii. Syracuse, NY: Syracuse University Press, 1990.

Preston, Samuel H., and Michael R. Haines. *Fatal Years: Child Mortality in Late Nineteenth-Century America*. Princeton, NJ: Princeton University Press, 1991.

Pym, Anthony. Review of Olson, *World on Paper*. *European Legacy* 3, no. 1 (February 1998): 134–35.

Quadrango, Jill. *The Color of Welfare: How Racism Undermined the War on Poverty*. New York: Oxford University Press, 1994.

"A Radio 'Newspaper.'" In Marx, ed., *Television and Radio*, 85–88.

Raeff, Marc. "Autocracy Tempered by Reform or by Regicide." *American Historical Review* 98, no. 4 (1993): 1143–55.

Raphaël, Freddy, and Roswitha Breckner. "The German Working Class and National Socialism: Two Reviews." In *Between Generations: Family Models, Myths, and Memories*, edited by Daniel Bertaux and Paul Thompson, 201–6. Oxford: Oxford University Press, 1993.

Rapport, Leonard. "How Valid Are the Federal Writers' Project Life Stories?: An Iconoclast among the True Believers." *Oral History Review* 7 (1979): 6–17.

Read, Peter. "Presenting Voices in Different Media: Print, Radio and CD-ROM." In Perks and Thomson, eds., *Oral History Reader*, 414–20.

Reich, Steve. *Writings about Music*. Halifax: Press of the Nova Scotia College of Art and Design, 1974.

Reid, Benjamin Lawrence. *Necessary Lives: Biographical Reflections*. Columbia: University of Missouri Press, 1990.

Reingold, Nathan. "A Critic Looks at Oral History." In Colman, ed., *Fourth National Colloquium*, 213–27.

Reinharz, Shulamit, and Lynn Davidman. *Feminist Methods in Social Research*. New York: Oxford University Press, 1992.

Rickard, Wendy. "Collaborating with Sex Workers in Oral History." *Oral History Review* 30, no. 1 (Winter–Spring 2003): 47–60.

Ricoeur, Paul. *Interpretation Theory: Discourse and the Surplus of Meaning.* Fort Worth: Texas Christian University Press, 1976.

——. *Time and Narrative.* Translated by Kathleen Blamey, David Pellauer, and Paul Rico. 3 vols. Chicago: University of Chicago Press, 1984–85.

Riley, Matilda White. "Age Stratification." *Encyclopedia of Gerontology: Age, Aging, and the Aged.* New York: Academic, 1996.

Riley, Matilda White, and Ann Foner. *Aging and Society.* New York: Russell Sage, 1968.

Ritchie, Donald A. *Doing Oral History.* New York: Twayne, 1995.

——. *Doing Oral History: A Practical Guide.* 2nd ed. New York: Oxford University Press, 2003.

Roach, Joseph R. *Cities of the Dead: Circum-Atlantic Performance.* New York: Columbia University Press, 1996.

Roberts, Brian. *Biographical Research.* Buckingham: Open University Press, 2002.

Rocha Lima, Valentina da. "Women in Exile: Becoming Feminist." *International Journal of Oral History* 5, no. 2 (June 1984): 81–99.

Rogers, Kim Lacy. "A Crisis of Opportunity: The Movement and Head Start." *Life and Death,* chap. 5. Forthcoming.

——. *Life and Death in the Delta: African American Narratives of Violence, Resilience, and Social Change.* New York: Palgrave, forthcoming.

——. *Righteous Lives: Narratives of the New Orleans Civil Rights Movement.* New York: New York University Press, 1993.

——. "Trauma Redeemed: The Narrative Construction of Social Violence." In McMahan and Rogers, eds., *Interactive Oral History Interviewing,* 31–46.

Rogers, Kim Lacy, Selma Leydesdorff, and Graham Dawson, eds. *Trauma and Life Stories: International Perspectives.* London: Routledge, 1999.

Romney, Joseph. "Legal Considerations in Oral History." *Oral History Review* 1 (1973): 66–76.

Roper, Michael. "Analysing the Analysed: Transference and Counter-Transference in the Oral History Interview." *Oral History: Journal of the Oral History Society* 31, no. 2 (Autumn 2003): 20–32.

Rosaldo, Renato. "Doing Oral History." *Social Analysis* 4 (September 1980): 89–99.

Rosen, Dale, and Theodore Rosengarten. "Shoot-Out at Reeltown: The Narrative of Jess Hull." *Radical America* 6 (November–December 1972): 65–85.

Rosengarten, Theodore. *All God's Dangers: The Life of Nate Shaw.* New York: Knopf, 1974.

——. "Stepping over Cockleburs: Conversations with Ned Cobb." In Edel, *Telling Lives,* 104–31.

Rosenwald, George C., and Richard L. Ochberg, eds. *Storied Lives: The Cultural Politics of Self-Understanding.* New Haven, CT: Yale University Press, 1992.

Rouverol, Alicia J. "Collaborative Oral History in a Correctional Setting: Promise and Pitfalls." *Oral History Review* 30, no. 1 (Winter–Spring 2003): 61–86.

Rubin, David C. "Beginnings of a Theory of Autobiographical Remembering." In Thompson, ed., *Autobiographical Memory*, 47–68.

Rudnick, Lois. "The Male-Identified Woman and Other Anxieties: The Life of Mabel Dodge Luhan." In Alpern et al., eds., *Challenge of Feminist Biography*, 116–38.

Rustin, Michael. "Reflections on the Biographical Turn in Social Science." In Chamberlayne, Bornat, and Wengraf, eds., *Biographical Methods*, 33–52.

Sacks, Oliver. *The Man Who Mistook His Wife for a Hat*. London: Picador, 1986.

Salazar, Claudia. "A Third World Woman's Text: Between the Politics of Criticism and Cultural Politics." In Gluck and Patai, eds., *Women's Words*, 93–106.

Samuel, Raphael. *East End Underworld: The Life of Arthur Harding*. London: Routledge, 1981.

———. "Local History and Oral History." *History Workshop Journal* 1 (Spring 1976): 191–208.

———. "People's History." In *People's History and Socialistic Theory*, xv–xxxix.

———, ed. *People's History and Socialistic Theory*. London: Routledge, 1981.

———. "Perils of the Transcript." *Oral History: Journal of the Oral History Society* 1, no. 2 (1971): 19–22.

———. "Perils of the Transcript." In Perks and Thomson, eds., *Oral History Reader* (1998), 389–92.

———. *Theatres of Memory*. Vol. 1, *Past and Present in Contemporary Culture*. London: Verso, 1994.

———. "Unofficial Knowledge." In *Theatres of Memory* 1: 3–51.

Samuel, Raphael, Alison Light, Sally Alexander, and Gareth Stedman Jones, eds. *Island Stories: Unraveling Britain*. Vol. 2, *Theatres of Memory*. London: Verso, 1998.

Samuel, Raphael, and Paul Thompson. Introduction. In *Myths We Live By*, 1–22.

———, eds. *The Myths We Live By*. London: Routledge, 1990.

Sangster, Joan. "Telling Our Stories: Feminist Debates and the Use of Oral History." *Women's History Review* 3, no. 1 (1994): 5–28.

Sarbin, Theodore R. "Steps to the Narratory Principle: An Autobiographical Essay." In *Life and Story: Autobiographies for a Narrative Psychology*, edited by D. John Lee, 7–38. Westport, CT: Praeger, 1994.

Sarris, Greg. "'The Woman Who Loved a Snake' and 'What People of Elem Saw': Orality in Mabel McKay's Stories." *American Indian Quarterly* 15, no. 2 (Spring 1991): 171–85.

Schacter, Daniel L. *The Seven Sins of Memory: How the Mind Forgets and Remembers*. Boston: Houghton Mifflin Company, 2001.

Schafer, R. Murray. *The Tuning of the World: Toward a Theory of Soundscape*. Philadelphia: University of Pennsylvania Press, 1980.

Schechner, Richard. *Performance Theory*. London: Routledge, 2003.

Schegloff, Emmanuel A. "What Next?: Language and Social Interaction Study at the Century's Turn." *Research on Language and Social Interaction* 32, no. 1/2 (1999): 141–49.

Schendler, Revan. "'They Made the Freedom Themselves': Popular Interpretations of Post-Communist Discourse in the Czech Republic." *Oral History: Journal of the Oral History Society* 29, no. 2 (Autumn 2001): 73–82.

Schiffrin, Deborah. "Linguistics and History: Oral History as Discourse." In *Linguistics, Language, and the Real World: Discourse and Beyond,* edited by Deborah Tannen and James E. Alatis, 84–113. Washington, DC: Georgetown University Press, 2003.

Schiffrin, Deborah, Deborah Tannen, and Heidi E. Hamilton, eds. *The Handbook of Discourse Analysis.* Malden, MA: Blackwell, 2001.

Schippers, Donald J. "Techniques of Oral History Interviewing." In Dixon and Mink, eds., *Oral History at Arrowhead,* 47–68.

Schlesinger, Arthur M., Jr. *The Disuniting of America: Reflections on a Multicultural Society.* New York: Norton, 1992.

———. *Robert Kennedy and His Times.* Vol. 1. Boston: Houghton Mifflin, 1978.

Schneider, William. "Lessons from Alaska Natives about Oral Tradition and Recordings." In *When Our Words Return: Writing, Hearing, and Remembering Oral Traditions of Alaska and the Yukon,* edited by Phyllis Morrow and William Schneider, 185–204. Logan: Utah State University Press, 1995.

———. *So They Understand: Cultural Issues in Oral History.* Logan: Utah State University Press, 2002.

Schorzman, Terri A., ed. *A Practical Introduction to Videohistory: The Smithsonian Institution and Alfred P. Sloan Foundation Experiment.* Malabar, FL: Krieger Publishing, 1993.

Schrager, Samuel. "What Is Social in Oral History?" *International Journal of Oral History* 4, no. 2 (June 1983): 76–98.

Schutz, Alfred. "Common-Sense and Scientific Interpretation of Human Action." In *Collected Papers I: The Problem of Social Reality,* 3–47. The Hague: Martinus Nijhoff, 1962.

Schwartz, Tony. *1, 2, and 3, and a Zing, Zing, Zing: Street Songs and Games of the Children of New York City.* Folkway Records FP 703, 1953. Microgroove.

———. *Media: The Second God.* New York: Random House, 1981.

———. *Nueva York: A Tape Documentary of Puerto Rican New Yorkers.* Folkways Records FP 58-2, 1956. Microgroove.

———. *Sounds of My City: The Stories, Music, and Sounds of the People of New York.* Folkways Records FC741, 1956. Microgroove.

———. *The Responsive Chord.* Garden City, NY: Anchor Press, 1973.

Schwarz, K. Robert. *Minimalists.* London: Phaidon, 1996.

Scott, Joan Wallach. "Gender: A Useful Category of Historical Analysis." In *Feminism and History,* edited by Joan Wallach Scott, 152–80. Oxford: Oxford University Press, 1996.

———. *Gender and the Politics of History.* Rev. ed. New York: Columbia University Press, 1999.

Scully, James. "In Defense of Ideology." In *Line Break: Poetry as Social Practice,* 9–22. Seattle: Bay Press, 1988.

Sewell, William H., Jr. "The Concept(s) of Culture." In Bonnell and Hunt, eds., *Beyond the Cultural Turn,* 35–61.

———. "Narratives and Social Identities." *Social Science History* 16, no. 3 (1992): 479–88.

Shariff, Shamsi. "Narrating History through Oral History Technique in Malaysia." *International Journal of Oral History* 9, no. 1 (February 1988): 40–42.

Sherbakova, Irena. "The Gulag in Memory." In Perks and Thomson, eds., *Oral History Reader*, 235–45.

Shircliffe, Barbara. "'We Got the Best of That World': A Case Study of Nostalgia in the Oral History of School Segregation." *Oral History Review* 28, no. 2 (Summer–Fall 2001): 59–84.

Shopes, Linda. "Commentary: Sharing Authority." *Oral History Review* 30, no. 1 (Winter–Spring 2003): 103–10.

———. "Developing a Critical Dialogue about Oral History: Some Notes Based on an Analysis of Book Reviews." *Oral History Review* 14 (1986): 9–25.

———. "Using Oral History for a Family History Project." In Dunaway and Baum, eds., *Oral History*, 2nd ed., 231–40.

Shore, Miles F. "Biography in the 1980s." *Journal of Interdisciplinary History* 12, no. 1 (Summer 1981): 89–113.

Shores, Louis. "Directions for Oral History." In Dixon and Mink, eds., *Oral History at Arrowhead*, 38–46.

Shortland, Michael, and Richard Yeo. Introduction. In *Telling Lives in Science*, 1–44.

———, eds. *Telling Lives in Science: Essays on Scientific Biography*. Cambridge: Cambridge University Press, 1996.

Siepmann, Charles A. "British, Canadian, and Other Systems." In *Radio, Television, and Society*, chap. 7. New York: Oxford University Press, 1950.

Silverman, David. *Interpreting Qualitative Data: Methods for Analysing Talk, Text, and Interaction*. Thousand Oaks, CA: Sage, 1993.

Sipe, Dan. "Media and Public History: The Future of Oral History and Moving Images." *Oral History Review* 19, nos. 1–2 (Spring–Fall 1991): 75–87.

Sitton, Thad. "The Descendants of *Foxfire*." *Oral History Review* 6 (1978): 20–35.

———, ed. *The Loblolly Book*. Austin: Texas Monthly Press, 1983.

Sitton, Thad, George L. Mehaffy, and O. L. Davis Jr. *Oral History: A Guide for Teachers (and Others)*. Austin: University of Texas Press, 1983.

Sitzia, Lorraine. "Shared Authority: An Impossible Goal?" *Oral History Review* 30, no. 1 (Winter–Spring 2003): 87–102.

Skotnes, Andor. Review of Bernhardt, *New Yorkers at Work*. *Oral History Review* 16, no. 1 (Spring 1989): 203–5.

Slim, Hugo, Paul Thompson, Olivia Bennett, and Nigel Cross. "Ways of Listening." In Perks and Thomson, eds., *Oral History Reader*, 114–25.

Smith, Anna Deavere. *Fires in the Mirror: Crown Heights, Brooklyn and Other Identities*. New York: Anchor/Doubleday, 1993.

Smith, Anthony. *Myths and Memories of the Nation*. Oxford: Oxford University Press, 1999.

Smith, Betty. *A Tree Grows in Brooklyn*. New York: Harper, 1943.

Smith, Bruce R. *The Acoustic World of Early Modern England: Attending to the O-Factor*. Chicago: University of Chicago Press, 1999.

Smith, Dorothy. *The Everyday World as Problematic: A Feminist Sociology*. Boston: Northeastern University Press, 1987.

———. "Some Implications of a Sociology for Women." In *Woman in a Man-made World: A Socioeconomic Handbook*, 2nd ed., edited by Nona Glazer and Helen Y. Washrer, 15–39. Chicago: Rand McNally, 1977.

Smith, Judi Moore. *Never a Man Spake Like This*. Washington, DC: National Federation of Community Broadcasters, 1982. Audiocassette.

Smith, Richard Cándida. "Popular Memory and Oral Narratives: Luisa Passerini's Reading of Oral History Interviews." *Oral History Review* 16, no. 2 (Fall 1988): 95–107.

Smith, S. A. "The Social Meanings of Swearing: Workers and Bad Language in Late Imperial and Early Soviet Russia." *Past & Present* 160 (August 1998): 167–202.

Smith, Sidonie, and Julia Watson. *Reading Autobiography: A Guide for Interpreting Life Narratives*. Minneapolis: University of Minnesota Press, 2001.

Smith, Stephen, and Deborah Amos. *Remembering Jim Crow: African Americans Tell about Life in the Segregated South*. St. Paul: Minnesota Public Radio, 2001. Compact disc.

Smith, Steven B. *Reading Althusser: An Essay on Structural Marxism*. Ithaca, NY: Cornell University Press, 1984.

Soapes, Thomas F. "The Federal Writers' Project Slave Interviews: Useful Data or Misleading Source." *Oral History Review* 5 (1977): 33–38.

Soderqvist, Thomas. "Existential Projects and Existential Choice in Science: Science Biography as an Edifying Genre." In Shortland and Yeo, eds., *Telling Lives in Science*, 45–84.

Somers, Margaret. "Narrativity, Narrative Identity and Social Action: Rethinking English Working Class Formation." *Social Science History* 16, no. 4 (Winter 1992): 591–630.

Sommer, Barbara W., and Mary Kay Quinlan. *The Oral History Manual*. Walnut Creek, CA: AltaMira, 2002.

Sommer, Doris. "'Not Just a Personal Story': Women's *Testimonios* and the Plural Self." In *Life/Lines: Theoretical Essays on Women's Autobiography*, edited by Bella Brodzki and Celeste Schenck, 107–30. Ithaca, NY: Cornell University Press, 1988.

Spence, Donald P. *Narrative Truth and Historical Truth: Meaning and Interpretation in Psychoanalysis*. New York: Norton, 1982.

Sperber, A. M. *Murrow: His Life and Times*. New York: Freundlich, 1986.

Spivak, Gayatri Chakravorty. "The Politics of Interpretation." In *The Politics of Interpretation*, edited by W. J. T. Mitchell, 347–66. Chicago: University of Chicago Press, 1983.

Stacey, Judith. "Can There Be a Feminist Ethnography?" In Gluck and Patai, eds., *Women's Words*, 111–19.

Stanley, Liz. *The Auto/Biographical 'I': Theory and Practice of Feminist Auto/Biography*. Manchester, England: Manchester University Press, 1992.

———. "How Do We Know About Past Lives? Methodological and Epistemological Matters Involving Prince Philip, the Russian Revolution, Emily Wilding Davison, My Mum and the Absent Sue." In *Women's Lives into Print: The Theory, Practice and Writing of Feminist Auto/Biography*, edited by Pauline Polkey, 3–21. London: Macmillan, 1999.

Stannard, David E. "Death and the Puritan Child." In *Death in America*, 9–29. Philadelphia: University of Pennsylvania Press, 1975.

Stannard, Martin. "A Matter of Life and Death." In *Writing the Lives of Writers,* edited by Warwick Gould and Thomas F. Staley, 1–17. New York: St. Martin's, 1998.

Starr, Louis. "Oral History." In Dunaway and Baum, eds., *Oral History* (1984), 3–26.

———. Review of *The Voice of the Past,* by Paul Thompson. *Oral History Review* 6 (1978): 67–68.

———. *The Second National Colloquium on Oral History.* New York: Oral History Association, 1968.

Steedman, Carolyn. "Enforced Narratives: Stories of Another Self." In Cosslett, Lury, and Summerfield, eds., *Feminism and Autobiography,* 25–39.

Stein, Jean. *American Journey: The Times of Robert Kennedy.* Edited by George Plimpton. New York: Harcourt, Brace, Jovanovich, 1970.

Steinmetz, George. "Reflections on the Role of Social Narrative in Working Class Formation: Narrative Theory in the Social Sciences." *Social Science History* 16, no. 3 (1992): 489–516.

Stephens, Carlene. "Videohistory at Waltham Clock Company: An Assessment." In Schorzman, ed., *Introduction to Videohistory,* 101–13.

Stevens, Anthony. *Private Myths: Dreams and Dreaming.* Cambridge, MA: Harvard University Press, 1995.

Stone, Lawrence. "The Revival of Narrative: Reflections on an Old New History." *Past and Present* 85 (1979): 3–24.

Storm-Clark, Christopher. "The Miners: The Relevance of Oral Evidence." *Oral History: Journal of the Oral History Society* 1, no. 4 (1970): 72–92.

Strassler, Robert B., ed. *The Landmark Thucydides: A Comprehensive Guide to the Peloponnesian War.* New York: Free Press, 1996.

Strauss, Anselm, and Juliet Corbin. *Basis of Qualitative Research: Grounded Theory Procedures and Techniques.* Thousand Oaks, CA: Sage, 1998.

Strouse, Jean. "The Real Reasons." In *Extraordinary Lives: The Art and Craft of American Biography,* edited by William Zinsser, 161–95. New York: American Heritage, 1986.

Strickland, Edward. *American Composers: Dialogues on Contemporary Music.* Bloomington: Indiana University Press, 1991.

Stricklin, David, and Rebecca Sharpless, eds. *The Past Meets the Present: Essays on Oral History.* Lanham, MD: University Press of America, 1988.

Summerfield, Penny. *Reconstructing Women's Wartime Lives: Discourse and Subjectivity in Oral Histories of the Second World War.* Manchester, England: Manchester University Press, 1998.

Susman, Warren I. "History and the American Intellectual: Uses of a Usable Past." *American Quarterly* 16, Part 2 (Summer 1964): 243–63.

Swedenburg, Ted. *Memories of Revolt.* Minneapolis: University of Minnesota Press, 1995.

Talsma, Jaap, and Selma Leydesdorff. "Oral History in the Netherlands." In Hartewig and Halbach, eds., "History of Oral History," 65–75.

Tannen, Deborah. "The Commingling of Orality and Literacy in Giving a Paper at a Scholarly Conference." *American Speech* 63, no. 1 (1988): 34–43.

———, ed. *Spoken and Written Language: Exploring Orality and Literacy*. Norwood, NJ: Ablex, 1982.

———. *You Just Don't Understand: Women and Men in Conversation*. New York: Ballantine, 1990.

Taylor, Jeremy. *Where People Fly and Water Runs Uphill*. New York: Warner, 1993.

Taylor, Shelley E., Laura Cousino Klein, Brian P. Lewis, Tara L. Gruenewald, Regan A. R. Gurung, and John A. Updegraff. "Biobehavioral Responses to Stress in Females: Tend-and-Befriend, Not Fight-or-Flight." *Psychological Review* 107, no. 3 (2000): 411–29.

Tedlock, Dennis. *Finding the Center: Narrative Poetry of the Zuni Indians*. New York: Dial, 1972.

———. "Learning to Listen: Oral History as Poetry." In Grele, *Envelopes of Sound*, 2nd ed., 106–25.

———. "On the Translation of Style in Oral Narrative." *Journal of American Folklore* 84 (1971): 114–33.

Terkel, Studs. *American Dreams: Lost and Found*. New York: Pantheon, 1980.

———. *Born to Live: Hiroshima, with Documentary Recordings*. Folkways Records FD5525, 1965. Microgroove.

———. *Division Street: America*. New York: Pantheon, 1967.

———. *"The Good War": An Oral History of World War Two*. New York: Pantheon, 1984.

———. *Hard Times: An Oral History of the Great Depression*. New York: Pantheon, 1970.

———. *Hard Times: The Story of the Depression in the Voices of Those Who Lived It. The Original Tapes on Which the Book Was Based*. Caedmon, 1971. Microgroove and audiocassette.

———. *Interviews with Interviewers—About Interviewing*. New York: In Motion Productions, 1985. Videorecording.

———. *Race: How Blacks and Whites Think and Feel about the American Obsession*. New York: Pantheon, 1992.

———. *Talking to Myself: A Memoir of My Times*. New York: Pantheon, 1973.

———. *Will the Circle Be Unbroken?: Reflections on Death, Rebirth, and Hunger for a Faith*. New York: Pantheon, 2001.

———. *Working: People Talk about What They Do All Day and How They Feel about What They Do*. New York: Pantheon, 1974.

Terrill, Tom E., and Jerrold Hirsch. "Replies to Leonard Rapport's 'How Valid Are the Federal Writers' Project Life Stories, An Iconoclast among the True Believers.'" *Oral History Review* 8 (1980): 81–92.

Thelen, David. "Memory and American History." *Journal of American History* 75, no. 4 (March 1989): 1117–29.

Therborn, Goran. *The Power of Ideology and The Ideology of Power*. London: Verso, 1980.

Thomas, Sherry. "Digging Beneath the Surface: Oral History Techniques." *Frontiers: Journal of Women Studies* 7, no. 1 (1983): 50–55.

———. *We Didn't Have Much, But We Sure Had Plenty: Stories of Rural Women*. Garden City, NY: Anchor, 1981.

Thomas, William Isaac, and Florian Znaniecki. *The Polish Peasant in Europe and America: Monograph of an Immigrant Group*. 5 vols. Chicago: University of Chicago Press, 1918–1920.

Thompson, Charles P., ed. *Autobiographical Memory: Theoretical and Applied Perspectives*. Mahwah, NJ: Erlbaum, 1998.

Thompson, Paul. "The Achievement of Oral History." In *Voice of the Past* (1978), 65–90.

———. "Believe It or Not: Rethinking the Historical Interpretation of Memory." In Jeffrey and Edwall, eds., *Memory and History*, 1–16.

———. *The Edwardians: The Remaking of British Society*. Bloomington: Indiana University Press, 1975.

———. "Evidence." In *Voice of the Past* (1978), 91–137.

———. "Oral History in North America." *Oral History: Journal of the Oral History Society* 3, no. 1 (1975): 26–40.

———. "Problems of Method in Oral History." *Oral History: Journal of the Oral History Society* 1, no. 4 (1971): 1–47.

———. "Projects." In *Voice of the Past*, 2nd ed., 166–95.

———. "Sharing and Reshaping Life Stories: Problems and Potential in Archiving Research Narratives." In Chamberlain and Thompson, eds., *Narrative and Genre*, 167–81.

———. *The Voice of the Past: Oral History*. Oxford: Oxford University Press, 1978.

———. *The Voice of the Past: Oral History*. 2nd ed. New York: Oxford University Press, 1988.

———. *The Voice of the Past: Oral History*. 3rd ed. Oxford: Oxford University Press, 2000.

Thompson, Paul, and Natasha Burchart, eds. *Our Common History: The Transformation of Europe*. Atlantic Highlands, NJ: Humanities Press, 1982.

Thompson, Paul, Luisa Passerini, Isabelle Bertaux-Wiame, and Alessandro Portelli. "Between Social Scientists: Responses to Louise A. Tilly." *International Journal of Oral History* 6, no. 1 (February 1985): 19–39.

Thomson, Alistair. "The Anzac Legend: Exploring National Myth and Memory in Australia." In Samuel and Thompson, eds., *Myths We Live By*, 73–82.

———. *Anzac Memories: Living with the Legend*. Oxford: Oxford University Press, 1994.

———. "Anzac Memories: Putting Popular Memory Theory into Practice in Australia." *Oral History: Journal of the Oral History Society* 18, no. 2 (1990): 25–31.

———. "Sharing Authority: Oral History and the Collaborative Process." *Oral History Review* 30, no. 1 (Winter–Spring 2003): 23–26.

Tilly, Louise. "Louise Tilly's Response to Thompson, Passerini, Bertaux-Wiame, and Portelli." *International Journal of Oral History* 6, no. 1 (February 1985): 40–42.

———. "People's History and Social History." *International Journal of Oral History* 6, no. 1 (February 1985): 5–18.

Tixier y Vigil, Yvonne, and Nan Elsasser. "The Effects of the Ethnicity of the Interviewer on Conversation: A Study of Chicana Women." In *Proceedings of the Conference on the Sociology of the Languages of American Women*, 2nd ed., edited by Betty DuBois and Isabel Crouch, 161–70. San Antonio, TX: Trinity University Press, 1983.

Tolnay, Stewart. *The Bottom Rung: African American Family Life on Southern Farms*. Urbana: University of Illinois Press, 1999.

Tonkin, Elizabeth. "The Boundaries of History in Oral Performance." *History in Africa* 9 (1982): 273–84.

———. "Implications of Oracy: An Anthropological View." *Oral History: Journal of the Oral History Society* 3, no. 1 (Spring 1975): 41–49.

———. *Narrating Our Pasts: The Social Construction of Oral History*. Cambridge: Cambridge University Press, 1992.

———. "Subjective or Objective? Debates on the Nature of Oral History." In *Narrating Our Pasts*, 83–96.

Torpey, John, ed. *Politics and the Past: On Repairing Historical Injustices*. New York: Rowman and Littlefield, 2003.

Treleven, Dale E. "An Interview with Jim Mink." *Oral History Review* 27, no. 1 (Winter–Spring 2000): 117–42.

———. "Oral History Audio Technology and the TAPE System." *International Journal of Oral History* 2, no. 1 (February 1981): 26–47.

Trouillot, Michel-Rolph. *Silencing the Past: Power and the Production of History*. Boston: Beacon, 1995.

Truax, Barry. *Acoustic Communication*. Norwood, NJ: Ablax, 1984.

Tuchman, Barbara. "Biography as a Prism of History." In Edel, *Telling Lives*, 132–47.

———. "Distinguishing the Significant from the Insignificant." In Dunaway and Baum, eds., *Oral History* (1984), 74–78.

———. "Distinguishing the Significant from the Insignificant." In Dunaway and Baum, eds., *Oral History*, 2nd ed. (1996), 94–98.

Tucker, Robert. "A Stalin Biographer's Memoir." In Baron and Pletsch, eds., *Introspection in Biography*, 249–71.

Turner, Victor Witter. *The Anthropology of Performance*. New York: PAJ, 1988.

Ullman, Maurice, and Nan Zimmerman. *Working with Dreams*. Los Angeles: Tarcher, 1985.

Vaillant, George E. *Adaptation to Life*. Boston: Little, Brown, 1977.

Van Bogart, John W. C. *Magnetic Tape Storage and Handling: A Guide for Libraries and Archives*. Washington, DC: Commission on Preservation and Access, 1995.

Van den Hoonaard, Will C., ed. *Walking the Tightrope: Ethical Issues for Qualitative Researchers*. Toronto: University of Toronto Press, 2002.

Vandiver, Frank E. "Biography as an Agent of Humanism." In Oates, ed., *Biography as High Adventure*, 50–64.

Van Maanen, John. *Representation in Ethnography*. Thousand Oaks, CA: Sage, 1995.

Vansina, Jan. *Oral Tradition*. Harmondsworth: Penguin, 1961.

———. *Oral Tradition: A Study in Historical Methodology*. Chicago: Aldine, 1965.

———. *Oral Tradition as History*. Madison: University of Wisconsin Press, 1985.

Vasari, Giorgio. *The Lives of the Artists*. New York : Oxford University Press, 1998.

Viagas, Robert, Baayork Lee, and Thommie Walsh. *On the Line: The Creation of a Chorus Line.* New York: William Morrow, 1990.

Vigne, Thea, ed. "Family History." Special issue, *Oral History: Journal of the Oral History Society* 3, no. 2 (Autumn 1975).

Vilanova, Mercedes. "The Struggle for a History without Adjectives: A Note on Using Oral History Sources in Spain." *Oral History Review* 24, no. 1 (Summer 1994): 81–90.

Wallot, Jean-Pierre, and Normand Fortier. "Archival Science and Oral Sources." In Perks and Thomson, eds., *Oral History Reader*, 365–78.

Wagner-Martin, Linda. *Telling Women's Lives: The New Biography.* New Brunswick, NJ: Rutgers University Press, 1994.

Ward, Alan. *A Manual of Sound Archive Administration.* Brookfield, VT: Gower, 1990.

Warner-Lewis, Maureen. *Guinea's Other Suns: The African Dynamic in Trinidad Culture.* Dover, MA: Majority, 1991.

Waserman, Manfred, comp. *Bibliography on Oral History.* New York: Oral History Association, 1971.

———. *Bibliography on Oral History.* Rev. ed. New York: Oral History Association, 1975.

Watson, Lawrence. "Understanding a Life History as a Subjective Document: Hermeneutical and Phenomenological Perspectives." *Ethos* 4, no. 1 (Spring 1976): 95–131.

Webb, Walter Prescott. "History as High Adventure." In *An Honest Preface and Other Essays*, 194–216. Boston: Houghton Mifflin, 1959.

Weidman, Bette S. "Oral History in Biography: A Shaping Source." *International Journal of Oral History* 8 (February 1987): 41–55.

Wekker, Gloria. "One Finger Does Not Drink Okra Soup: Afro-Surinamese Women and Critical Agency." In *Feminist Genealogies, Colonial Legacies, Democratic Futures*, edited by M. Jacqui Alexander and Chandra Talpade Mohanty, 330–52. London: Routledge, 1997.

Welch, H. Mason. "A Lawyer Looks at Oral History." In Colman, ed., *Fourth National Colloquium*, 182–95.

White, Hayden. *The Content of the Form: Narrative Discourse and Historical Representation.* Baltimore, MD: Johns Hopkins University Press, 1987.

———. "Foucault Decoded: Notes from Underground." *History and Theory* 12, no. 1 (1973): 23–54.

———. *Metahistory: The Historical Imagination in Nineteenth Century Europe.* Baltimore, MD: Johns Hopkins University Press, 1973.

White, Naomi Rosh. "Marking Absences: Holocaust Testimony and History." In Perks and Thomson, eds., *Oral History Reader*, 172–82.

Whorf, Benjamin. "Language, Mind, and Reality." In Carroll, *Language, Thought, and Reality*, 246–70.

———. "The Relation of Habitual Thought and Behavior to Language." In Carroll, *Language, Thought and Reality*, 134–59.

Wigginton, Eliot, ed. *The Foxfire Book.* Garden City, NY: Doubleday, 1972.

———. *Sometimes a Shining Moment: The Foxfire Experience, Twenty Years Teaching in a High School Classroom.* Garden City, NY: Anchor Books/Doubleday, 1985.

Williams, Brien. "Recording Videohistory: A Perspective." In Schorzman, ed., *Introduction to Videohistory*, 138–54.

Williams, T. Harry. *Huey Long*. New York: Knopf, 1969.

Wilmsen, Carl. "For the Record: Editing and the Production of Meaning in Oral History." *Oral History Review* 28, no. 1 (Winter/Spring 2001): 65–85.

Winograd, Eugene. "The Authenticity and Utility of Memories." In Neisser and Fivush, eds., *Remembering Self*, 243–51.

Winslow, Donald J. *Life-Writing: A Glossary of Terms*. Honolulu: University Press of Hawaii, 1980.

Winter, J. M., and Emmanuel Sivan. "Setting the Framework." In *War and Remembrance in the Twentieth Century*, 6–39. Cambridge: Cambridge University Press, 1999.

Witherspoon, John, and Roselle Kovitz. *The History of Public Broadcasting*. Washington, DC: Current, 1987.

Wood, Linda P. *Oral History Projects in Your Classroom*. Dickinson, PA: Oral History Association, 2001.

Woodruff, Nan Elizabeth. *American Congo: The African American Freedom Struggle in the Delta*. Cambridge, MA: Harvard University Press, 2003.

Woods, Clyde. *Development Arrested: The Blues and Plantation Power in the Mississippi Delta*. London: Verso, 1999.

Woolf, Virginia. *A Writer's Diary: Being Extracts from the Diary of Virginia Woolf*. Edited by Leonard Woolf. New York: Harcourt, Brace, 1954.

Wrong, Dennis. "The Over-socialized Concept of Man in Modern Sociology." *American Journal of Sociology* 26, no. 2 (1961): 183–93.

X, Malcolm. *The Autobiography of Malcolm X*. With Alex Haley. New York: Grove, 1965.

Yans-McLaughlin, Virginia. "Metaphors of Self in History: Subjectivity, Oral Narrative, and Immigration Studies." In *Immigration Reconsidered: History, Sociology, and Politics*, 254–92. New York: Oxford University Press, 1990.

Yeo, Stephen. "The Politics of Community Publications." In Samuel, *People's History and Socialist Theory*, 44–46.

Yow, Valerie Raleigh. *Bernice Kelly Harris: A Good Life Was Writing*. Baton Rouge: Louisiana State University Press, 1999.

———. "Betty Smith and *A Tree Grows in Brooklyn*." Unpublished manuscript.

———. "'Do I Like Them Too Much?': Effects of the Oral History Interview on the Interviewer and Vice-Versa." *Oral History Review* 24 (Summer 1997): 55–79.

———. "Ethics and Interpersonal Relationships in Oral History Research." *Oral History Review* 22, no. 1 (Summer 1995): 51–66.

———. *Recording Oral History: A Guide for the Humanities and Social Sciences*. 2nd ed. New York: Rowman and Littlefield, 2005.

———. *Recording Oral History: A Practical Guide for Social Scientists*. Thousand Oaks, CA: Sage, 1994.

Zimmerman, Don H. "On Conversation: The Conversation Analytic Perspective." In *Communication Yearbook* 11, edited by J. A. Anderson, 406–32. Newbury Park, CA: Sage, 1988.

Zorbaugh, Harvey. *The Gold Coast and the Slum: A Sociological Study of Chicago's Near North Side*. Chicago: University of Chicago Press, 1929.

Index

About the Editors
and Contributors

An Arkansas native and naturalized Texan, **Thomas L. Charlton** holds degrees in history from Baylor University (B.A.) and the University of Texas at Austin (M.A. and Ph.D.). He has been on the Baylor faculty since 1970, specializing in the history of Texas and the Southwest, the American South, public history/historic preservation, and oral history. He has been an active member of the Department of History, directed the Institute for Oral History (1970–1993), served as vice provost in three capacities (1992–2003), and has served as director of the Texas Collection library/archival center since 2003. Charlton has been active in oral history research and teaching at both the state level (co-founder of the Texas Oral History Association) and the national level (active in the Oral History Association, OHA president in 1990–1991). The Texas Oral History Association honored him with its first lifetime achievement award in 1999. He is the author of *Oral History for Texans* (1981, 1985) and co-editor of *Handbook of Oral History* (2006).

James E. Fogerty is head of the Acquisitions and Curatorial Department of the Minnesota Historical Society, which includes the society's Oral History Office. He has directed oral history projects with a number of immigrant communities and for individual corporations, on issues relating to agriculture, the environment, the recreation industry, and the medical device industry. He teaches workshops on the use of oral history and videohistory in archives, corporations, and cultural organizations. Fogerty is a fellow of the Society of American Archivists and has served on its governing council and on the council of the Oral History Association. He chaired the Oral Sources Committee of the International Council on Archives and is currently a member of its Business Archives Section. He has authored numerous articles, especially on the development of oral history and archives in business.

Ronald J. Grele is the former director of the Columbia University Oral History Research Office in New York City and a former president of the Oral History Association. He is the author of *Envelopes of Sound: The Art of Oral History* (1975, 1985) and editor of *Subjectivity and Multiculturalism in Oral History* (1992). For many years he was editor of the *International Journal of Oral History* and taught a graduate seminar in oral history with the Columbia University Department of History. The essay in this volume is part of a larger project on the state of the art of oral history.

Mary A. Larson, who earned her Ph.D. from Brown University, came to oral history from a background in anthropology. She is the assistant director at the University of Nevada Oral History Program, having worked previously with the oral history office at the University of Alaska, Fairbanks. After serving as media review editor for the *Oral History Review* and on many committees of the Oral History Association, she has moved to elected membership on the OHA Council (2003–2006). She is currently an editor for the H-Oralhist discussion list. On the regional level, Mary served six years on the board of the Southwest Oral History Association. Her research interests include the geographical areas of the Intermountain West and the Arctic as well as issues pertaining to the methods and ethics of digitizing oral histories and increasing their accessibility.

Elinor A. Mazé is a member of the faculty of Baylor University and serves as senior editor at the university's Institute for Oral History. She is an editor for H-Oralhist, the Internet discussion forum for the oral history community. She holds an M.L.S. degree from Texas Woman's University and M.A. and B.A. degrees from the University of Texas at Austin. She taught English in Japan and served as a technical reference librarian in Saudi Arabia before joining Baylor in 2001.

A past president of the Oral History Association, **Charles T. Morrissey** began his career in 1962 by interviewing former members of the White House staff during the Truman administration for the Truman Library, and he subsequently directed the John F. Kennedy Library Oral History Project. He has also directed projects for and about the Ford Foundation, the Pew Charitable Trusts, the Howard Hughes Medical Institute, the Bush Foundation of Minnesota, Baylor College of Medicine in Houston, and a Washington group, Former Members of Congress. He frequently teaches oral history workshops and has published more than fifty articles about oral history skills and applications.

Lois E. Myers is associate director of the Baylor University Institute for Oral History, in Waco, Texas, where since 1986 she has participated in all the steps of creating oral history, from planning to publication. Secretary/treasurer of the Texas Oral History Association since 1987, she consults with a wide variety of people involved in recording the histories of their communities, occupations, families, and businesses. She has conducted numerous workshops on oral history methodology and is active in the national Oral History Association. She is author of *Letters by Lamplight: A Woman's View of Everyday Life in South Texas 1873–1883* (1991); co-author, with historian Rebecca Sharpless and photographer Clark Baker, of *Rock Beneath the Sand: The Country Church in Texas* (2003); and co-editor of *Handbook of Oral History* (2006).

Rebecca Sharpless directed the Baylor University Institute for Oral History from 1993 to 2006 and served as president of the Oral History Association in 2005–2006. She began her work in oral history at Baylor in 1977, transcribing interviews on an electric typewriter with lots of Liquid Paper. She is author of *Fertile Ground, Narrow Choices: Women on Texas Cotton Farms, 1900–1940*

(1999); co-author of *Rock Beneath the Sand: Country Churches in Texas* (2003); and co-editor of *Handbook of Oral History* (2006). In 2006 Sharpless joined the Department of History at Texas Christian University, where she teaches women's history.

A historian at the Pennsylvania Historical and Museum Commission, **Linda Shopes** has participated in and consulted on dozens of oral history projects. She has written widely on both oral and public history, including, most recently, "Making Sense of Oral History" for the Historymatters Web site, available at http://historymatters.gmu.edu/sme/oral. Shopes is a past president of the Oral History Association, for which she also co-chaired the committee that drafted the legal and ethical guidelines in the *Oral History Evaluation Guidelines*. She currently co-edits the Palgrave Studies in Oral History Series. Also, Shopes has been active in efforts throughout the United States to exclude oral history from regulations governing research on what are termed human subjects.

Breinigsville, PA USA
04 August 2010
242990BV00005B/1/P